ONE
PRESENTS

モブサイコ100

MOB PSYCHO 100

VOLUME 7

DARK HORSE MANGA

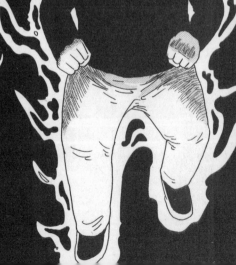

MOB PSYCHO 100
VOLUME 7

Translated by
KUMAR SIVASUBRAMANIAN

Lettering and Retouch by
JOHN CLARK

Edited by
CARL GUSTAV HORN

CHAPTER 53: URBAN LEGENDS

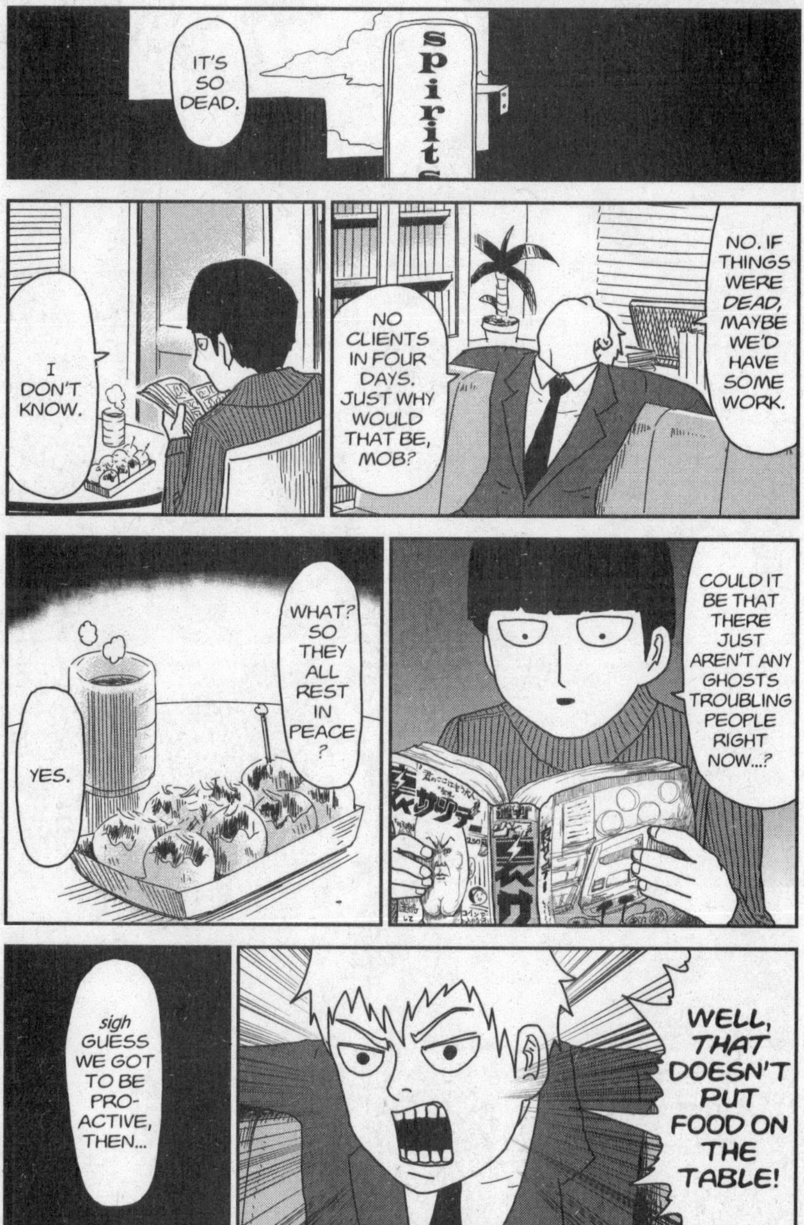

IT'S SO DEAD.
spirits
NO. IF THINGS WERE *DEAD*, MAYBE WE'D HAVE SOME WORK.
NO CLIENTS IN FOUR DAYS. JUST WHY WOULD THAT BE, MOB?
I DON'T KNOW.
COULD IT BE THAT THERE JUST AREN'T ANY GHOSTS TROUBLING PEOPLE RIGHT NOW...?
WHAT? SO THEY ALL REST IN PEACE?
YES.
WELL, THAT DOESN'T PUT FOOD ON THE TABLE!
sigh GUESS WE GOT TO BE PRO-ACTIVE, THEN...

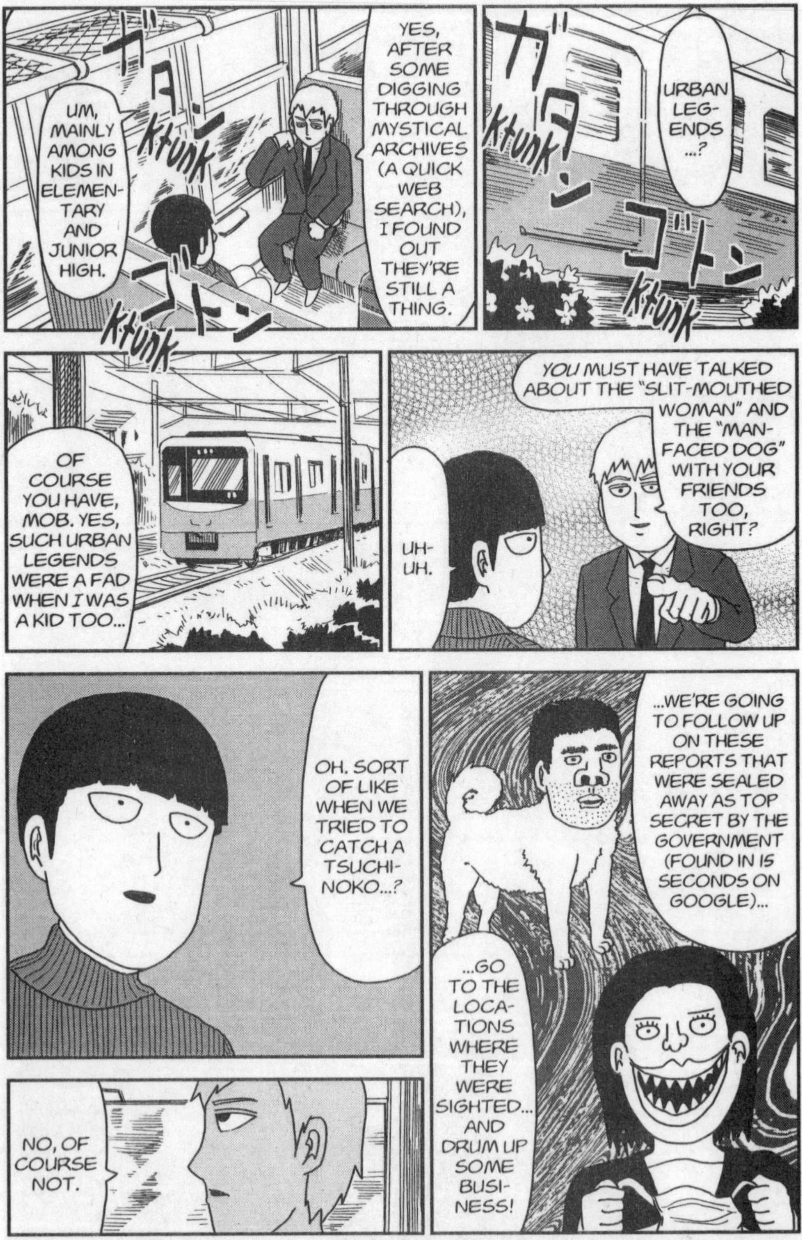
ガタン
ktunk
ゴトン
ktunk
URBAN LEG-ENDS ...?
YES, AFTER SOME DIGGING THROUGH MYSTICAL ARCHIVES (A QUICK WEB SEARCH), I FOUND OUT THEY'RE STILL A THING.
UM, MAINLY AMONG KIDS IN ELEMEN-TARY AND JUNIOR HIGH.
ガタン
ktunk
ゴトン
ktunk
YOU MUST HAVE TALKED ABOUT THE "SLIT-MOUTHED WOMAN" AND THE "MAN-FACED DOG" WITH YOUR FRIENDS TOO, RIGHT?
UH-UH.
OF COURSE YOU HAVE, MOB. YES, SUCH URBAN LEGENDS WERE A FAD WHEN *I* WAS A KID TOO...
...WE'RE GOING TO FOLLOW UP ON THESE REPORTS THAT WERE SEALED AWAY AS TOP SECRET BY THE GOVERNMENT (FOUND IN 15 SECONDS ON GOOGLE)...
...GO TO THE LOCA-TIONS WHERE THEY WERE SIGHTED... AND DRUM UP SOME BUSI-NESS!
OH. SORT OF LIKE WHEN WE TRIED TO CATCH A TSUCHI-NOKO...?
NO, OF COURSE NOT.

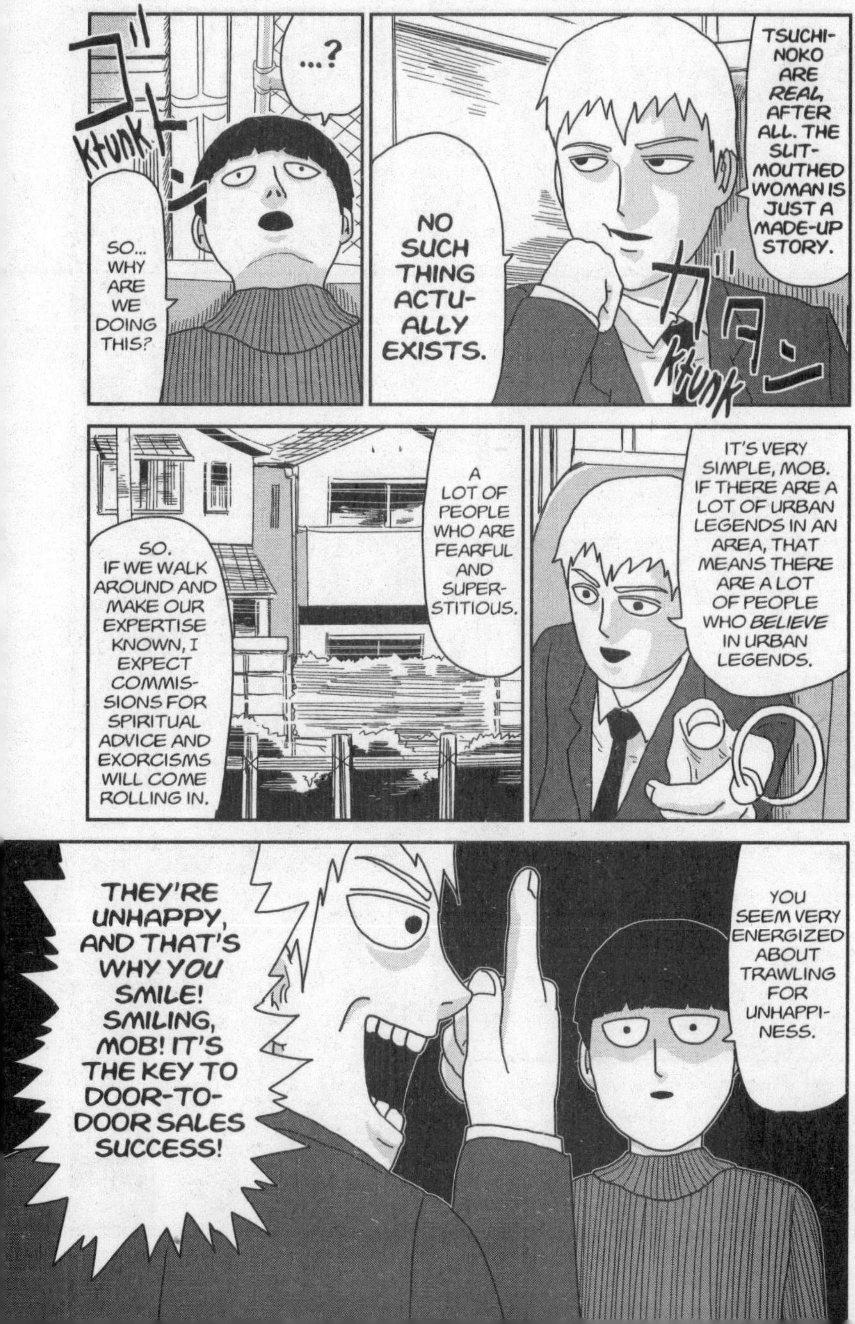
TSUCHINOKO ARE *REAL*, AFTER ALL. THE SLIT-MOUTHED WOMAN IS JUST A MADE-UP STORY.
NO SUCH THING ACTUALLY EXISTS.
ktunk
...?
ktunk
SO... WHY ARE WE DOING THIS?
IT'S VERY SIMPLE, MOB. IF THERE ARE A LOT OF URBAN LEGENDS IN AN AREA, THAT MEANS THERE ARE A LOT OF PEOPLE WHO *BELIEVE* IN URBAN LEGENDS.
A LOT OF PEOPLE WHO ARE FEARFUL AND SUPERSTITIOUS.
SO. IF WE WALK AROUND AND MAKE OUR EXPERTISE KNOWN, I EXPECT COMMISSIONS FOR SPIRITUAL ADVICE AND EXORCISMS WILL COME ROLLING IN.
YOU SEEM VERY ENERGIZED ABOUT TRAWLING FOR UNHAPPINESS.
THEY'RE UNHAPPY, AND THAT'S WHY *YOU* SMILE! SMILING, MOB! IT'S THE KEY TO DOOR-TO-DOOR SALES SUCCESS!

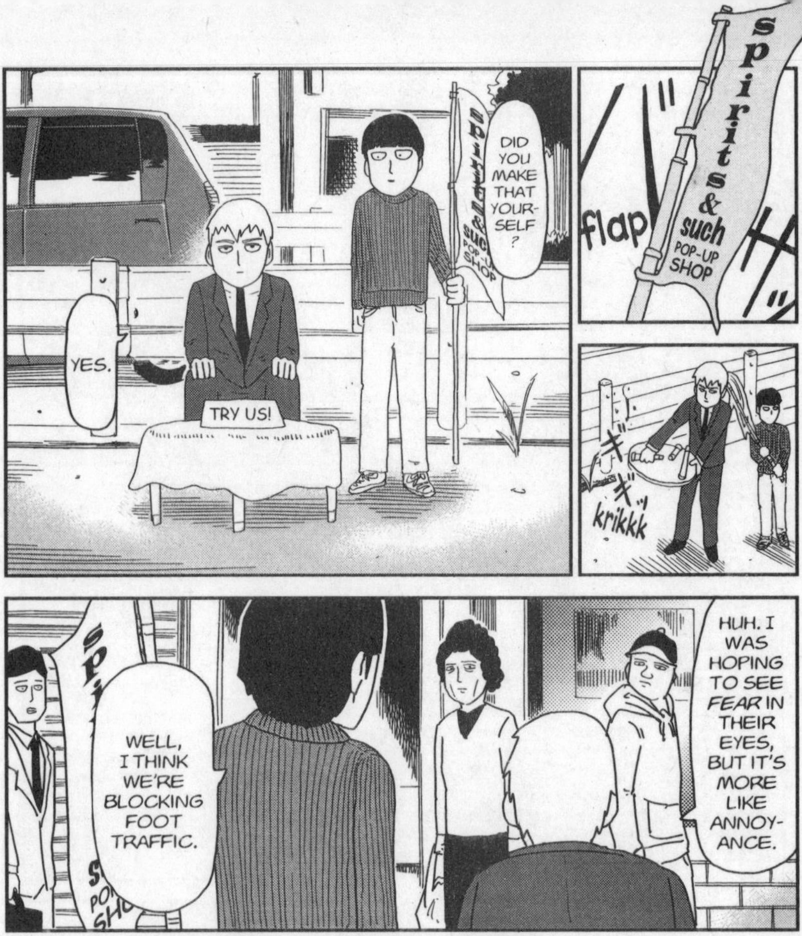
spirits & such POP-UP SHOP
flap
krikkk
DID YOU MAKE THAT YOURSELF?
YES.
TRY US!
spirits & such POP-UP SHOP
HUH. I WAS HOPING TO SEE FEAR IN THEIR EYES, BUT IT'S MORE LIKE ANNOYANCE.
WELL, I THINK WE'RE BLOCKING FOOT TRAFFIC.
...HEY, YOU! WHO GAVE YOU PERMISSION TO DO BUSINESS HERE...?!
ピク
twitch
...!
DON'T YOU KNOW THAT THIS JURISDICTION BELONGS TO ME-- BANSHOMARU SHINRA, PSYCHIC MEDIUM OF THE 21st CENTURY!
WHAT DO YOU MEAN?
THIS GUY'S AN "OF THE 21st CENTURY" TOO...

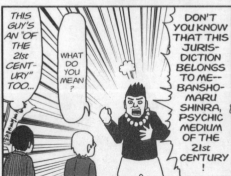

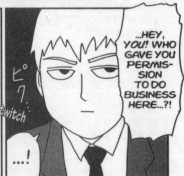

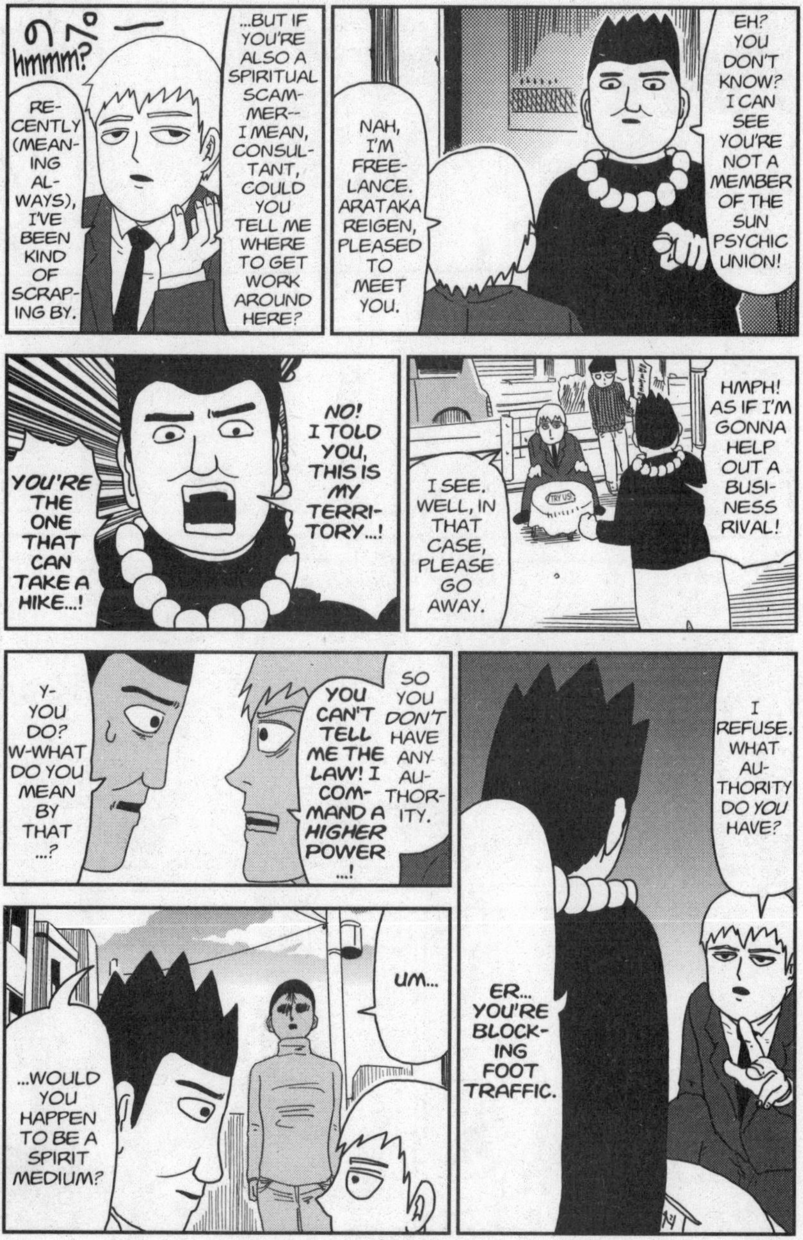
EH? YOU DON'T KNOW? I CAN SEE YOU'RE NOT A MEMBER OF THE SUN PSYCHIC UNION!
NAH, I'M FREELANCE. ARATAKA REIGEN, PLEASED TO MEET YOU.
hmmm?
RECENTLY (MEANING ALWAYS), I'VE BEEN KIND OF SCRAPING BY.
...BUT IF YOU'RE ALSO A SPIRITUAL SCAMMER-- I MEAN, CONSULTANT, COULD YOU TELL ME WHERE TO GET WORK AROUND HERE?
HMPH! AS IF I'M GONNA HELP OUT A BUSINESS RIVAL!
TRY US
I SEE. WELL, IN THAT CASE, PLEASE GO AWAY.
NO! I TOLD YOU, THIS IS MY TERRITORY...!
YOU'RE THE ONE THAT CAN TAKE A HIKE...!
I REFUSE. WHAT AUTHORITY DO YOU HAVE?
ER... YOU'RE BLOCKING FOOT TRAFFIC.
SO YOU DON'T HAVE ANY AUTHORITY.
YOU CAN'T TELL ME THE LAW! I COMMAND A HIGHER POWER...!
Y-YOU DO? W-WHAT DO YOU MEAN BY THAT...?
UM...
...WOULD YOU HAPPEN TO BE A SPIRIT MEDIUM?

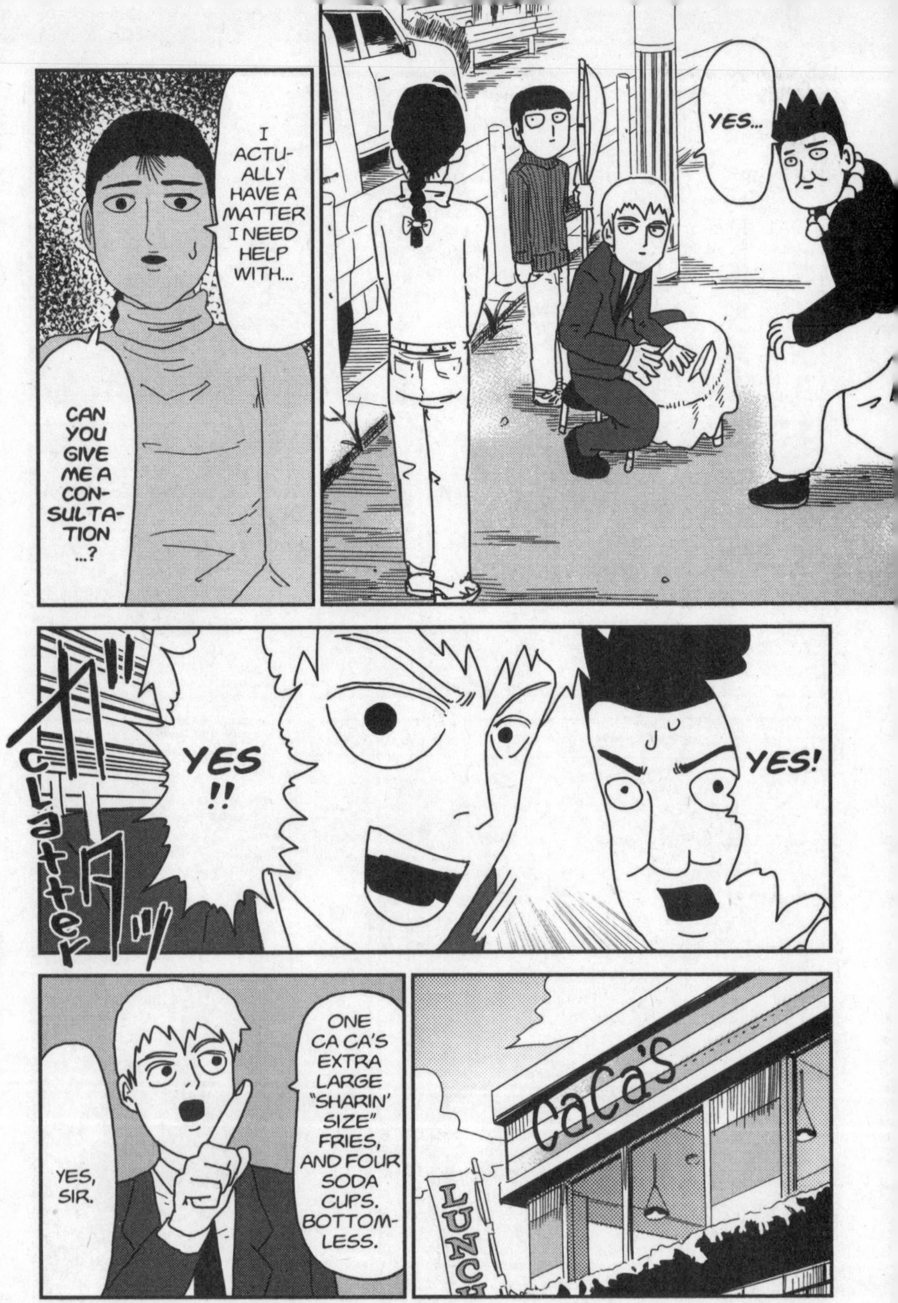
YES...
I ACTUALLY HAVE A MATTER I NEED HELP WITH...
CAN YOU GIVE ME A CONSULTATION...?
YES!
YES!!
CLATTER
CaCa's
LUNCH
ONE CA CA'S EXTRA LARGE "SHARIN' SIZE" FRIES, AND FOUR SODA CUPS. BOTTOMLESS.
YES, SIR.

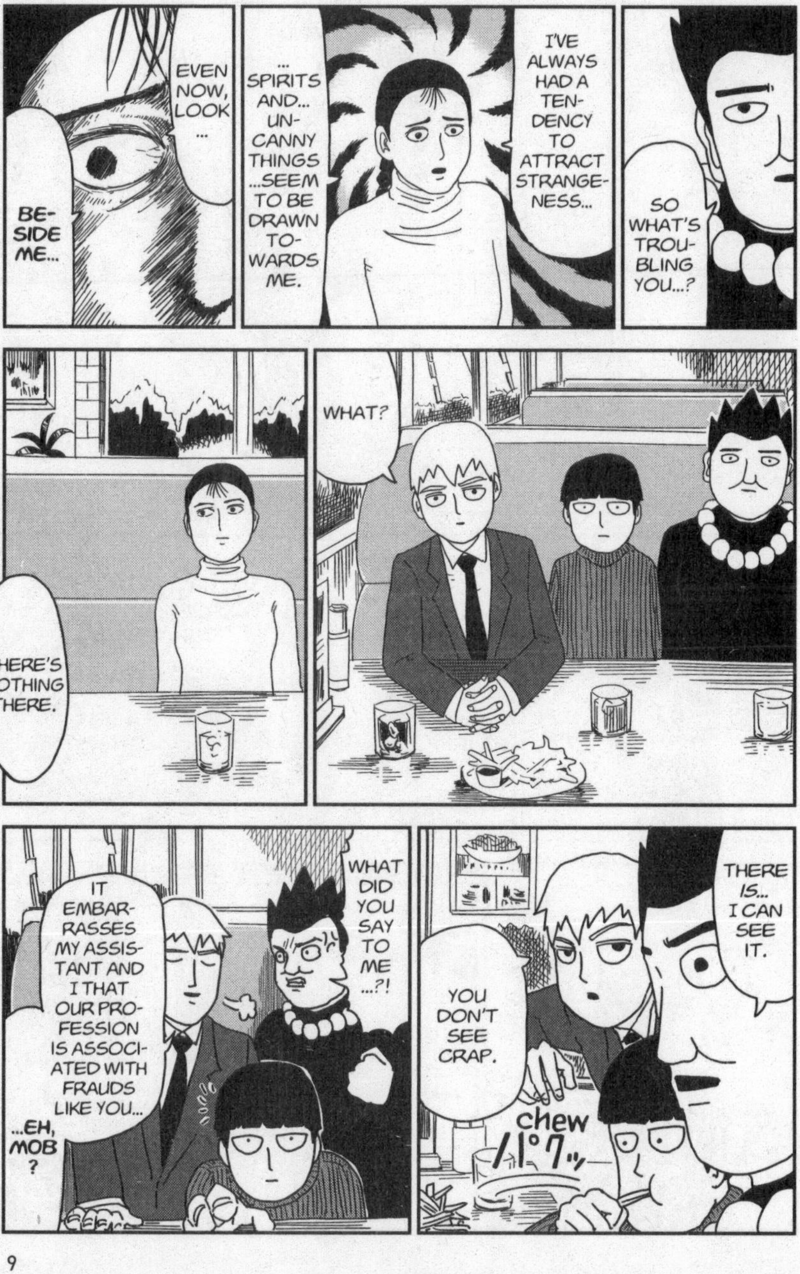
SO WHAT'S TROUBLING YOU...?
I'VE ALWAYS HAD A TENDENCY TO ATTRACT STRANGENESS...
... SPIRITS AND... UNCANNY THINGS ...SEEM TO BE DRAWN TOWARDS ME.
EVEN NOW, LOOK ...
BESIDE ME...
WHAT?
THERE'S NOTHING THERE.
THERE IS... I CAN SEE IT.
YOU DON'T SEE CRAP.
chew
パクッ
WHAT DID YOU SAY TO ME ...?!
IT EMBARRASSES MY ASSISTANT AND I THAT OUR PROFESSION IS ASSOCIATED WITH FRAUDS LIKE YOU...
...EH, MOB ?

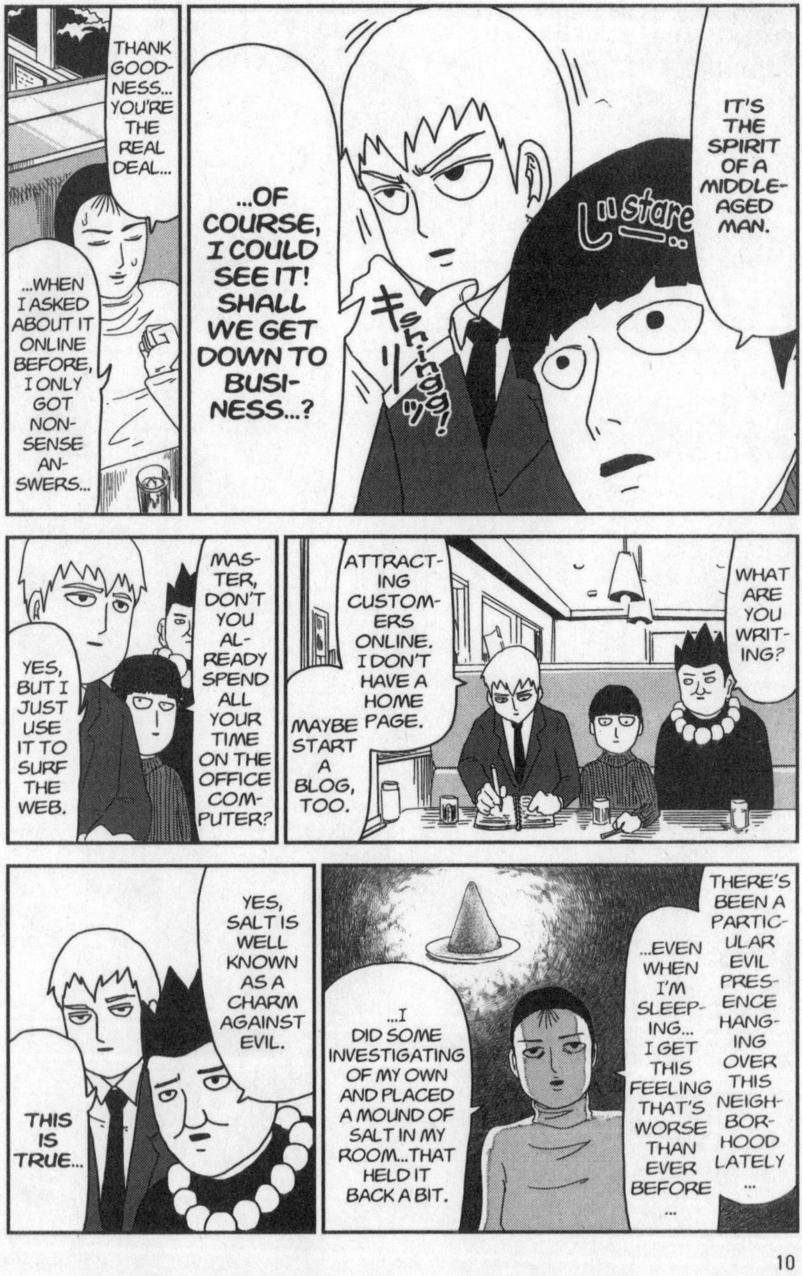
IT'S THE SPIRIT OF A MIDDLE-AGED MAN.
stare
...OF COURSE, I COULD SEE IT! SHALL WE GET DOWN TO BUSINESS...?
shingg!
THANK GOODNESS... YOU'RE THE REAL DEAL...
...WHEN I ASKED ABOUT IT ONLINE BEFORE, I ONLY GOT NONSENSE ANSWERS...
WHAT ARE YOU WRITING?
ATTRACTING CUSTOMERS ONLINE. I DON'T HAVE A HOME PAGE.
MAYBE START A BLOG, TOO.
MASTER, DON'T YOU ALREADY SPEND ALL YOUR TIME ON THE OFFICE COMPUTER?
YES, BUT I JUST USE IT TO SURF THE WEB.
THERE'S BEEN A PARTICULAR EVIL PRESENCE HANGING OVER THIS NEIGHBORHOOD LATELY...
...EVEN WHEN I'M SLEEPING... I GET THIS FEELING THAT'S WORSE THAN EVER BEFORE...
...I DID SOME INVESTIGATING OF MY OWN AND PLACED A MOUND OF SALT IN MY ROOM...THAT HELD IT BACK A BIT.
YES, SALT IS WELL KNOWN AS A CHARM AGAINST EVIL.
THIS IS TRUE...

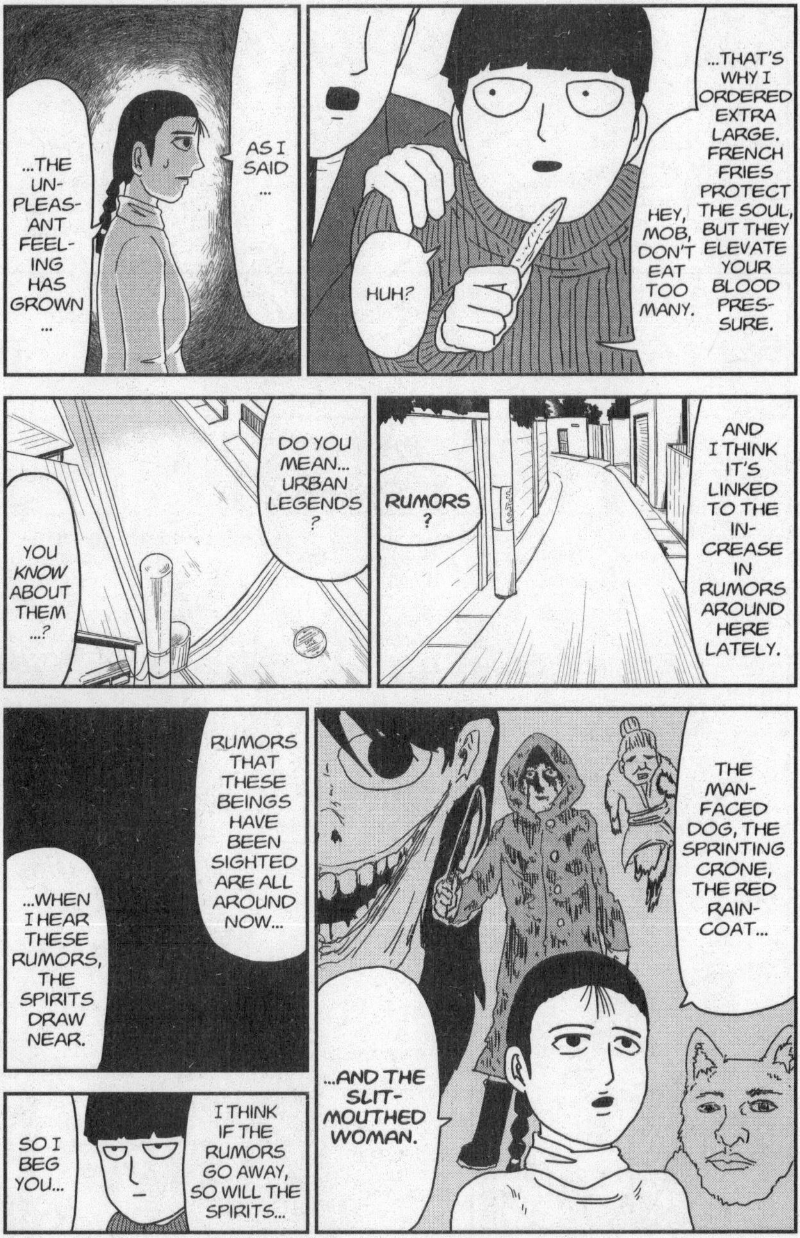
...THAT'S WHY I ORDERED EXTRA LARGE. FRENCH FRIES PROTECT THE SOUL, BUT THEY ELEVATE YOUR BLOOD PRESSURE.
HEY, MOB, DON'T EAT TOO MANY.
HUH?
AS I SAID ...
...THE UNPLEASANT FEELING HAS GROWN ...
AND I THINK IT'S LINKED TO THE INCREASE IN RUMORS AROUND HERE LATELY.
RUMORS ?
DO YOU MEAN... URBAN LEGENDS ?
YOU KNOW ABOUT THEM ...?
THE MAN-FACED DOG, THE SPRINTING CRONE, THE RED RAINCOAT...
...AND THE SLIT-MOUTHED WOMAN.
RUMORS THAT THESE BEINGS HAVE BEEN SIGHTED ARE ALL AROUND NOW...
...WHEN I HEAR THESE RUMORS, THE SPIRITS DRAW NEAR.
I THINK IF THE RUMORS GO AWAY, SO WILL THE SPIRITS...
SO I BEG YOU...

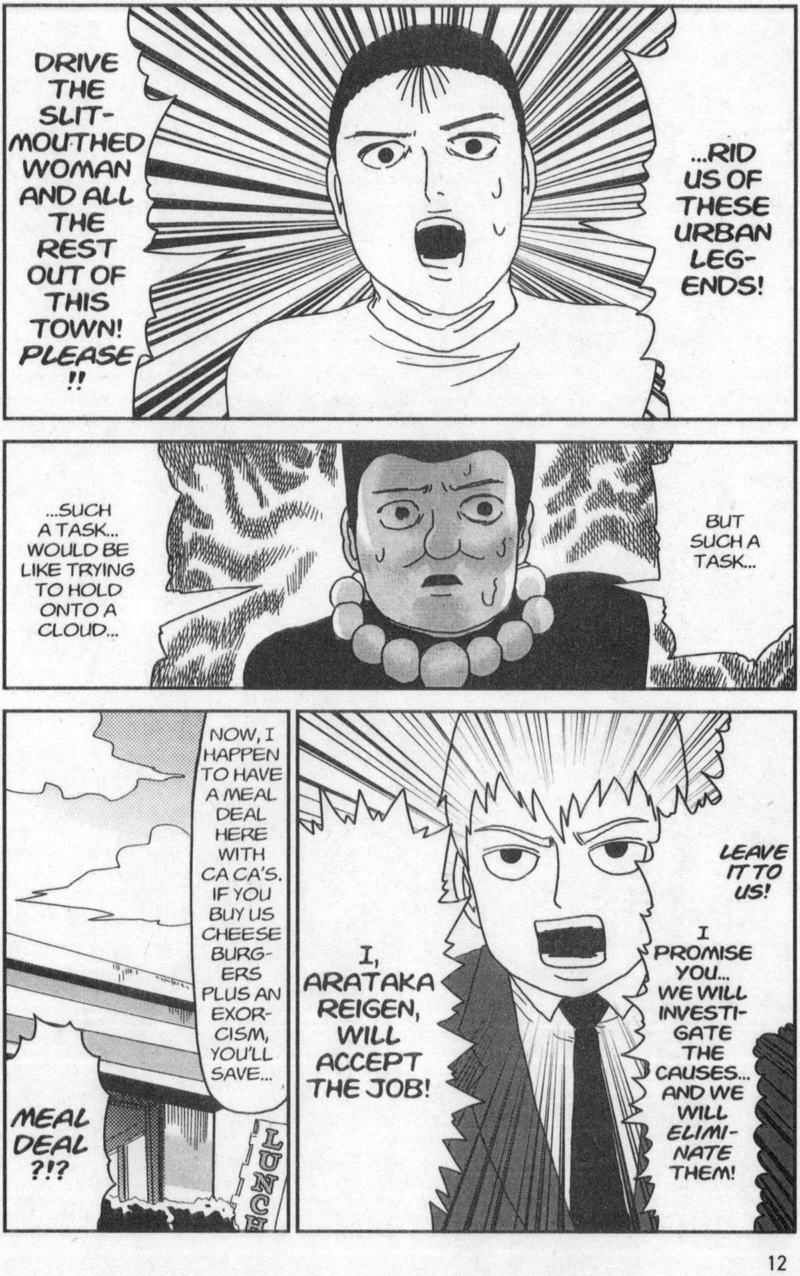
...RID US OF THESE URBAN LEG-ENDS!
DRIVE THE SLIT-MOUTHED WOMAN AND ALL THE REST OUT OF THIS TOWN! PLEASE!!
BUT SUCH A TASK...
...SUCH A TASK... WOULD BE LIKE TRYING TO HOLD ONTO A CLOUD...
LEAVE IT TO US!
I PROMISE YOU... WE WILL INVESTI-GATE THE CAUSES... AND WE WILL ELIMI-NATE THEM!
I, ARATAKA REIGEN, WILL ACCEPT THE JOB!
NOW, I HAPPEN TO HAVE A MEAL DEAL HERE WITH CA CA'S. IF YOU BUY US CHEESE BURG-ERS PLUS AN EXOR-CISM, YOU'LL SAVE...
MEAL DEAL ?!?
LUNCH

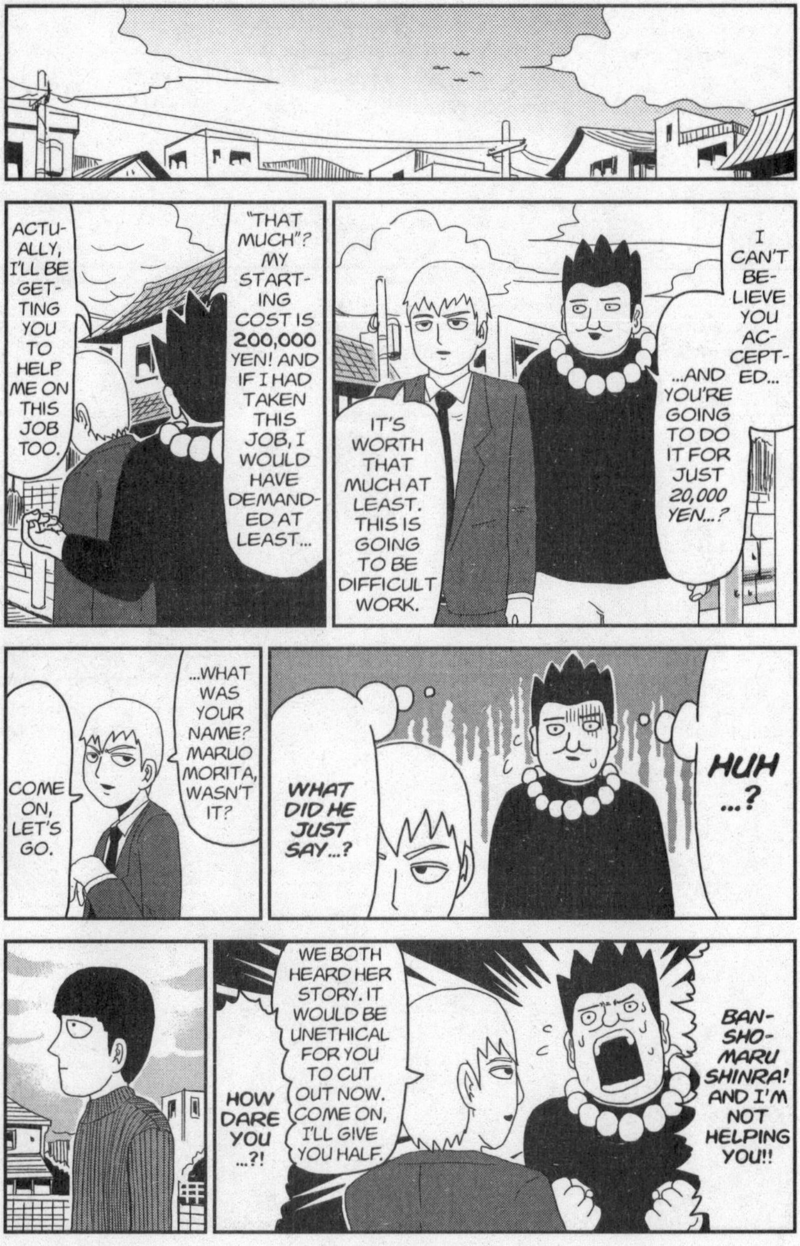
I CAN'T BELIEVE YOU ACCEPTED...
...AND YOU'RE GOING TO DO IT FOR JUST 20,000 YEN...?
IT'S WORTH THAT MUCH AT LEAST. THIS IS GOING TO BE DIFFICULT WORK.
"THAT MUCH"? MY STARTING COST IS 200,000 YEN! AND IF I HAD TAKEN THIS JOB, I WOULD HAVE DEMANDED AT LEAST...
ACTUALLY, I'LL BE GETTING YOU TO HELP ME ON THIS JOB TOO.
HUH ...?
WHAT DID HE JUST SAY...?
...WHAT WAS YOUR NAME? MARUO MORITA, WASN'T IT?
COME ON, LET'S GO.
BANSHOMARU SHINRA! AND I'M NOT HELPING YOU!!
WE BOTH HEARD HER STORY. IT WOULD BE UNETHICAL FOR YOU TO CUT OUT NOW. COME ON, I'LL GIVE YOU HALF.
HOW DARE YOU ...?!

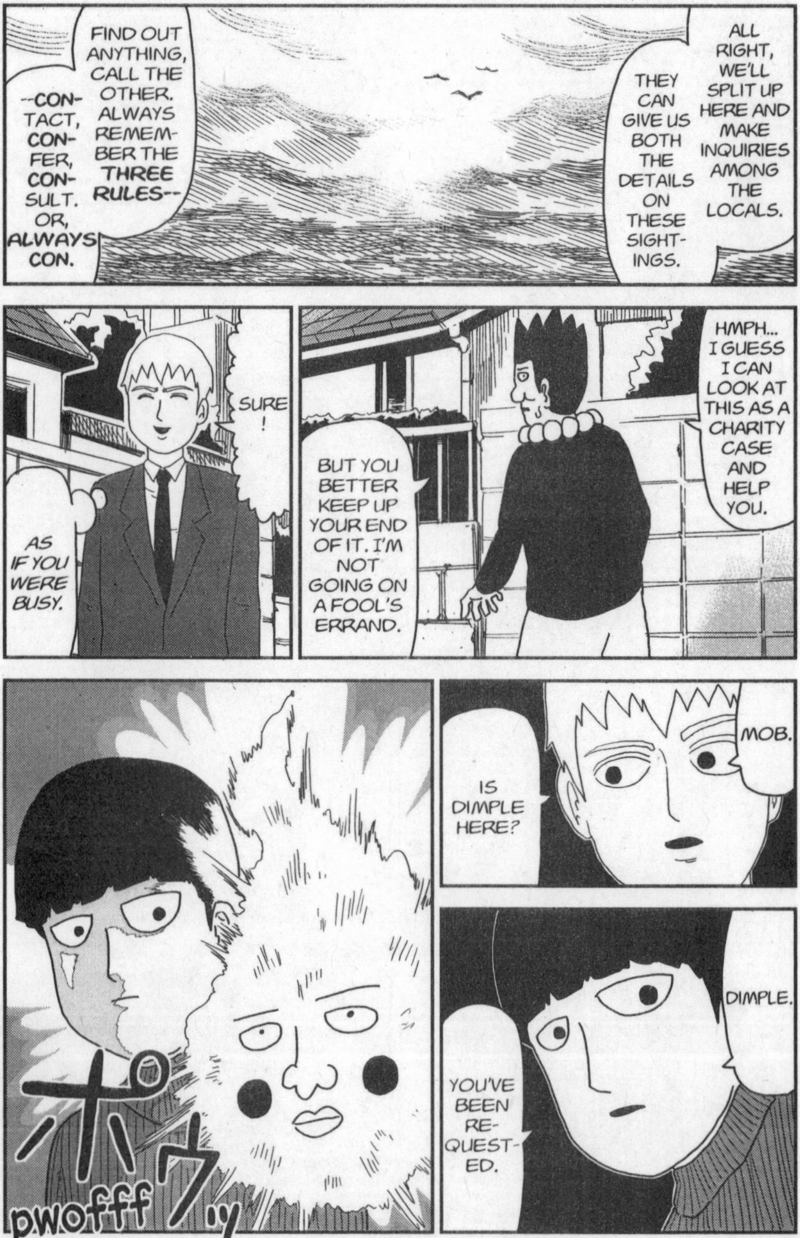
ALL RIGHT, WE'LL SPLIT UP HERE AND MAKE INQUIRIES AMONG THE LOCALS.
THEY CAN GIVE US BOTH THE DETAILS ON THESE SIGHTINGS.
FIND OUT ANYTHING, CALL THE OTHER. ALWAYS REMEMBER THE THREE RULES--
--CONTACT, CONFER, CONSULT. OR, ALWAYS CON.
HMPH... I GUESS I CAN LOOK AT THIS AS A CHARITY CASE AND HELP YOU.
BUT YOU BETTER KEEP UP YOUR END OF IT. I'M NOT GOING ON A FOOL'S ERRAND.
SURE!
AS IF YOU WERE BUSY.
MOB.
IS DIMPLE HERE?
DIMPLE.
YOU'VE BEEN REQUESTED.
ポワウッ
pwofff

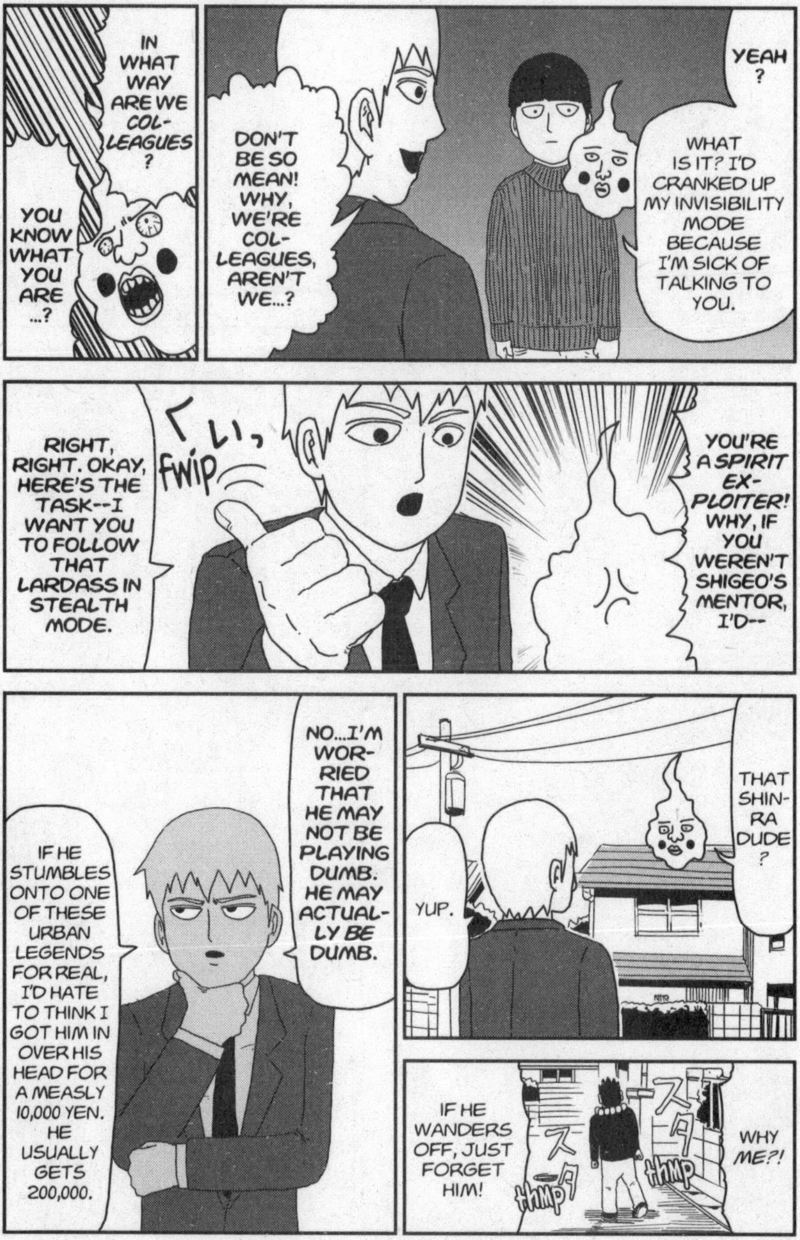

YEAH?
WHAT IS IT? I'D CRANKED UP MY INVISIBILITY MODE BECAUSE I'M SICK OF TALKING TO YOU.
DON'T BE SO MEAN! WHY, WE'RE COL-LEAGUES, AREN'T WE...?
IN WHAT WAY ARE WE *COL-LEAGUES*?
YOU KNOW WHAT YOU ARE...?
YOU'RE A *SPIRIT EX-PLOITER!* WHY, IF YOU WEREN'T SHIGEO'S MENTOR, I'D--
くい fwip
RIGHT, RIGHT. OKAY, HERE'S THE TASK--I WANT YOU TO FOLLOW THAT LARDASS IN STEALTH MODE.
THAT SHIN-RA DUDE?
YUP.
WHY *ME?!*
IF HE WANDERS OFF, JUST FORGET HIM!
スタ thmp
スタ thmp
NO...I'M WOR-RIED THAT HE MAY NOT BE PLAYING DUMB. HE MAY ACTUAL-LY *BE* DUMB.
IF HE STUMBLES ONTO ONE OF THESE URBAN LEGENDS FOR REAL, I'D HATE TO THINK I GOT HIM IN OVER HIS HEAD FOR A MEASLY 10,000 YEN. HE USUALLY GETS 200,000.

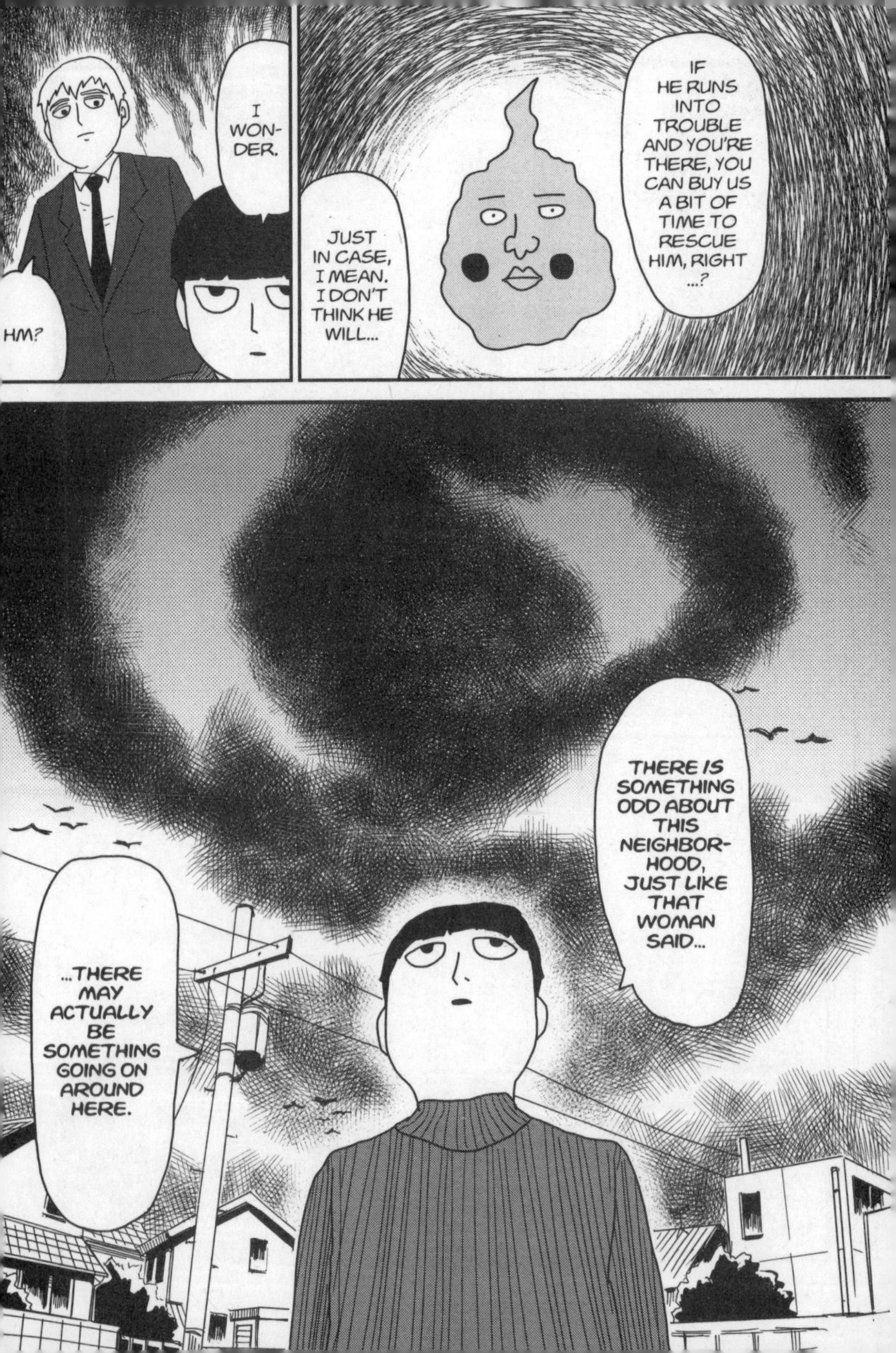
IF HE RUNS INTO TROUBLE AND YOU'RE THERE, YOU CAN BUY US A BIT OF TIME TO RESCUE HIM, RIGHT ...?
JUST IN CASE, I MEAN. I DON'T THINK HE WILL...
I WONDER.
HM?
THERE IS SOMETHING ODD ABOUT THIS NEIGHBORHOOD, JUST LIKE THAT WOMAN SAID...
...THERE MAY ACTUALLY BE SOMETHING GOING ON AROUND HERE.

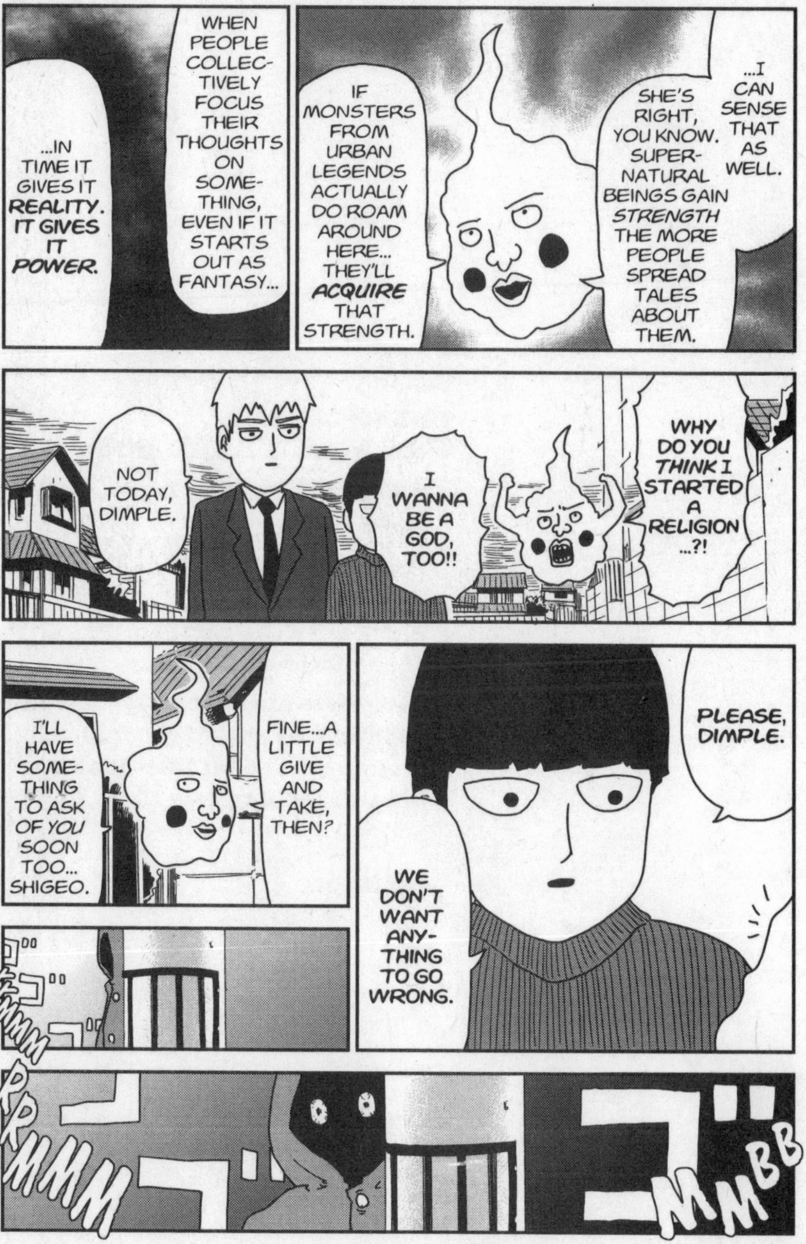
...I CAN SENSE THAT AS WELL.
SHE'S RIGHT, YOU KNOW. SUPER-NATURAL BEINGS GAIN STRENGTH THE MORE PEOPLE SPREAD TALES ABOUT THEM.
IF MONSTERS FROM URBAN LEGENDS ACTUALLY DO ROAM AROUND HERE... THEY'LL ACQUIRE THAT STRENGTH.
WHEN PEOPLE COLLEC-TIVELY FOCUS THEIR THOUGHTS ON SOME-THING, EVEN IF IT STARTS OUT AS FANTASY...
...IN TIME IT GIVES IT REALITY. IT GIVES IT POWER.
WHY DO YOU THINK I STARTED A RELIGION ...?!
I WANNA BE A GOD, TOO!!
NOT TODAY, DIMPLE.
PLEASE, DIMPLE.
WE DON'T WANT ANY-THING TO GO WRONG.
FINE...A LITTLE GIVE AND TAKE, THEN?
I'LL HAVE SOME-THING TO ASK OF YOU SOON TOO... SHIGEO.
RMMMM
RRMMMM
MMBB

URBAN LEGEND:

THE MAN-FACED DOG

- **A dog with the face of a middle-aged man.**
- **A dog with the voice of a middle-aged man.**
- **A dog with the personality of a middle-aged man.**
- **Occultists are currently debating whether it should be renamed "The Middle-Aged Man-Faced Dog."**

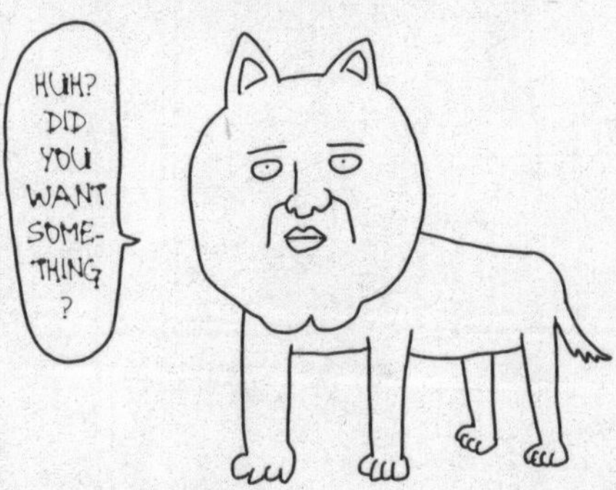
HUH? DID YOU WANT SOME-THING ?

CHAPTER 54: RUMORS AND CONFRONTATIONS

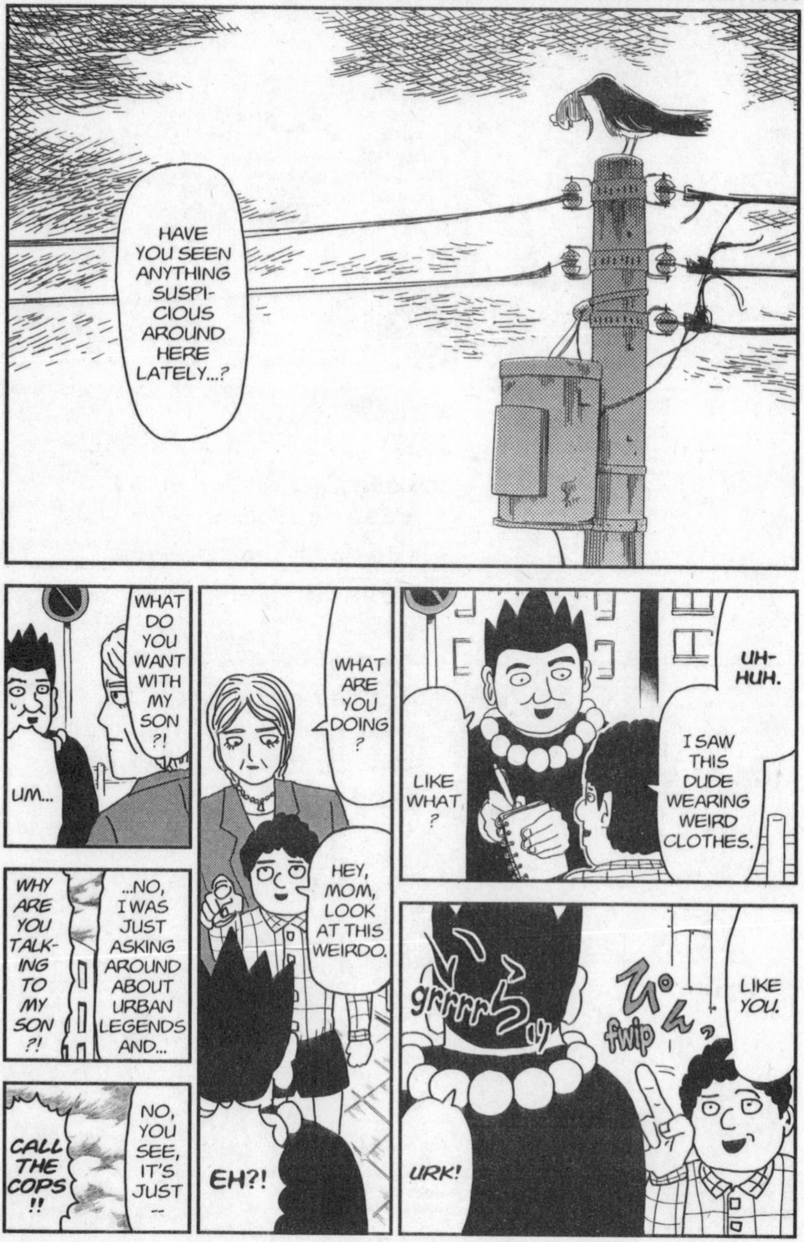
HAVE YOU SEEN ANYTHING SUSPICIOUS AROUND HERE LATELY...?
UH-HUH.
I SAW THIS DUDE WEARING WEIRD CLOTHES.
LIKE WHAT?
LIKE YOU.
fwip
grrrr
URK!
WHAT ARE YOU DOING?
HEY, MOM, LOOK AT THIS WEIRDO.
EH?!
WHAT DO YOU WANT WITH MY SON?!
UM...
...NO, I WAS JUST ASKING AROUND ABOUT URBAN LEGENDS AND...
WHY ARE YOU TALKING TO MY SON?!
NO, YOU SEE, IT'S JUST --
CALL THE COPS!!

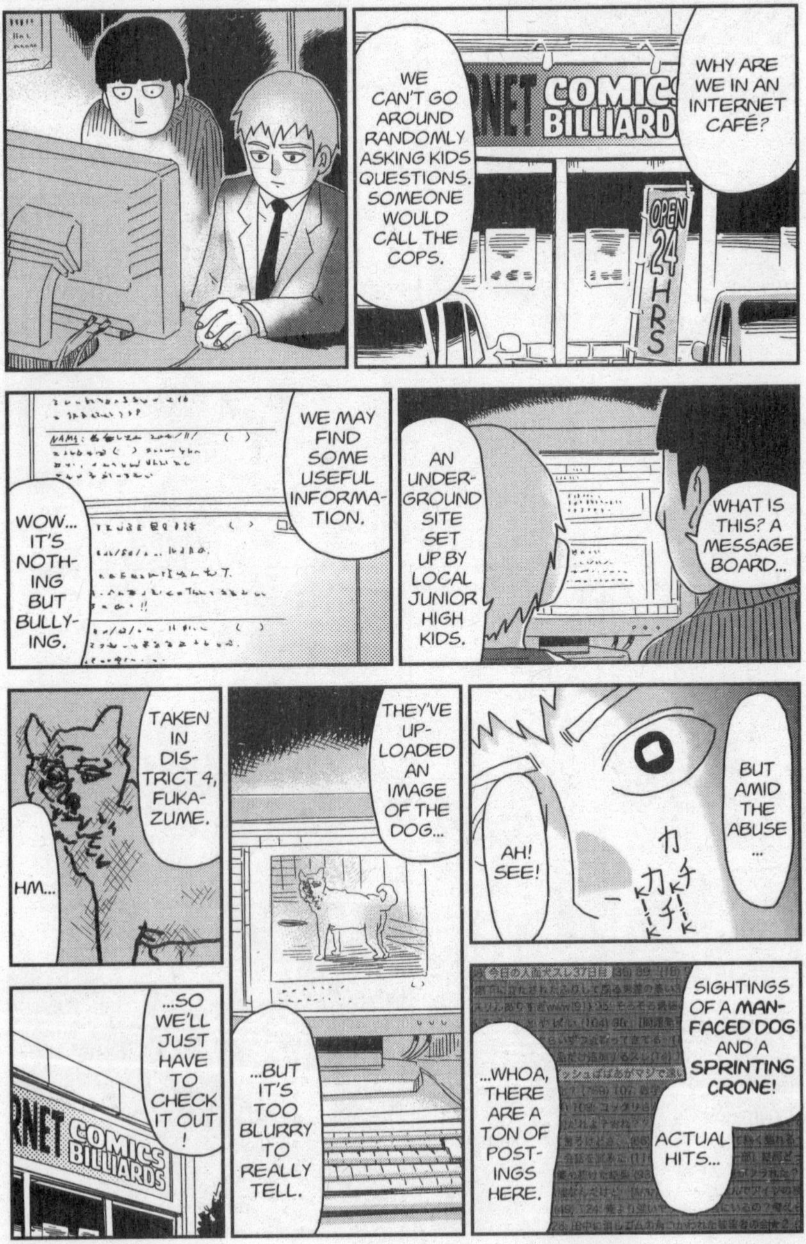
WHY ARE WE IN AN INTERNET CAFÉ?
WE CAN'T GO AROUND RANDOMLY ASKING KIDS QUESTIONS. SOMEONE WOULD CALL THE COPS.
OPEN 24 HRS
WHAT IS THIS? A MESSAGE BOARD...
AN UNDERGROUND SITE SET UP BY LOCAL JUNIOR HIGH KIDS.
WE MAY FIND SOME USEFUL INFORMATION.
WOW... IT'S NOTHING BUT BULLYING.
BUT AMID THE ABUSE...
AH! SEE!
カチカチ KLIK KLIK
SIGHTINGS OF A MAN-FACED DOG AND A SPRINTING CRONE!
ACTUAL HITS...
...WHOA, THERE ARE A TON OF POSTINGS HERE.
THEY'VE UPLOADED AN IMAGE OF THE DOG...
...BUT IT'S TOO BLURRY TO REALLY TELL.
TAKEN IN DISTRICT 4, FUKAZUME.
HM...
...SO WE'LL JUST HAVE TO CHECK IT OUT!
COMICS BILLIARDS

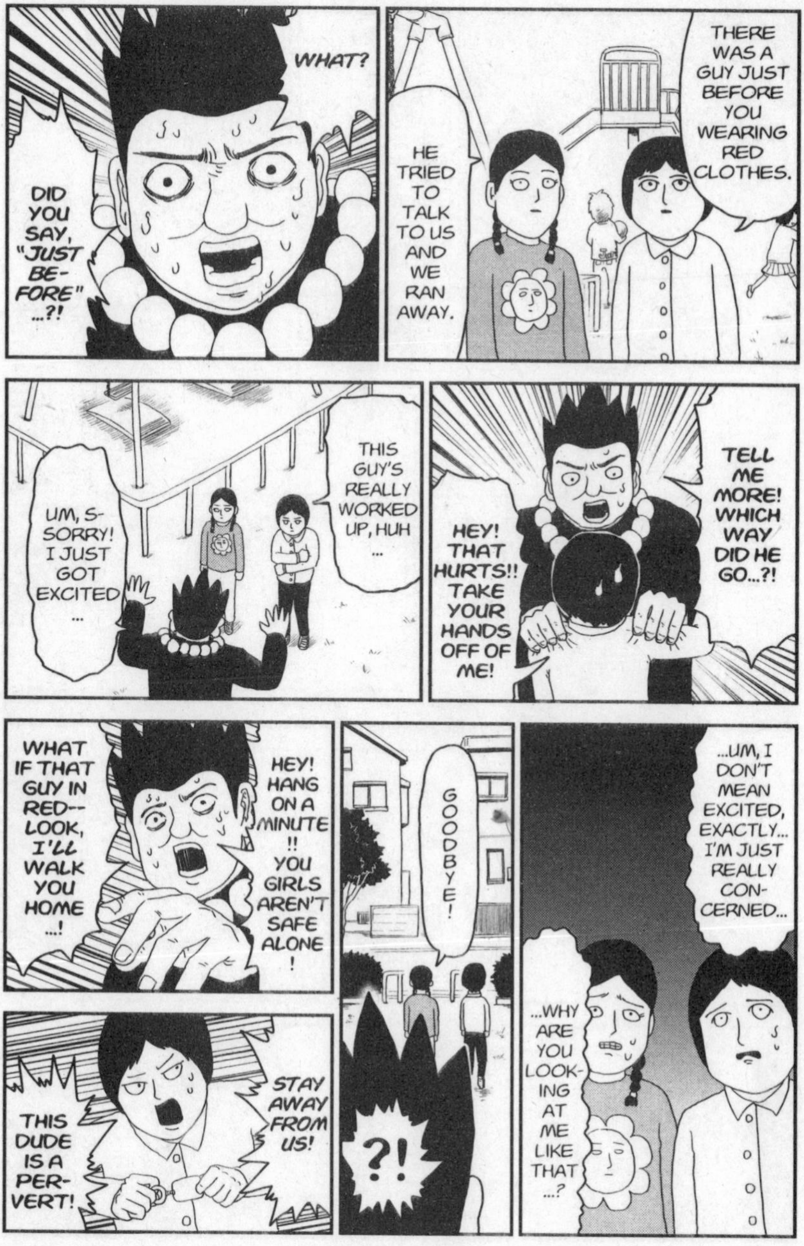
THERE WAS A GUY JUST BEFORE YOU WEARING RED CLOTHES.
HE TRIED TO TALK TO US AND WE RAN AWAY.
WHAT?
DID YOU SAY, "JUST BEFORE" ...?!
TELL ME MORE! WHICH WAY DID HE GO...?!
HEY! THAT HURTS!! TAKE YOUR HANDS OFF OF ME!
THIS GUY'S REALLY WORKED UP, HUH ...
UM, S-SORRY! I JUST GOT EXCITED ...
...UM, I DON'T MEAN EXCITED, EXACTLY... I'M JUST REALLY CONCERNED...
...WHY ARE YOU LOOKING AT ME LIKE THAT ...?
GOODBYE!
?!
HEY! HANG ON A MINUTE!! YOU GIRLS AREN'T SAFE ALONE!
WHAT IF THAT GUY IN RED-- LOOK, I'LL WALK YOU HOME ...!
STAY AWAY FROM US!
THIS DUDE IS A PERVERT!

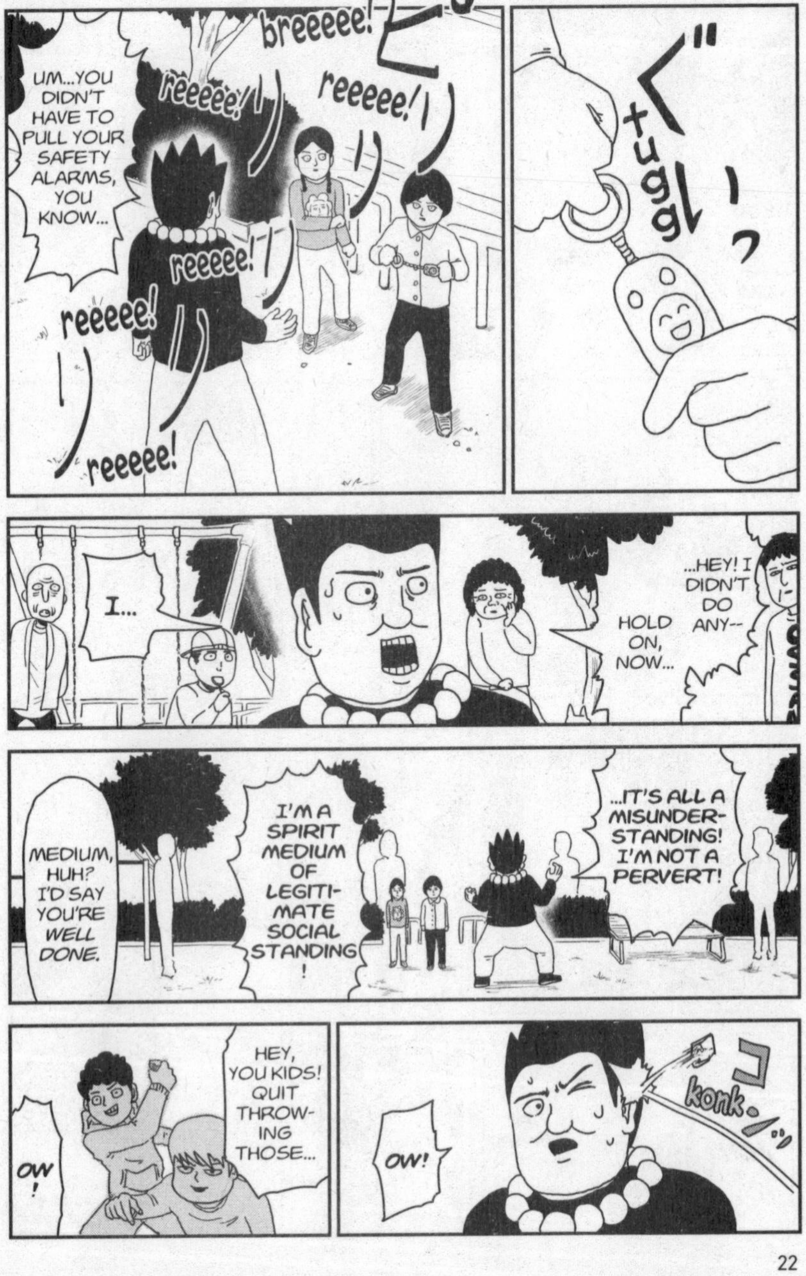
tug
breeeee!
reeeee!
reeeee!
UM...YOU DIDN'T HAVE TO PULL YOUR SAFETY ALARMS, YOU KNOW...
reeeee!
reeeee!
reeeee!
...HEY! I DIDN'T DO ANY--
HOLD ON, NOW...
I...
...IT'S ALL A MISUNDERSTANDING! I'M NOT A PERVERT!
I'M A SPIRIT MEDIUM OF LEGITIMATE SOCIAL STANDING!
MEDIUM, HUH? I'D SAY YOU'RE WELL DONE.
konk
OW!
HEY, YOU KIDS! QUIT THROWING THOSE...
OW!

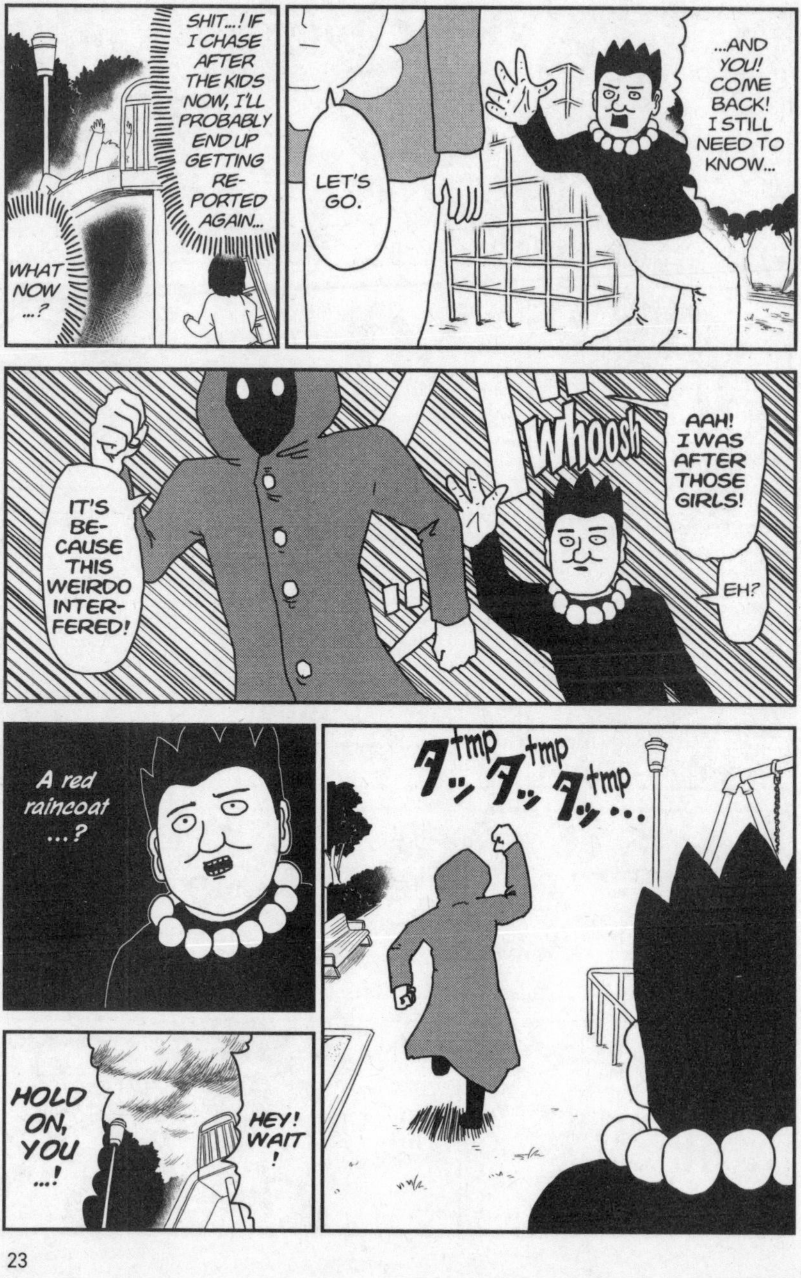
...AND YOU! COME BACK! I STILL NEED TO KNOW...
LET'S GO.
SHIT...! IF I CHASE AFTER THE KIDS NOW, I'LL PROBABLY END UP GETTING RE-PORTED AGAIN...
WHAT NOW ...?
AAH! I WAS AFTER THOSE GIRLS!
Whoosh
EH?
IT'S BE-CAUSE THIS WEIRDO INTER-FERED!
タッタッタッ...
tmp tmp tmp
A red raincoat ...?
HEY! WAIT!
HOLD ON, YOU ...!

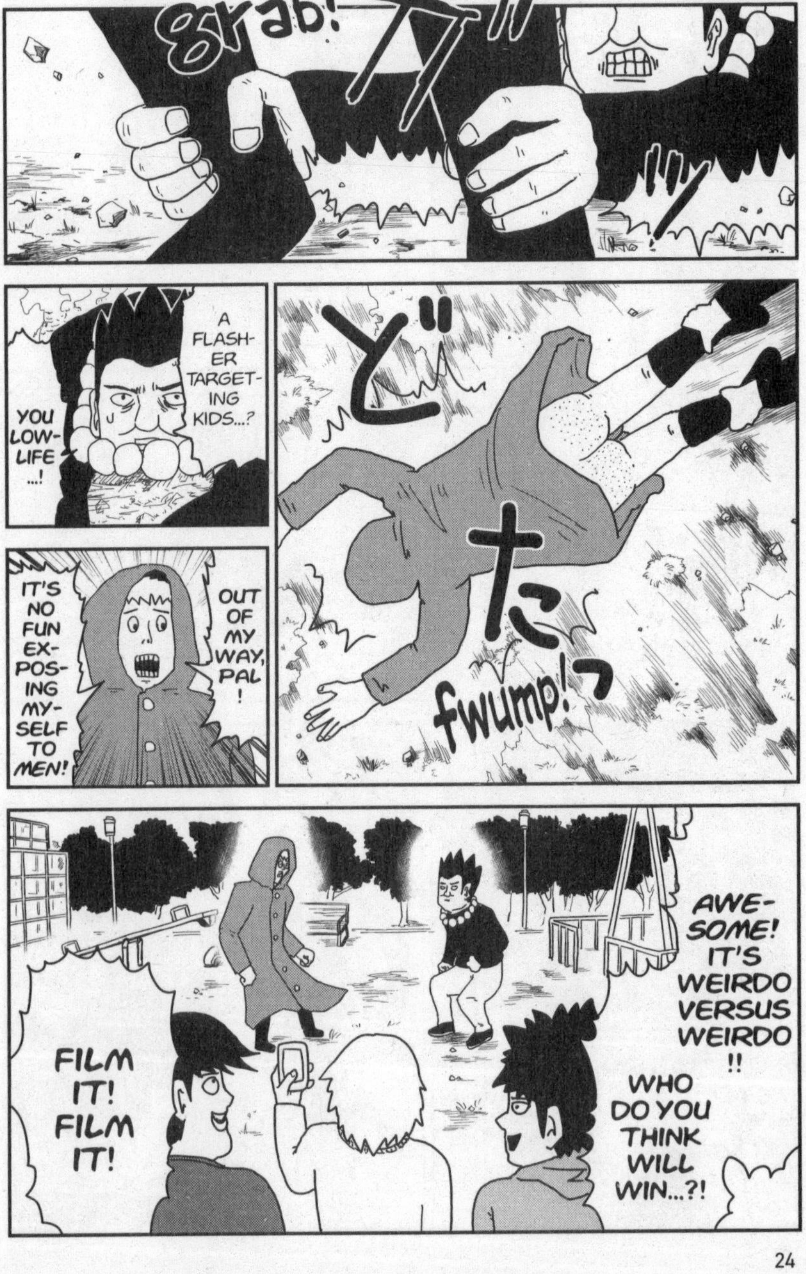

grab! カッ
どた
fwump!
A FLASHER TARGETING KIDS...?
YOU LOWLIFE...!
OUT OF MY WAY, PAL!
IT'S NO FUN EXPOSING MYSELF TO MEN!
AWESOME! IT'S WEIRDO VERSUS WEIRDO!!
WHO DO YOU THINK WILL WIN...?!
FILM IT! FILM IT!

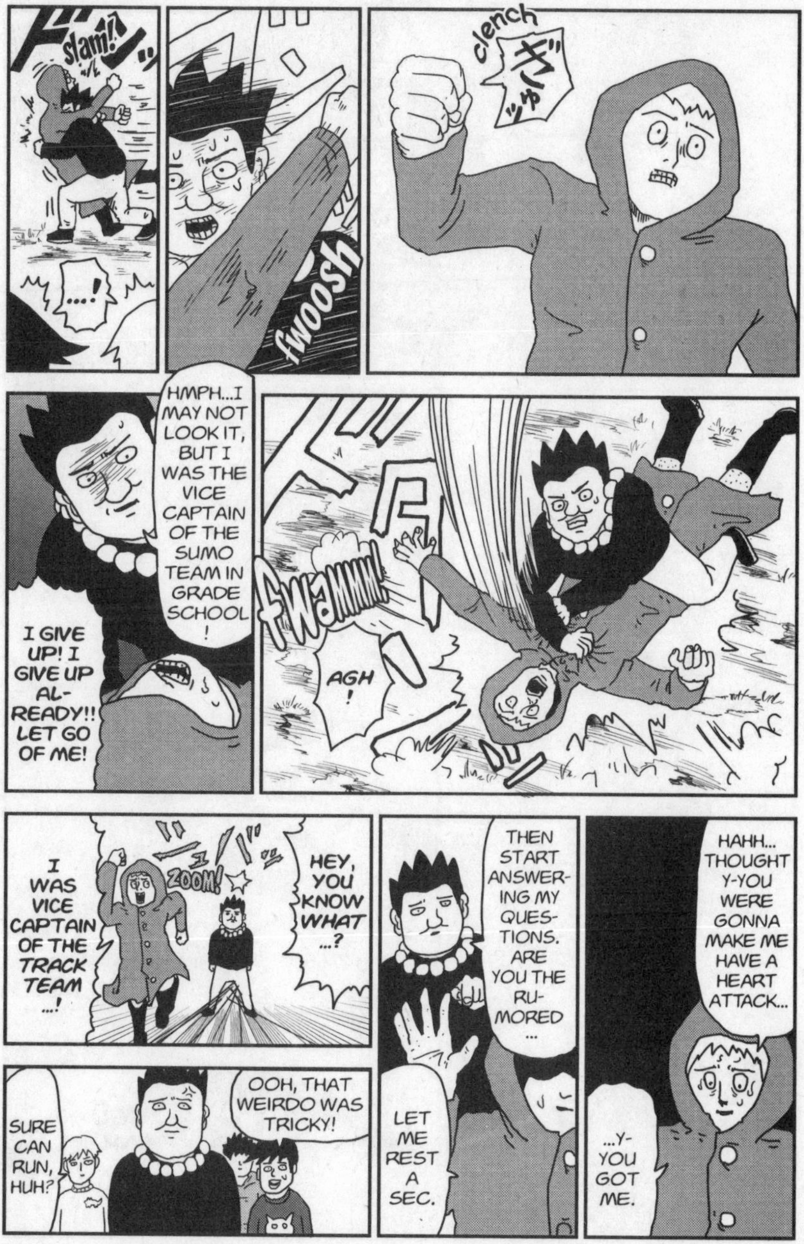
clench
ぎゅッ
fwoosh
slam!?
...!
fwammm!
AGH!
HMPH...I MAY NOT LOOK IT, BUT I WAS THE VICE CAPTAIN OF THE SUMO TEAM IN GRADE SCHOOL!
I GIVE UP! I GIVE UP ALREADY!! LET GO OF ME!
HAHH... THOUGHT Y-YOU WERE GONNA MAKE ME HAVE A HEART ATTACK...
...Y-YOU GOT ME.
THEN START ANSWERING MY QUESTIONS. ARE YOU THE RUMORED...
LET ME REST A SEC.
HEY, YOU KNOW WHAT...?
ZOOM!
I WAS VICE CAPTAIN OF THE TRACK TEAM...!
OOH, THAT WEIRDO WAS TRICKY!
SURE CAN RUN, HUH?

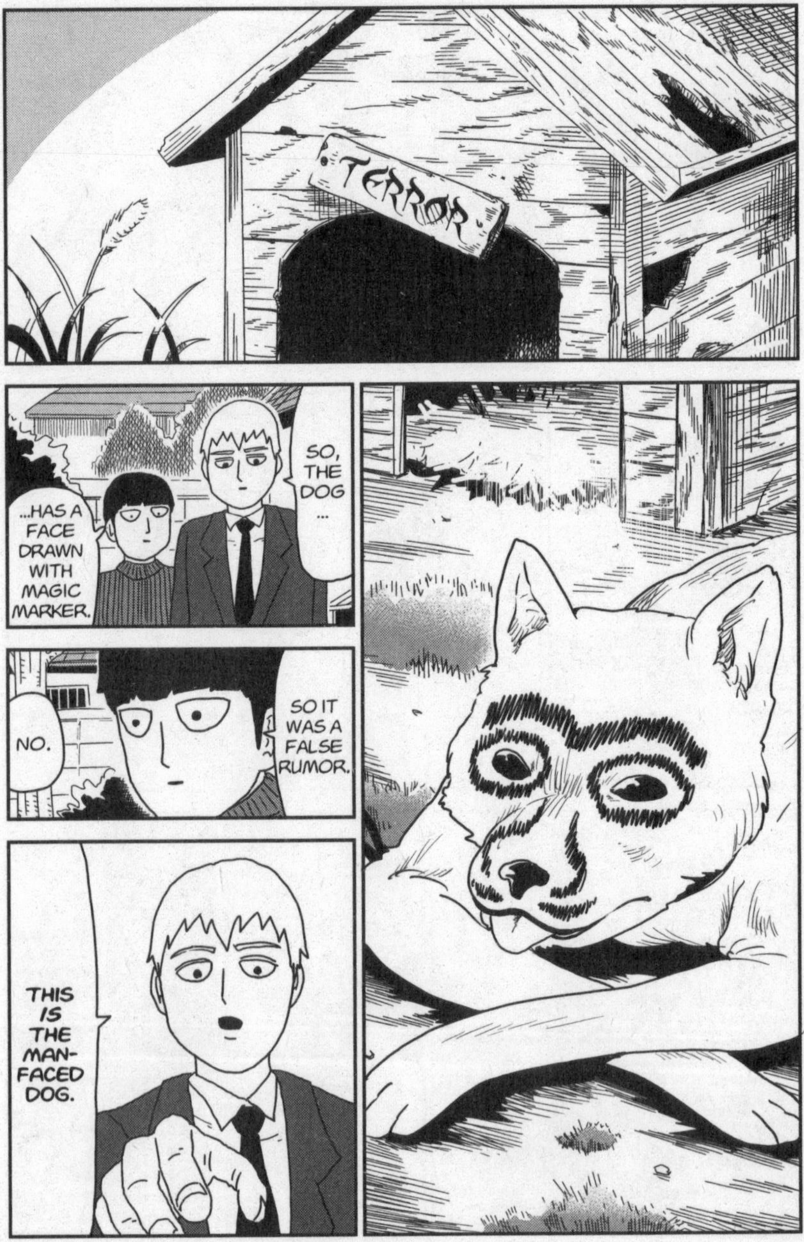
TERROR
SO, THE DOG ...
...HAS A FACE DRAWN WITH MAGIC MARKER.
SO IT WAS A FALSE RUMOR.
NO.
THIS IS THE MAN-FACED DOG.

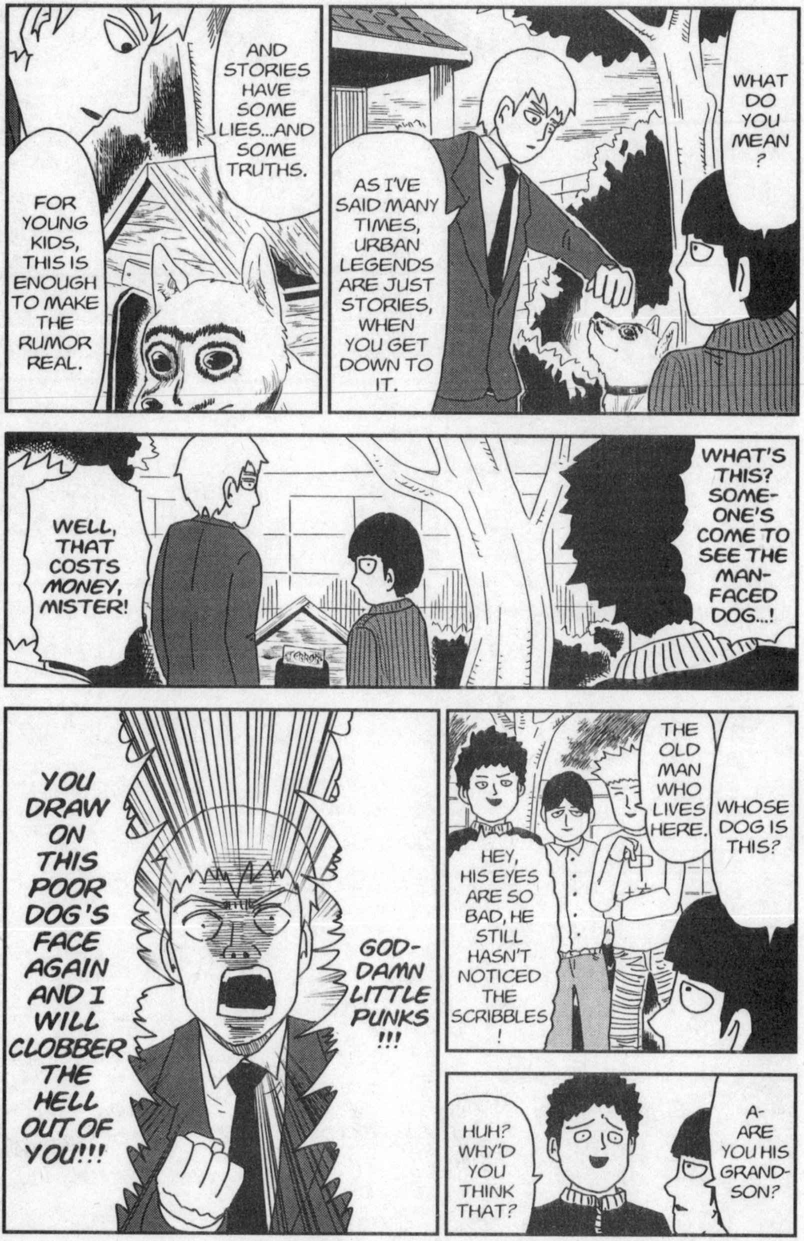

WHAT DO YOU MEAN?
AS I'VE SAID MANY TIMES, URBAN LEGENDS ARE JUST STORIES, WHEN YOU GET DOWN TO IT.
AND STORIES HAVE SOME LIES...AND SOME TRUTHS.
FOR YOUNG KIDS, THIS IS ENOUGH TO MAKE THE RUMOR REAL.
WHAT'S THIS? SOME-ONE'S COME TO SEE THE MAN-FACED DOG...!
WELL, THAT COSTS *MONEY*, MISTER!
WHOSE DOG IS THIS?
THE OLD MAN WHO LIVES HERE.
HEY, HIS EYES ARE SO BAD, HE STILL HASN'T NOTICED THE SCRIBBLES!
A- ARE YOU HIS GRAND-SON?
HUH? WHY'D YOU THINK THAT?
GOD-DAMN LITTLE PUNKS!!!
YOU DRAW ON THIS POOR DOG'S FACE AGAIN AND I WILL CLOBBER THE HELL OUT OF YOU!!!

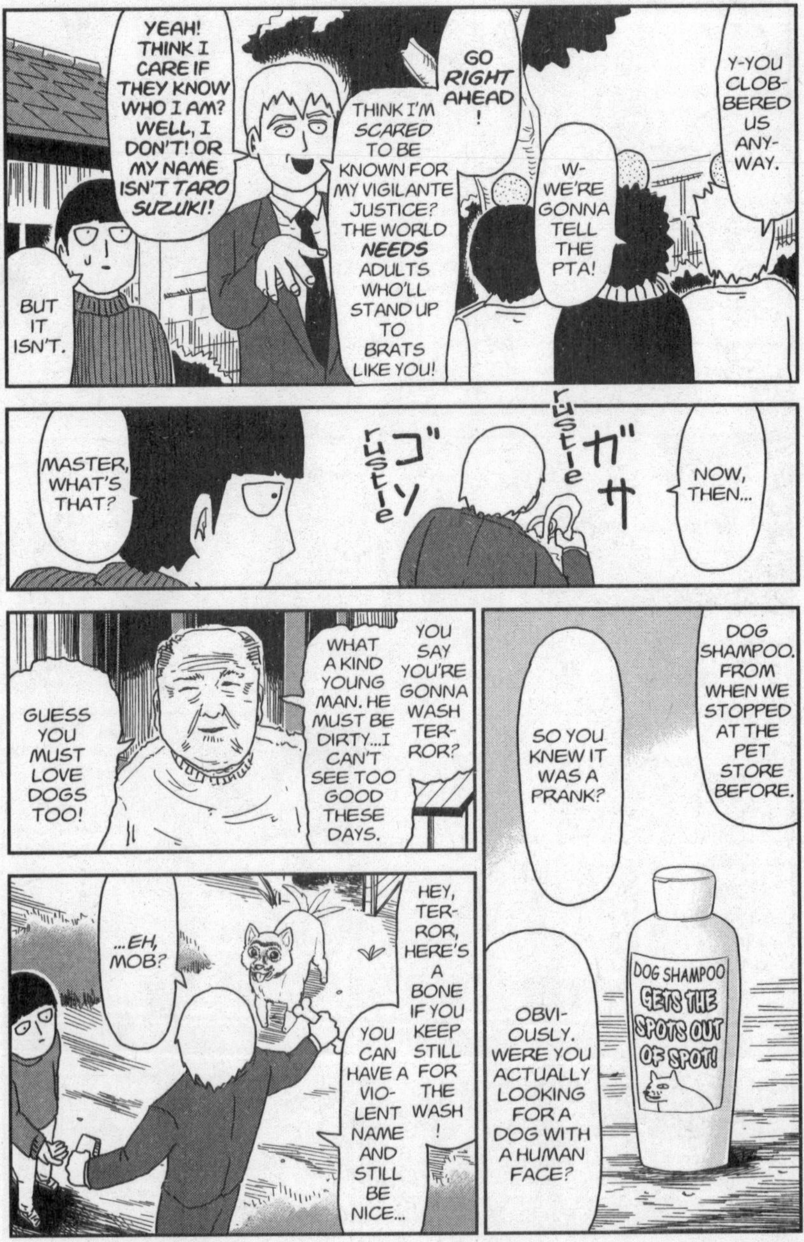
Y-YOU CLOBBERED US ANYWAY.
W-WE'RE GONNA TELL THE PTA!
GO RIGHT AHEAD!
THINK I'M SCARED TO BE KNOWN FOR MY VIGILANTE JUSTICE? THE WORLD NEEDS ADULTS WHO'LL STAND UP TO BRATS LIKE YOU!
YEAH! THINK I CARE IF THEY KNOW WHO I AM? WELL, I DON'T! OR MY NAME ISN'T TARO SUZUKI!
BUT IT ISN'T.
NOW, THEN...
ガサ rustle
ゴソ rustle
MASTER, WHAT'S THAT?
DOG SHAMPOO. FROM WHEN WE STOPPED AT THE PET STORE BEFORE.
SO YOU KNEW IT WAS A PRANK?
DOG SHAMPOO
GETS THE SPOTS OUT OF SPOT!
OBVIOUSLY. WERE YOU ACTUALLY LOOKING FOR A DOG WITH A HUMAN FACE?
YOU SAY YOU'RE GONNA WASH TERROR?
WHAT A KIND YOUNG MAN. HE MUST BE DIRTY...I CAN'T SEE TOO GOOD THESE DAYS.
GUESS YOU MUST LOVE DOGS TOO!
HEY, TERROR, HERE'S A BONE IF YOU KEEP STILL FOR THE WASH!
YOU CAN HAVE A VIOLENT NAME AND STILL BE NICE...
...EH, MOB?

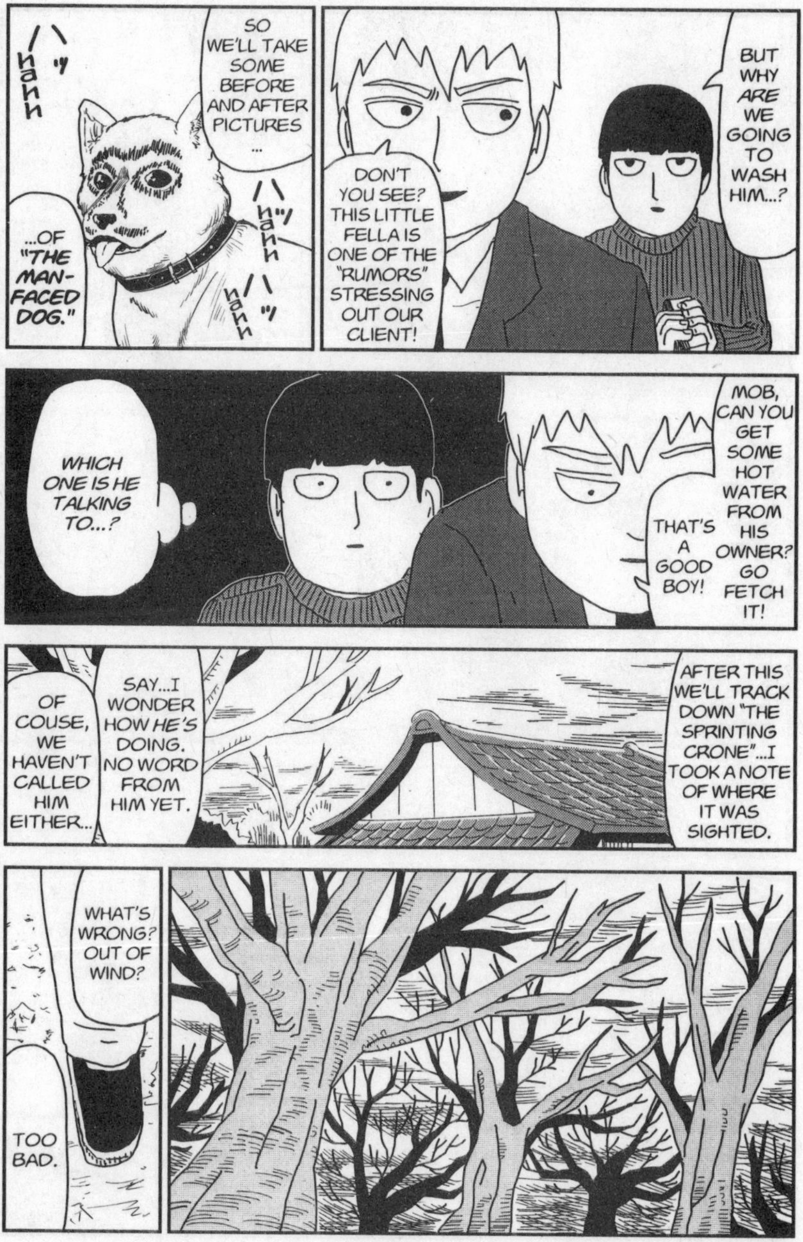
BUT WHY ARE WE GOING TO WASH HIM...?
DON'T YOU SEE? THIS LITTLE FELLA IS ONE OF THE "RUMORS" STRESSING OUT OUR CLIENT!
SO WE'LL TAKE SOME BEFORE AND AFTER PICTURES ...
...OF "THE MAN-FACED DOG."
ハッ hahh
ハッ hahh
ハッ hahh
MOB, CAN YOU GET SOME HOT WATER FROM HIS OWNER? GO FETCH IT!
THAT'S A GOOD BOY!
WHICH ONE IS HE TALKING TO...?
AFTER THIS WE'LL TRACK DOWN "THE SPRINTING CRONE"...I TOOK A NOTE OF WHERE IT WAS SIGHTED.
SAY...I WONDER HOW HE'S DOING. NO WORD FROM HIM YET.
OF COUSE, WE HAVEN'T CALLED HIM EITHER...
WHAT'S WRONG? OUT OF WIND?
TOO BAD.

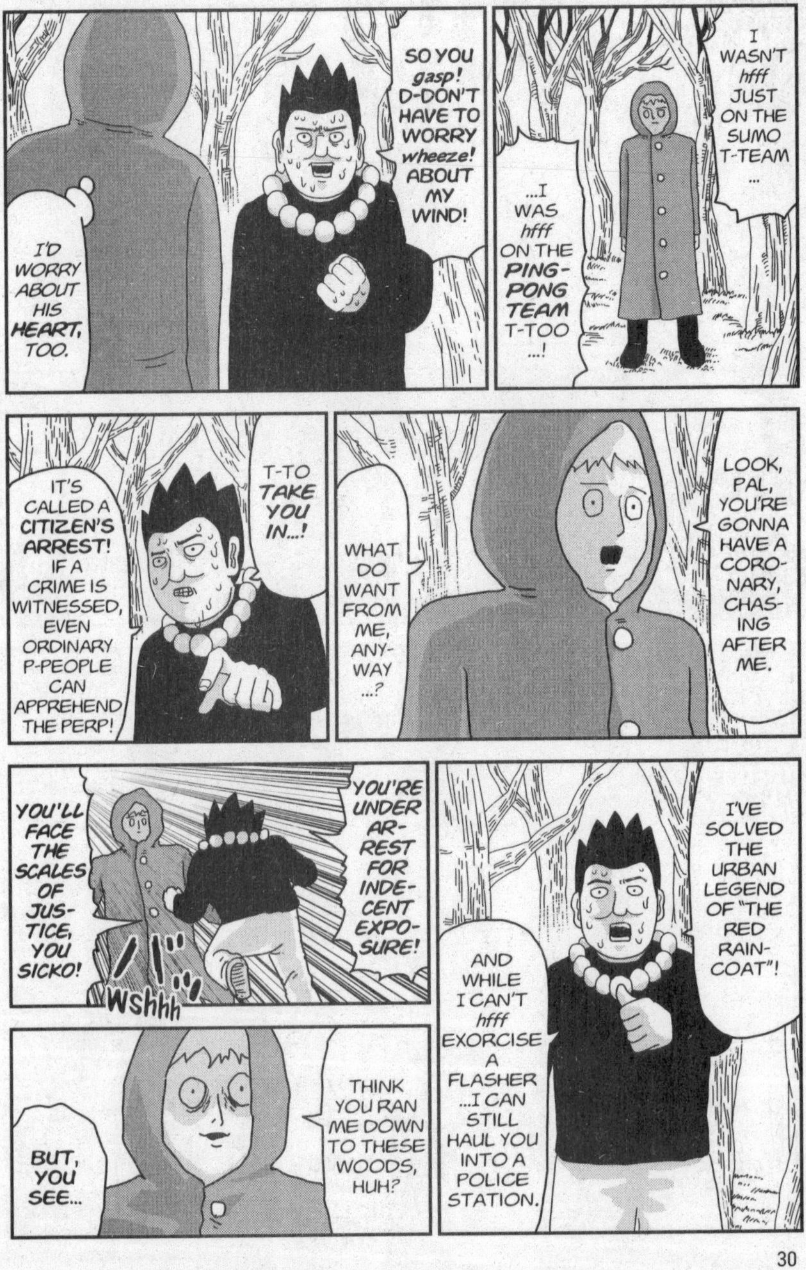
I WASN'T *hfff* JUST ON THE SUMO T-TEAM ...
...I WAS *hfff* ON THE **PING-PONG TEAM** T-TOO ...!
SO YOU *gasp!* D-DON'T HAVE TO WORRY *wheeze!* ABOUT MY WIND!
*I'D WORRY ABOUT HIS **HEART,** TOO.*
LOOK, PAL, YOU'RE GONNA HAVE A CORONARY, CHASING AFTER ME.
WHAT DO WANT FROM ME, ANYWAY ...?
T-TO ***TAKE YOU IN...!***
IT'S CALLED A **CITIZEN'S ARREST!** IF A CRIME IS WITNESSED, EVEN ORDINARY P-PEOPLE CAN APPREHEND THE PERP!
I'VE SOLVED THE URBAN LEGEND OF "THE RED RAINCOAT"!
AND WHILE I CAN'T *hfff* EXORCISE A FLASHER ...I CAN STILL HAUL YOU INTO A POLICE STATION.
YOU'RE UNDER ARREST FOR INDECENT EXPOSURE!
YOU'LL FACE THE SCALES OF JUSTICE, YOU SICKO!
WSHHH
THINK YOU RAN ME DOWN TO THESE WOODS, HUH?
BUT, YOU SEE...

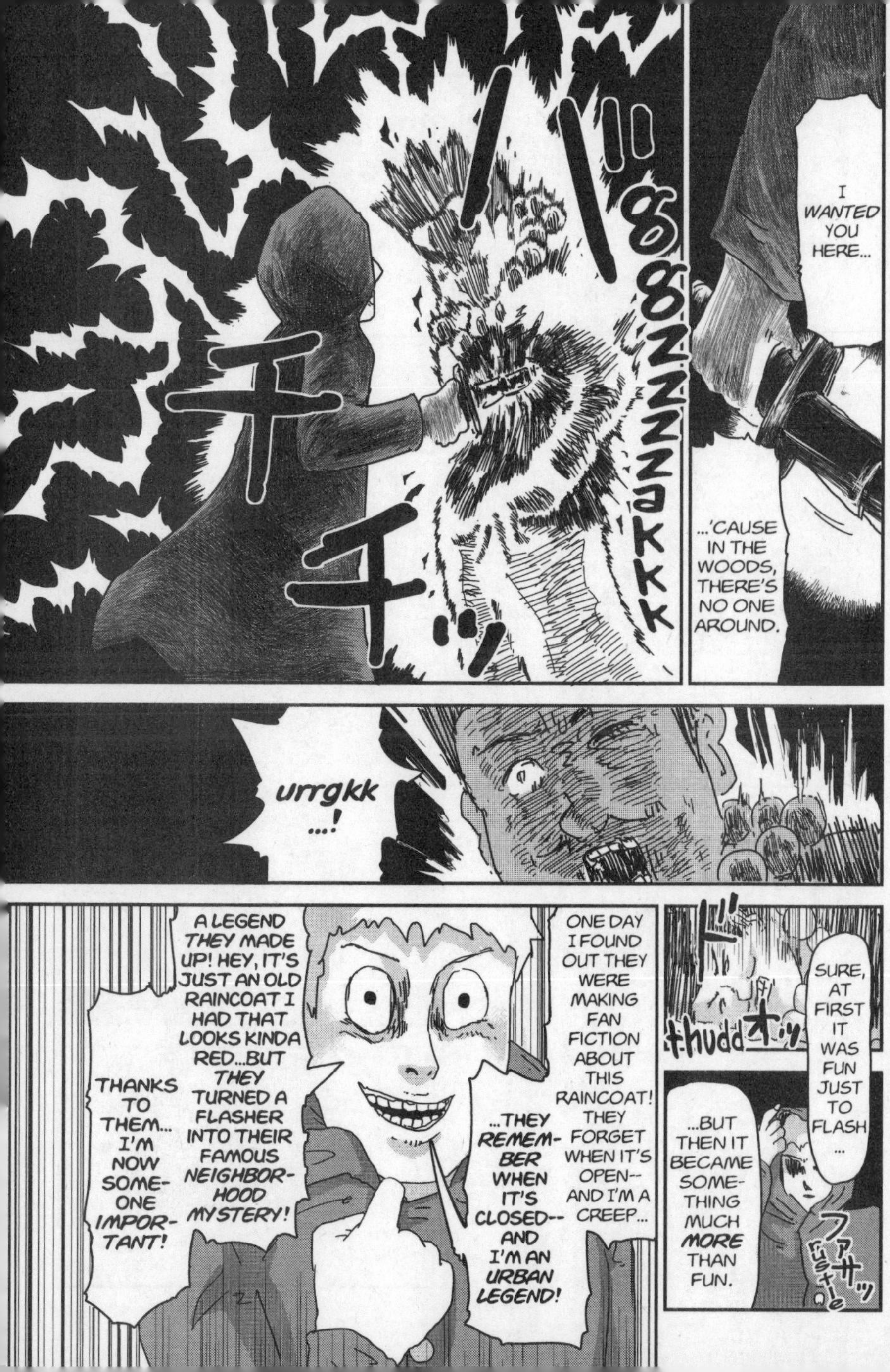
I WANTED YOU HERE...
...'CAUSE IN THE WOODS, THERE'S NO ONE AROUND.
urrgkk ...!
thudd
SURE, AT FIRST IT WAS FUN JUST TO FLASH...
...BUT THEN IT BECAME SOMETHING MUCH MORE THAN FUN.
rustle
ONE DAY I FOUND OUT THEY WERE MAKING FAN FICTION ABOUT THIS RAINCOAT! THEY FORGET WHEN IT'S OPEN--AND I'M A CREEP...
...THEY REMEMBER WHEN IT'S CLOSED--AND I'M AN URBAN LEGEND!
A LEGEND THEY MADE UP! HEY, IT'S JUST AN OLD RAINCOAT I HAD THAT LOOKS KINDA RED...BUT THEY TURNED A FLASHER INTO THEIR FAMOUS NEIGHBORHOOD MYSTERY!
THANKS TO THEM... I'M NOW SOMEONE IMPORTANT!

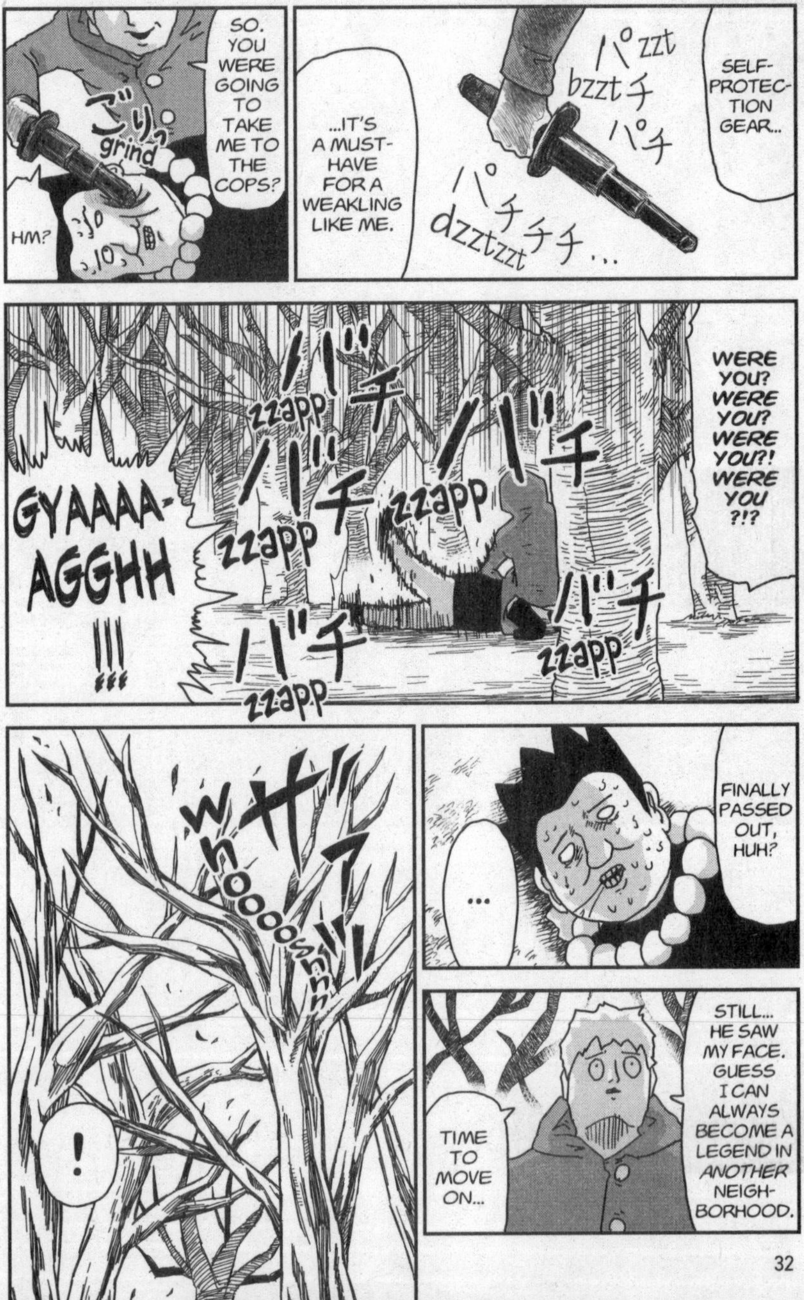
SELF-PROTECTION GEAR...
パzzt
bzztチ
パチ
パチ
チチ...
dzztzzt
...IT'S A MUST-HAVE FOR A WEAKLING LIKE ME.
SO. YOU WERE GOING TO TAKE ME TO THE COPS?
ごりっ
grind
HM?
WERE YOU? WERE YOU? WERE YOU?! WERE YOU ?!?
バチ
zzapp
バチ
zzapp
バチ
zzapp
バチ
zzapp
バチ
zzapp
GYAAAA-AGGHH!!!
FINALLY PASSED OUT, HUH?
...
STILL... HE SAW MY FACE. GUESS I CAN ALWAYS BECOME A LEGEND IN ANOTHER NEIGHBORHOOD.
TIME TO MOVE ON...
ザアッ
whoooooshhh
!

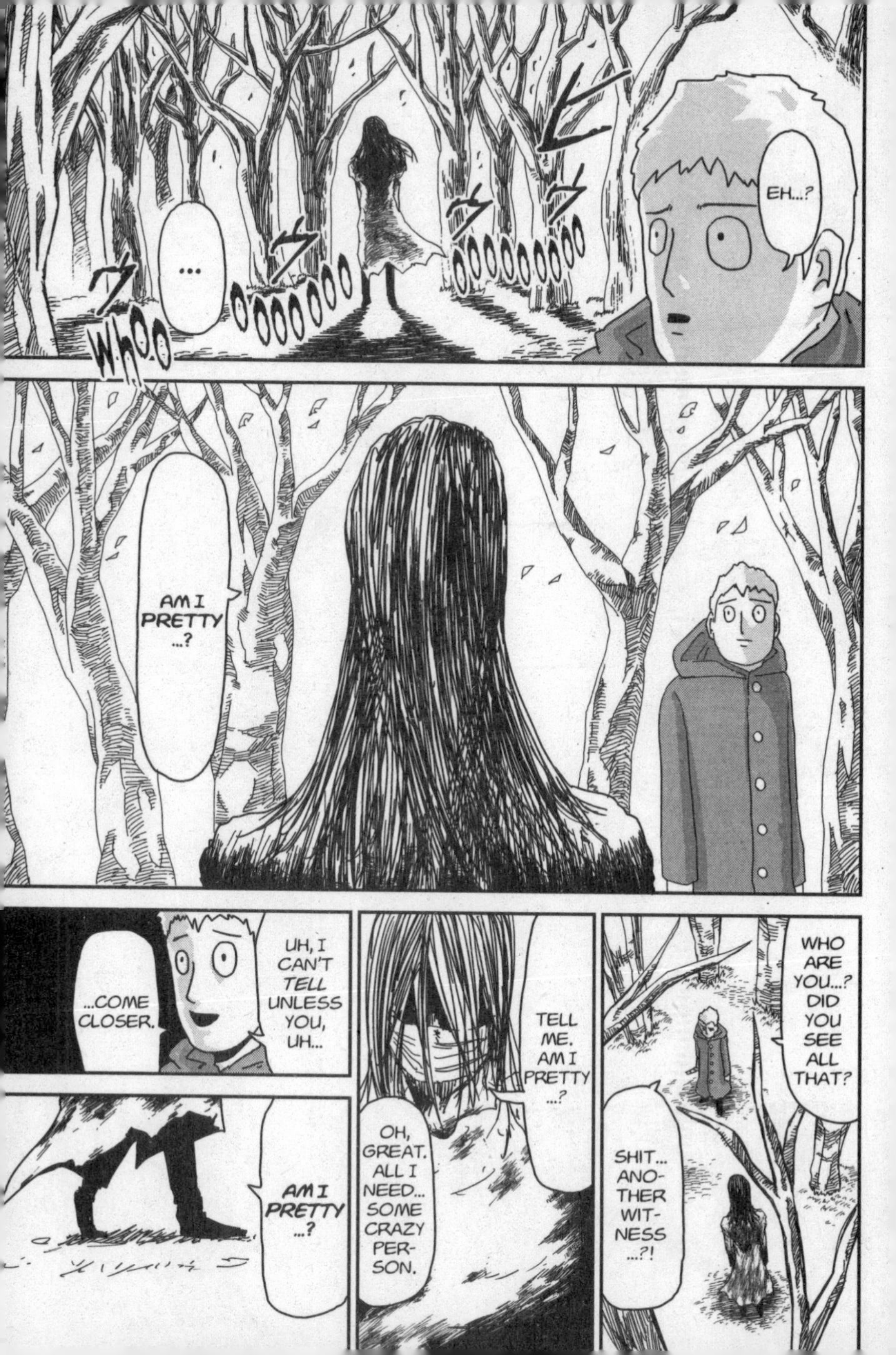
EH...?
...
WHOOOOOOOOOOOOOOOOOO
AM I PRETTY ...?
WHO ARE YOU...? DID YOU SEE ALL THAT?
SHIT... ANO-THER WIT-NESS ...?!
TELL ME. AM I PRETTY ...?
OH, GREAT. ALL I NEED... SOME CRAZY PER-SON.
UH, I CAN'T TELL UNLESS YOU, UH...
...COME CLOSER.
AM I PRETTY ...?

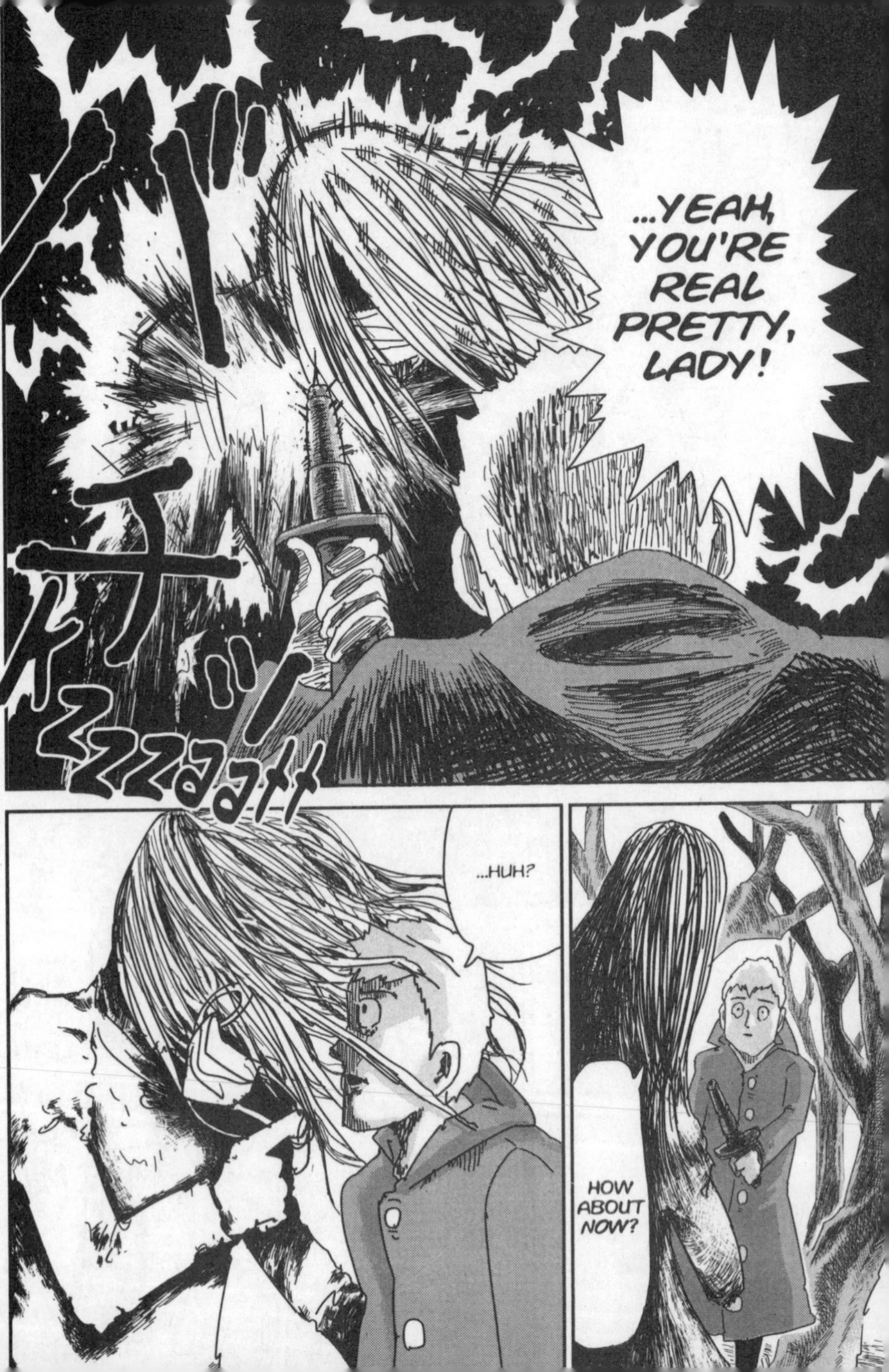
...YEAH, YOU'RE REAL PRETTY, LADY!
ZZZAATT
HOW ABOUT NOW?
...HUH?

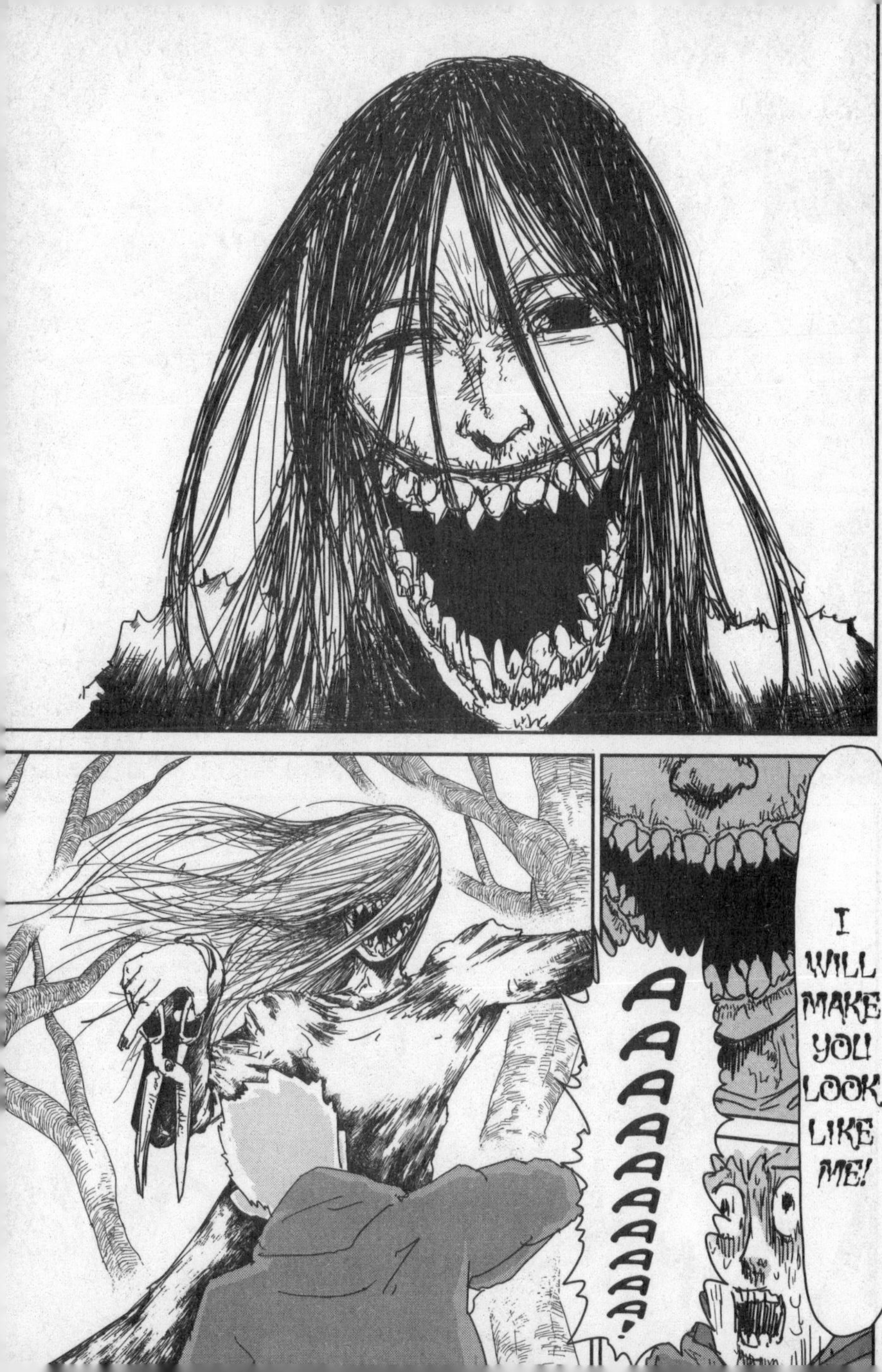
I WILL MAKE YOU LOOK LIKE ME!
AAAAAAAAAAAA!

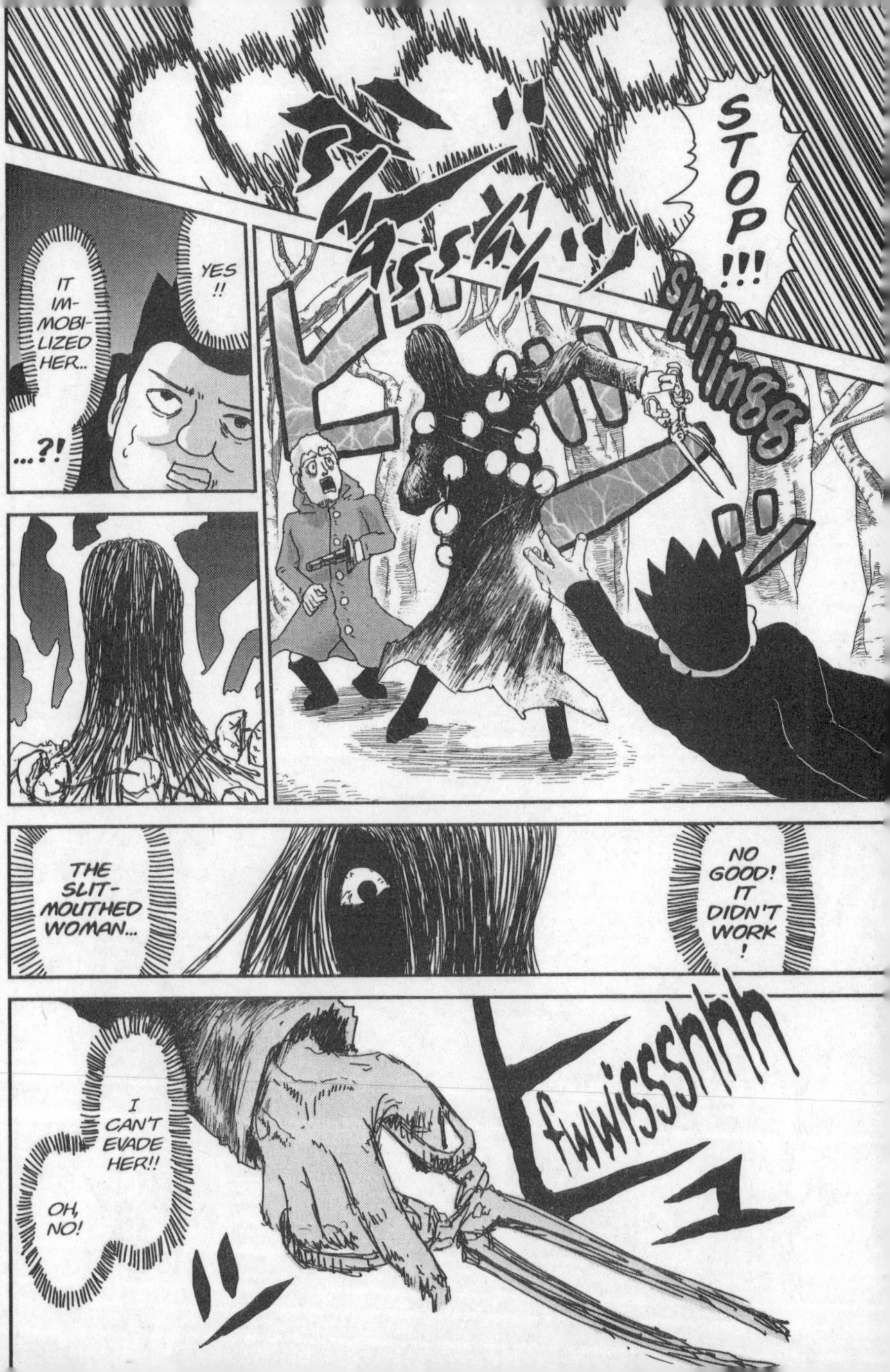
STOP!!!
shiiingg
YES!!
IT IMMOBILIZED HER...
...?!
NO GOOD! IT DIDN'T WORK!
THE SLIT-MOUTHED WOMAN...
fwiissshhh
I CAN'T EVADE HER!!
OH, NO!

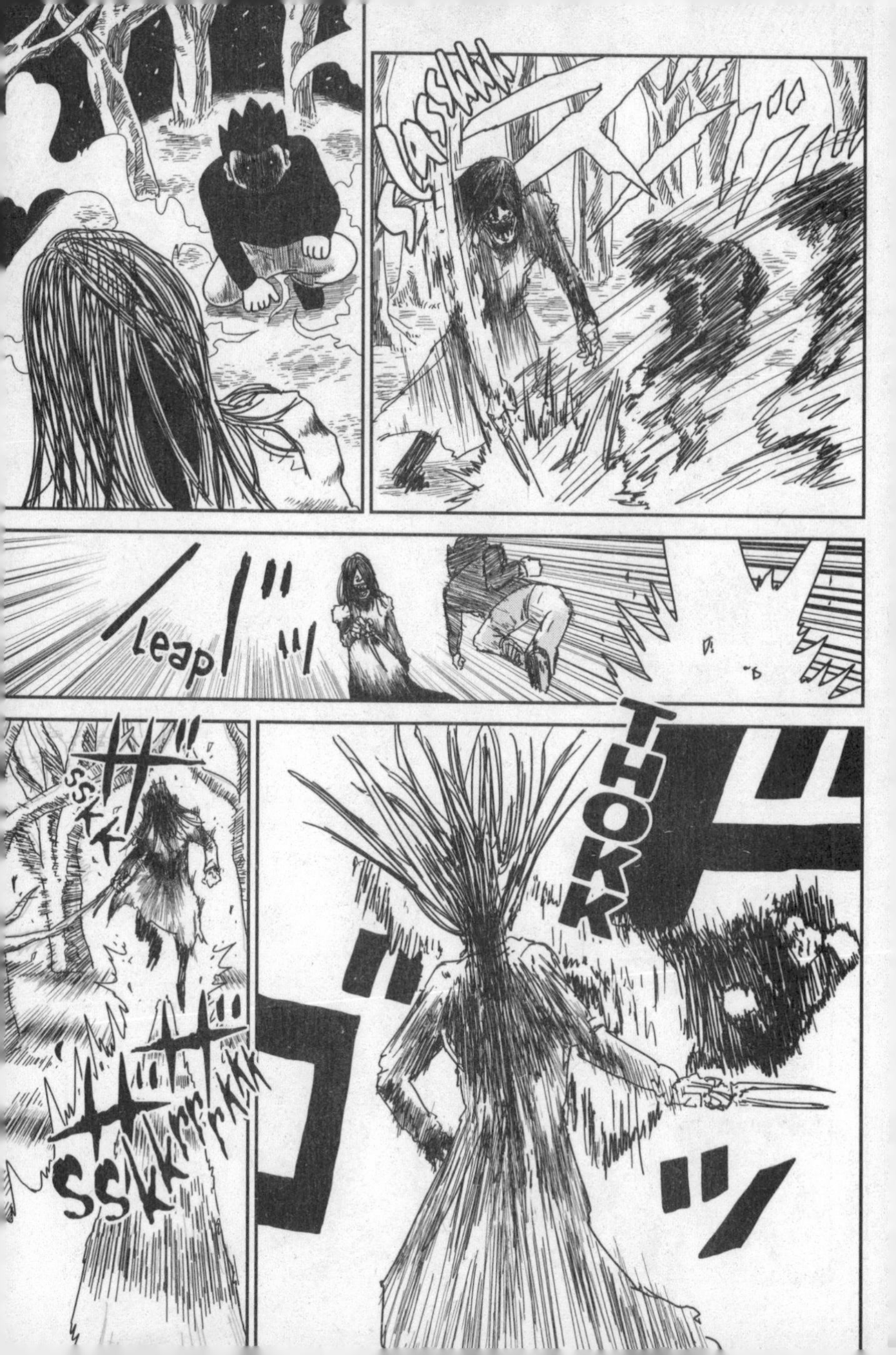
SLASSHHH
leap
THOKK
SSKK
SSKKRRRKKK

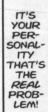

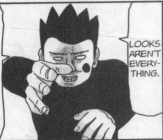

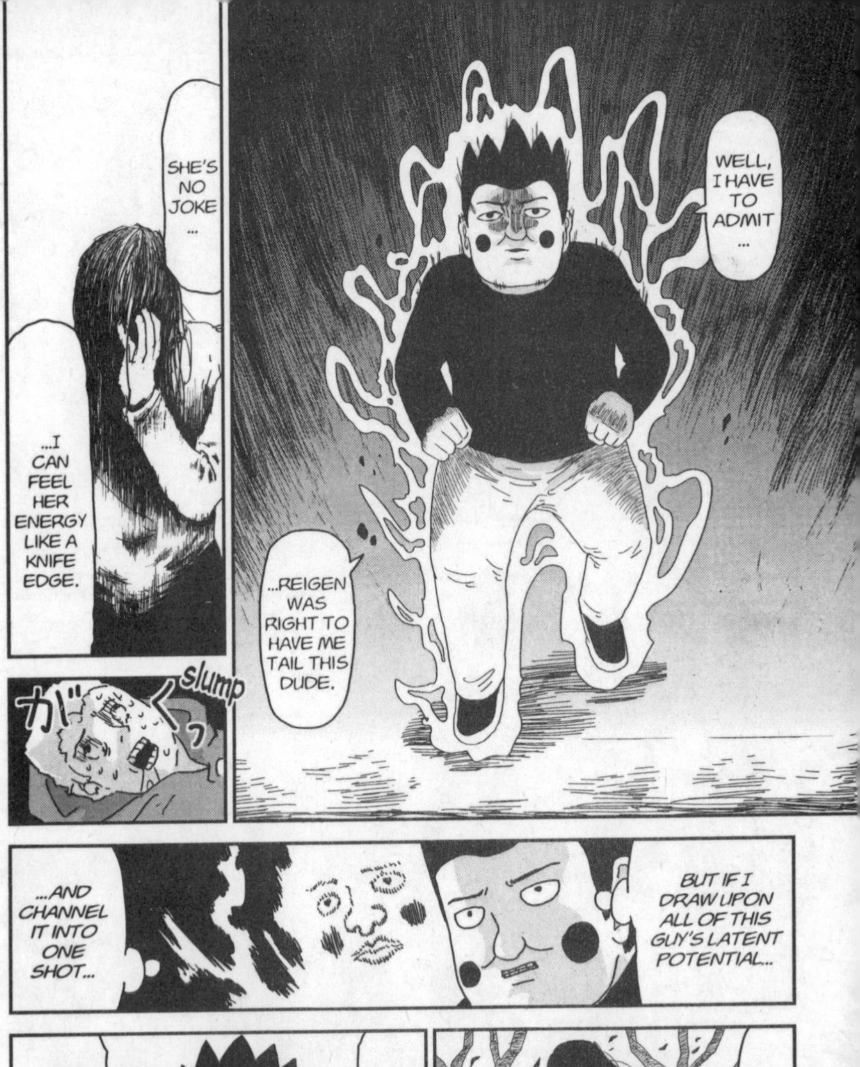
WELL, I HAVE TO ADMIT ...
...REIGEN WAS RIGHT TO HAVE ME TAIL THIS DUDE.
SHE'S NO JOKE ...
...I CAN FEEL HER ENERGY LIKE A KNIFE EDGE.
ガくっ
slump
BUT IF I DRAW UPON ALL OF THIS GUY'S LATENT POTENTIAL...
...AND CHANNEL IT INTO ONE SHOT...
AM I PRETTY ?
LOOKS AREN'T EVERY-THING.
IT'S YOUR PER-SONAL-ITY THAT'S THE *REAL* PROB-LEM!

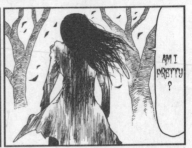

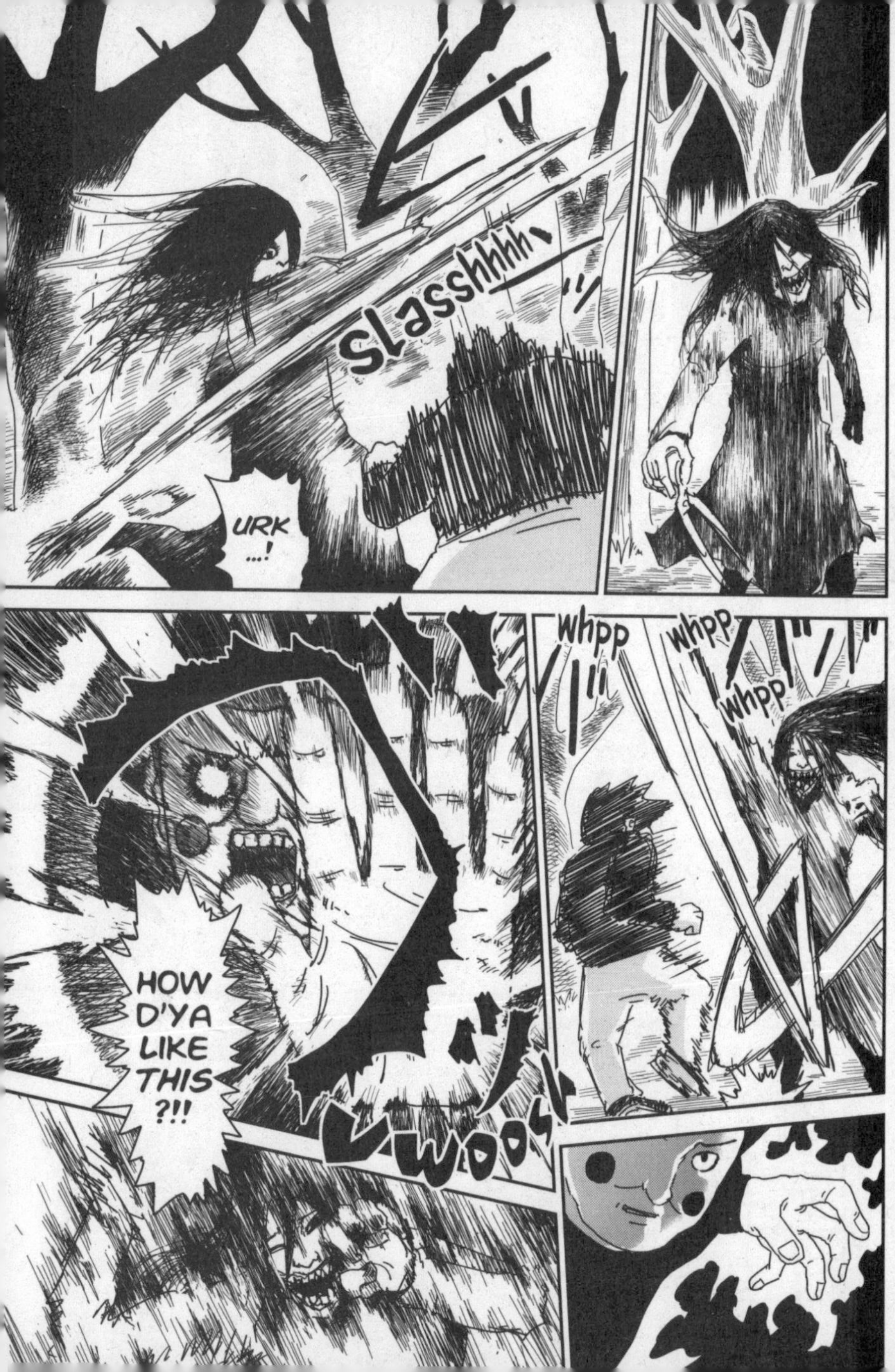
SLASSHHHH
URK ...!
whpp
whpp
whpp
HOW D'YA LIKE THIS?!!
WOOSH

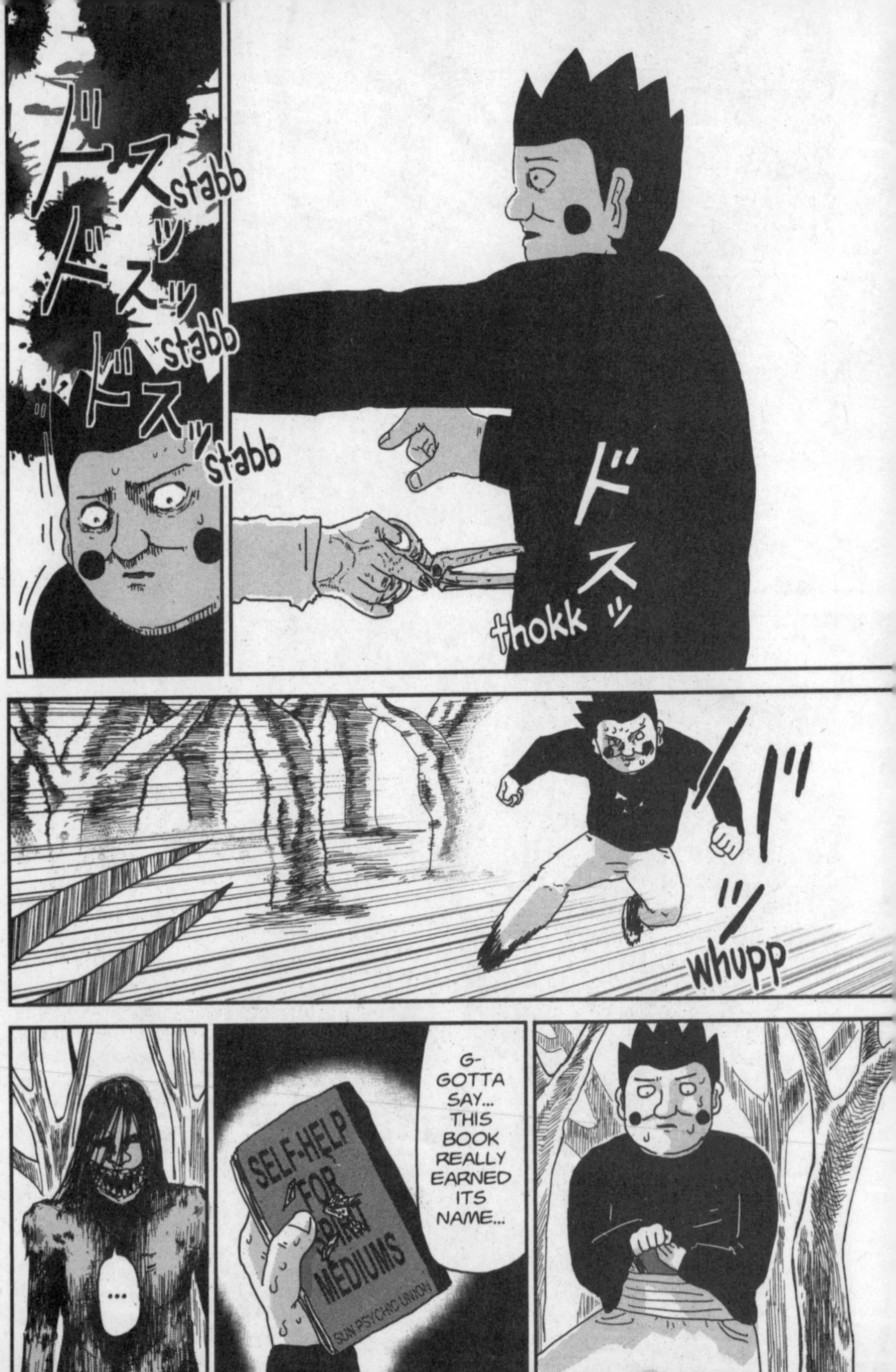
ドスッ
thokk
ドスッ
stabb
ドスッ
stabb
ドスッ
stabb
ダッ
whupp
G-GOTTA SAY... THIS BOOK REALLY EARNED ITS NAME...
SELF-HELP FOR
MEDIUMS
SUN PSYCHIC UNION
...

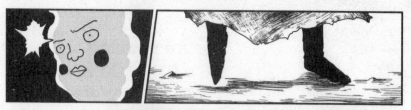

WELL ...
leap!
leap!
leap!
...TIME TO CALL FOR BACK-UP!!!
SWOOOSH
SOS!
beep!
SO! ALL CLEAN NOW!
OH! CALL FROM SHIN-RA.
brrrrrrrrr
CAN YOU PICK THAT UP, MOB?
NO, WAIT. YOU'RE SOAK-ING WET.
HOW DID YOU GET SO MESSY?
I SHOULD NOT HAVE HELPED ...
fwippp
fwipp
fwipp

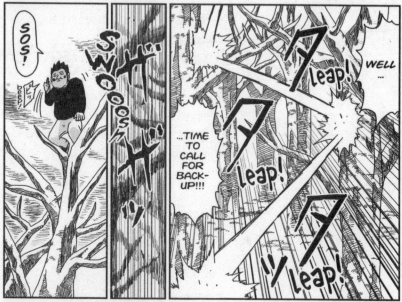

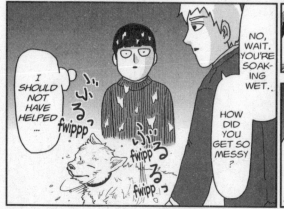

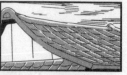

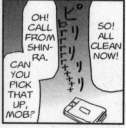

URBAN LEGEND:

THE RED RAINCOAT

- Wears the raincoat on sunny days.
- Walks around with a carving knife.
- Loves bathing in the blood of children.
- The raincoat keeps him dry when it's all wet.
- The raincoat wasn't red when he bought it.

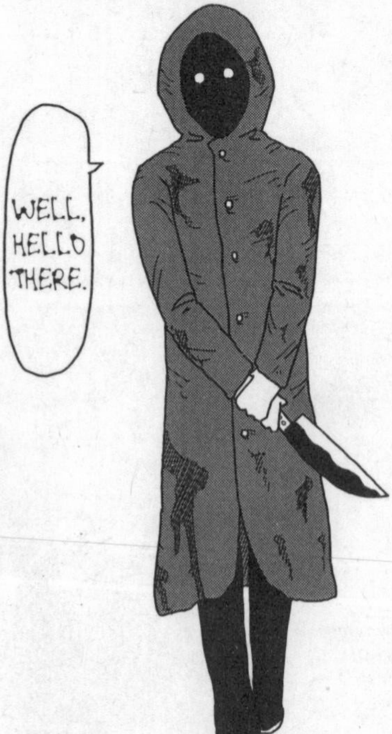
WELL, HELLO THERE.

CHAPTER 55: HE HAS NO IDEA

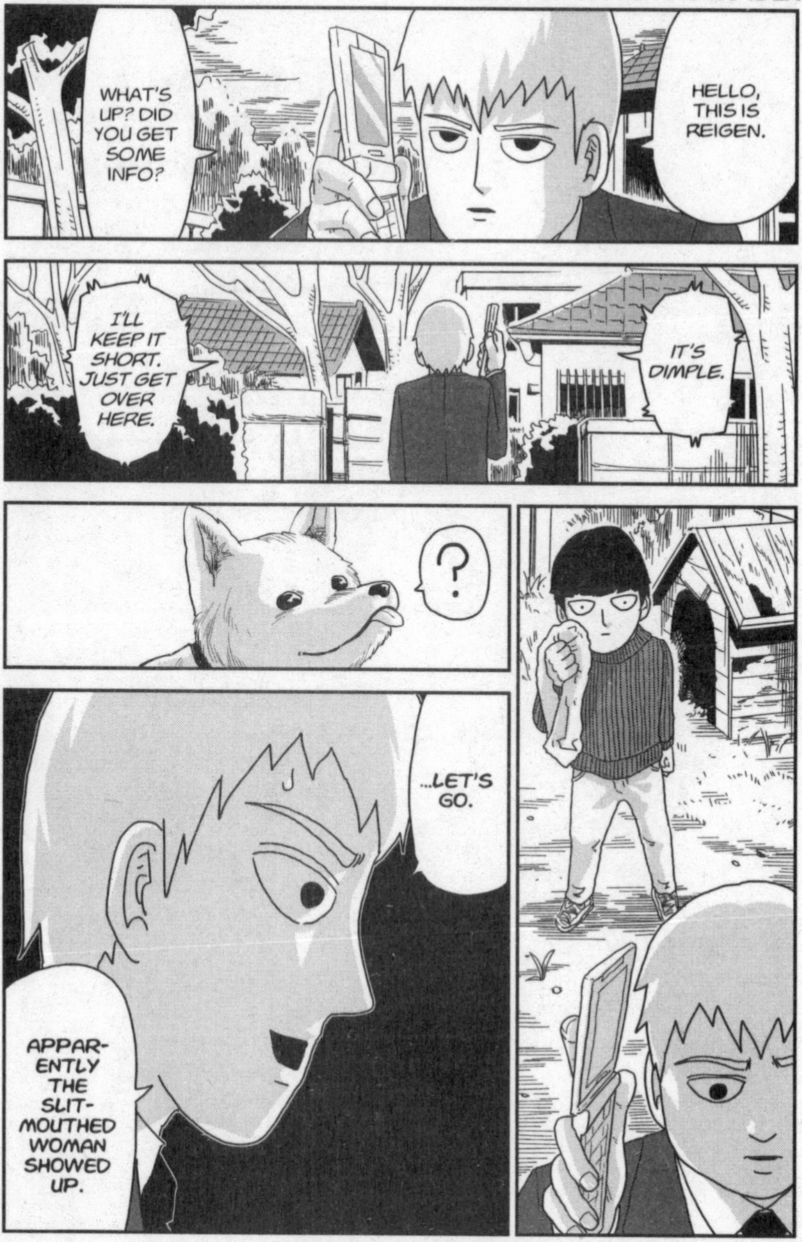
HELLO, THIS IS REIGEN.
WHAT'S UP? DID YOU GET SOME INFO?
IT'S DIMPLE.
I'LL KEEP IT SHORT. JUST GET OVER HERE.
?
...LET'S GO.
APPAR-ENTLY THE SLIT-MOUTHED WOMAN SHOWED UP.

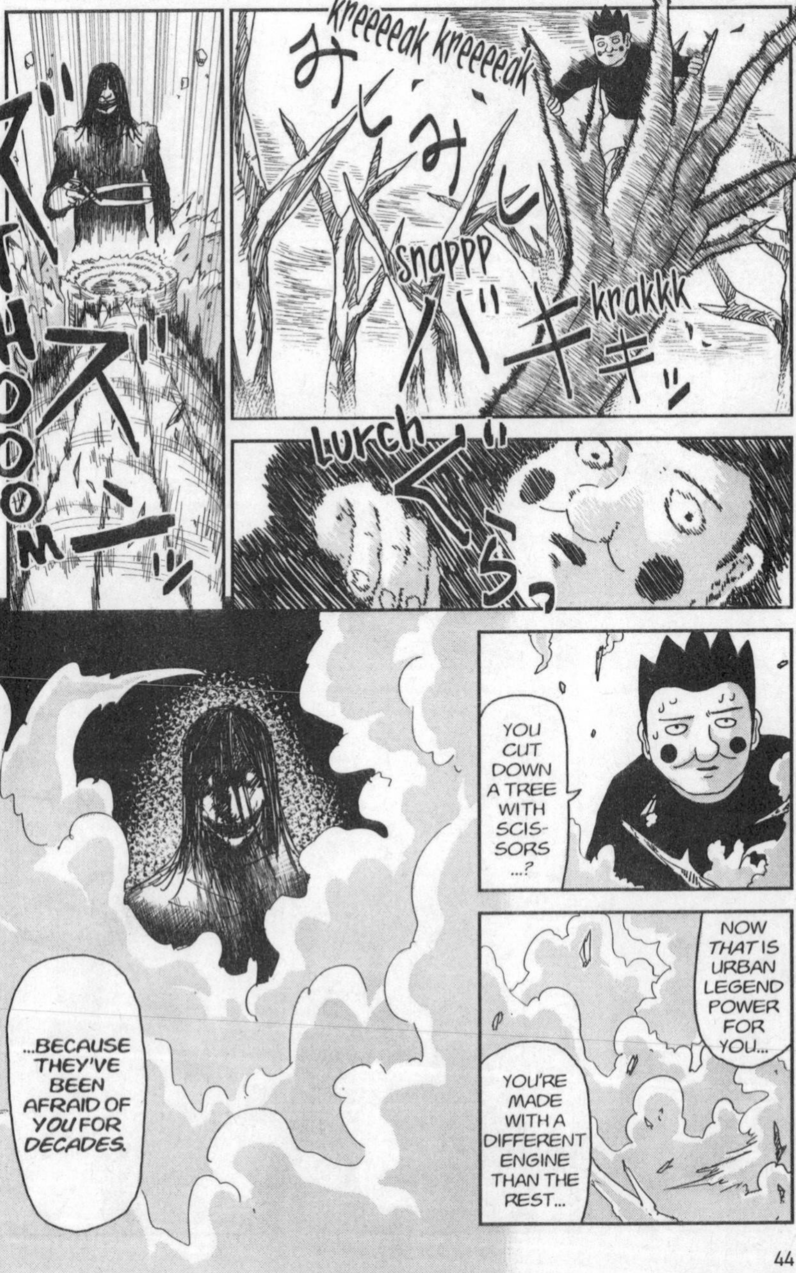

kreeeeak kreeeeak
snappp
krakkk
Lurch
THOOOOM
YOU CUT DOWN A TREE WITH SCISSORS ...?
NOW *THAT* IS URBAN LEGEND POWER FOR YOU...
YOU'RE MADE WITH A DIFFERENT ENGINE THAN THE REST...
...BECAUSE THEY'VE BEEN AFRAID OF *YOU* FOR DECADES.

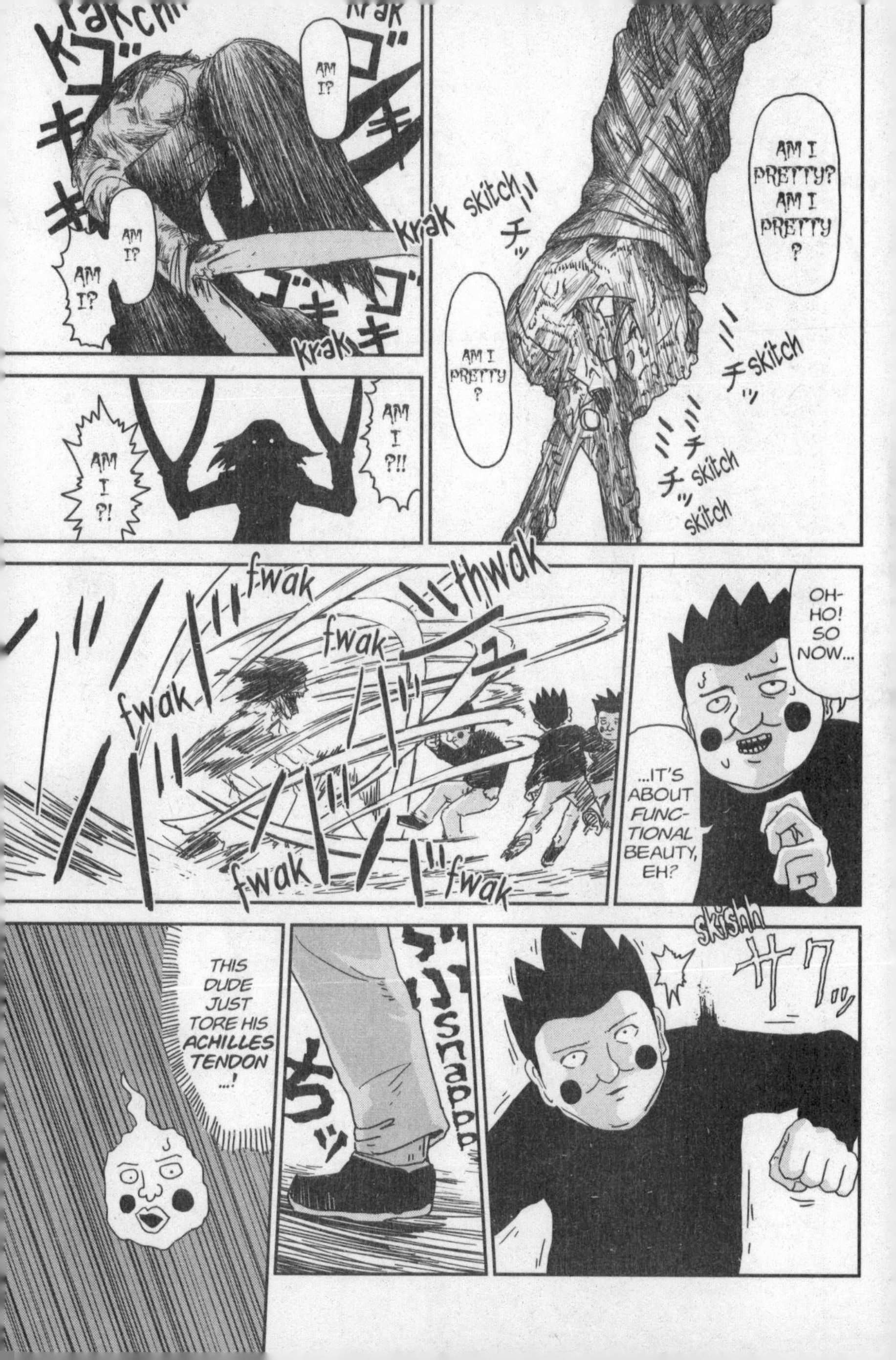
AM I PRETTY? AM I PRETTY ?
skitch
AM I PRETTY ?
skitch
skitch
skitch
krak
AM I?
krak
AM I?
AM I?
krak
AM I ?!!
AM I ?!
OH-HO! SO NOW...
...IT'S ABOUT FUNCTIONAL BEAUTY, EH?
thwak
fwak
fwak
fwak
fwak
fwak
THIS DUDE JUST TORE HIS ACHILLES TENDON ...!

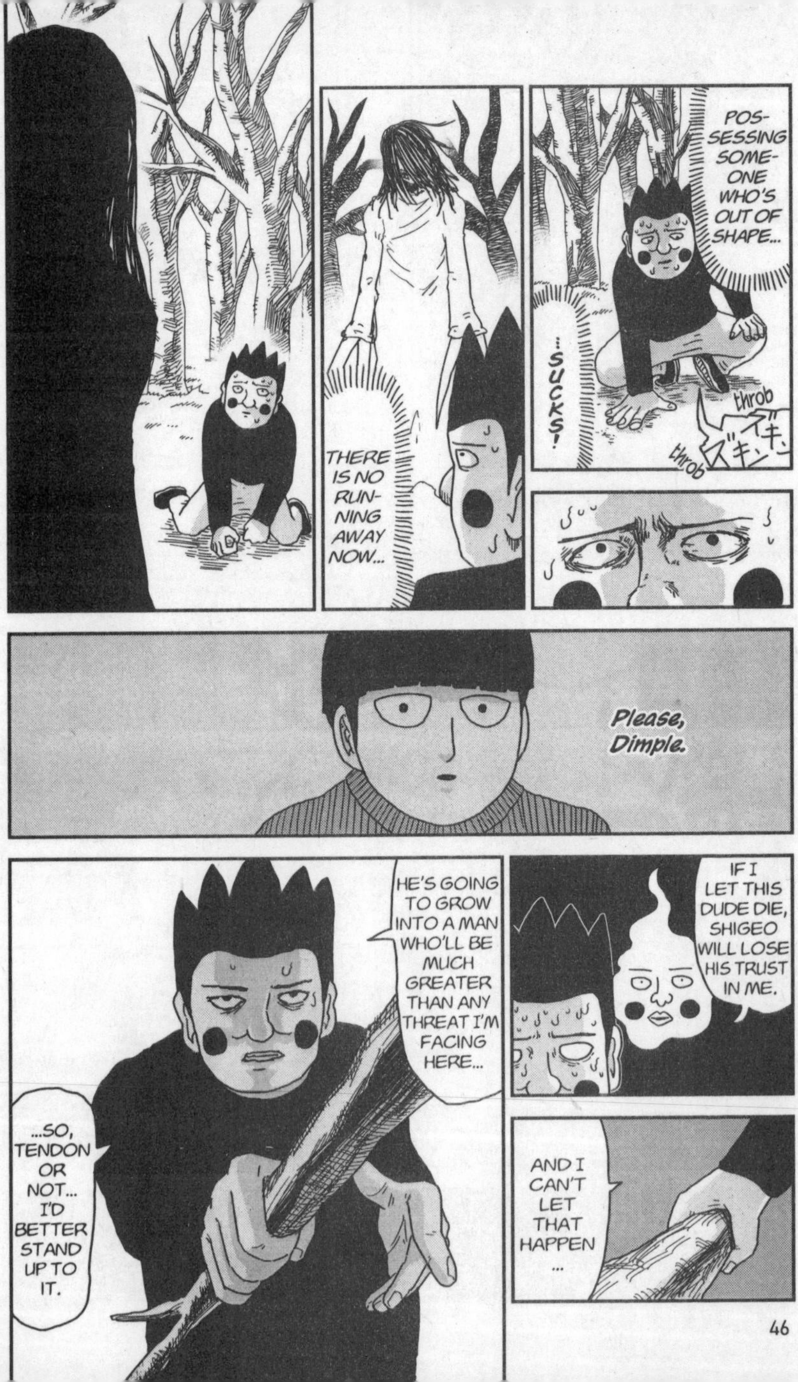

POS-SESSING SOMEONE WHO'S OUT OF SHAPE...
...SUCKS!
throb
throb
THERE IS NO RUN-NING AWAY NOW...
Please, Dimple.
IF I LET THIS DUDE DIE, SHIGEO WILL LOSE HIS TRUST IN ME.
AND I CAN'T LET THAT HAPPEN...
HE'S GOING TO GROW INTO A MAN WHO'LL BE MUCH GREATER THAN ANY THREAT I'M FACING HERE...
...SO, TENDON OR NOT... I'D BETTER STAND UP TO IT.

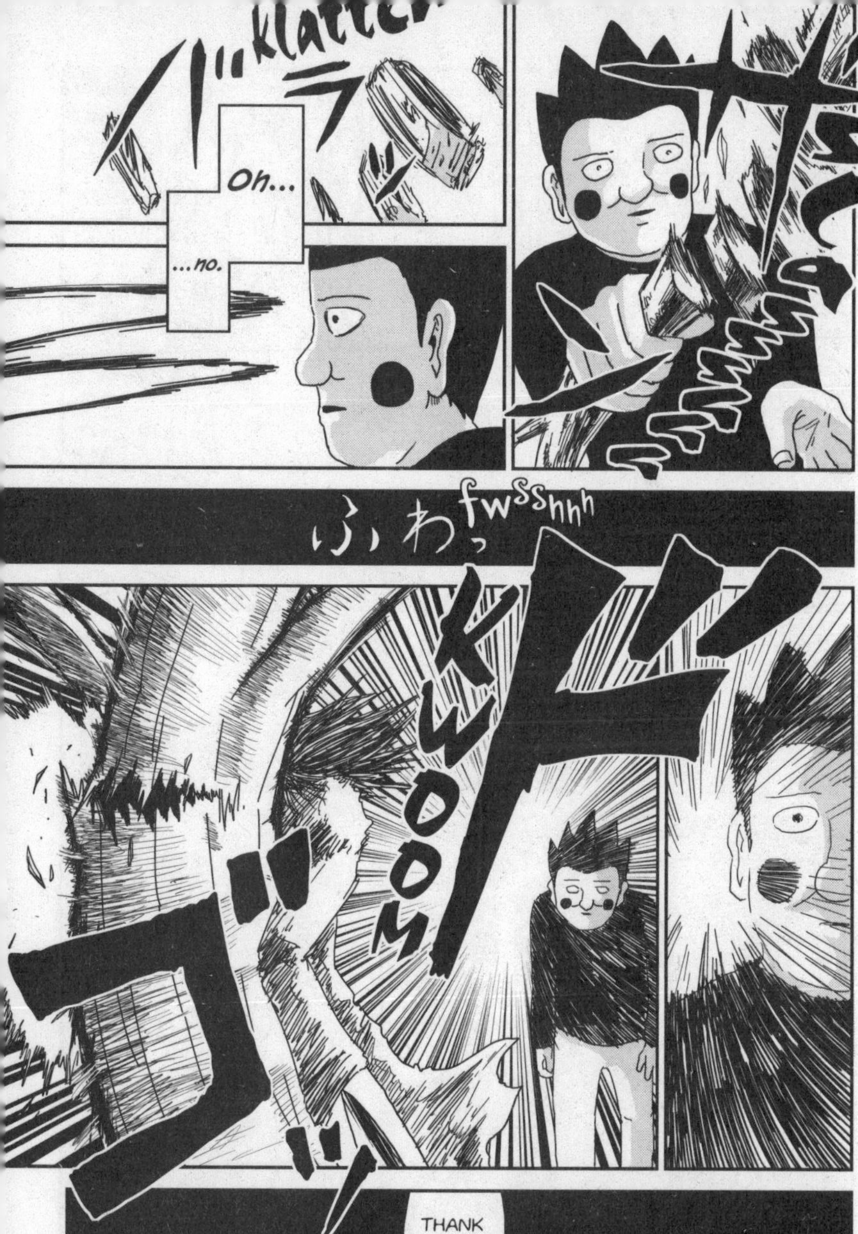

klatter
Oh...
...no.
fwsshhh
KWOOM
THANK YOU, DIMPLE.

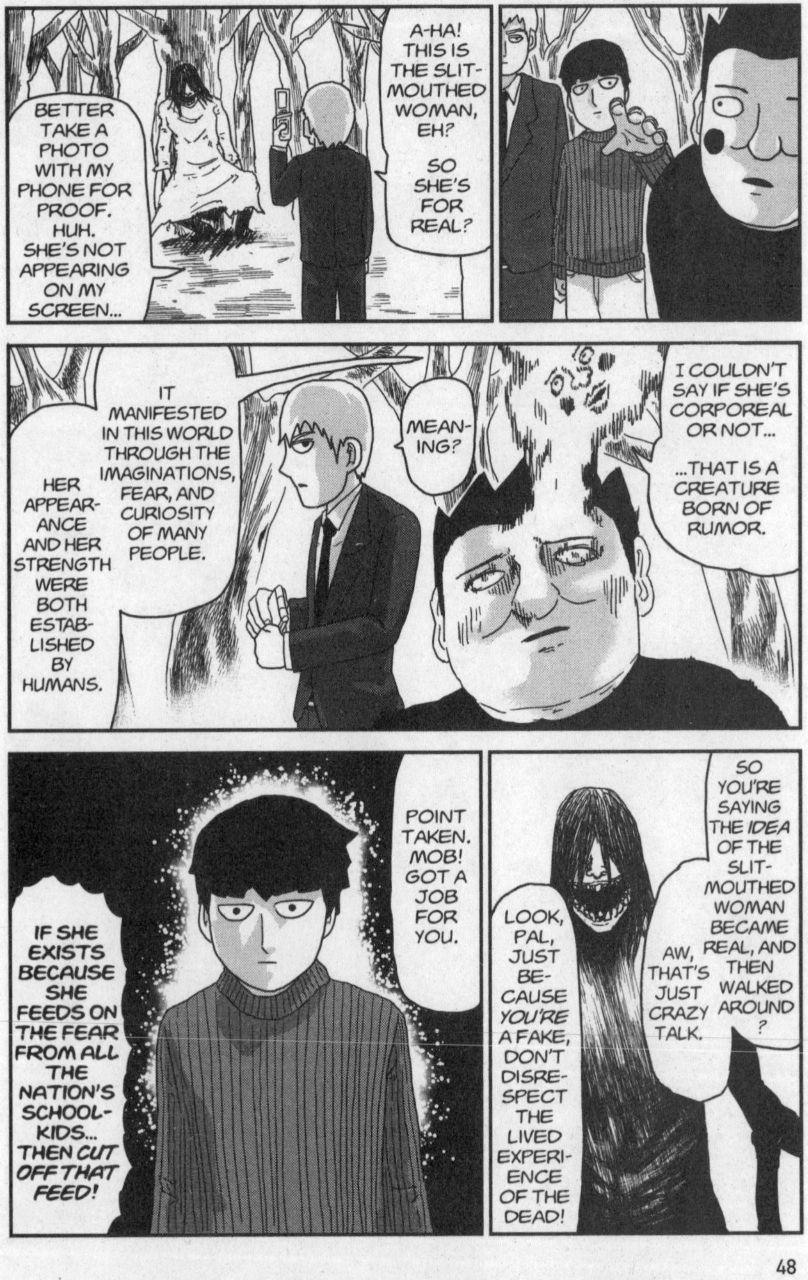

A-HA! THIS IS THE SLIT-MOUTHED WOMAN, EH?
SO SHE'S FOR REAL?
BETTER TAKE A PHOTO WITH MY PHONE FOR PROOF. HUH. SHE'S NOT APPEARING ON MY SCREEN...
I COULDN'T SAY IF SHE'S CORPOREAL OR NOT...
...THAT IS A CREATURE BORN OF RUMOR.
MEANING?
IT MANIFESTED IN THIS WORLD THROUGH THE IMAGINATIONS, FEAR, AND CURIOSITY OF MANY PEOPLE.
HER APPEARANCE AND HER STRENGTH WERE BOTH ESTABLISHED BY HUMANS.
SO YOU'RE SAYING THE *IDEA* OF THE SLIT-MOUTHED WOMAN BECAME REAL, AND THEN WALKED AROUND?
AW, THAT'S JUST CRAZY TALK.
LOOK, PAL, JUST BECAUSE *YOU'RE* A FAKE, DON'T DISRESPECT THE LIVED EXPERIENCE OF THE DEAD!
POINT TAKEN. MOB! GOT A JOB FOR YOU.
IF SHE EXISTS BECAUSE SHE FEEDS ON THE FEAR FROM ALL THE NATION'S SCHOOLKIDS... THEN *CUT OFF THAT FEED!*

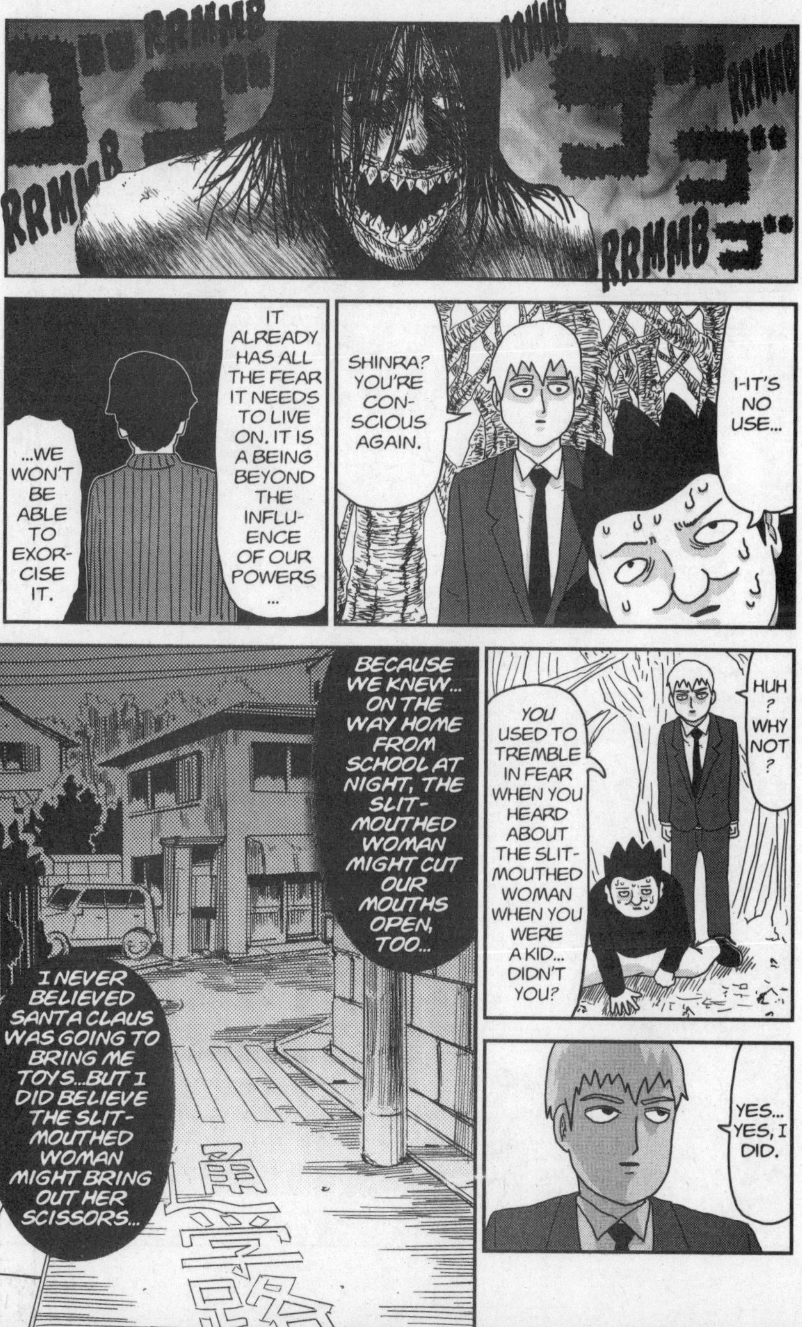
RRMMB
RRMMB
RRMMB
RRMMB
RRMMB
I-IT'S NO USE...
SHINRA? YOU'RE CONSCIOUS AGAIN.
IT ALREADY HAS ALL THE FEAR IT NEEDS TO LIVE ON. IT IS A BEING BEYOND THE INFLUENCE OF OUR POWERS...
...WE WON'T BE ABLE TO EXORCISE IT.
HUH? WHY NOT?
YOU USED TO TREMBLE IN FEAR WHEN YOU HEARD ABOUT THE SLIT-MOUTHED WOMAN WHEN YOU WERE A KID... DIDN'T YOU?
YES... YES, I DID.
BECAUSE WE KNEW... ON THE WAY HOME FROM SCHOOL AT NIGHT, THE SLIT-MOUTHED WOMAN MIGHT CUT OUR MOUTHS OPEN, TOO...
I NEVER BELIEVED SANTA CLAUS WAS GOING TO BRING ME TOYS...BUT I DID BELIEVE THE SLIT-MOUTHED WOMAN MIGHT BRING OUT HER SCISSORS...

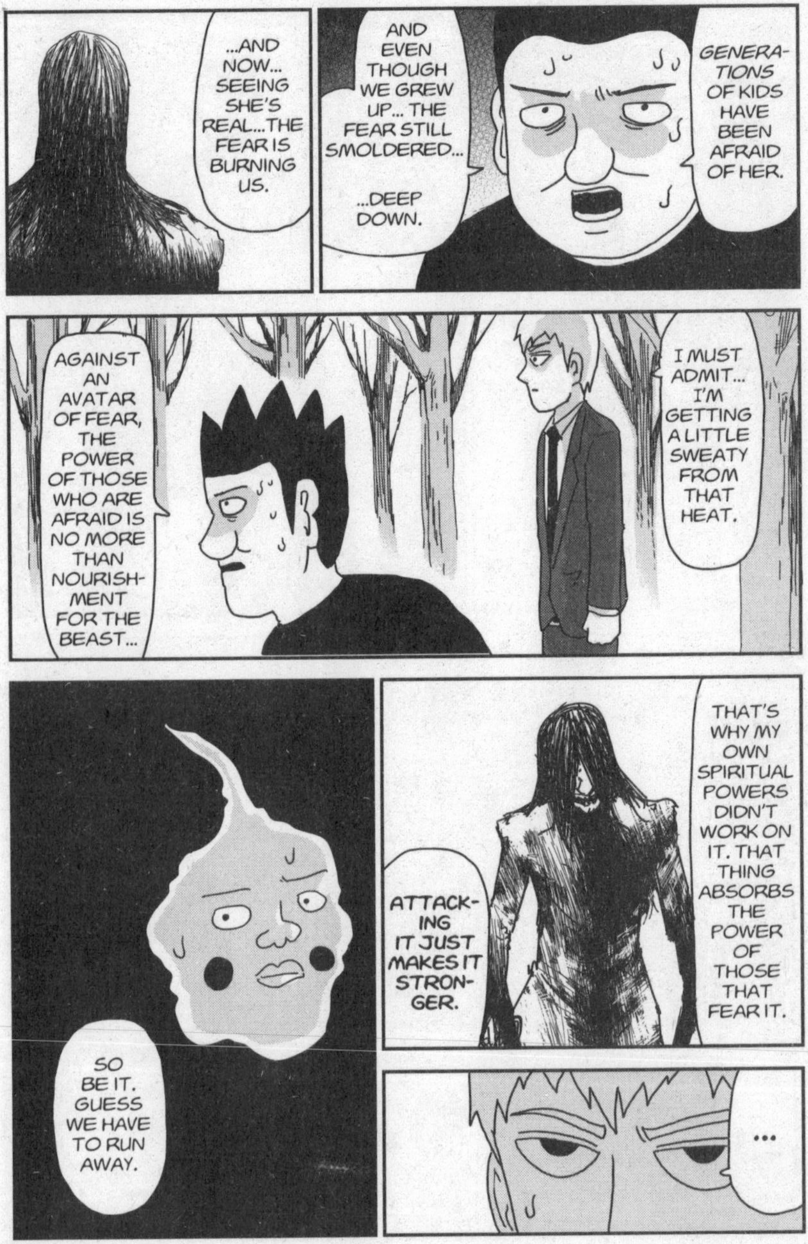

GENERATIONS OF KIDS HAVE BEEN AFRAID OF HER.
AND EVEN THOUGH WE GREW UP... THE FEAR STILL SMOLDERED...
...DEEP DOWN.
...AND NOW... SEEING SHE'S REAL...THE FEAR IS BURNING US.
I MUST ADMIT... I'M GETTING A LITTLE SWEATY FROM THAT HEAT.
AGAINST AN AVATAR OF FEAR, THE POWER OF THOSE WHO ARE AFRAID IS NO MORE THAN NOURISHMENT FOR THE BEAST...
THAT'S WHY MY OWN SPIRITUAL POWERS DIDN'T WORK ON IT. THAT THING ABSORBS THE POWER OF THOSE THAT FEAR IT.
ATTACKING IT JUST MAKES IT STRONGER.
...
SO BE IT. GUESS WE HAVE TO RUN AWAY.

HEY, MOB! DIDN'T YOU HEAR ME? IT'S TIME FOR A RETREAT --

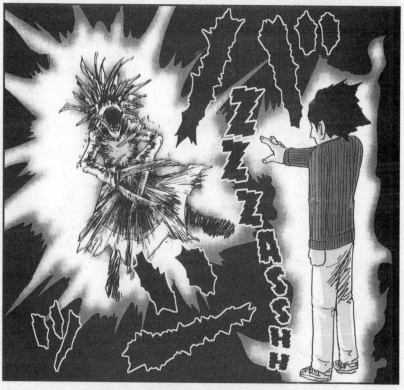

ZZZZASSHH

NO, WAIT...

MOB, THAT WON'T WORK! SHE'LL ABSORB YOUR POWER TOO...

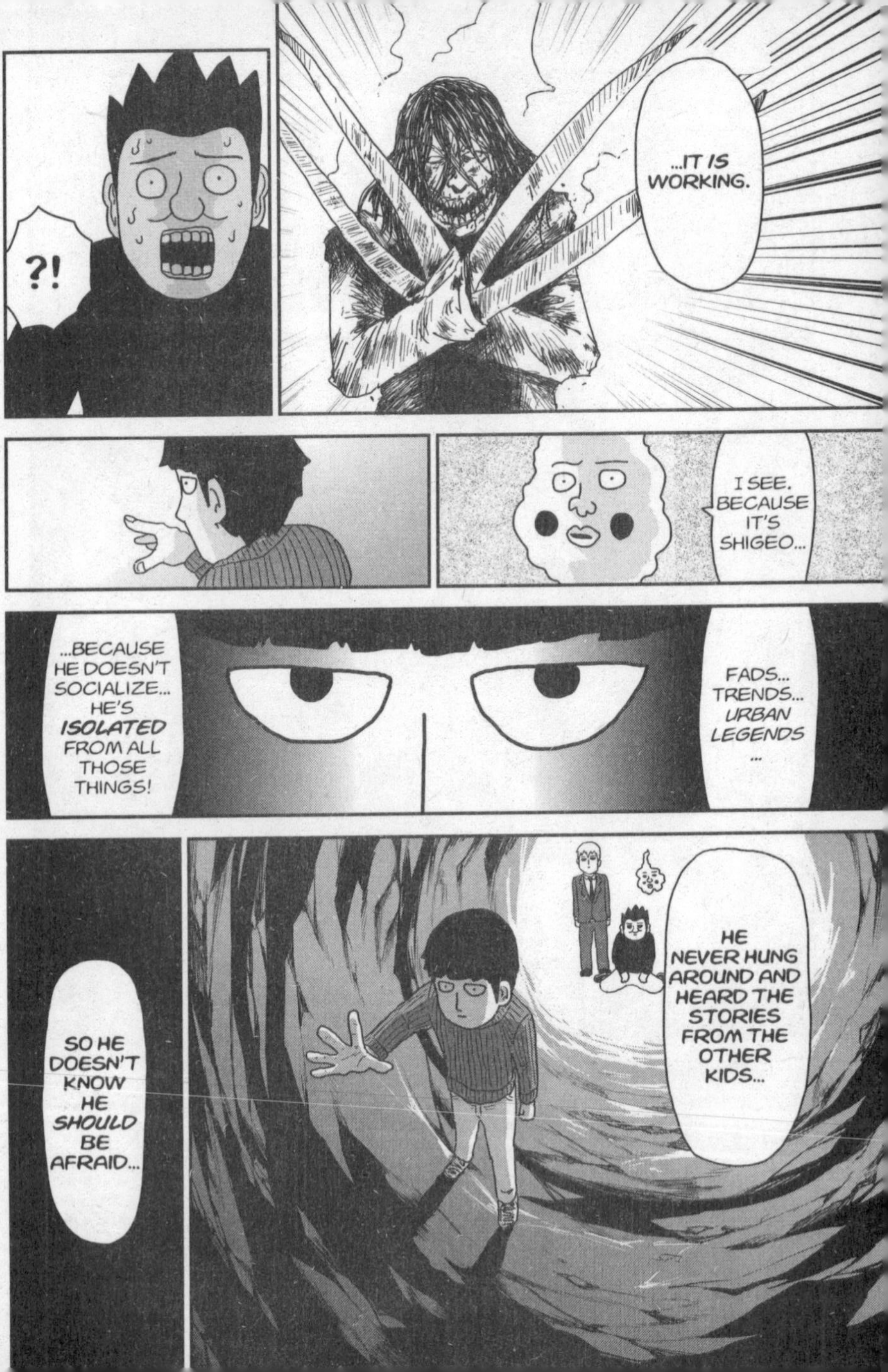
...IT IS WORKING.
?!
I SEE. BECAUSE IT'S SHIGEO...
FADS... TRENDS... URBAN LEGENDS ...
...BECAUSE HE DOESN'T SOCIALIZE... HE'S ISOLATED FROM ALL THOSE THINGS!
HE NEVER HUNG AROUND AND HEARD THE STORIES FROM THE OTHER KIDS...
SO HE DOESN'T KNOW HE SHOULD BE AFRAID...

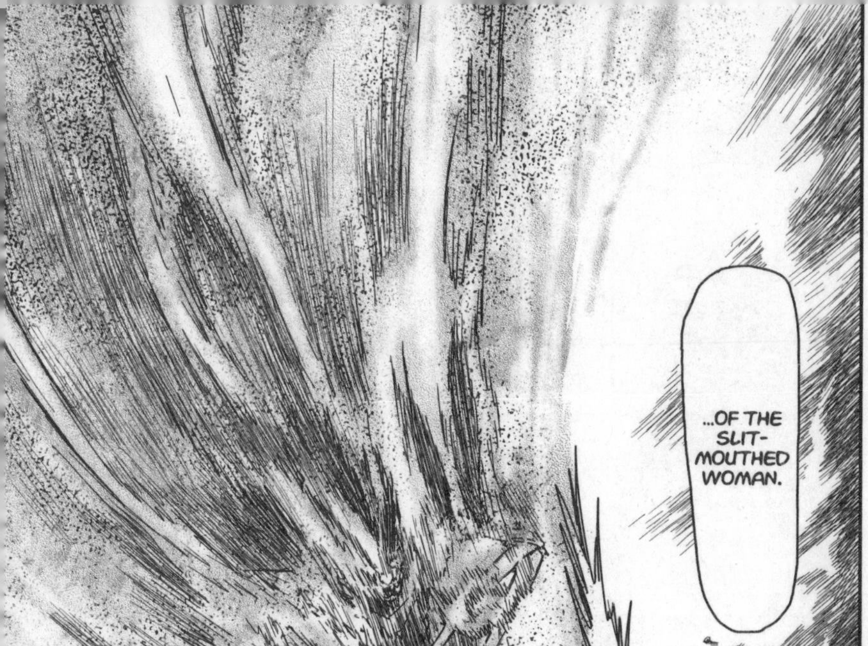
...OF THE SLIT-MOUTHED WOMAN.

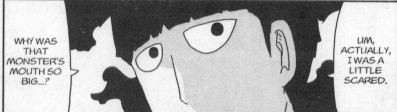

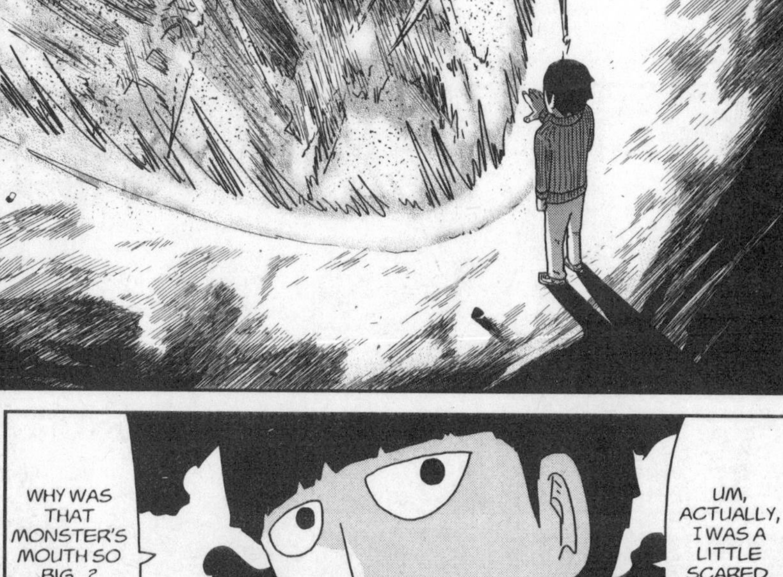
UM, ACTUALLY, I WAS A LITTLE SCARED.
WHY WAS THAT MONSTER'S MOUTH SO BIG...?

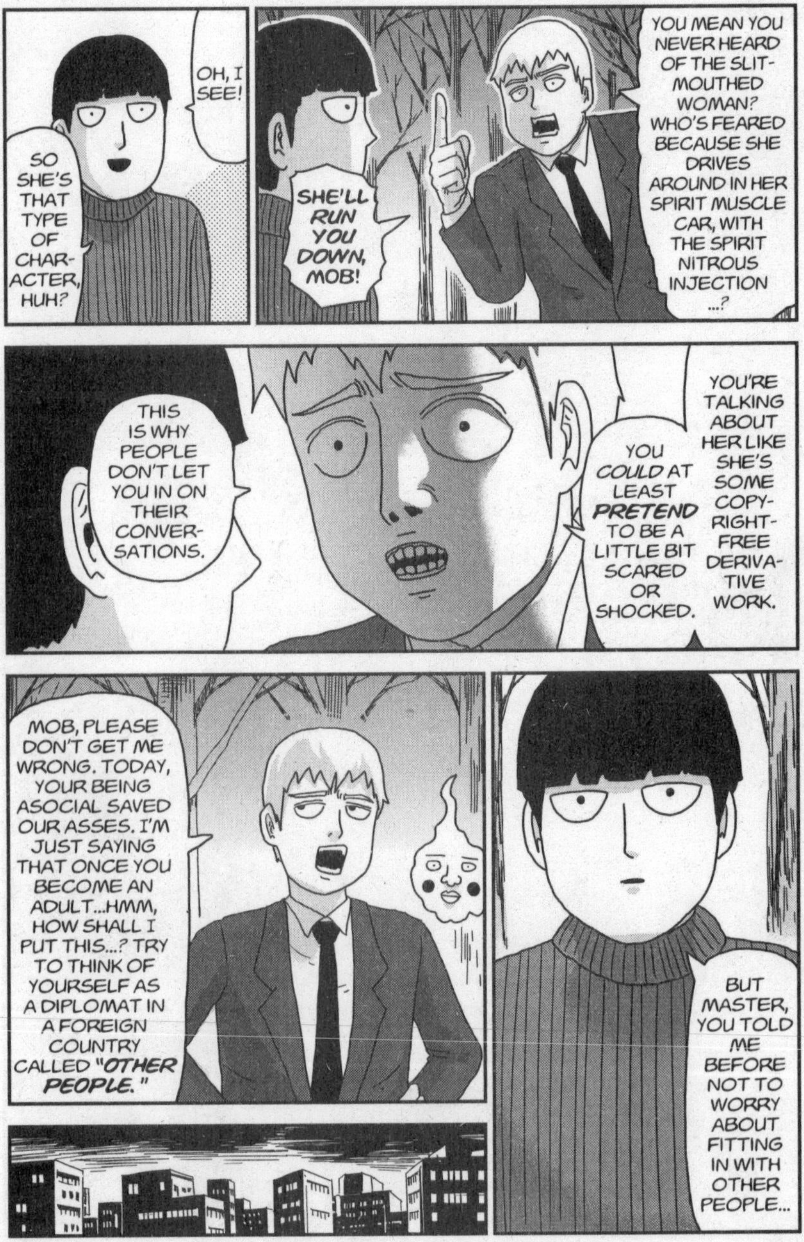
YOU MEAN YOU NEVER HEARD OF THE SLIT-MOUTHED WOMAN? WHO'S FEARED BECAUSE SHE DRIVES AROUND IN HER SPIRIT MUSCLE CAR, WITH THE SPIRIT NITROUS INJECTION ...?
SHE'LL RUN YOU DOWN, MOB!
OH, I SEE!
SO SHE'S THAT TYPE OF CHARACTER, HUH?
YOU'RE TALKING ABOUT HER LIKE SHE'S SOME COPYRIGHT-FREE DERIVATIVE WORK.
YOU *COULD* AT LEAST **PRETEND** TO BE A LITTLE BIT SCARED OR SHOCKED.
THIS IS WHY PEOPLE DON'T LET YOU IN ON THEIR CONVERSATIONS.
MOB, PLEASE DON'T GET ME WRONG. TODAY, YOUR BEING ASOCIAL SAVED OUR ASSES. I'M JUST SAYING THAT ONCE YOU BECOME AN ADULT...HMM, HOW SHALL I PUT THIS...? TRY TO THINK OF YOURSELF AS A DIPLOMAT IN A FOREIGN COUNTRY CALLED "*OTHER PEOPLE.*"
BUT MASTER, YOU TOLD ME BEFORE NOT TO WORRY ABOUT FITTING IN WITH OTHER PEOPLE...

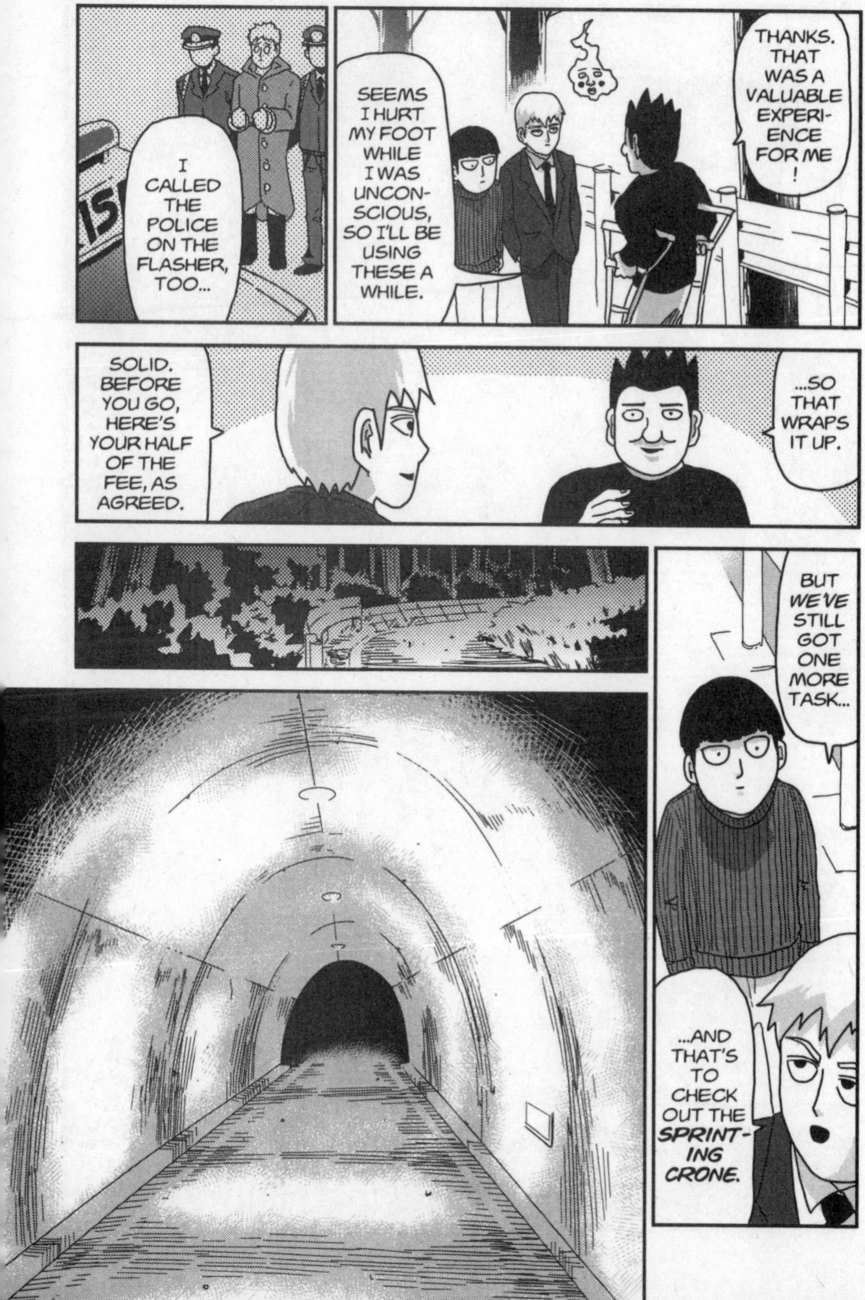
THANKS. THAT WAS A VALUABLE EXPERIENCE FOR ME!
SEEMS I HURT MY FOOT WHILE I WAS UNCONSCIOUS, SO I'LL BE USING THESE A WHILE.
I CALLED THE POLICE ON THE FLASHER, TOO...
...SO THAT WRAPS IT UP.
SOLID. BEFORE YOU GO, HERE'S YOUR HALF OF THE FEE, AS AGREED.
BUT *WE'VE* STILL GOT ONE MORE TASK...
...AND THAT'S TO CHECK OUT THE ***SPRINTING CRONE***.

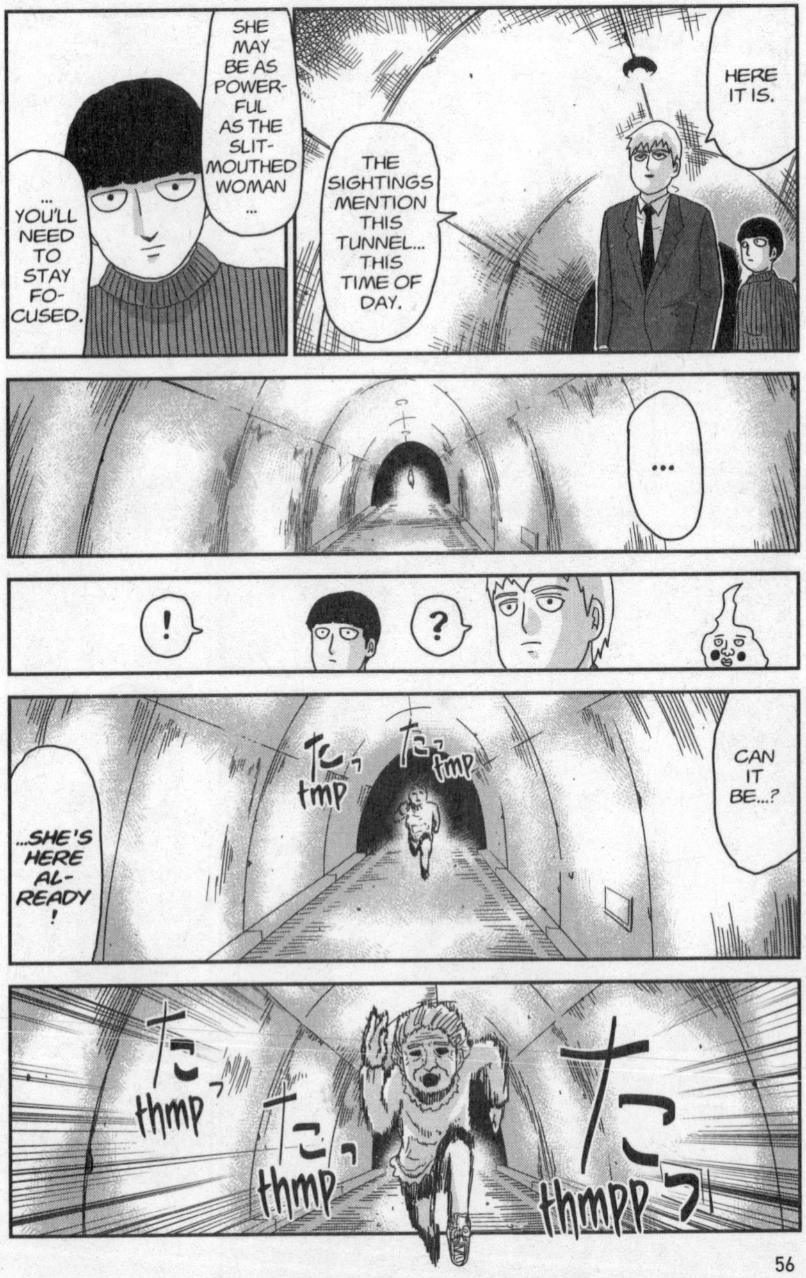
HERE IT IS.
THE SIGHTINGS MENTION THIS TUNNEL... THIS TIME OF DAY.
SHE MAY BE AS POWERFUL AS THE SLIT-MOUTHED WOMAN...
...YOU'LL NEED TO STAY FOCUSED.
...
?
!
CAN IT BE...?
tmp
tmp
...SHE'S HERE ALREADY!
thmpp
thmp
thmp

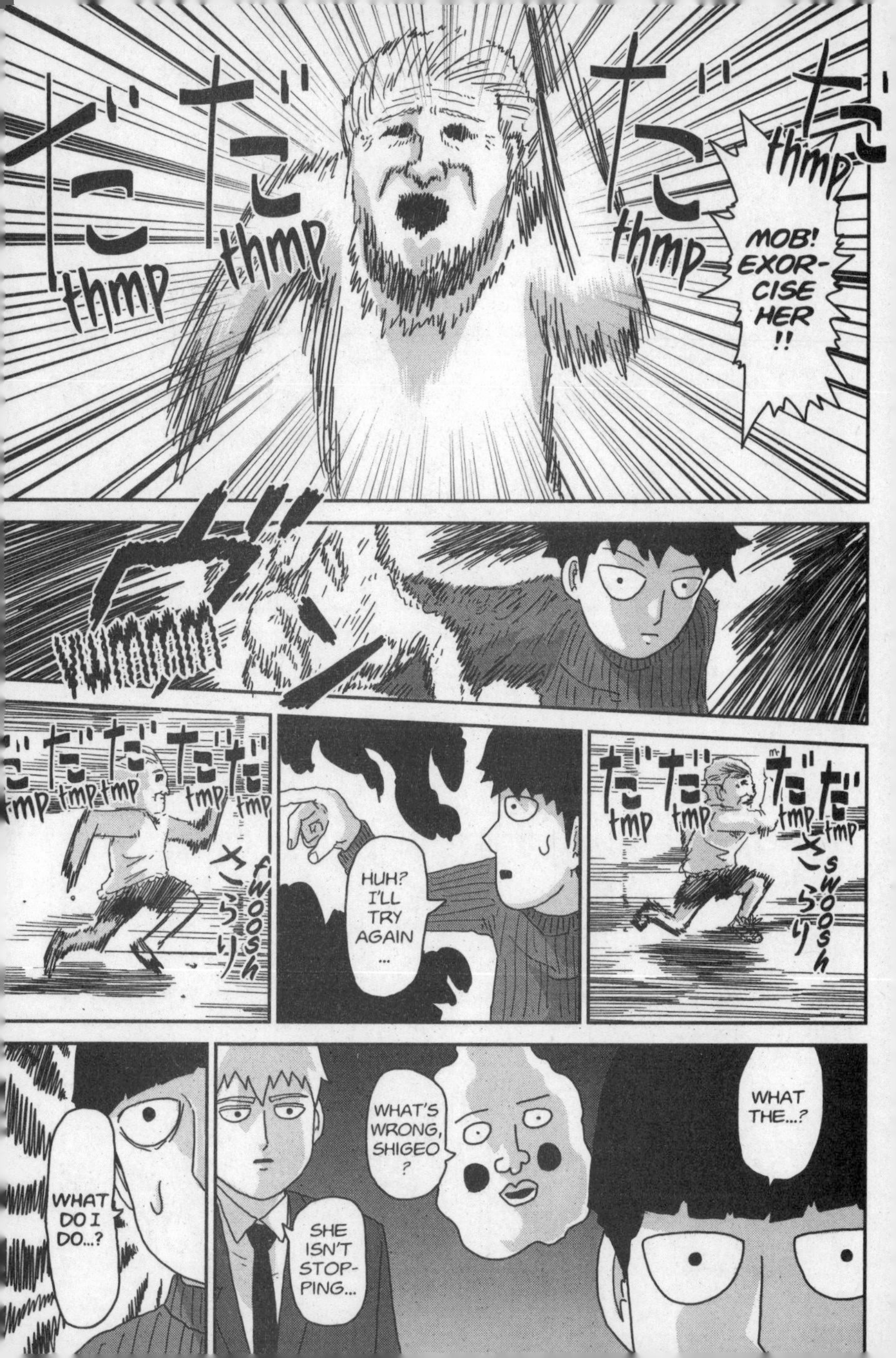
thmp
thmp
thmp
thmp
MOB! EXOR-CISE HER!!
VUMMMM
tmp
tmp
tmp
tmp
SWOOSH
HUH? I'LL TRY AGAIN...
tmp
tmp
tmp
tmp
tmp
fWOOSH
WHAT THE...?
WHAT'S WRONG, SHIGEO?
SHE ISN'T STOP-PING...
WHAT DO I DO...?

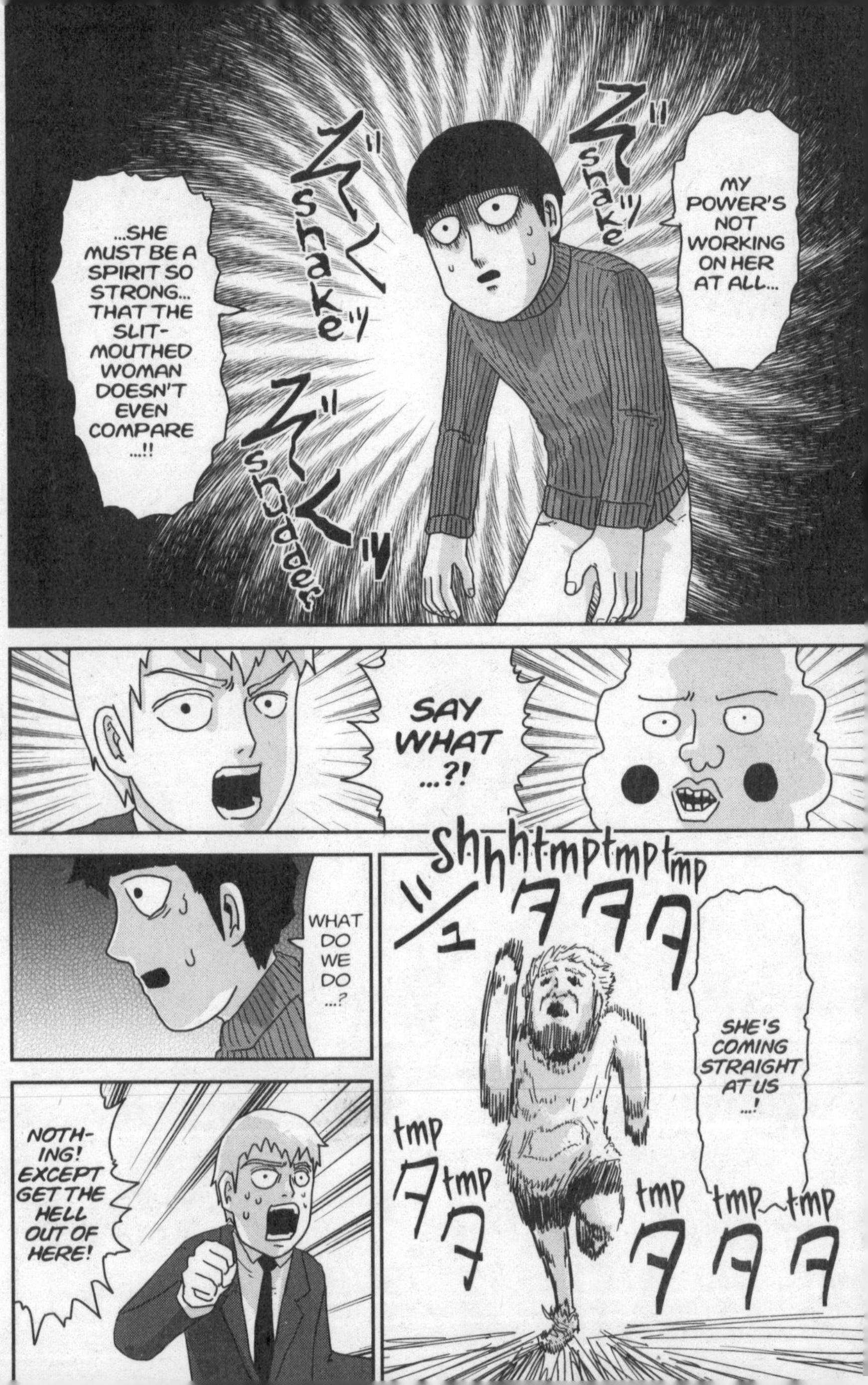
MY POWER'S NOT WORKING ON HER AT ALL...
shake
shake
shudder
...SHE MUST BE A SPIRIT SO STRONG... THAT THE SLIT-MOUTHED WOMAN DOESN'T EVEN COMPARE ...!!
SAY WHAT ...?!
shhh tmp tmp tmp
SHE'S COMING STRAIGHT AT US ...!
tmp tmp tmp tmp~tmp
WHAT DO WE DO ...?
NOTH-ING! EXCEPT GET THE HELL OUT OF HERE!

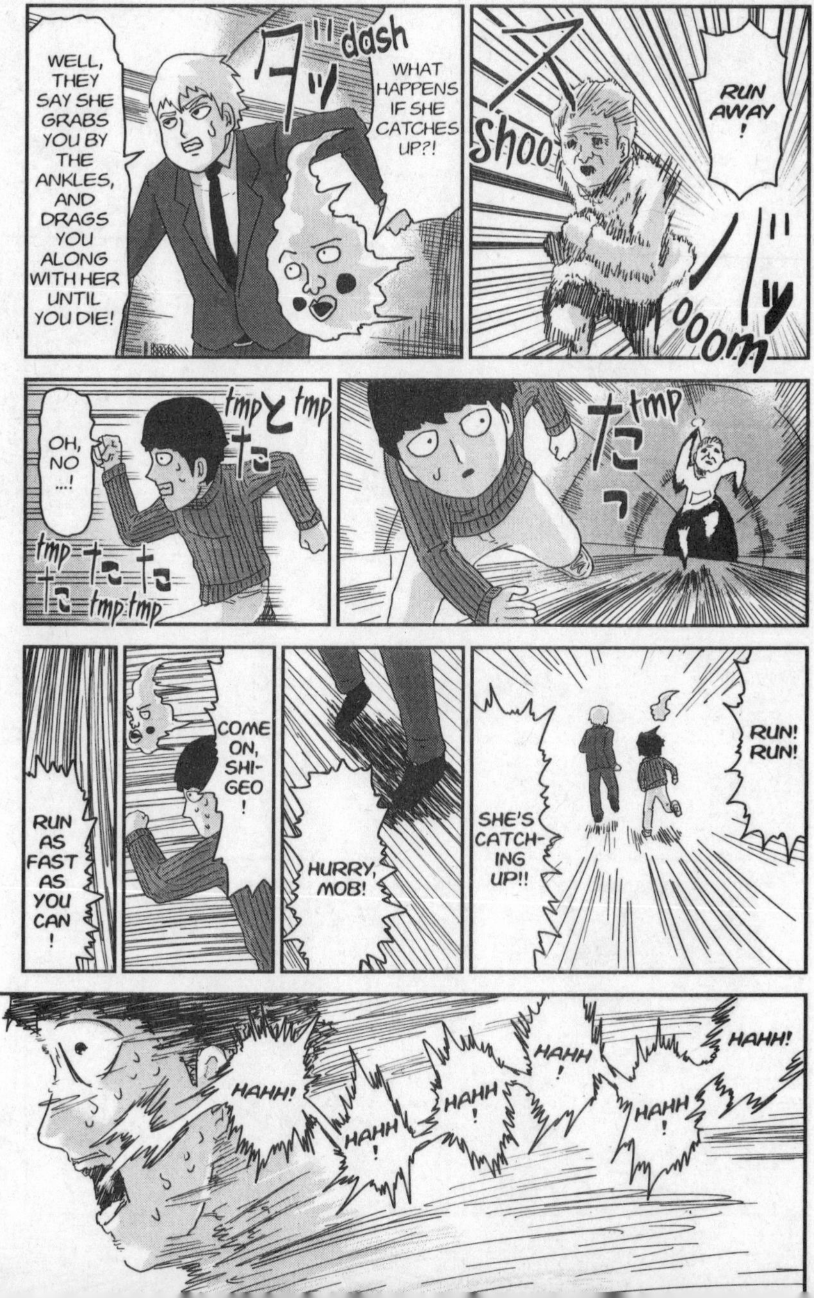
RUN AWAY!
shoo
ooom
dash
WHAT HAPPENS IF SHE CATCHES UP?!
WELL, THEY SAY SHE GRABS YOU BY THE ANKLES, AND DRAGS YOU ALONG WITH HER UNTIL YOU DIE!
tmp
tmp tmp
OH, NO ...!
tmp tmp tmp
RUN! RUN!
SHE'S CATCHING UP!!
HURRY, MOB!
COME ON, SHIGEO!
RUN AS FAST AS YOU CAN!
HAHH!
HAHH!
HAHH!
HAHH!
HAHH!
HAHH!
HAHH!

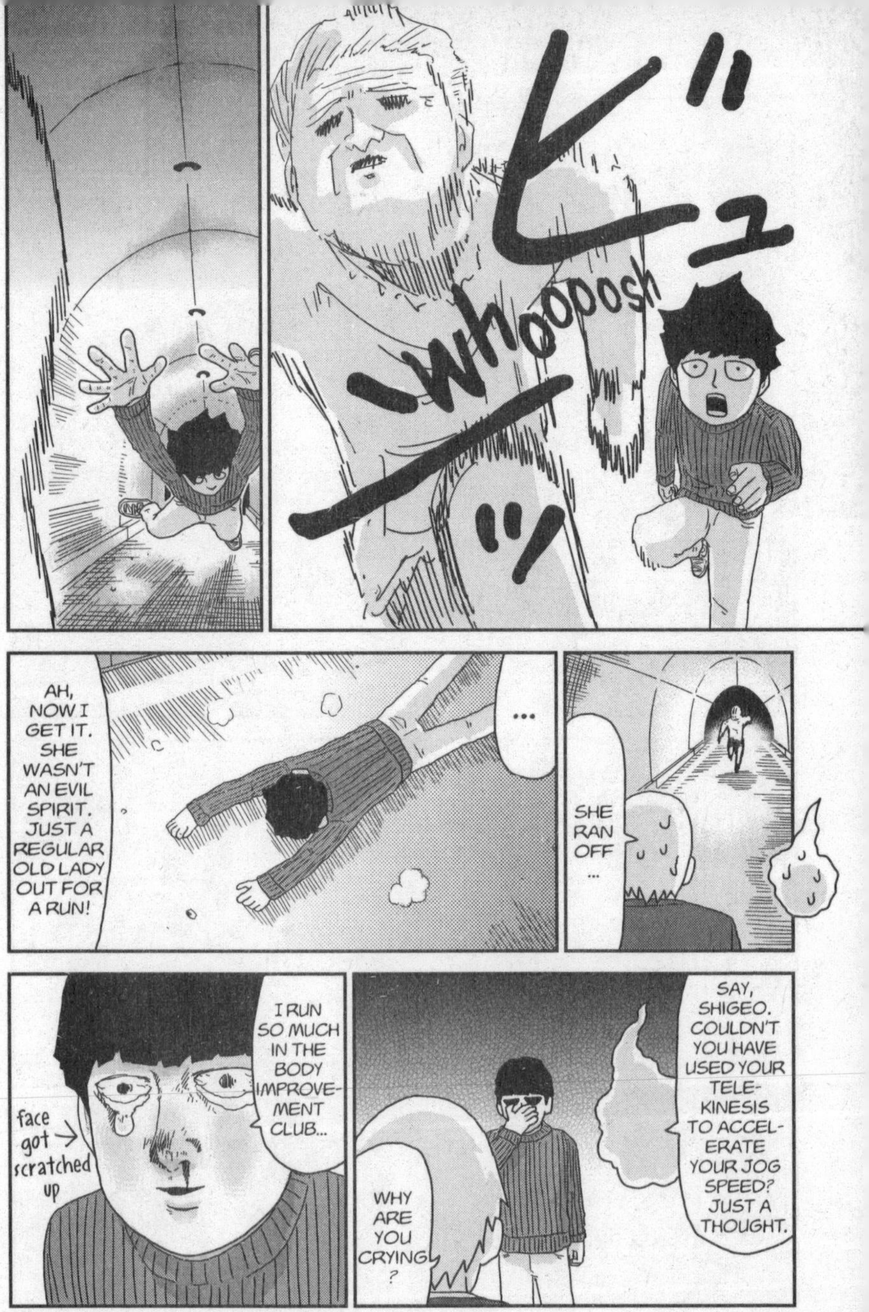
ビュッ
whooosh
SHE RAN OFF...
...
AH, NOW I GET IT. SHE WASN'T AN EVIL SPIRIT. JUST A REGULAR OLD LADY OUT FOR A RUN!
SAY, SHIGEO. COULDN'T YOU HAVE USED YOUR TELE-KINESIS TO ACCEL-ERATE YOUR JOG SPEED? JUST A THOUGHT.
WHY ARE YOU CRYING?
I RUN SO MUCH IN THE BODY IMPROVE-MENT CLUB...
face got scratched up

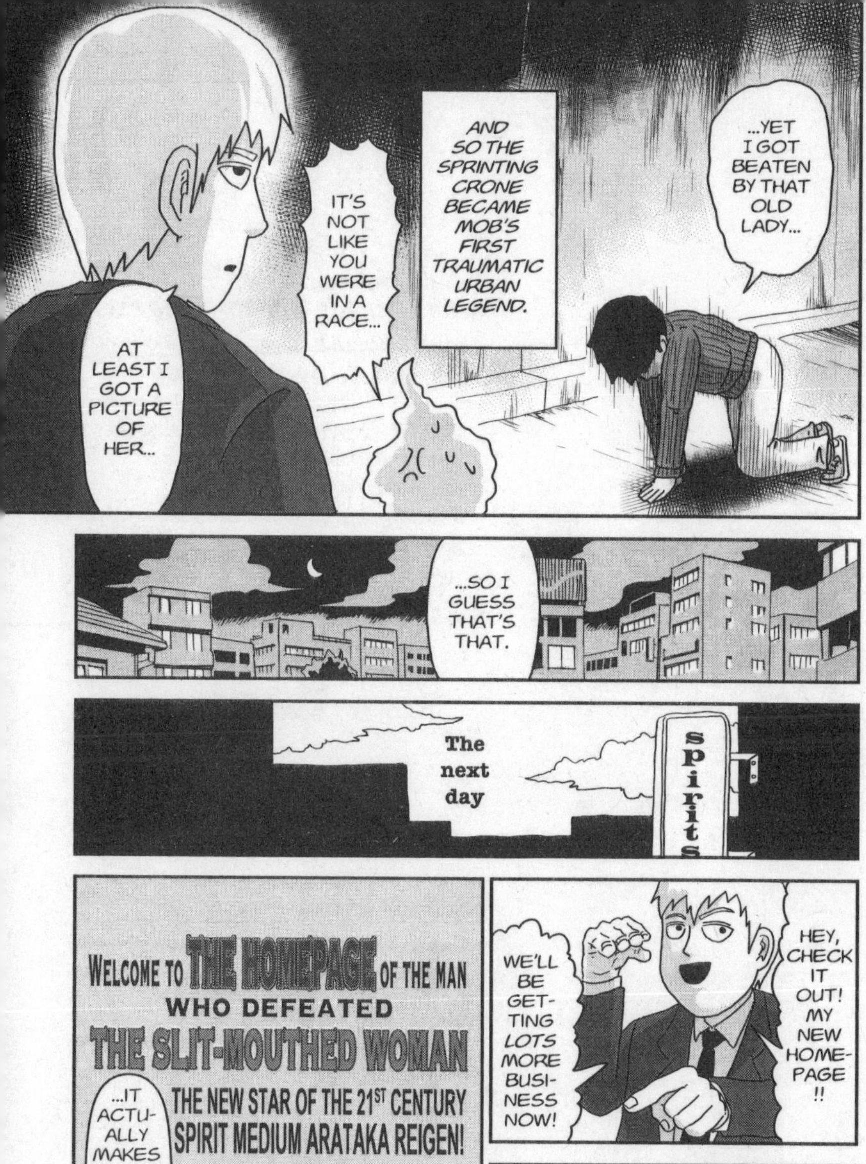
...YET I GOT BEATEN BY THAT OLD LADY...
AND SO THE SPRINTING CRONE BECAME MOB'S FIRST TRAUMATIC URBAN LEGEND.
IT'S NOT LIKE YOU WERE IN A RACE...
AT LEAST I GOT A PICTURE OF HER...
...SO I GUESS THAT'S THAT.
The next day
spirits
HEY, CHECK IT OUT! MY NEW HOMEPAGE!!
WE'LL BE GETTING LOTS MORE BUSINESS NOW!
WELCOME TO THE HOMEPAGE OF THE MAN WHO DEFEATED THE SLIT-MOUTHED WOMAN
THE NEW STAR OF THE 21ST CENTURY SPIRIT MEDIUM ARATAKA REIGEN!
ENTER
YOU ARE VISITOR NUMBER 000000002
...IT ACTUALLY MAKES YOU LOOK MORE SHADY.

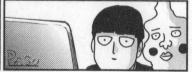

URBAN LEGEND:

THE SLIT-MOUTHED WOMAN

- Approaches grade school kids walking home.
- Asks them a question: "Am I pretty?"
- Choose "YES" and she takes off her mask.
- Then slits your mouth with her scissors.
- Choose "NO" and she gets angry.
- Then kills you with her scissors.
- Basically no good answers to the question.
- But that's grownups for you.

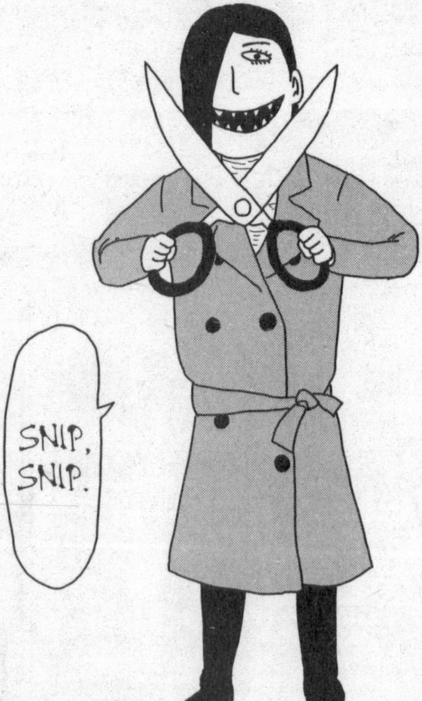
SNIP, SNIP.

CHAPTER 56: SOLO MISSION

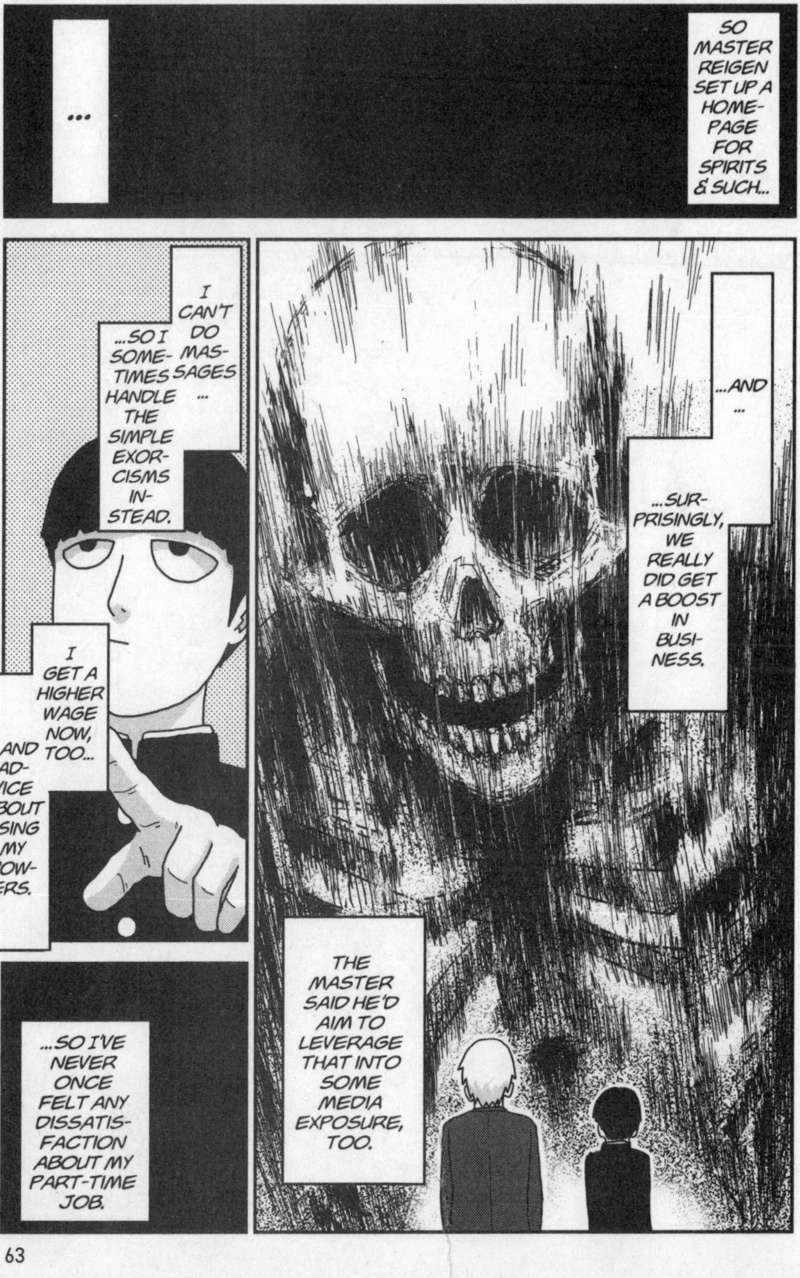

SO MASTER REIGEN SET UP A HOMEPAGE FOR SPIRITS & SUCH...
...
...AND ...
...SURPRISINGLY, WE REALLY DID GET A BOOST IN BUSINESS.
THE MASTER SAID HE'D AIM TO LEVERAGE THAT INTO SOME MEDIA EXPOSURE, TOO.
I CAN'T DO MASSAGES ...
...SO I SOMETIMES HANDLE THE SIMPLE EXORCISMS INSTEAD.
I GET A HIGHER WAGE NOW, TOO...
...AND ADVICE ABOUT USING MY POWERS.
...SO I'VE NEVER ONCE FELT ANY DISSATISFACTION ABOUT MY PART-TIME JOB.

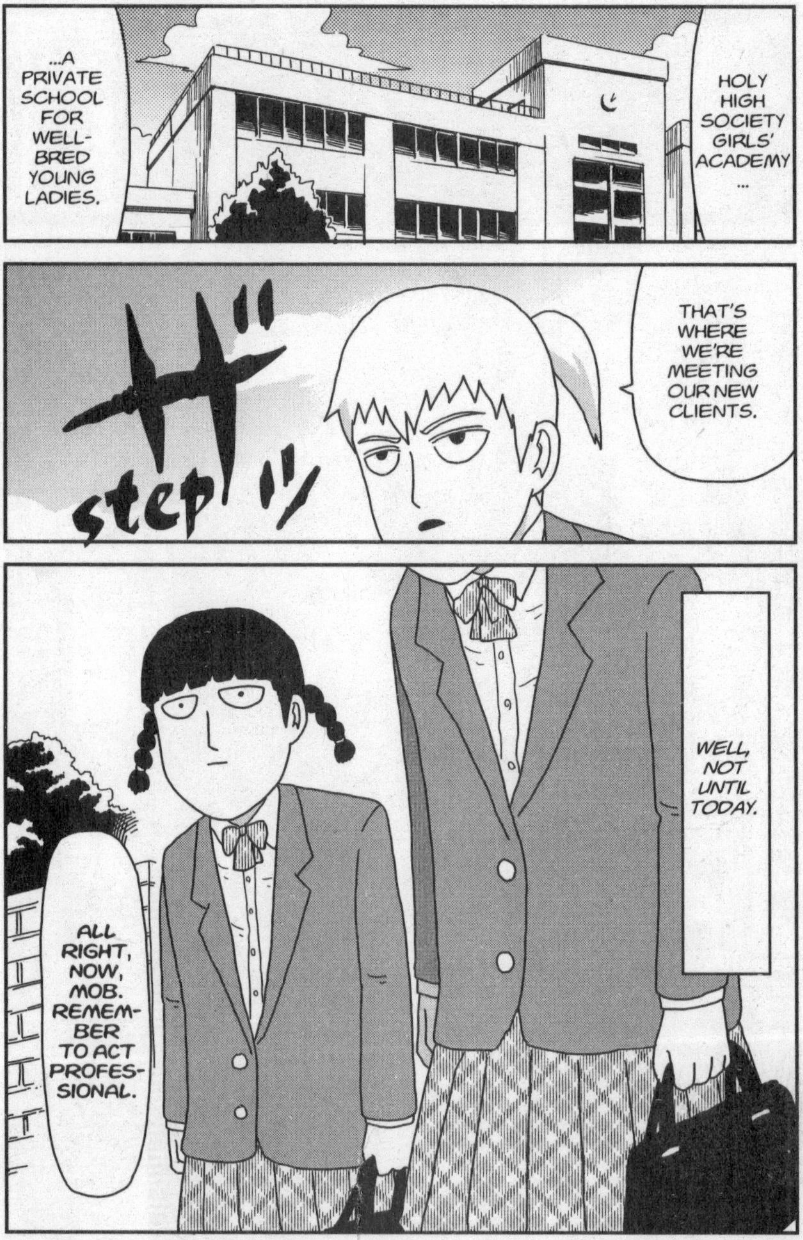
HOLY HIGH SOCIETY GIRLS' ACADEMY ...
...A PRIVATE SCHOOL FOR WELL-BRED YOUNG LADIES.
THAT'S WHERE WE'RE MEETING OUR NEW CLIENTS.
step
WELL, NOT UNTIL TODAY.
ALL RIGHT, NOW, MOB. REMEMBER TO ACT PROFESSIONAL.

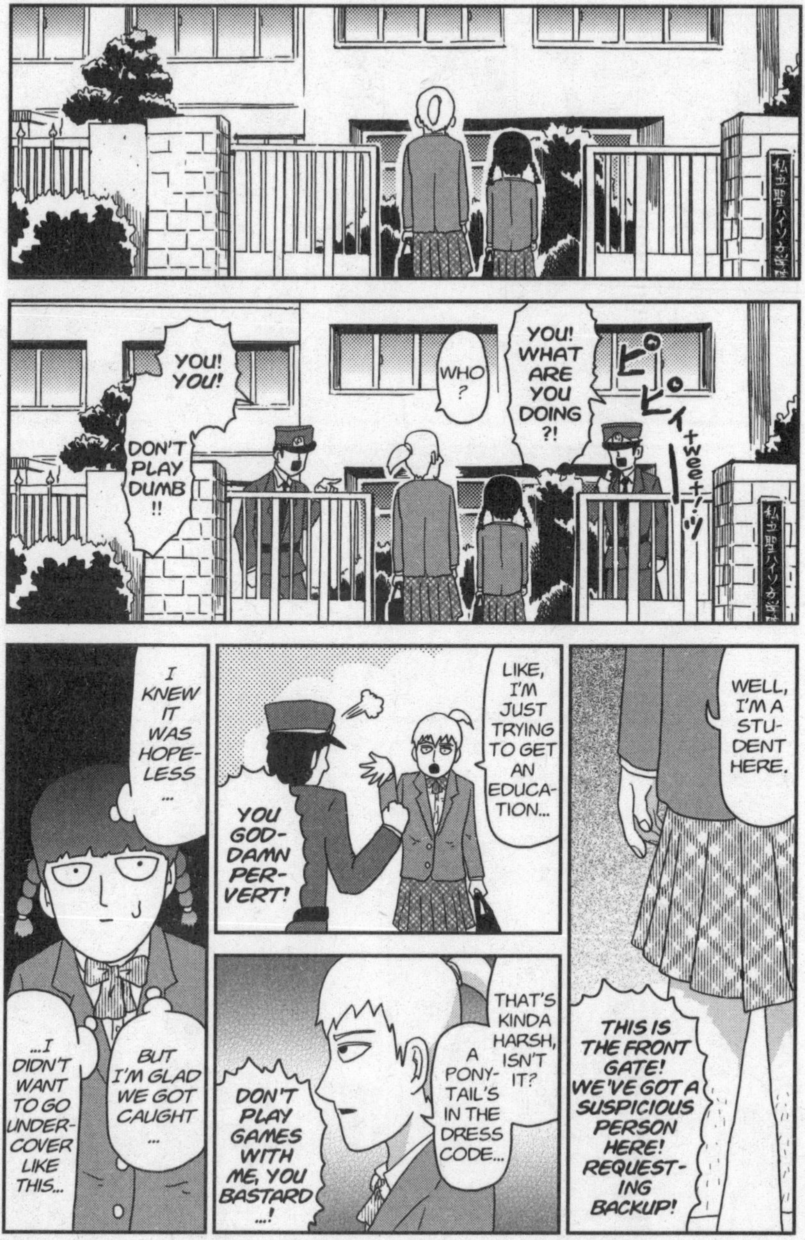
ピ ピイー
tweet!! ッ
YOU! WHAT ARE YOU DOING?!
WHO?
YOU! YOU!
DON'T PLAY DUMB!!
WELL, I'M A STUDENT HERE.
THIS IS THE FRONT GATE! WE'VE GOT A SUSPICIOUS PERSON HERE! REQUESTING BACKUP!
LIKE, I'M JUST TRYING TO GET AN EDUCATION...
YOU GODDAMN PERVERT!
THAT'S KINDA HARSH, ISN'T IT?
A PONYTAIL'S IN THE DRESS CODE...
DON'T PLAY GAMES WITH ME, YOU BASTARD...!
I KNEW IT WAS HOPELESS...
BUT I'M GLAD WE GOT CAUGHT...
...I DIDN'T WANT TO GO UNDERCOVER LIKE THIS...

UM...

HUH?

ARE YOU OKAY, MISS?

WE'LL DEAL WITH THAT CREEPY GUY WHO WAS STALKING YOU.

GO ON IN, YOUNG LADY. CLASS HAS ALREADY STARTED.

"GO."

...

ペコッ thap

ペコッ thap

ON MY OWN? SERIOUSLY...?

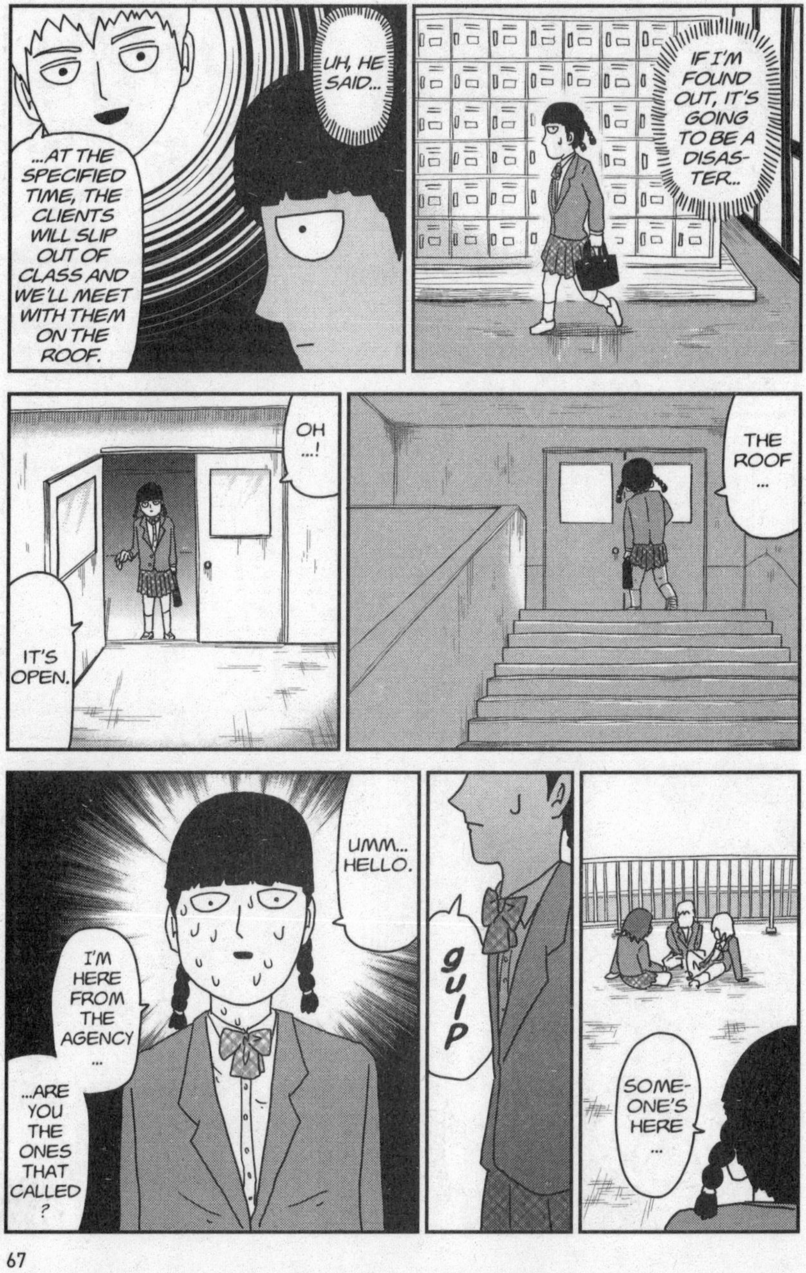
IF I'M FOUND OUT, IT'S GOING TO BE A DISASTER...
UH, HE SAID...
...AT THE SPECIFIED TIME, THE CLIENTS WILL SLIP OUT OF CLASS AND WE'LL MEET WITH THEM ON THE ROOF.
THE ROOF ...
OH ...!
IT'S OPEN.
SOME-ONE'S HERE ...
gulp
UMM... HELLO.
I'M HERE FROM THE AGENCY ...
...ARE YOU THE ONES THAT CALLED?

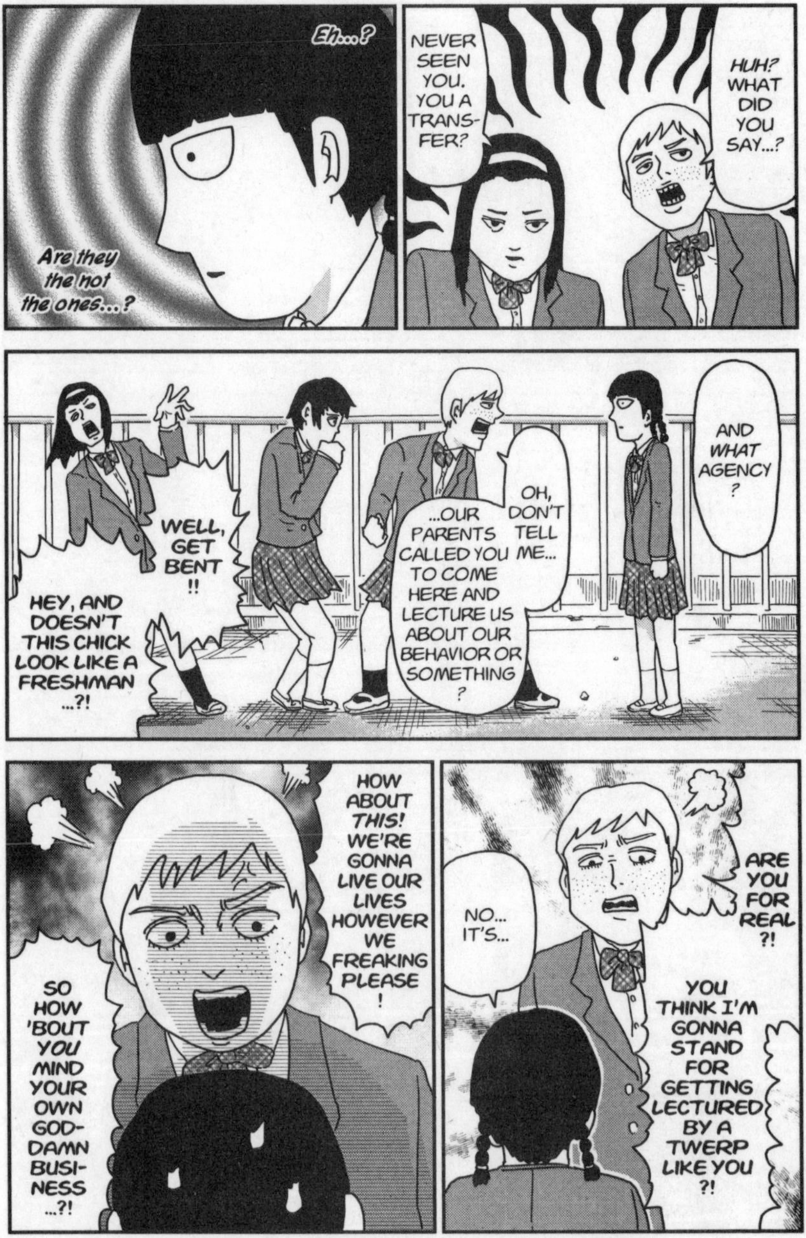
HUH? WHAT DID YOU SAY...?
NEVER SEEN YOU. YOU A TRANSFER?
Eh...?
Are they the not the ones...?
AND WHAT AGENCY?
OH, DON'T TELL ME...
...OUR PARENTS CALLED YOU TO COME HERE AND LECTURE US ABOUT OUR BEHAVIOR OR SOMETHING?
WELL, GET BENT!!
HEY, AND DOESN'T THIS CHICK LOOK LIKE A FRESHMAN...?!
ARE YOU FOR REAL?!
NO... IT'S...
YOU THINK I'M GONNA STAND FOR GETTING LECTURED BY A TWERP LIKE YOU?!
HOW ABOUT THIS! WE'RE GONNA LIVE OUR LIVES HOWEVER WE FREAKING PLEASE!
SO HOW 'BOUT YOU MIND YOUR OWN GOD-DAMN BUSI-NESS...?!

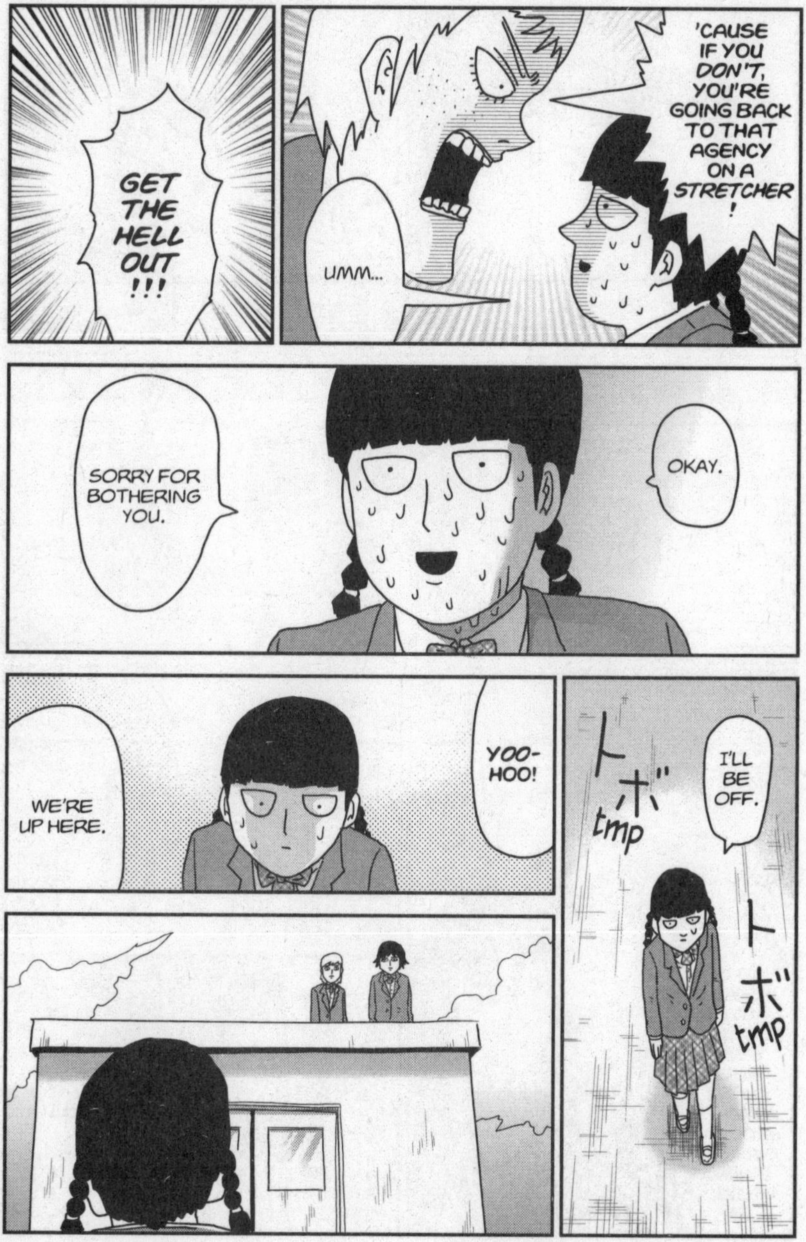

'CAUSE IF YOU DON'T, YOU'RE GOING BACK TO THAT AGENCY ON A STRETCHER!
UMM...
GET THE HELL OUT!!!
OKAY.
SORRY FOR BOTHERING YOU.
I'LL BE OFF.
トボ tmp
トボ tmp
YOO-HOO!
WE'RE UP HERE.

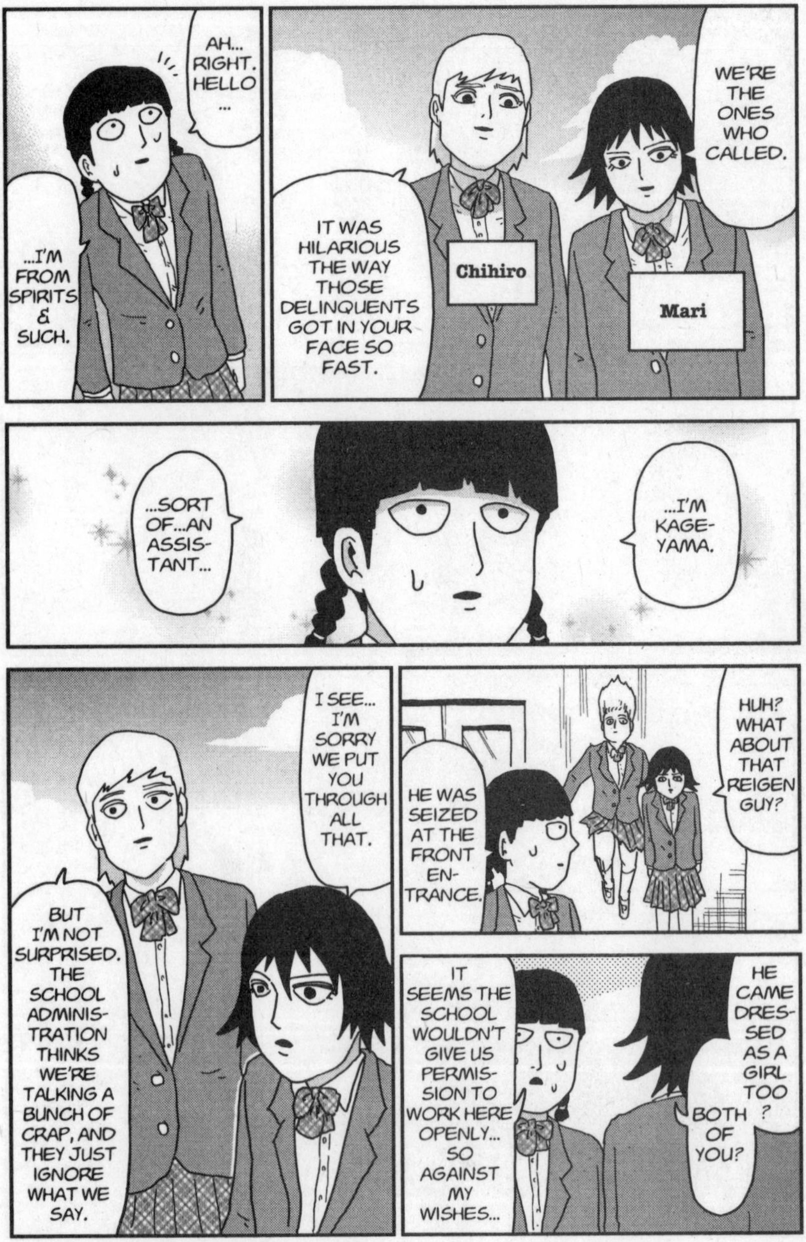
WE'RE THE ONES WHO CALLED.
IT WAS HILARIOUS THE WAY THOSE DELINQUENTS GOT IN YOUR FACE SO FAST.
Chihiro
Mari
AH... RIGHT. HELLO ...
...I'M FROM SPIRITS & SUCH.
...I'M KAGE-YAMA.
...SORT OF...AN ASSIS-TANT...
HUH? WHAT ABOUT THAT REIGEN GUY?
HE WAS SEIZED AT THE FRONT EN-TRANCE.
HE CAME DRES-SED AS A GIRL TOO ?
BOTH OF YOU?
IT SEEMS THE SCHOOL WOULDN'T GIVE US PERMIS-SION TO WORK HERE OPENLY... SO AGAINST MY WISHES...
I SEE... I'M SORRY WE PUT YOU THROUGH ALL THAT.
BUT I'M NOT SURPRISED. THE SCHOOL ADMINIS-TRATION THINKS WE'RE TALKING A BUNCH OF CRAP, AND THEY JUST IGNORE WHAT WE SAY.

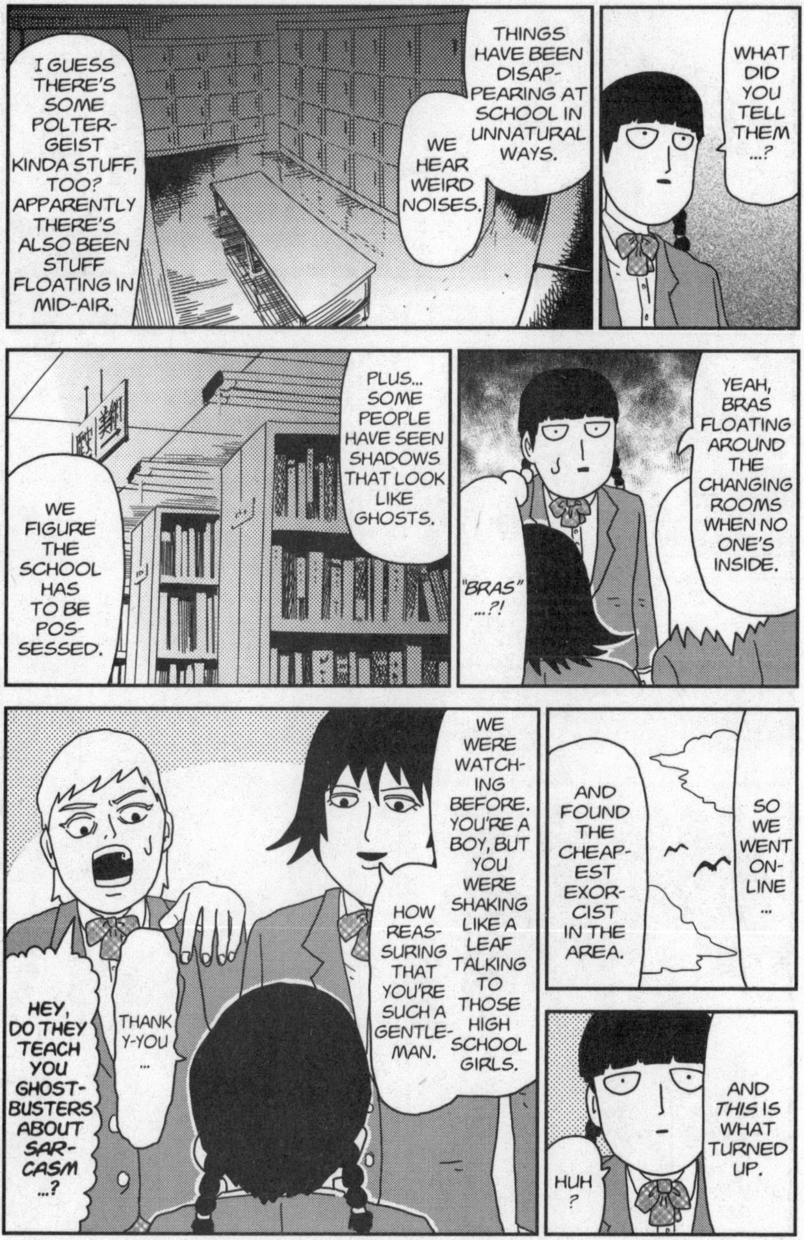
WHAT DID YOU TELL THEM ...?
THINGS HAVE BEEN DISAPPEARING AT SCHOOL IN UNNATURAL WAYS.
WE HEAR WEIRD NOISES.
I GUESS THERE'S SOME POLTERGEIST KINDA STUFF, TOO? APPARENTLY THERE'S ALSO BEEN STUFF FLOATING IN MID-AIR.
YEAH, BRAS FLOATING AROUND THE CHANGING ROOMS WHEN NO ONE'S INSIDE.
"BRAS" ...?!
PLUS... SOME PEOPLE HAVE SEEN SHADOWS THAT LOOK LIKE GHOSTS.
WE FIGURE THE SCHOOL HAS TO BE POSSESSED.
SO WE WENT ONLINE ...
AND FOUND THE CHEAPEST EXORCIST IN THE AREA.
AND *THIS* IS WHAT TURNED UP.
HUH?
WE WERE WATCHING BEFORE. YOU'RE A BOY, BUT YOU WERE SHAKING LIKE A LEAF TALKING TO THOSE HIGH SCHOOL GIRLS.
HOW REASSURING THAT YOU'RE SUCH A GENTLEMAN.
THANK Y-YOU ...
HEY, DO THEY TEACH YOU GHOSTBUSTERS ABOUT *SARCASM* ...?

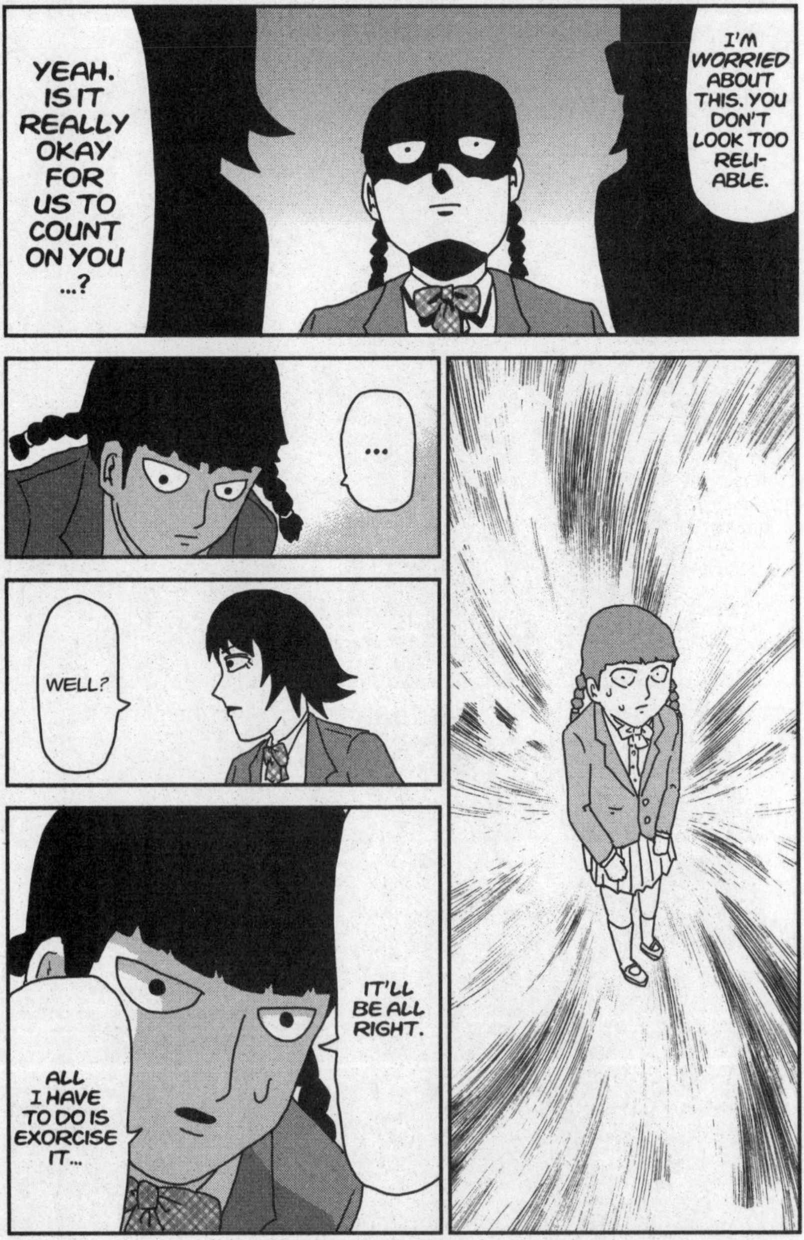
I'M WORRIED ABOUT THIS. YOU DON'T LOOK TOO RELI-ABLE.
YEAH. IS IT REALLY OKAY FOR US TO COUNT ON YOU ...?
...
WELL?
IT'LL BE ALL RIGHT.
ALL I HAVE TO DO IS EXORCISE IT...

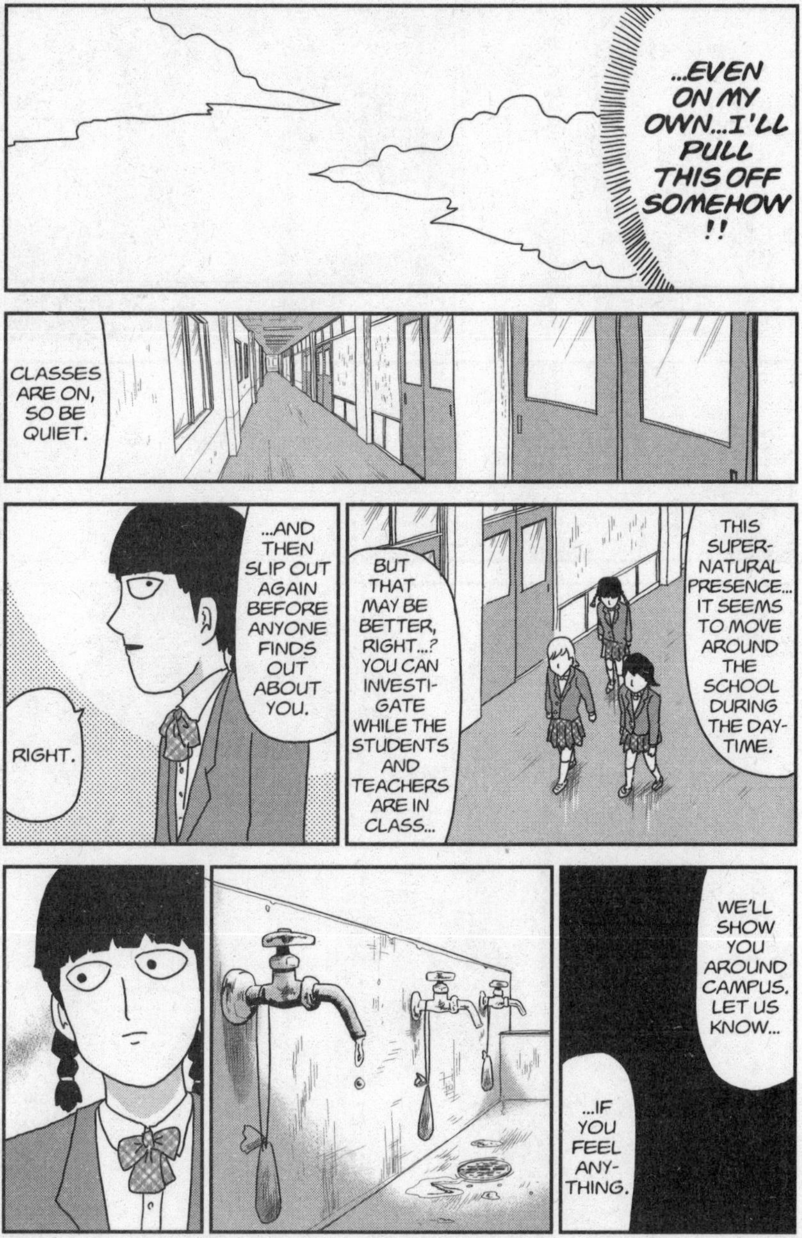
...EVEN ON MY OWN...I'LL PULL THIS OFF SOMEHOW!!
CLASSES ARE ON, SO BE QUIET.
THIS SUPER-NATURAL PRESENCE... IT SEEMS TO MOVE AROUND THE SCHOOL DURING THE DAY-TIME.
BUT THAT MAY BE BETTER, RIGHT...? YOU CAN INVESTI-GATE WHILE THE STUDENTS AND TEACHERS ARE IN CLASS...
...AND THEN SLIP OUT AGAIN BEFORE ANYONE FINDS OUT ABOUT YOU.
RIGHT.
WE'LL SHOW YOU AROUND CAMPUS. LET US KNOW...
...IF YOU FEEL ANY-THING.

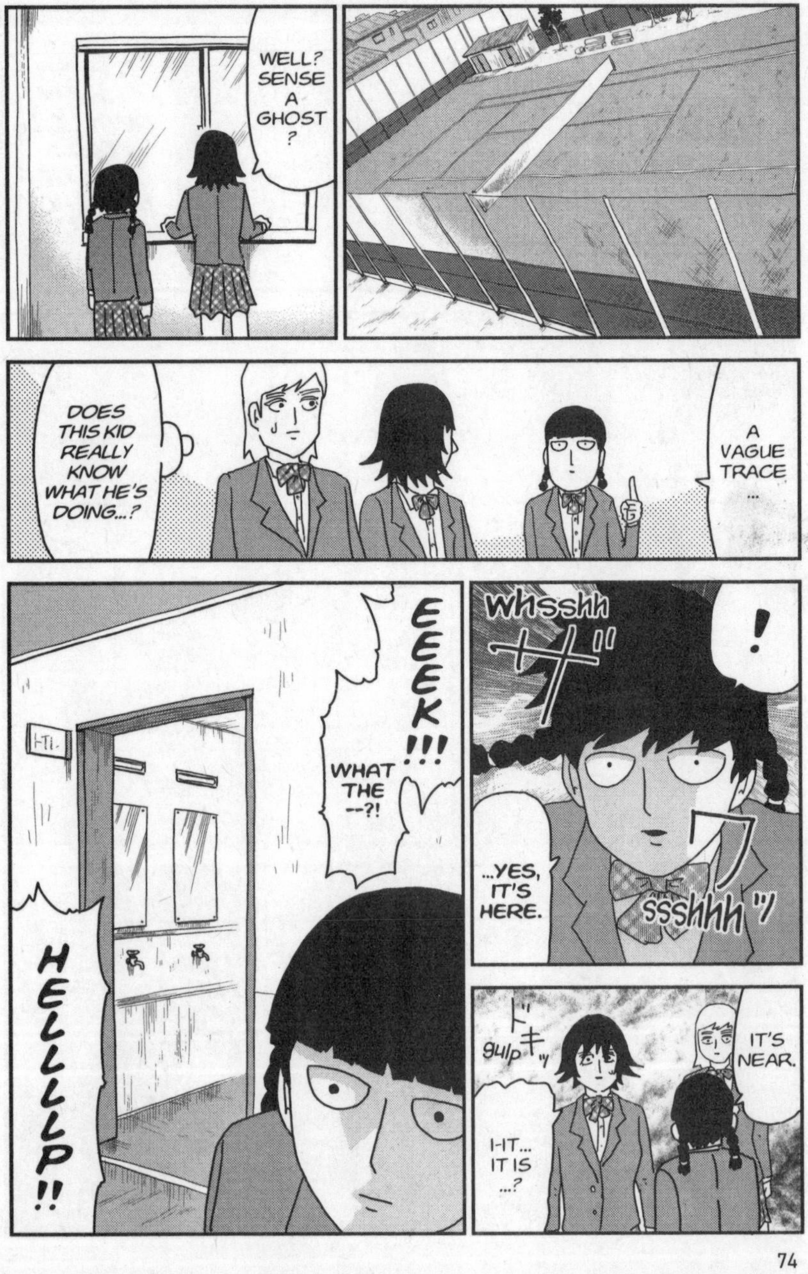

WELL? SENSE A GHOST?
A VAGUE TRACE ...
DOES THIS KID REALLY KNOW WHAT HE'S DOING...?
!
whsshh
...YES, IT'S HERE.
ssshhh
IT'S NEAR.
gulp
I-IT... IT IS ...?
EEEEK!!!
WHAT THE --?!
HELLLLP!!

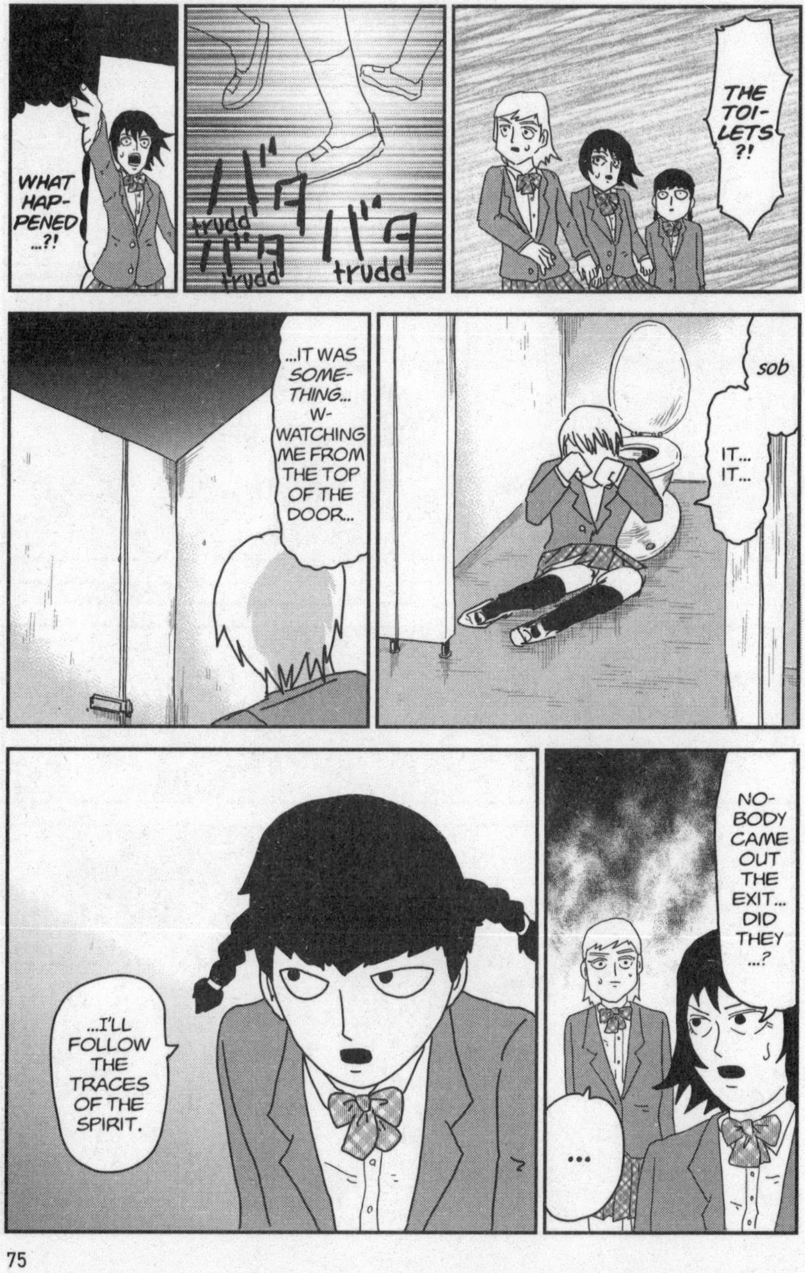
THE TOI-LETS?!
バタ trudd
バタ trudd
バタ trudd
WHAT HAP-PENED...?!
sob
IT... IT...
...IT WAS SOME-THING... W-WATCHING ME FROM THE TOP OF THE DOOR...
NO-BODY CAME OUT THE EXIT... DID THEY...?
...
...I'LL FOLLOW THE TRACES OF THE SPIRIT.

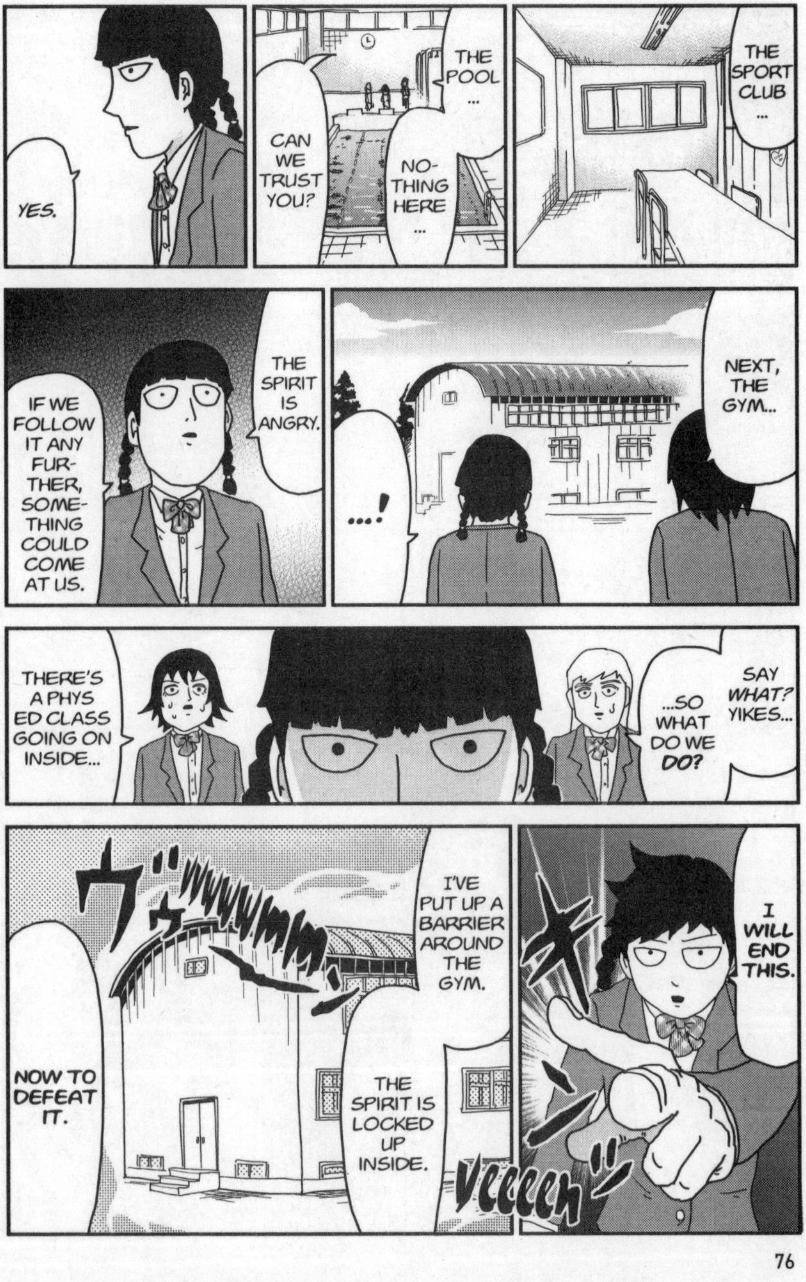
THE SPORT CLUB ...
THE POOL ...
NO-THING HERE ...
CAN WE TRUST YOU?
YES.
NEXT, THE GYM...
...!
THE SPIRIT IS ANGRY.
IF WE FOLLOW IT ANY FUR-THER, SOME-THING COULD COME AT US.
SAY WHAT? YIKES...
...SO WHAT DO WE DO?
THERE'S A PHYS ED CLASS GOING ON INSIDE...
I WILL END THIS.
VEEEEN
I'VE PUT UP A BARRIER AROUND THE GYM.
THE SPIRIT IS LOCKED UP INSIDE.
NOW TO DEFEAT IT.

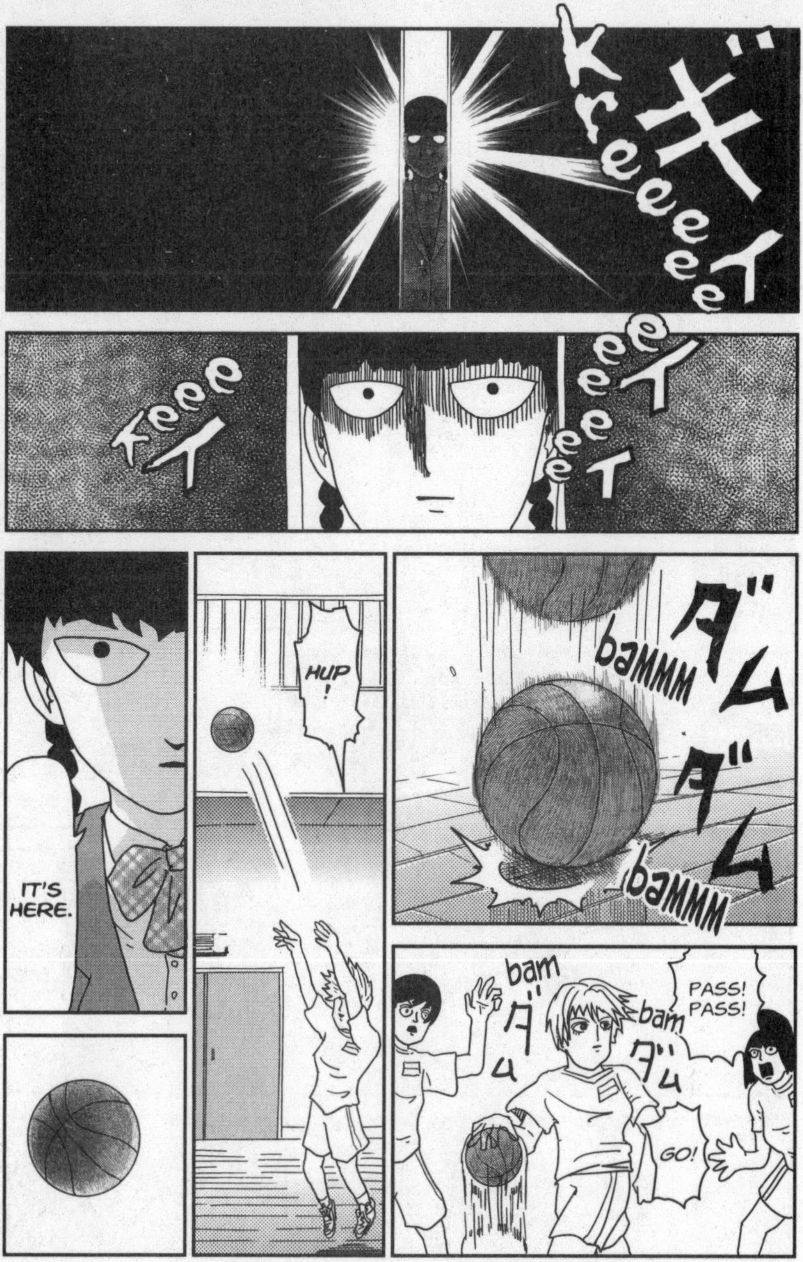
ギイ
Kreeeeeeeeeeeee
イイ
Keee
ダム
bammm
ダム
bammm
PASS! PASS!
bam
ダム
bam
ダム
GO!
HUP!
IT'S HERE.

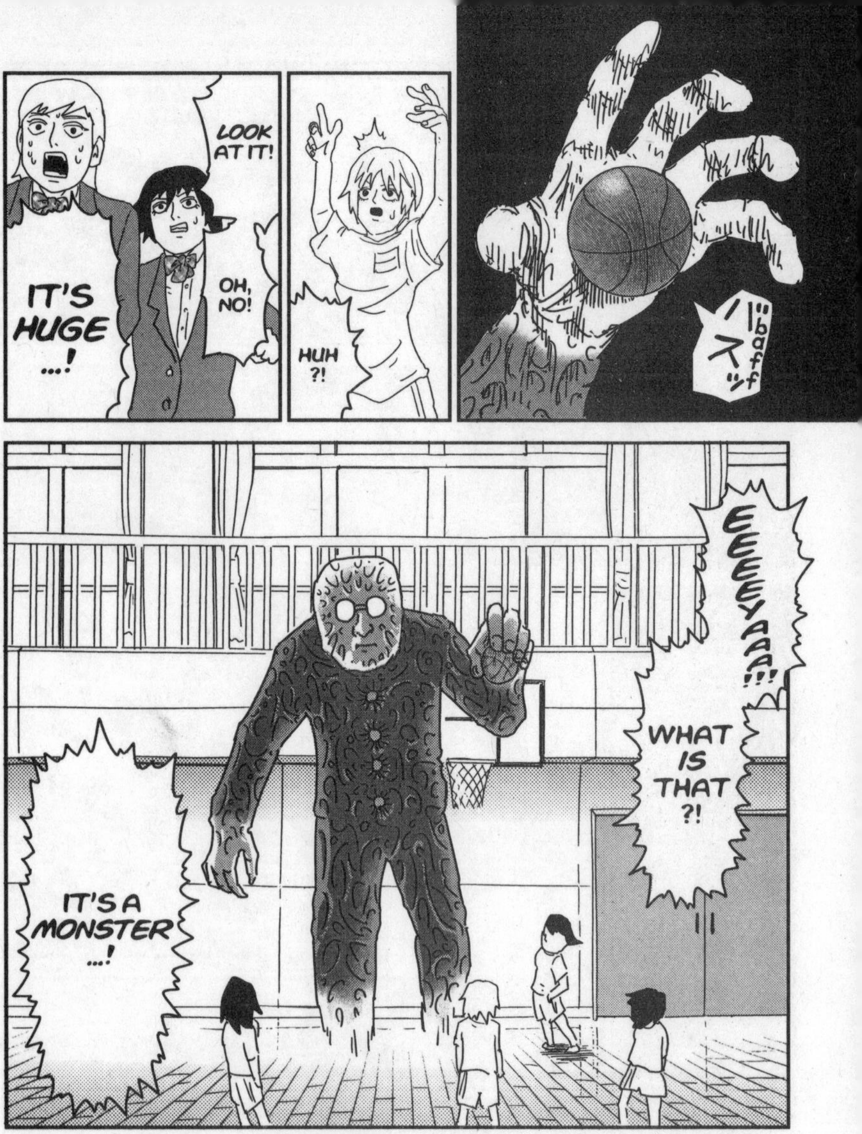

バスッ
baff
HUH ?!
LOOK AT IT!
OH, NO!
IT'S HUGE ...!
EEEEYAAA?!!
WHAT IS THAT ?!
IT'S A MONSTER ...!
HEY, KID...
...YOU'VE GOT SOME NERVE SEALING ME IN HERE.

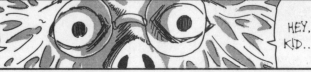

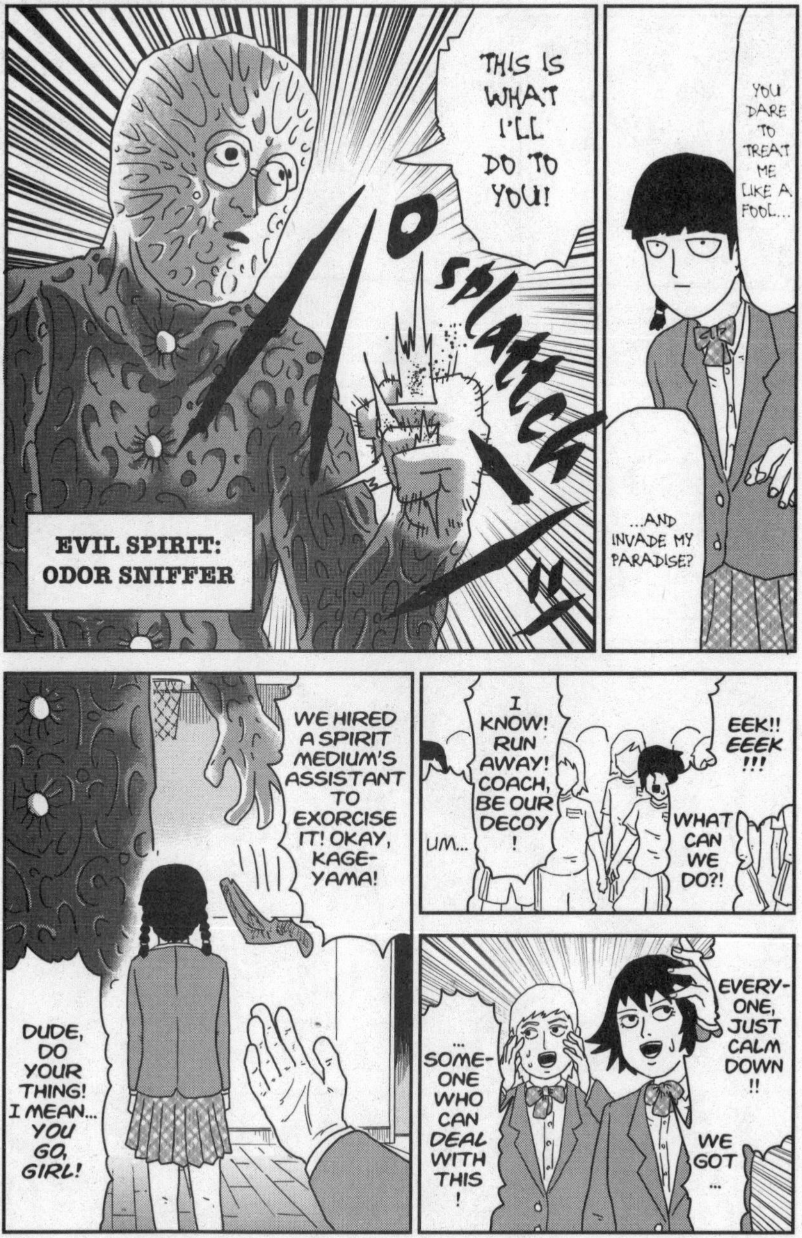
YOU DARE TO TREAT ME LIKE A FOOL...
...AND INVADE MY PARADISE?
THIS IS WHAT I'LL DO TO YOU!
SPLATCH
EVIL SPIRIT: ODOR SNIFFER
EEK!! EEEK!!!
WHAT CAN WE DO?!
I KNOW! RUN AWAY! COACH, BE OUR DECOY!
UM...
EVERYONE, JUST CALM DOWN!!
WE GOT...
...SOMEONE WHO CAN DEAL WITH THIS!
WE HIRED A SPIRIT MEDIUM'S ASSISTANT TO EXORCISE IT! OKAY, KAGEYAMA!
DUDE, DO YOUR THING! I MEAN... YOU GO, GIRL!

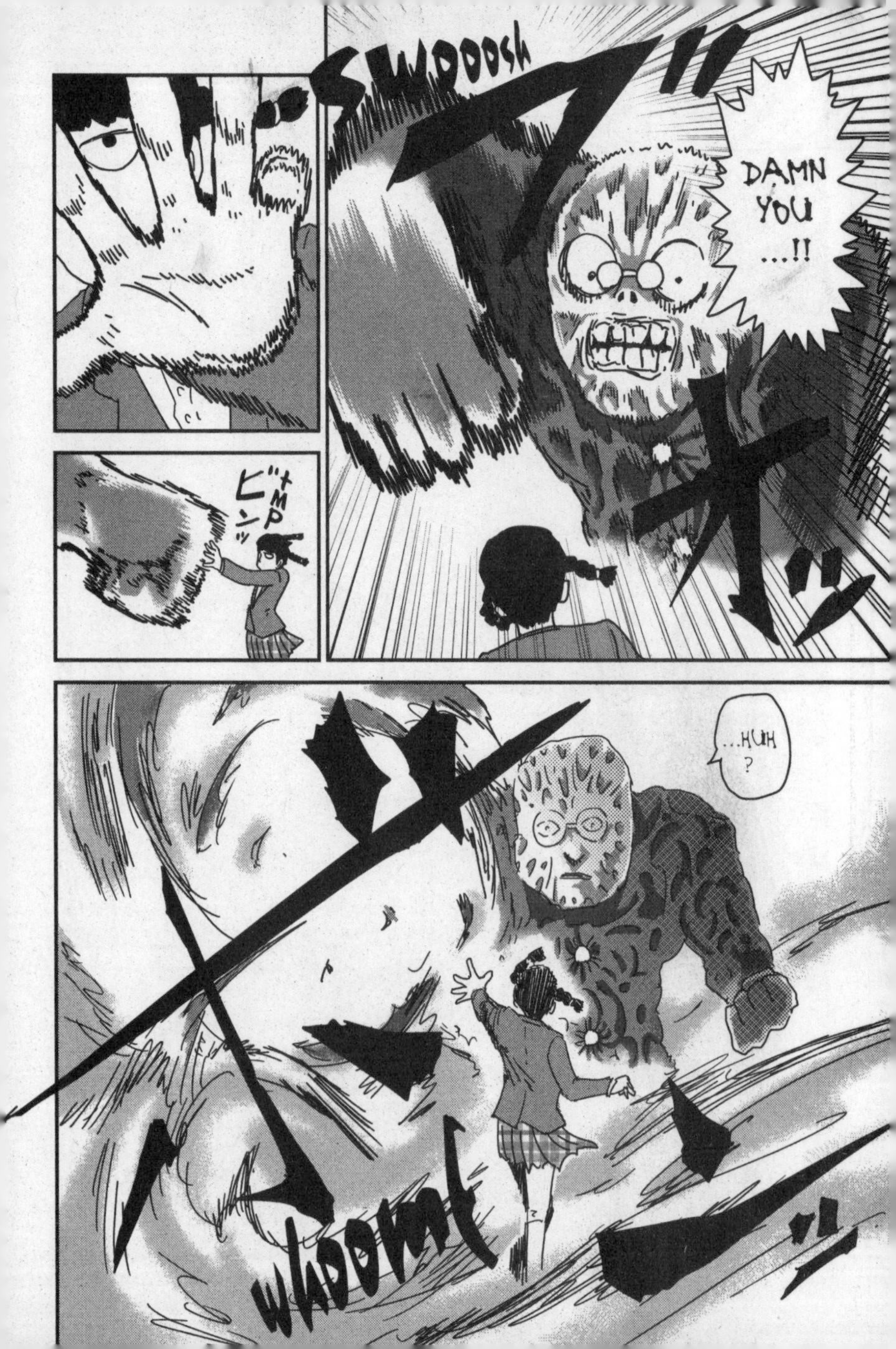
SWOOOSH
DAMN YOU ...!!
TMP
ビンッ
...HUH ?
WHOOMP

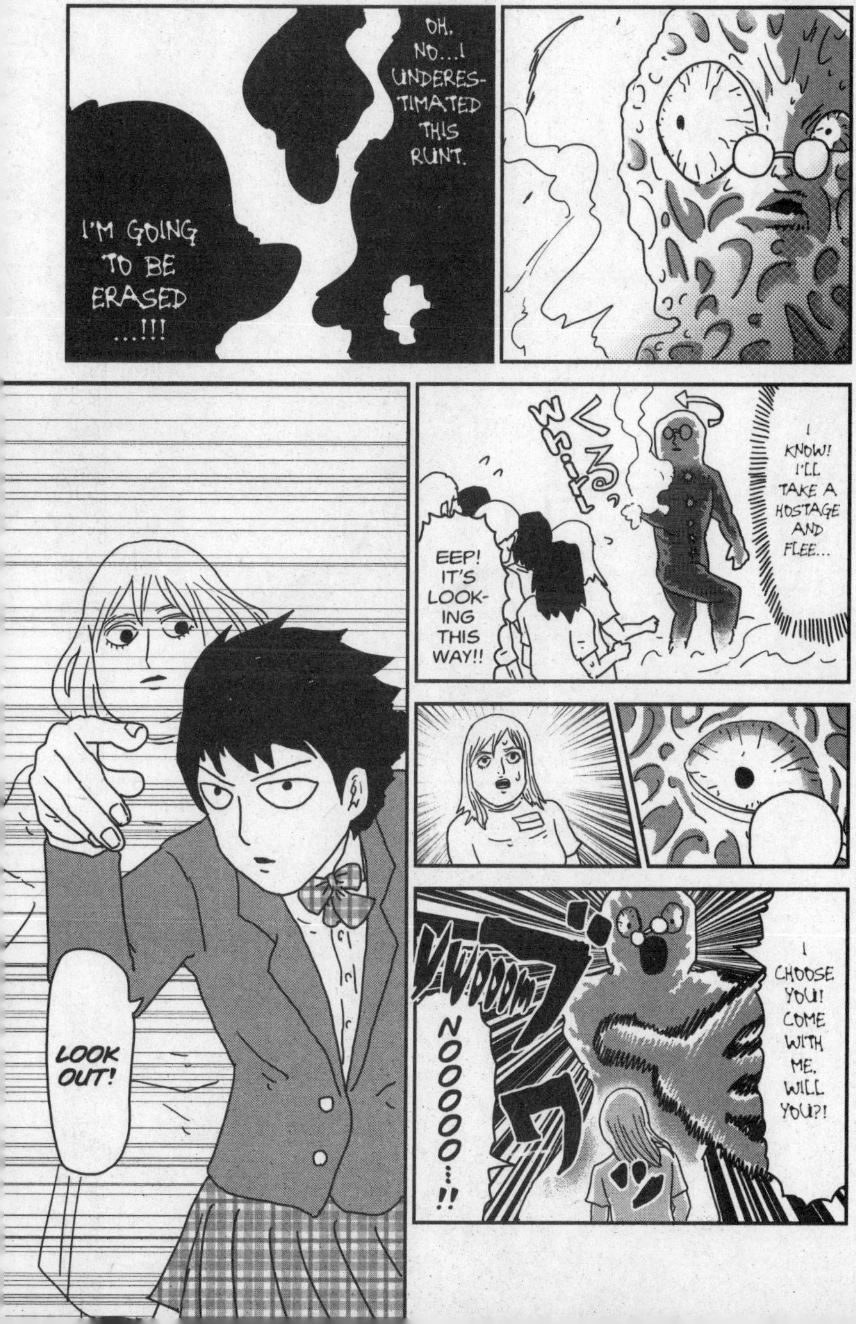
OH, NO...I UNDERESTIMATED THIS RUNT.
I'M GOING TO BE ERASED ...!!!
I KNOW! I'LL TAKE A HOSTAGE AND FLEE...
whirl
EEP! IT'S LOOKING THIS WAY!!
I CHOOSE YOU! COME WITH ME, WILL YOU?!
NOOOOOO...!!
LOOK OUT!

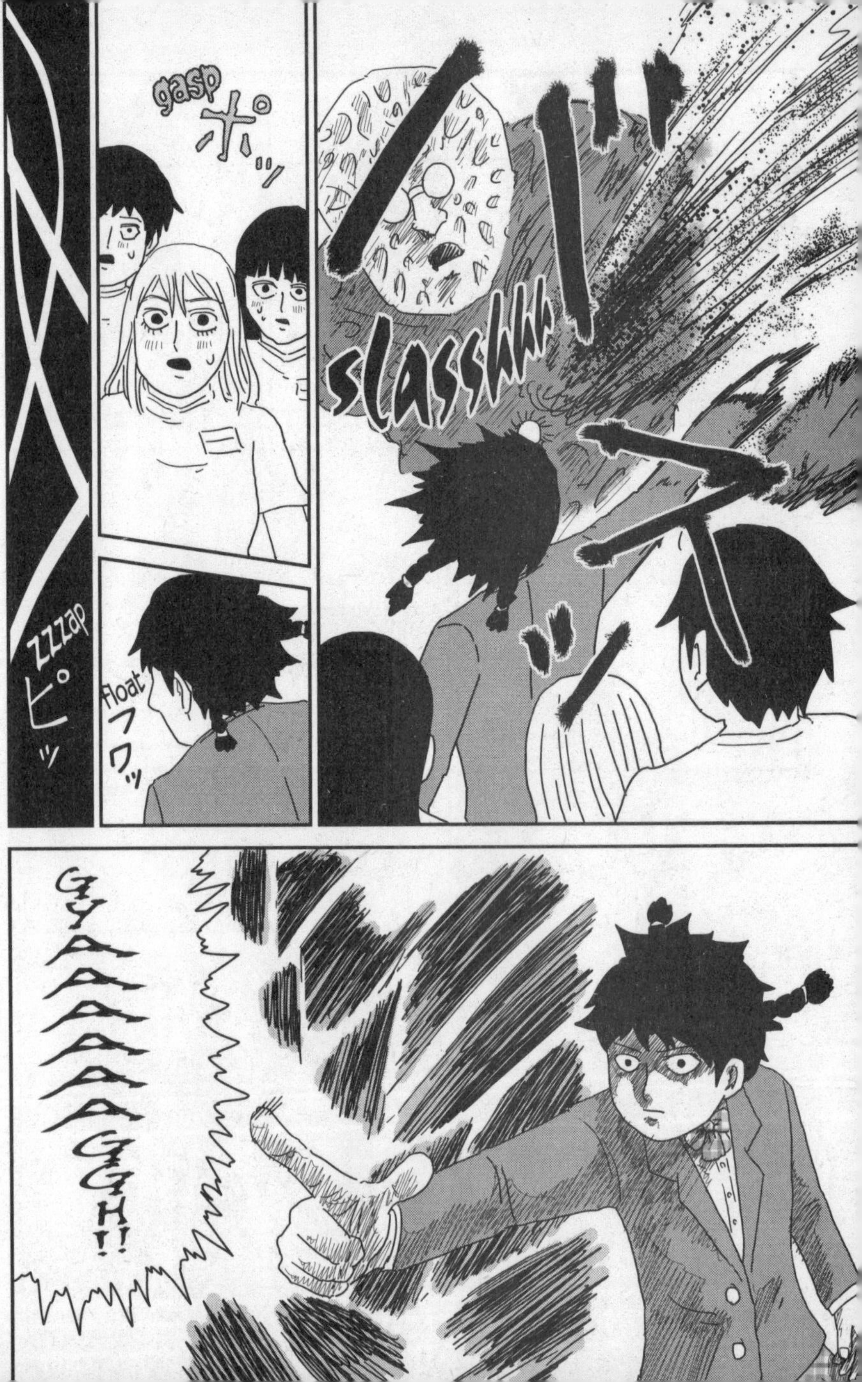
slasshhh
gasp
ポッ
float
フワッ
zzzap
ピッ
GYAAAAAAAAGGH!!

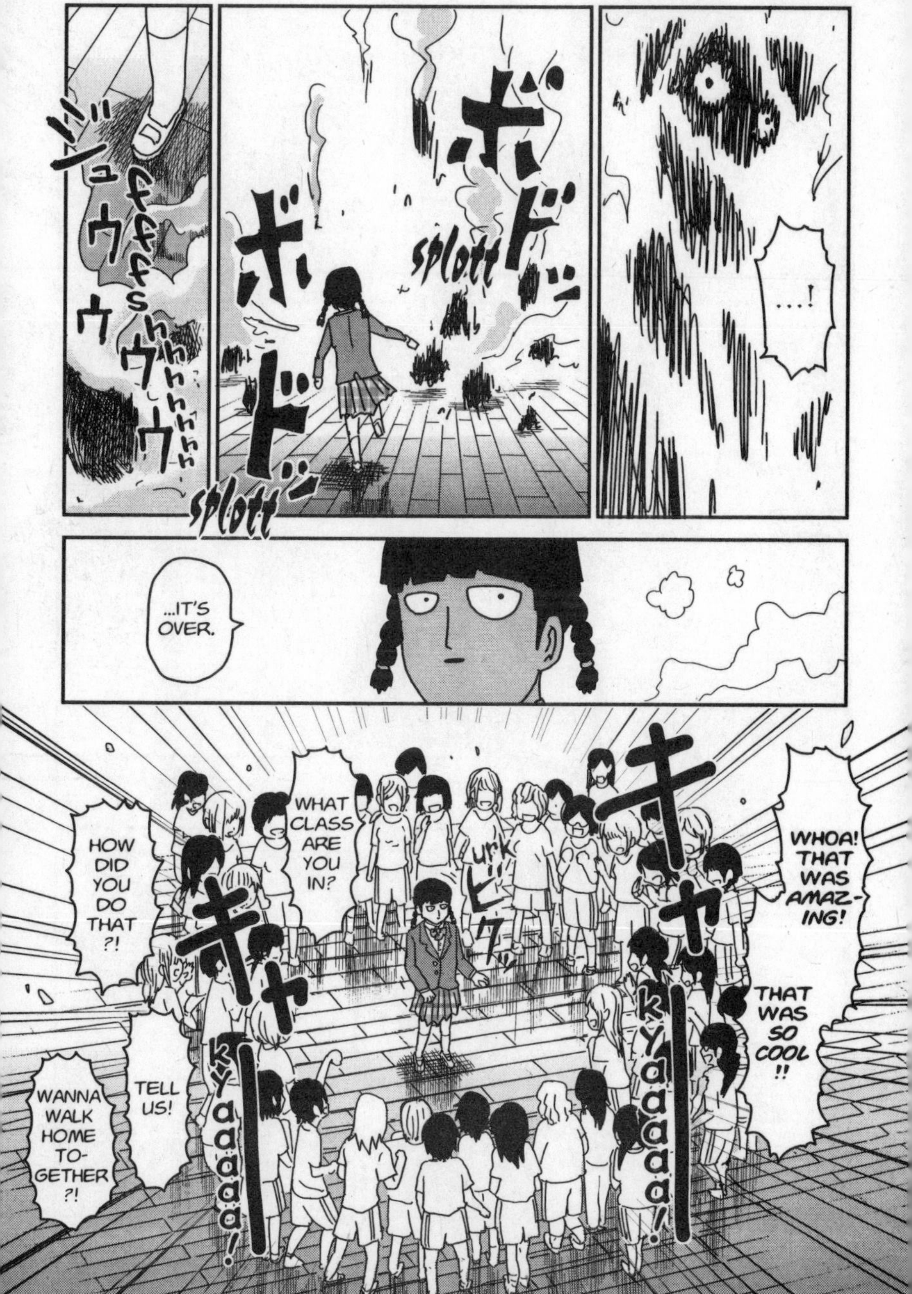

...!
ボドッ
splott
ボドッ
splott
ジュウウウ
fffshhhhhhhhh
...IT'S OVER.
WHOA! THAT WAS AMAZ-ING!
キャー
kyaaaaaa!
THAT WAS SO COOL!!
WHAT CLASS ARE YOU IN?
urk
ビクッ
HOW DID YOU DO THAT?!
キャー
kyaaaa!
TELL US!
WANNA WALK HOME TO-GETHER?!

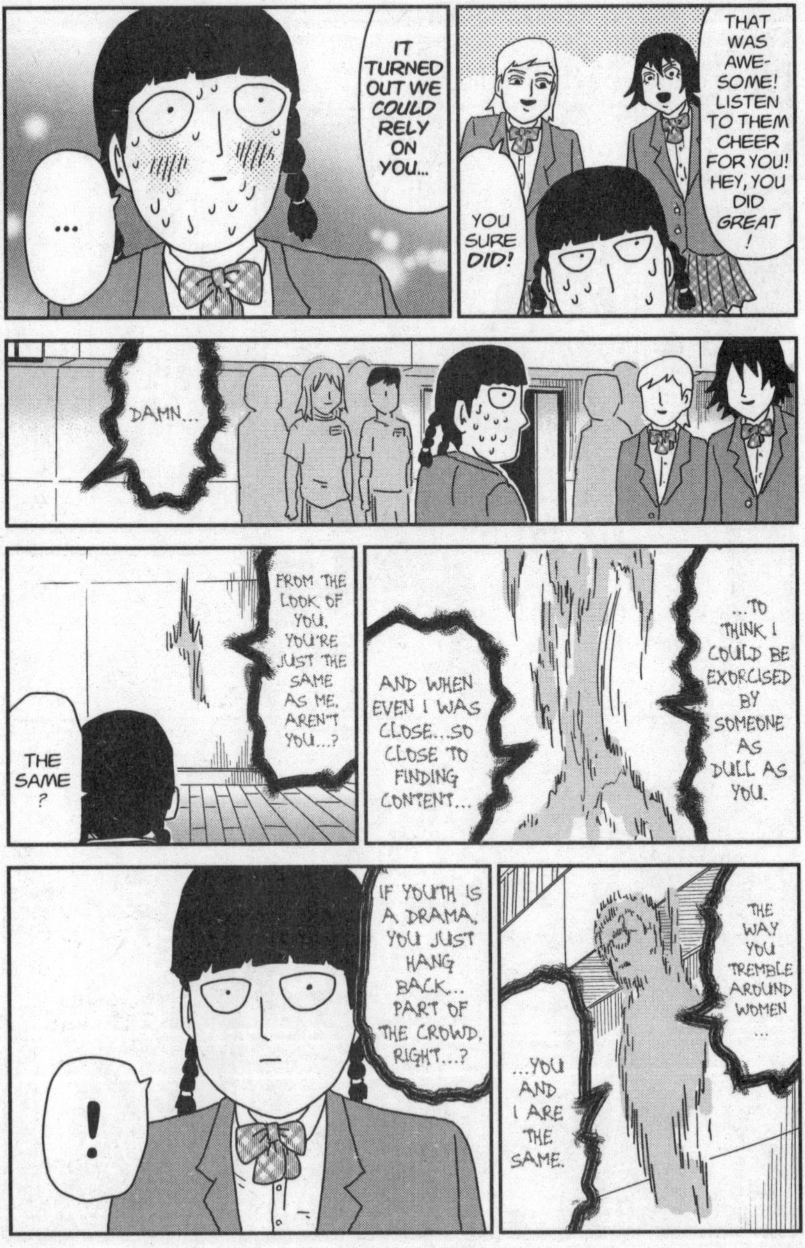
THAT WAS AWE-SOME! LISTEN TO THEM CHEER FOR YOU! HEY, YOU DID GREAT!
YOU SURE DID!
IT TURNED OUT WE COULD RELY ON YOU...
...
DAMN...
...TO THINK I COULD BE EXORCISED BY SOMEONE AS DULL AS YOU.
AND WHEN EVEN I WAS CLOSE...SO CLOSE TO FINDING CONTENT...
FROM THE LOOK OF YOU, YOU'RE JUST THE SAME AS ME, AREN'T YOU...?
THE SAME?
THE WAY YOU TREMBLE AROUND WOMEN...
...YOU AND I ARE THE SAME.
IF YOUTH IS A DRAMA, YOU JUST HANG BACK... PART OF THE CROWD, RIGHT...?
!

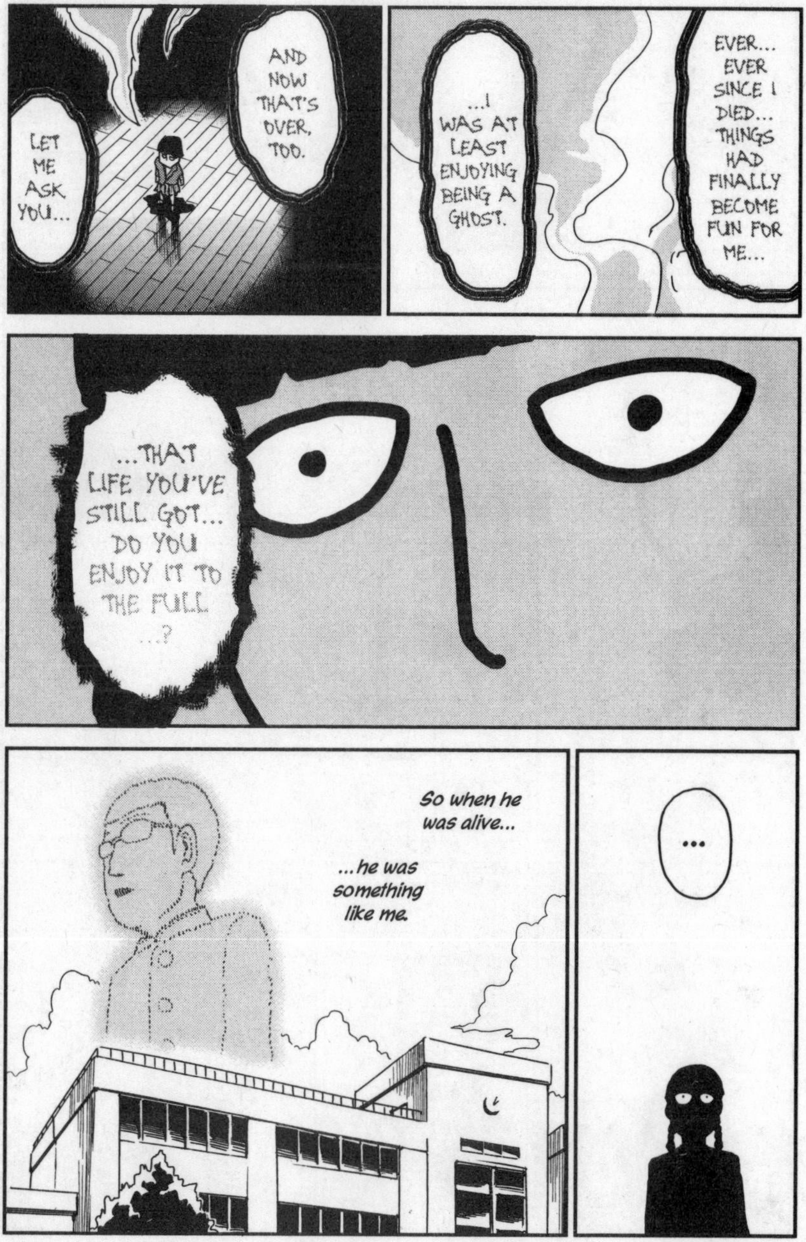
EVER... EVER SINCE I DIED... THINGS HAD FINALLY BECOME FUN FOR ME...
...I WAS AT LEAST ENJOYING BEING A GHOST.
AND NOW THAT'S OVER, TOO.
LET ME ASK YOU...
...THAT LIFE YOU'VE STILL GOT... DO YOU ENJOY IT TO THE FULL ...?
...
So when he was alive...
...he was something like me.

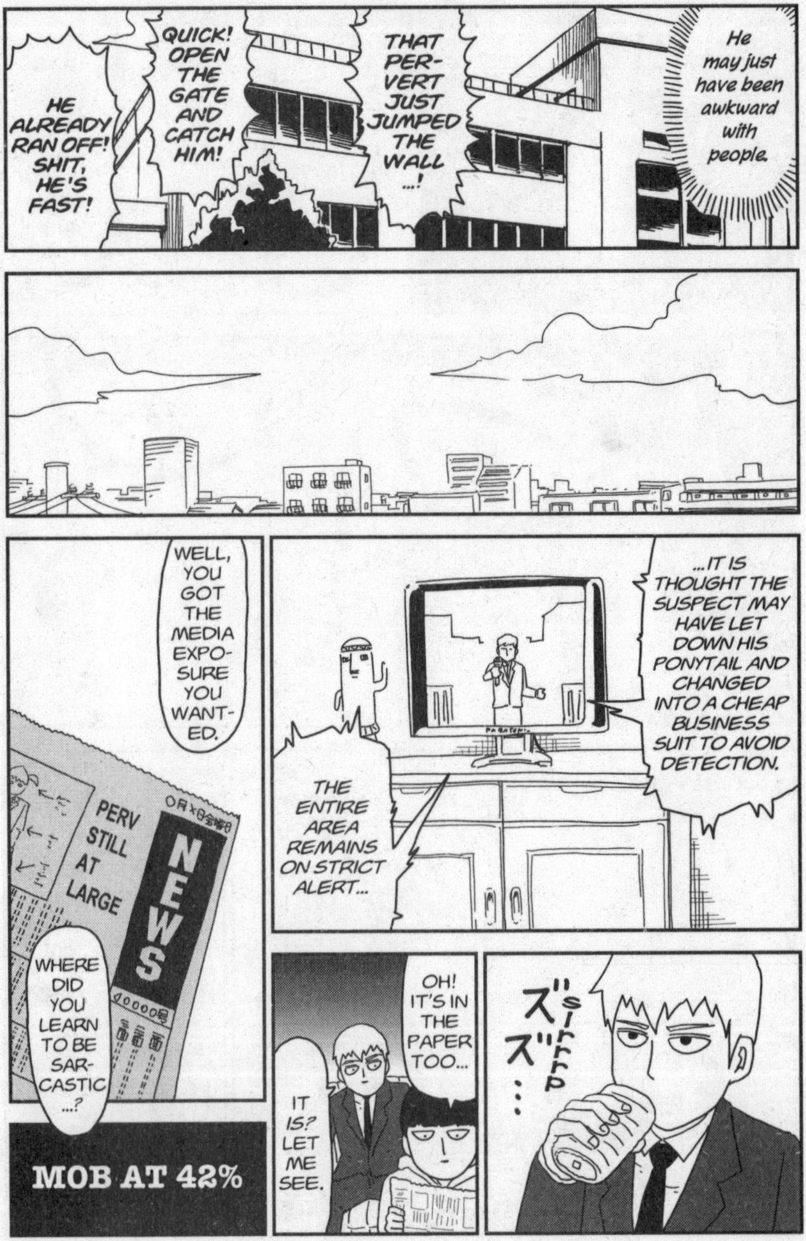
He may just have been awkward with people.
THAT PER-VERT JUST JUMPED THE WALL ...!
QUICK! OPEN THE GATE AND CATCH HIM!
HE ALREADY RAN OFF! SHIT, HE'S FAST!
...IT IS THOUGHT THE SUSPECT MAY HAVE LET DOWN HIS PONYTAIL AND CHANGED INTO A CHEAP BUSINESS SUIT TO AVOID DETECTION.
THE ENTIRE AREA REMAINS ON STRICT ALERT...
ズズ…
slrrp
OH! IT'S IN THE PAPER TOO...
IT IS? LET ME SEE.
WELL, YOU GOT THE MEDIA EXPO-SURE YOU WANT-ED.
PERV STILL AT LARGE
NEWS
WHERE DID YOU LEARN TO BE SAR-CASTIC ...?
MOB AT 42%

CHAPTER 57: ROOTS

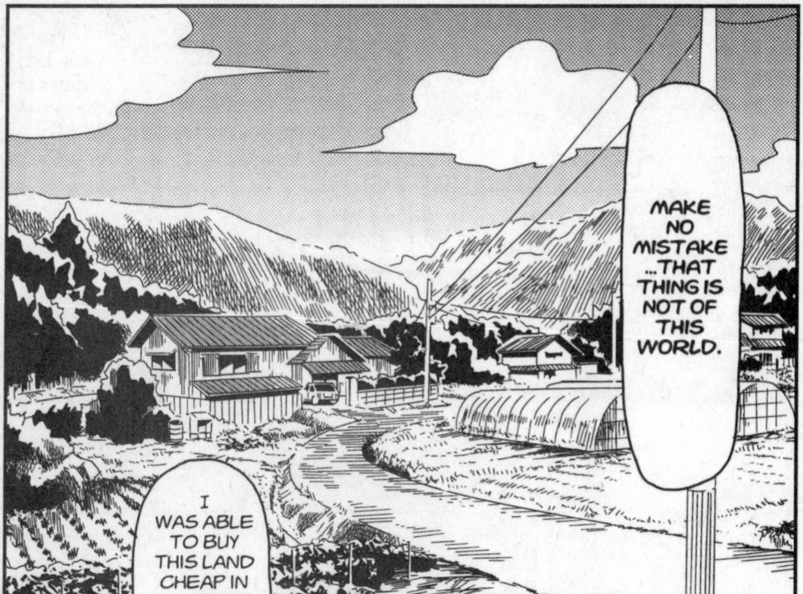
MAKE NO MISTAKE ...THAT THING IS NOT OF THIS WORLD.
I WAS ABLE TO BUY THIS LAND CHEAP IN THE FIRST PLACE BECAUSE IT HAD SOME KIND OF "SHADY HISTORY"...
...BUT IT'S NOT IN MY NATURE TO CARE ABOUT STUFF LIKE THAT.

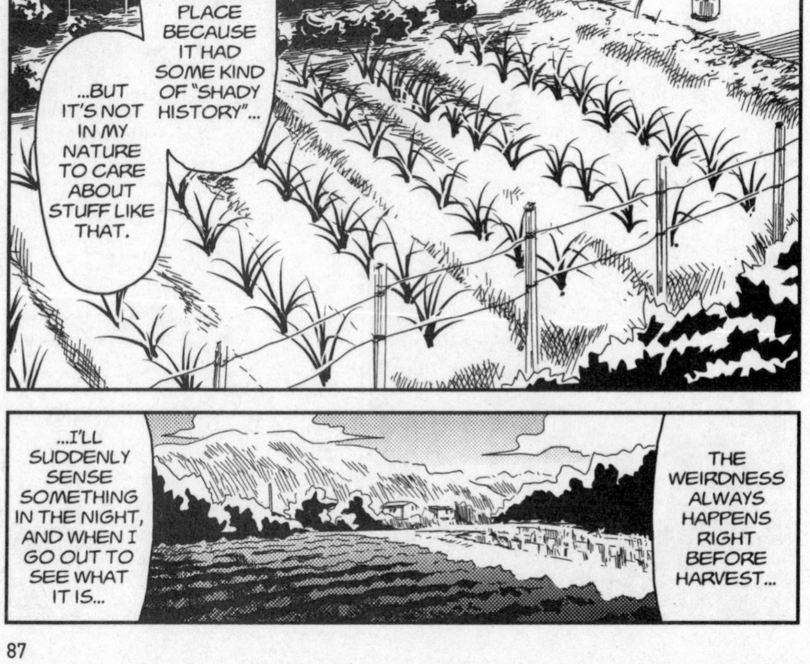
THE WEIRDNESS ALWAYS HAPPENS RIGHT BEFORE HARVEST...
...I'LL SUDDENLY SENSE SOMETHING IN THE NIGHT, AND WHEN I GO OUT TO SEE WHAT IT IS...

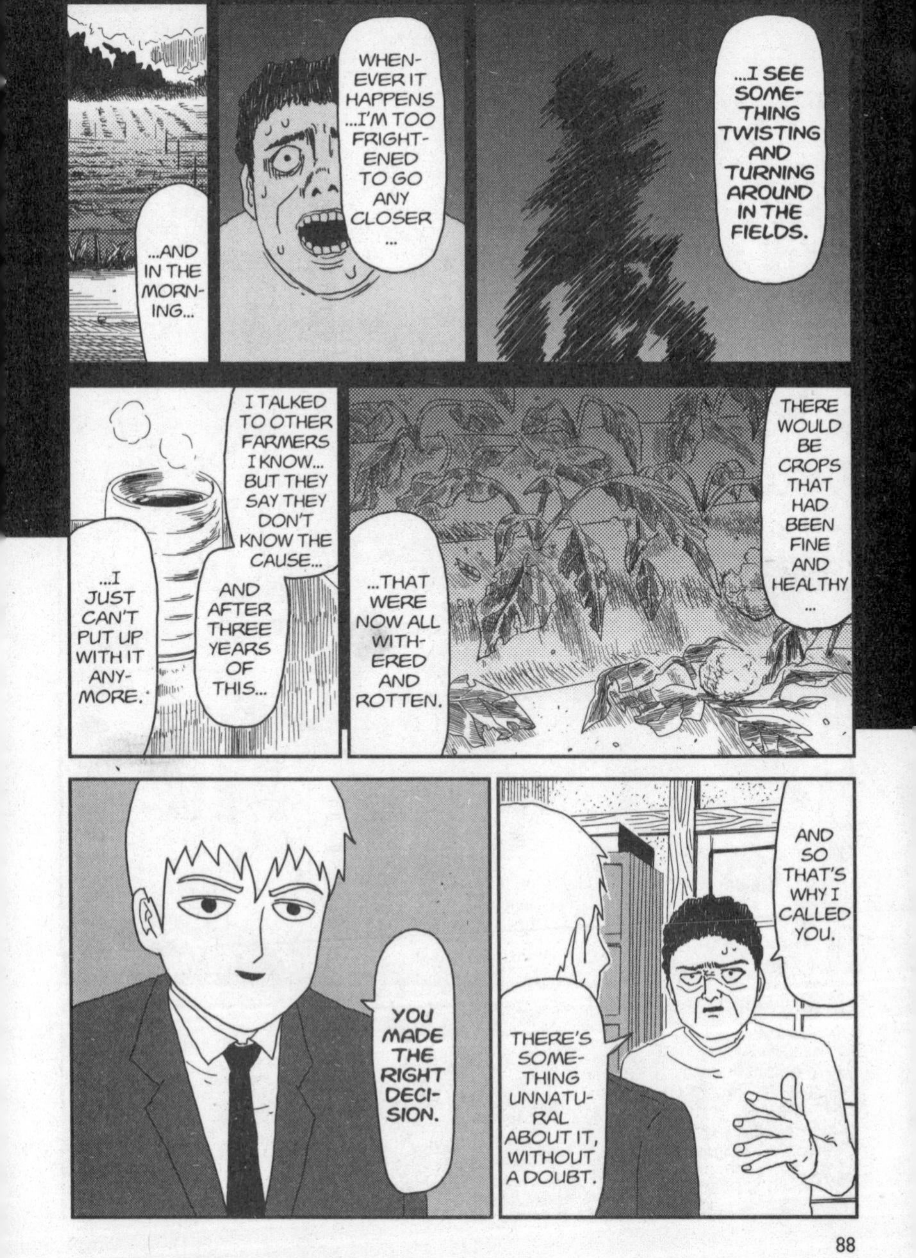
...I SEE SOMETHING TWISTING AND TURNING AROUND IN THE FIELDS.
WHENEVER IT HAPPENS ...I'M TOO FRIGHTENED TO GO ANY CLOSER ...
...AND IN THE MORNING...
THERE WOULD BE CROPS THAT HAD BEEN FINE AND HEALTHY ...
...THAT WERE NOW ALL WITHERED AND ROTTEN.
I TALKED TO OTHER FARMERS I KNOW... BUT THEY SAY THEY DON'T KNOW THE CAUSE...
AND AFTER THREE YEARS OF THIS...
...I JUST CAN'T PUT UP WITH IT ANYMORE.
AND SO THAT'S WHY I CALLED YOU.
THERE'S SOMETHING UNNATURAL ABOUT IT, WITHOUT A DOUBT.
YOU MADE THE RIGHT DECISION.

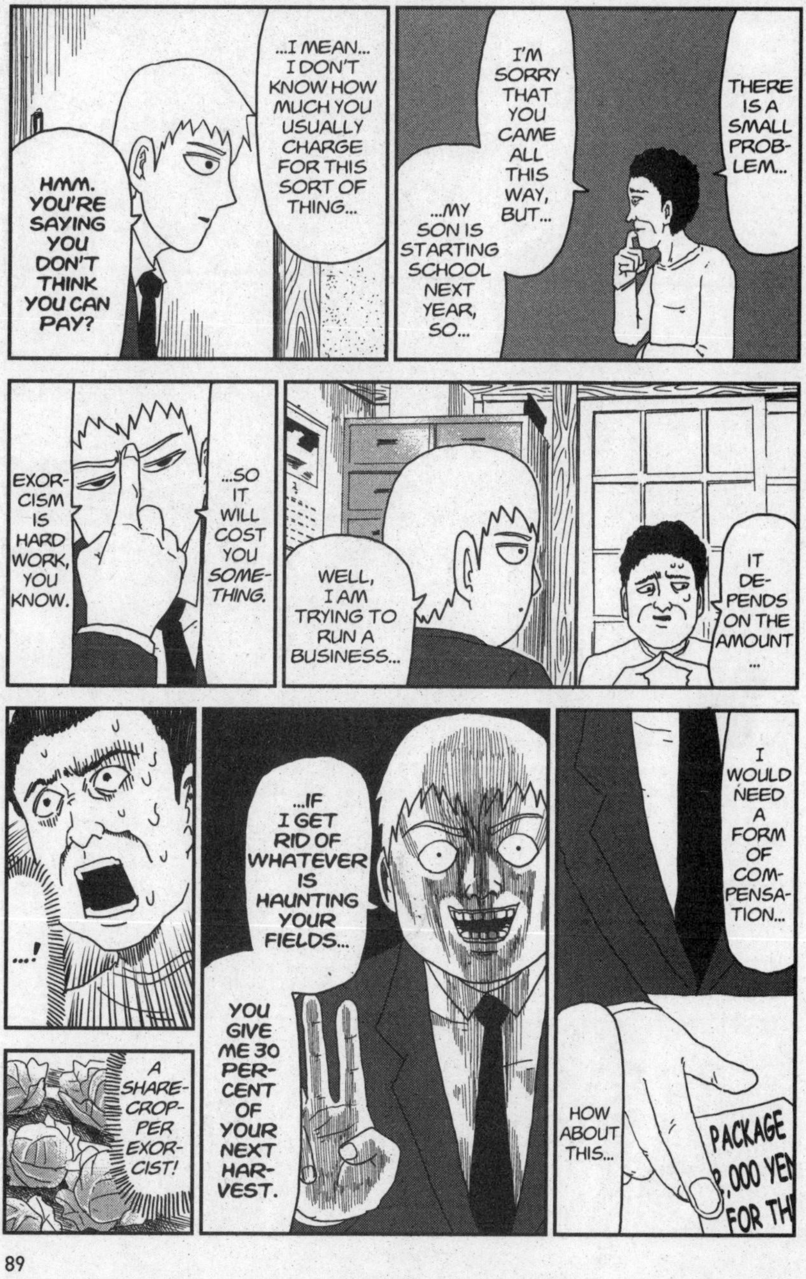
THERE IS A SMALL PROB-LEM...
I'M SORRY THAT YOU CAME ALL THIS WAY, BUT...
...MY SON IS STARTING SCHOOL NEXT YEAR, SO...
...I MEAN... I DON'T KNOW HOW MUCH YOU USUALLY CHARGE FOR THIS SORT OF THING...
HMM. YOU'RE SAYING YOU DON'T THINK YOU CAN PAY?
IT DE-PENDS ON THE AMOUNT...
WELL, I AM TRYING TO RUN A BUSINESS...
...SO IT WILL COST YOU SOME-THING.
EXOR-CISM IS HARD WORK, YOU KNOW.
I WOULD NEED A FORM OF COM-PENSA-TION...
HOW ABOUT THIS...
PACKAGE
...IF I GET RID OF WHATEVER IS HAUNTING YOUR FIELDS...
YOU GIVE ME 30 PER-CENT OF YOUR NEXT HAR-VEST.
...!
A SHARE-CROP-PER EXOR-CIST!

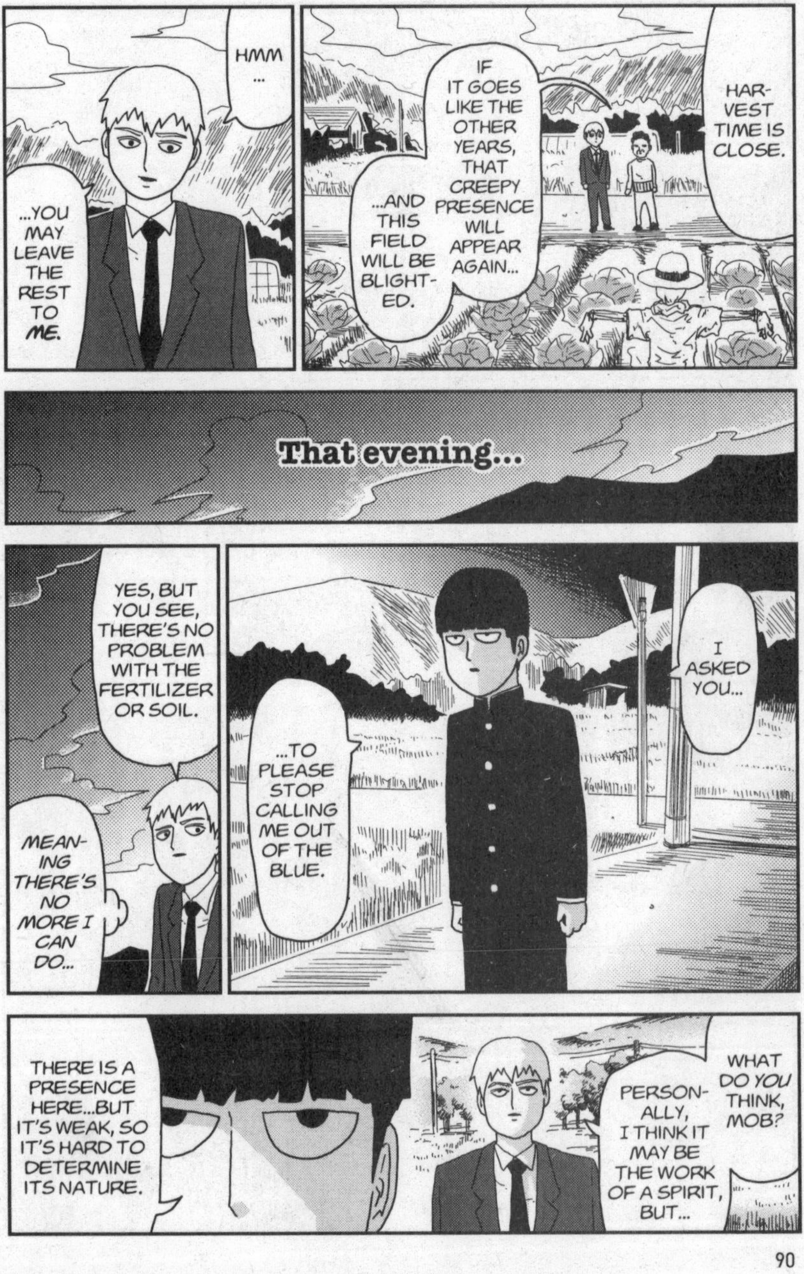
HARVEST TIME IS CLOSE.
IF IT GOES LIKE THE OTHER YEARS, THAT CREEPY PRESENCE WILL APPEAR AGAIN...
...AND THIS FIELD WILL BE BLIGHTED.
HMM...
...YOU MAY LEAVE THE REST TO *ME*.
That evening...
I ASKED YOU...
...TO PLEASE STOP CALLING ME OUT OF THE BLUE.
YES, BUT YOU SEE, THERE'S NO PROBLEM WITH THE FERTILIZER OR SOIL.
MEANING THERE'S NO MORE I CAN DO...
WHAT DO *YOU* THINK, MOB?
PERSONALLY, I THINK IT *MAY* BE THE WORK OF A SPIRIT, BUT...
THERE IS A PRESENCE HERE...BUT IT'S WEAK, SO IT'S HARD TO DETERMINE ITS NATURE.

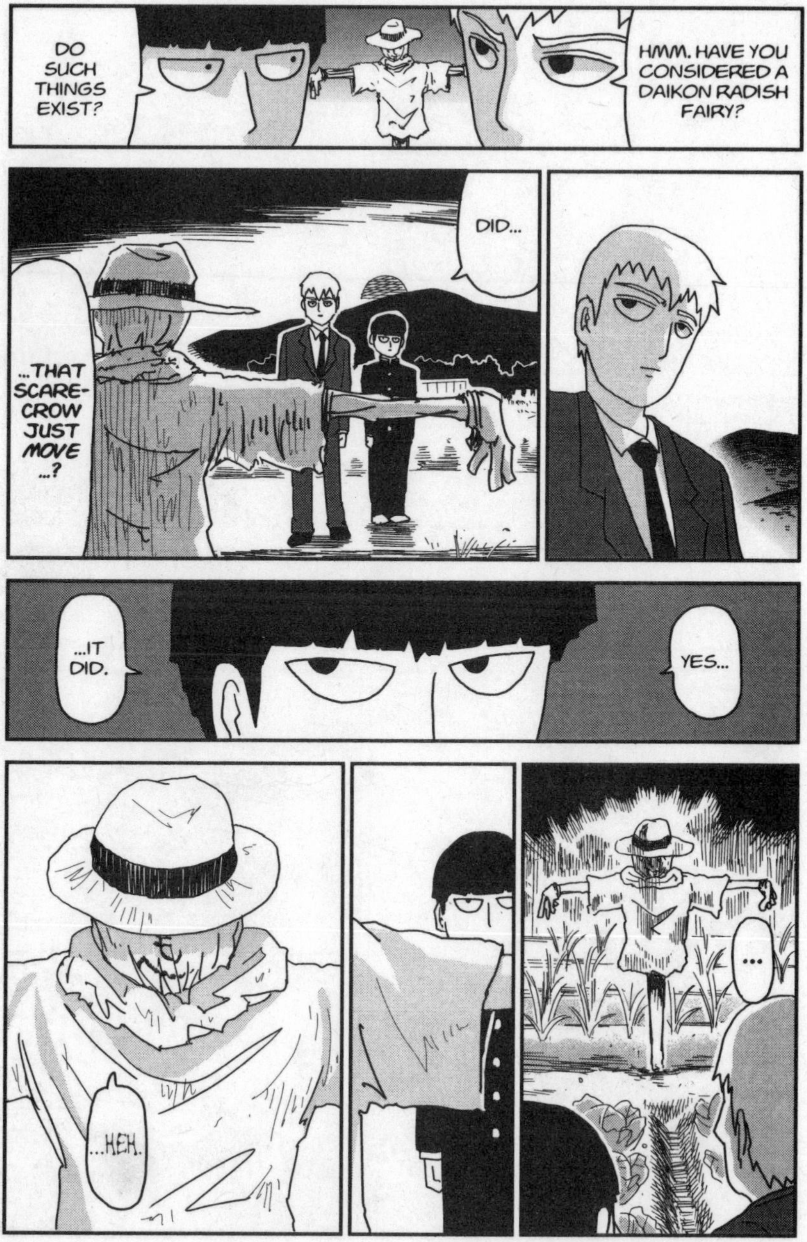
HMM. HAVE YOU CONSIDERED A DAIKON RADISH FAIRY?
DO SUCH THINGS EXIST?
DID...
...THAT SCARE-CROW JUST *MOVE* ...?
YES...
...IT DID.
...
...HEH.

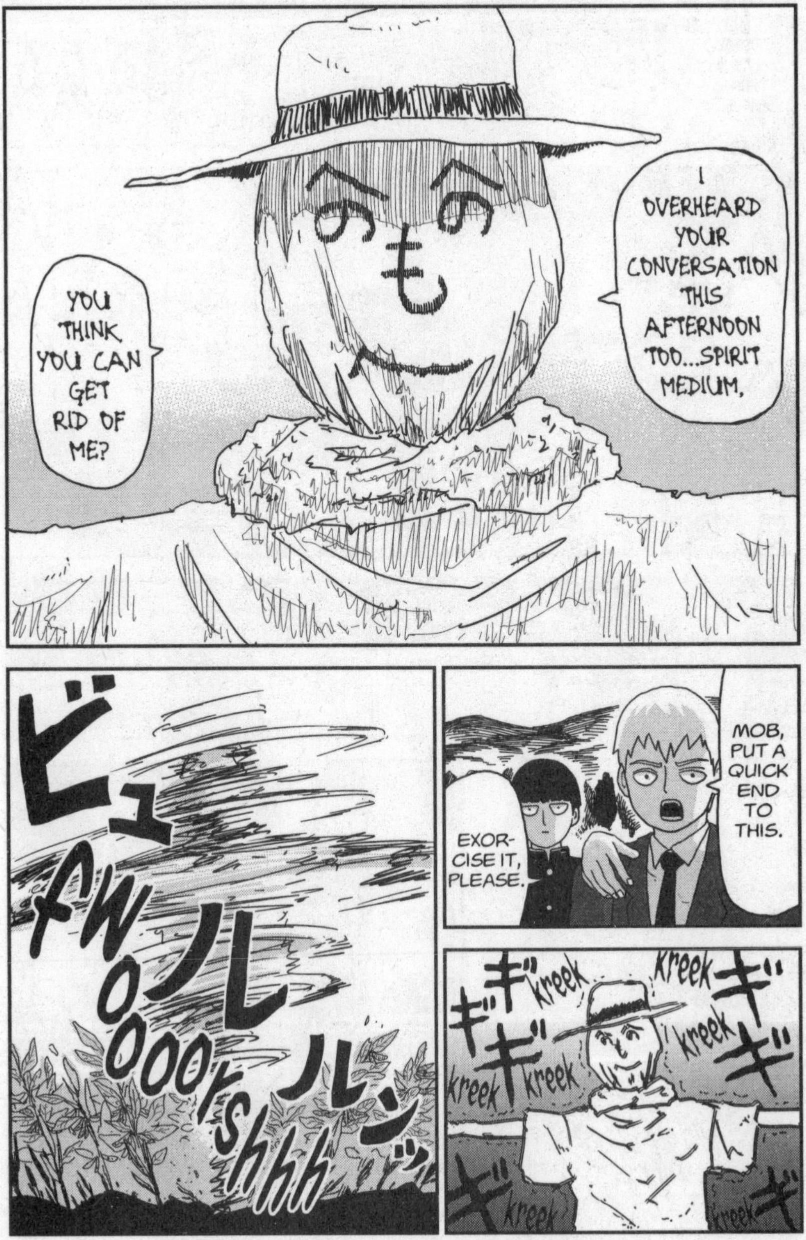
I OVERHEARD YOUR CONVERSATION THIS AFTERNOON TOO...SPIRIT MEDIUM,
YOU THINK YOU CAN GET RID OF ME?
MOB, PUT A QUICK END TO THIS.
EXORCISE IT, PLEASE.
ギ kreek
ギ kreek
ギ kreek
ギ kreek
ギ kreek
ギ kreek
ビュルルンッ
fwoooorshhh

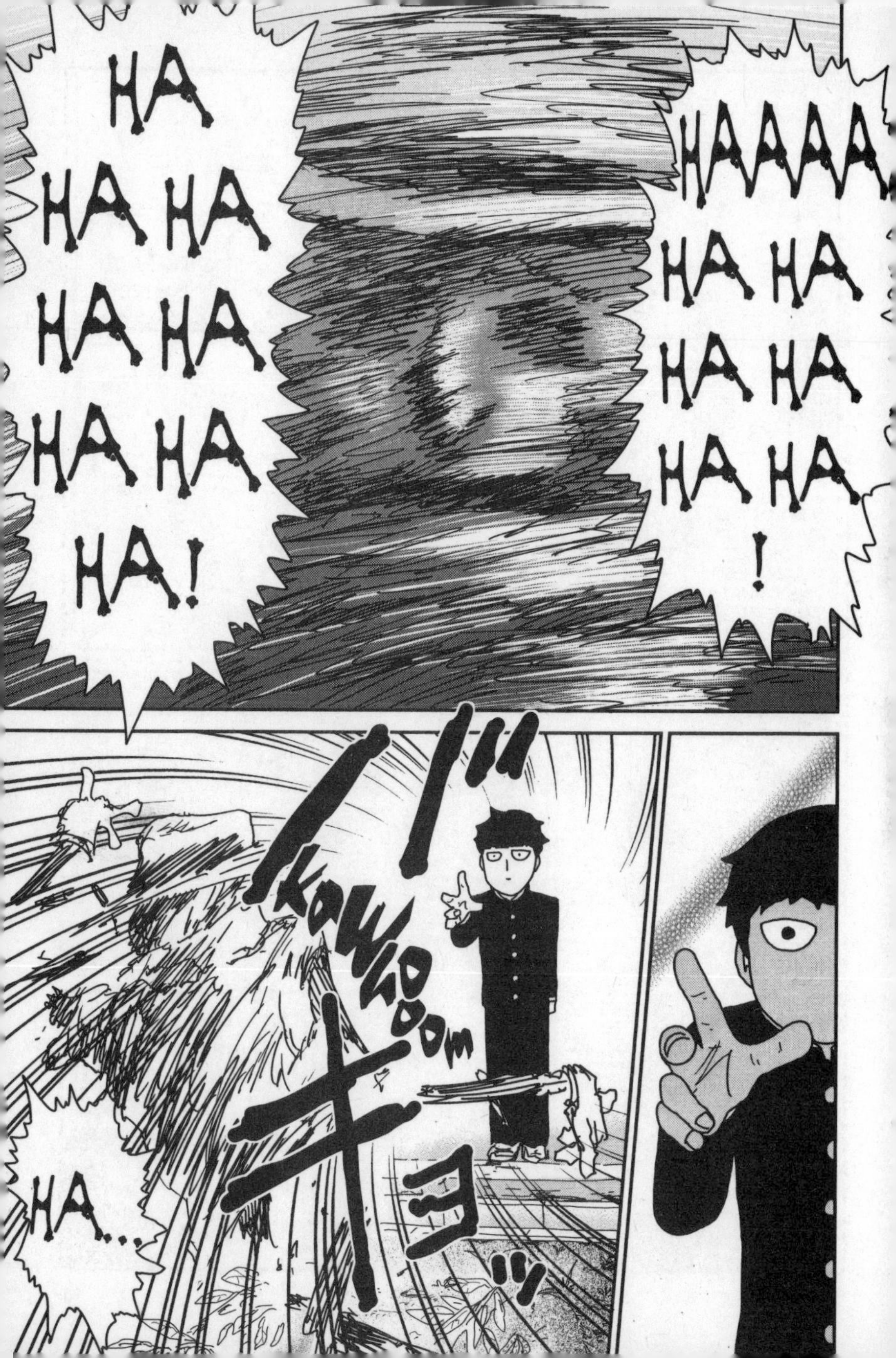
HAAAA HA HA HA HA HA HA !
HA HA HA HA HA HA HA HA HA!
KAWLOOOM
キョッ
HA...

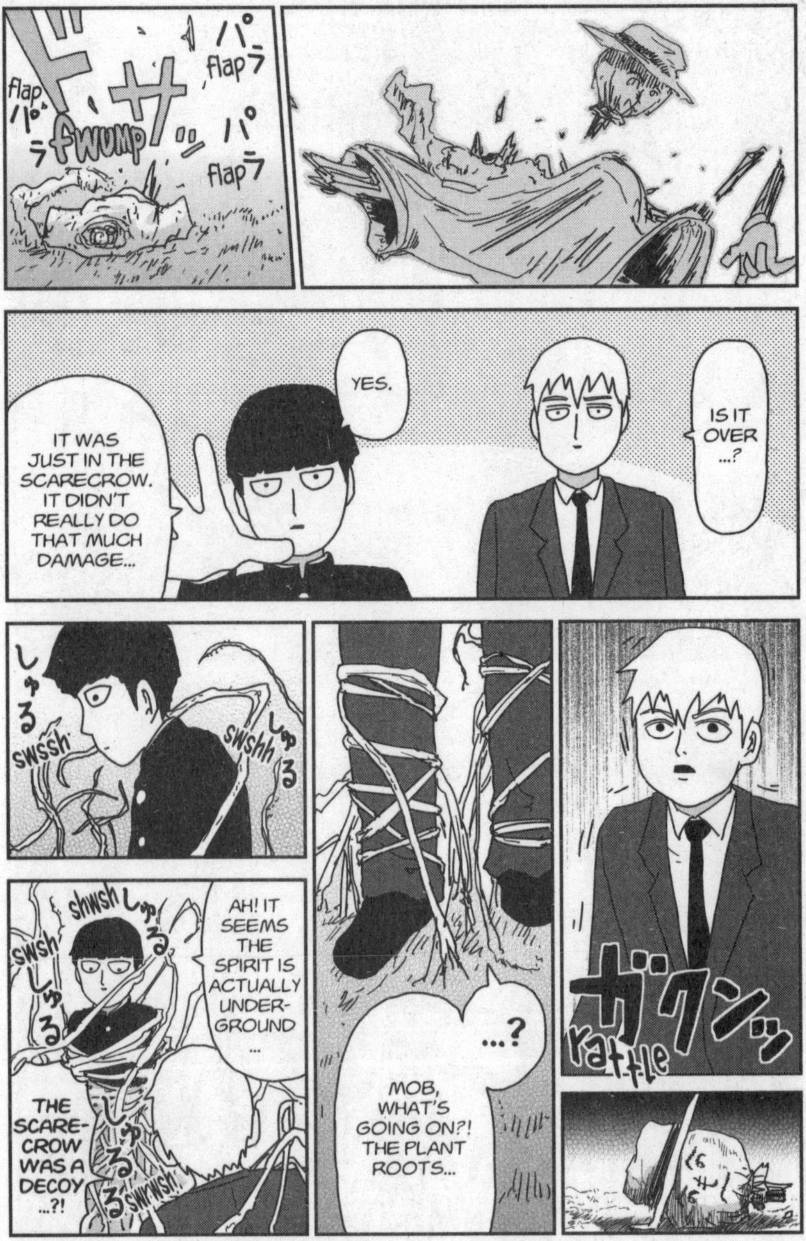
flap
fwump
flap
flap
IS IT OVER ...?
YES.
IT WAS JUST IN THE SCARECROW. IT DIDN'T REALLY DO THAT MUCH DAMAGE...
rattle
...?
MOB, WHAT'S GOING ON?! THE PLANT ROOTS...
swshh
swssh
shwsh
swsh
AH! IT SEEMS THE SPIRIT IS ACTUALLY UNDER-GROUND ...
THE SCARE-CROW WAS A DECOY ...?!
swrwsh

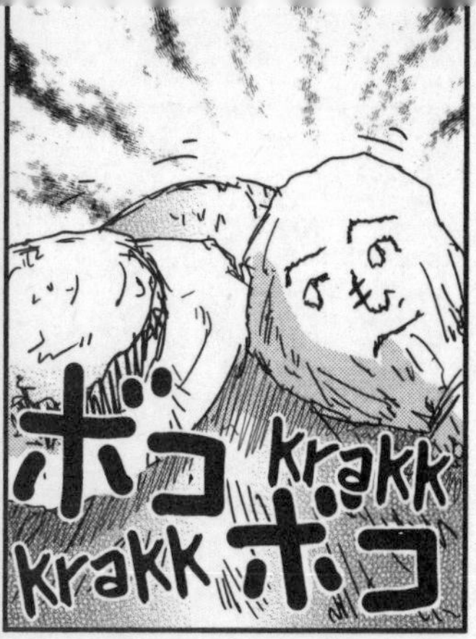
ボコ
krakk
krakk
ボコ

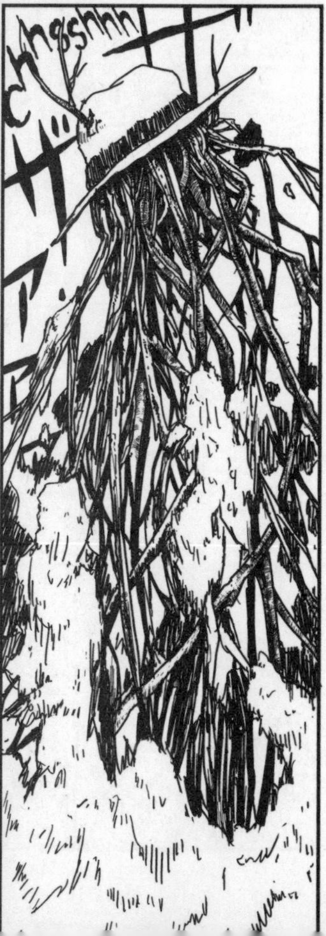
chngshhh
ザァ

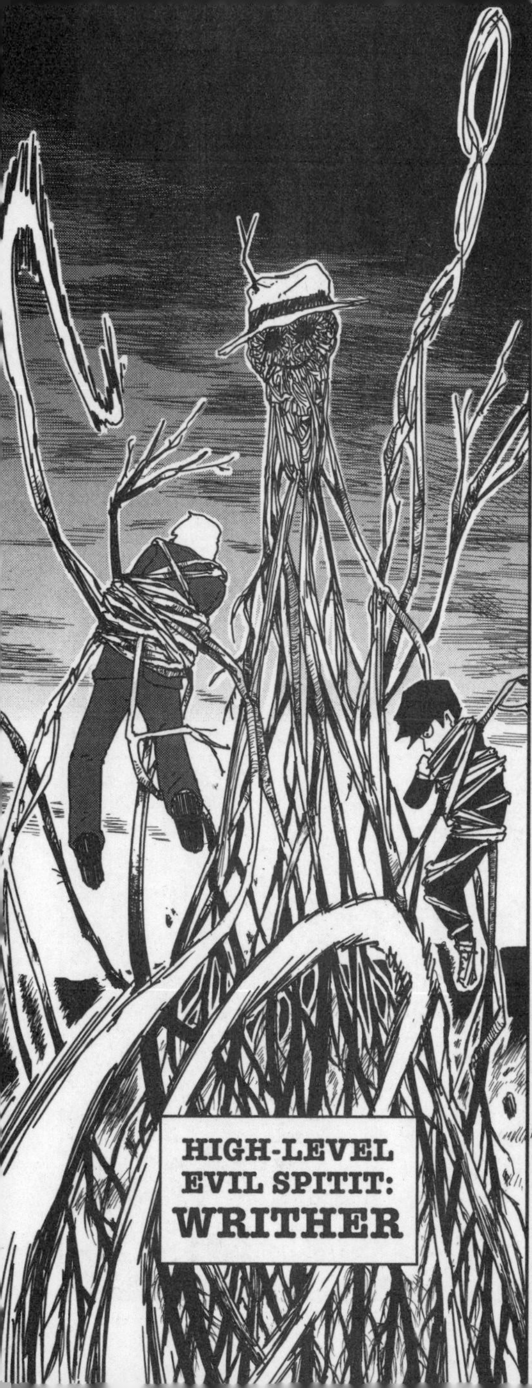
HIGH-LEVEL
EVIL SPITIT:
WRITHER

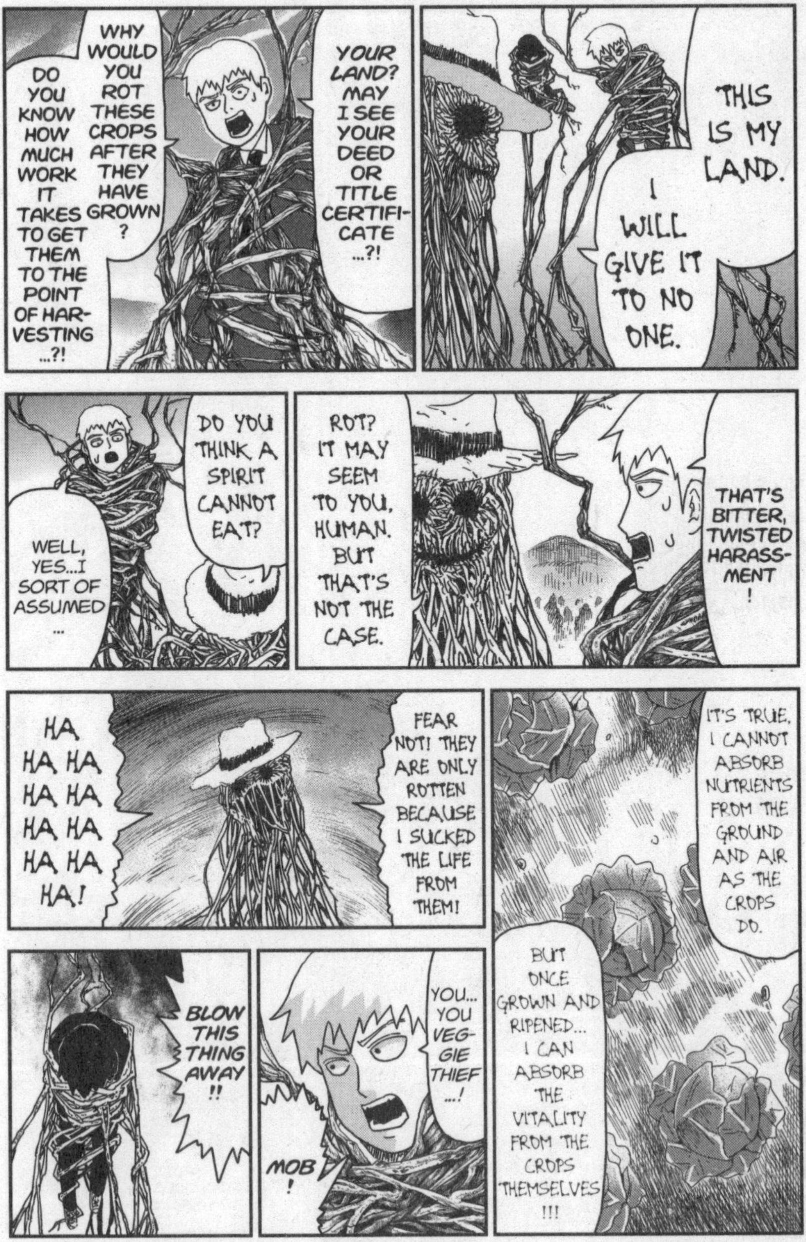
THIS IS MY LAND.
I WILL GIVE IT TO NO ONE.
YOUR LAND? MAY I SEE YOUR DEED OR TITLE CERTIFICATE ...?!
WHY WOULD YOU ROT THESE CROPS AFTER THEY HAVE GROWN?
DO YOU KNOW HOW MUCH WORK IT TAKES TO GET THEM TO THE POINT OF HARVESTING ...?!
THAT'S BITTER, TWISTED HARASSMENT!
ROT? IT MAY SEEM TO YOU, HUMAN. BUT THAT'S NOT THE CASE.
DO YOU THINK A SPIRIT CANNOT EAT?
WELL, YES...I SORT OF ASSUMED...
IT'S TRUE. I CANNOT ABSORB NUTRIENTS FROM THE GROUND AND AIR AS THE CROPS DO.
BUT ONCE GROWN AND RIPENED... I CAN ABSORB THE VITALITY FROM THE CROPS THEMSELVES!!!
FEAR NOT! THEY ARE ONLY ROTTEN BECAUSE I SUCKED THE LIFE FROM THEM!
HA HA HA HA HA HA HA HA HA HA HA!
YOU... YOU VEGGIE THIEF...!
MOB!
BLOW THIS THING AWAY!!

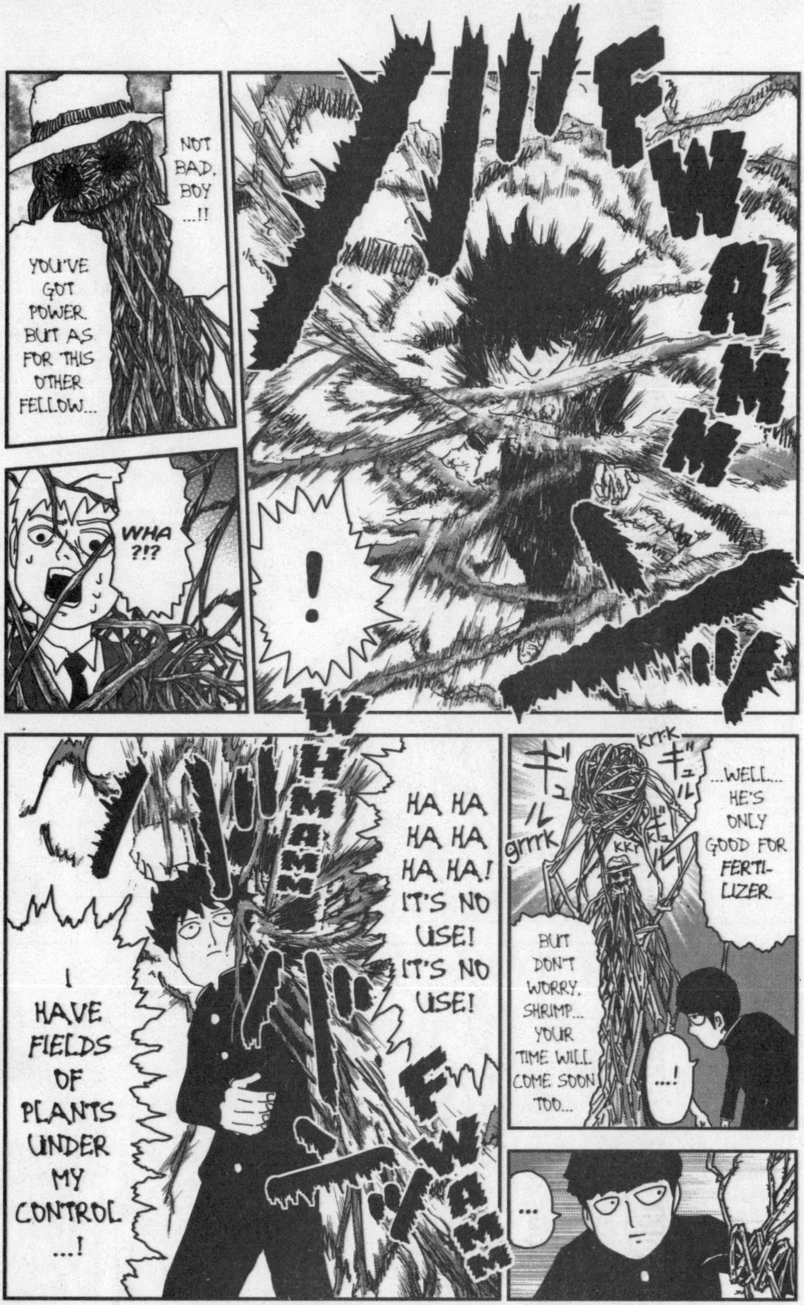
FWAMMM
!
NOT BAD, BOY ...!!
YOU'VE GOT POWER. BUT AS FOR THIS OTHER FELLOW...
WHA ?!?
ギュル
krrk
ギュル
grrrk
ギュル
KKI
...WELL... HE'S ONLY GOOD FOR FERTILIZER.
BUT DON'T WORRY, SHRIMP... YOUR TIME WILL COME SOON TOO...
...!
...
WHMAMM
HA HA HA HA HA HA! IT'S NO USE! IT'S NO USE!
I HAVE FIELDS OF PLANTS UNDER MY CONTROL ...!
FWAM

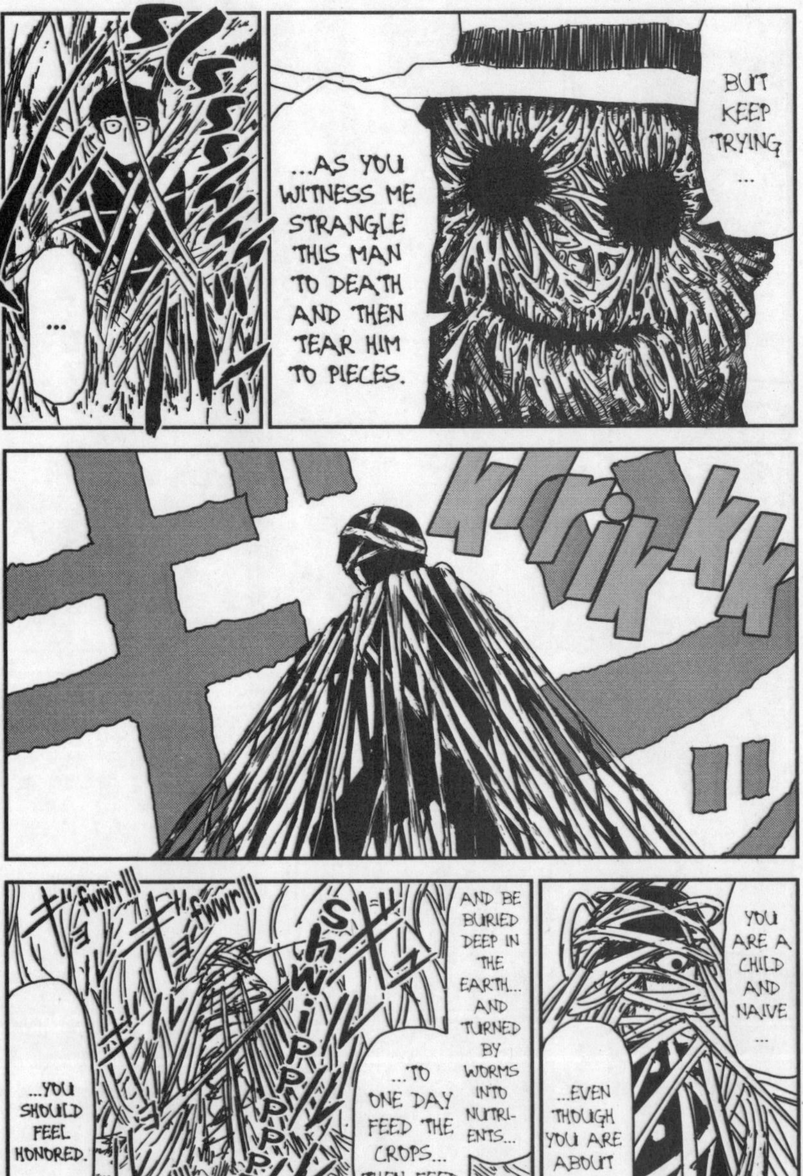
BUT KEEP TRYING ...
...AS YOU WITNESS ME STRANGLE THIS MAN TO DEATH AND THEN TEAR HIM TO PIECES.
...
krikkk
YOU ARE A CHILD AND NAIVE ...
...EVEN THOUGH YOU ARE ABOUT TO DIE...
AND BE BURIED DEEP IN THE EARTH... AND TURNED BY WORMS INTO NUTRI-ENTS...
...TO ONE DAY FEED THE CROPS... THEN FEED ME...
shwiPPPPP
fwwr
fwwr
fwwr
...YOU SHOULD FEEL HONORED.

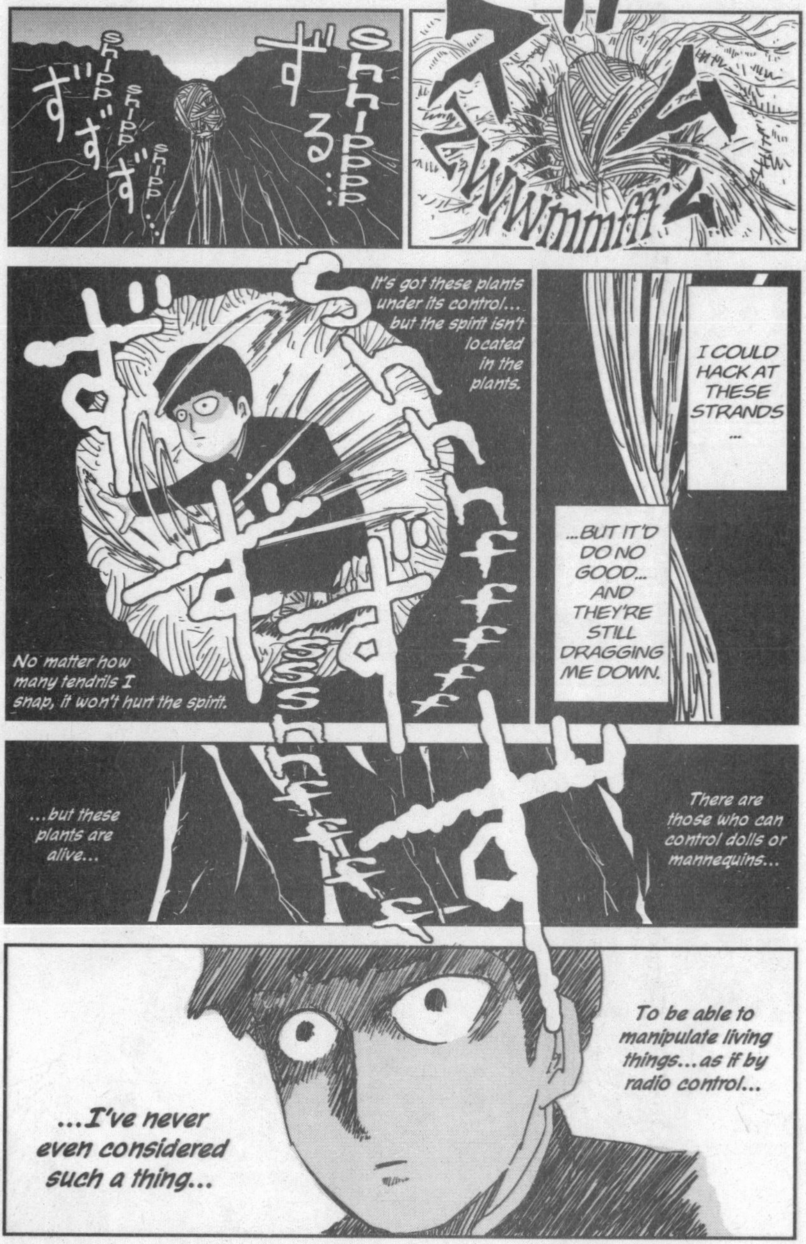
WWmmfff
shhipppp…
shipp shipp shipp…
I COULD HACK AT THESE STRANDS…
…BUT IT'D DO NO GOOD… AND THEY'RE STILL DRAGGING ME DOWN.
It's got these plants under its control… but the spirit isn't located in the plants.
No matter how many tendrils I snap, it won't hurt the spirit.
There are those who can control dolls or mannequins…
…but these plants are alive…
To be able to manipulate living things…as if by radio control…
…I've never even considered such a thing…

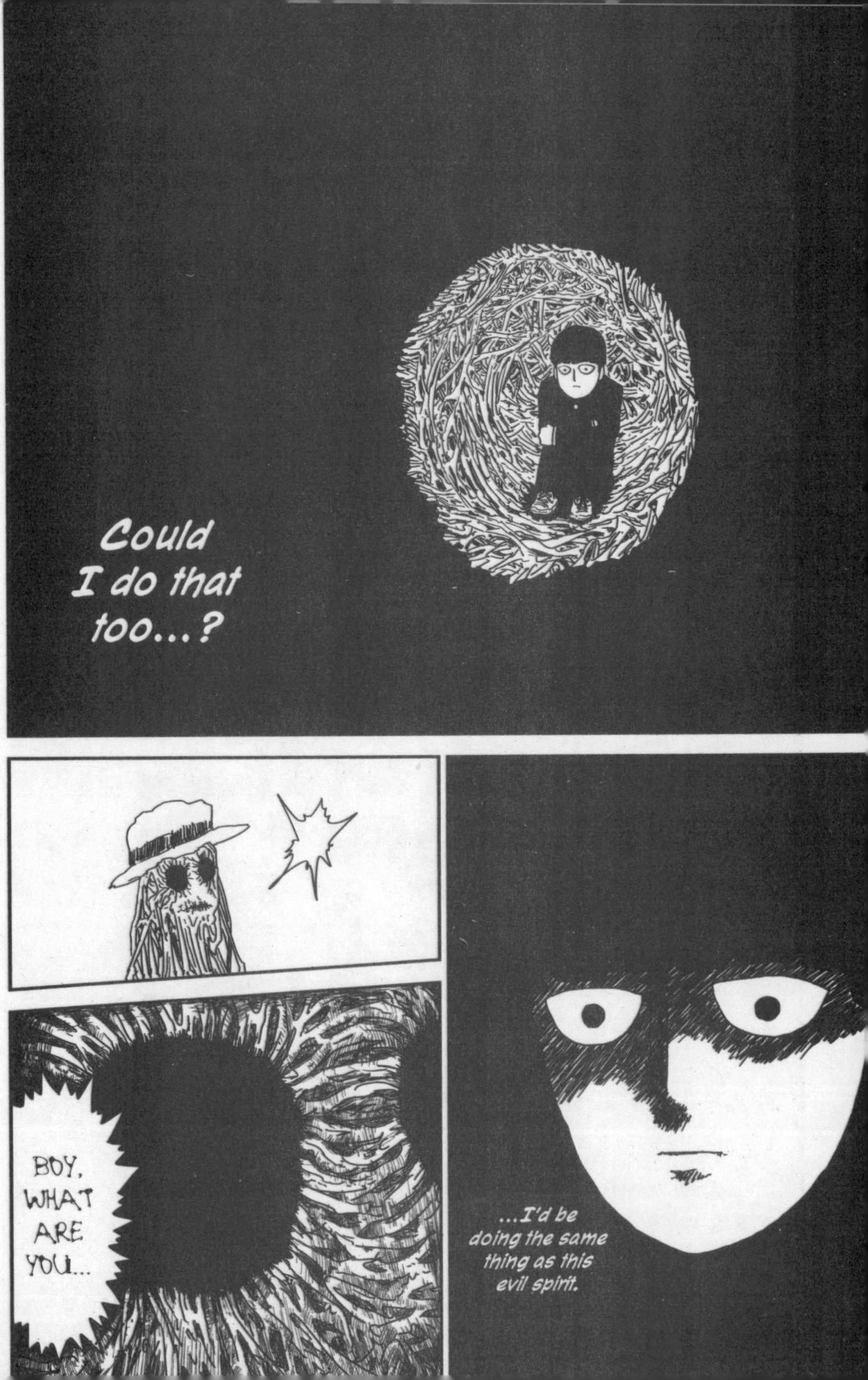
Could I do that too...?
...I'd be doing the same thing as this evil spirit.
BOY, WHAT ARE YOU...

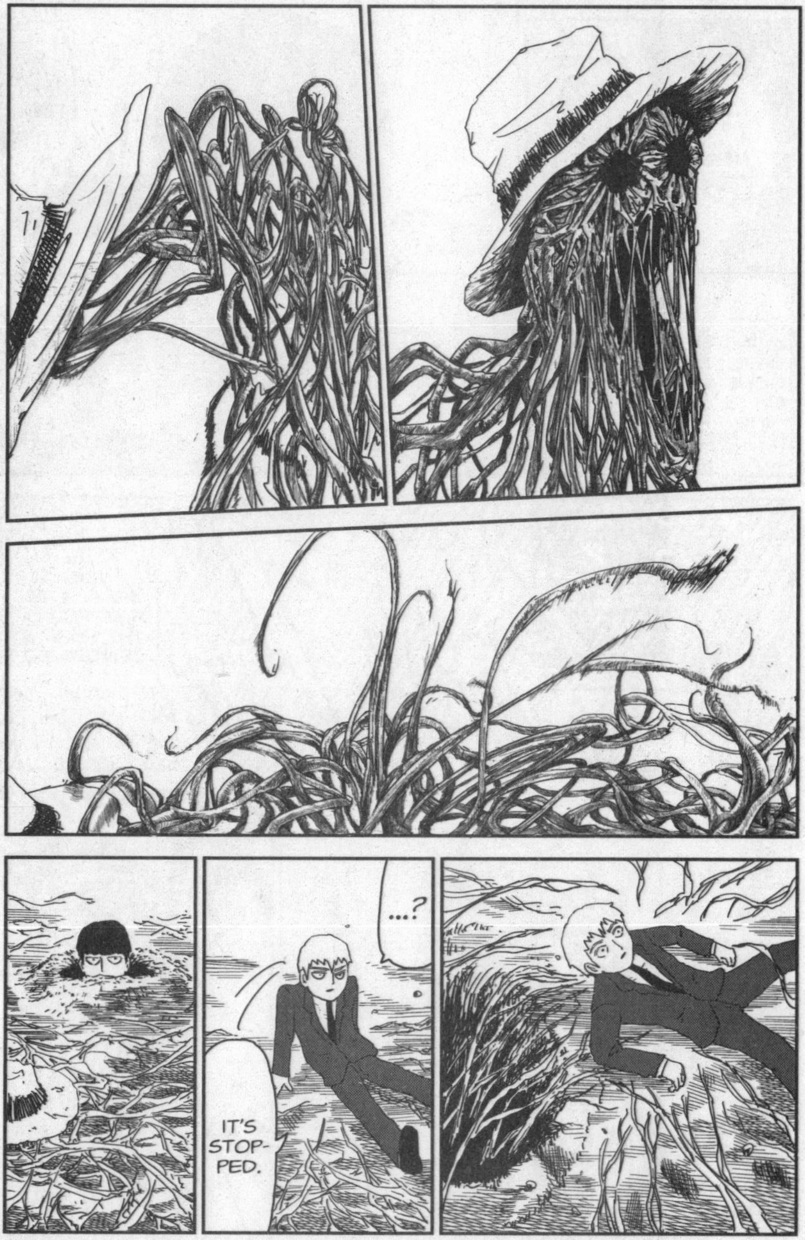
...?
IT'S STOP-PED.

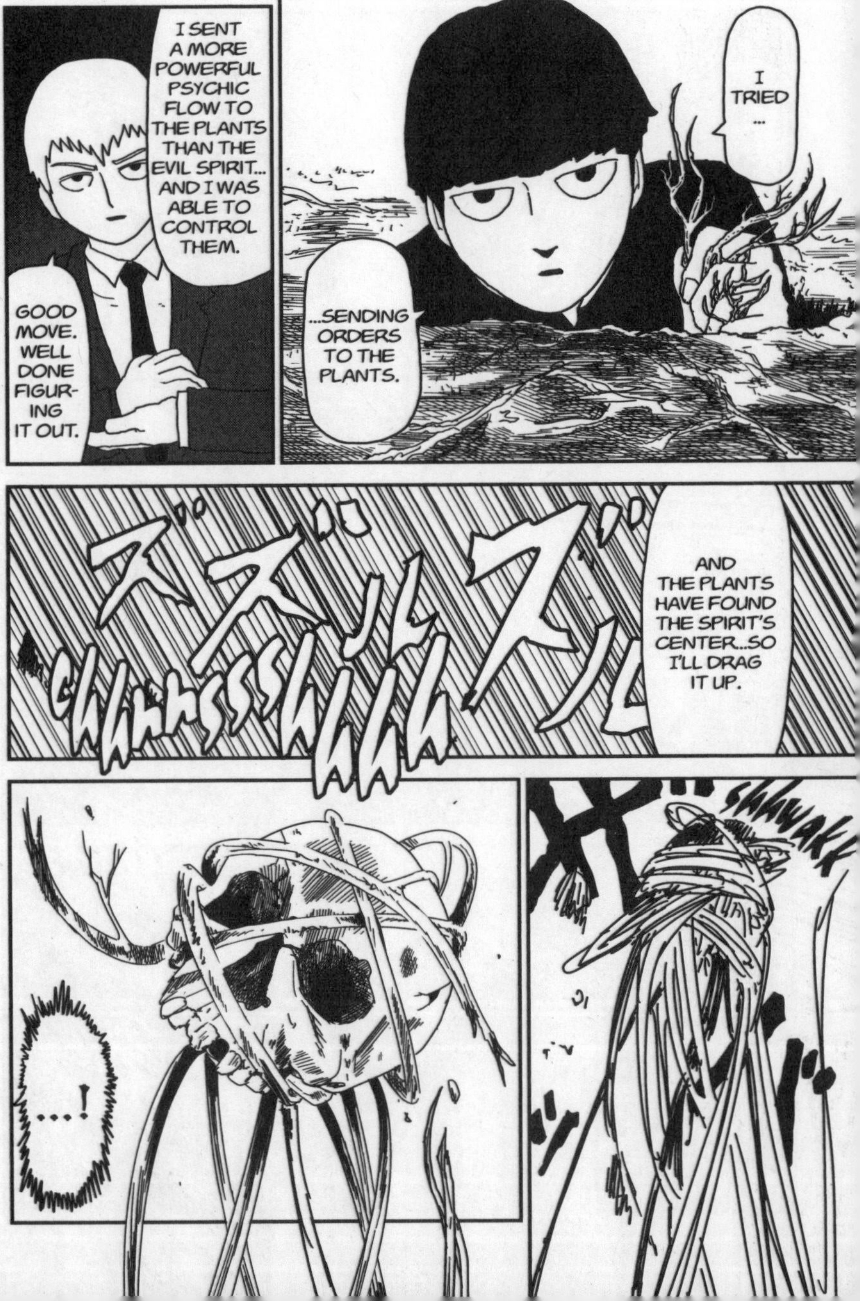
I TRIED ...
...SENDING ORDERS TO THE PLANTS.
I SENT A MORE POWERFUL PSYCHIC FLOW TO THE PLANTS THAN THE EVIL SPIRIT... AND I WAS ABLE TO CONTROL THEM.
GOOD MOVE. WELL DONE FIGUR-ING IT OUT.
AND THE PLANTS HAVE FOUND THE SPIRIT'S CENTER...SO I'LL DRAG IT UP.
SHWAKK
...!

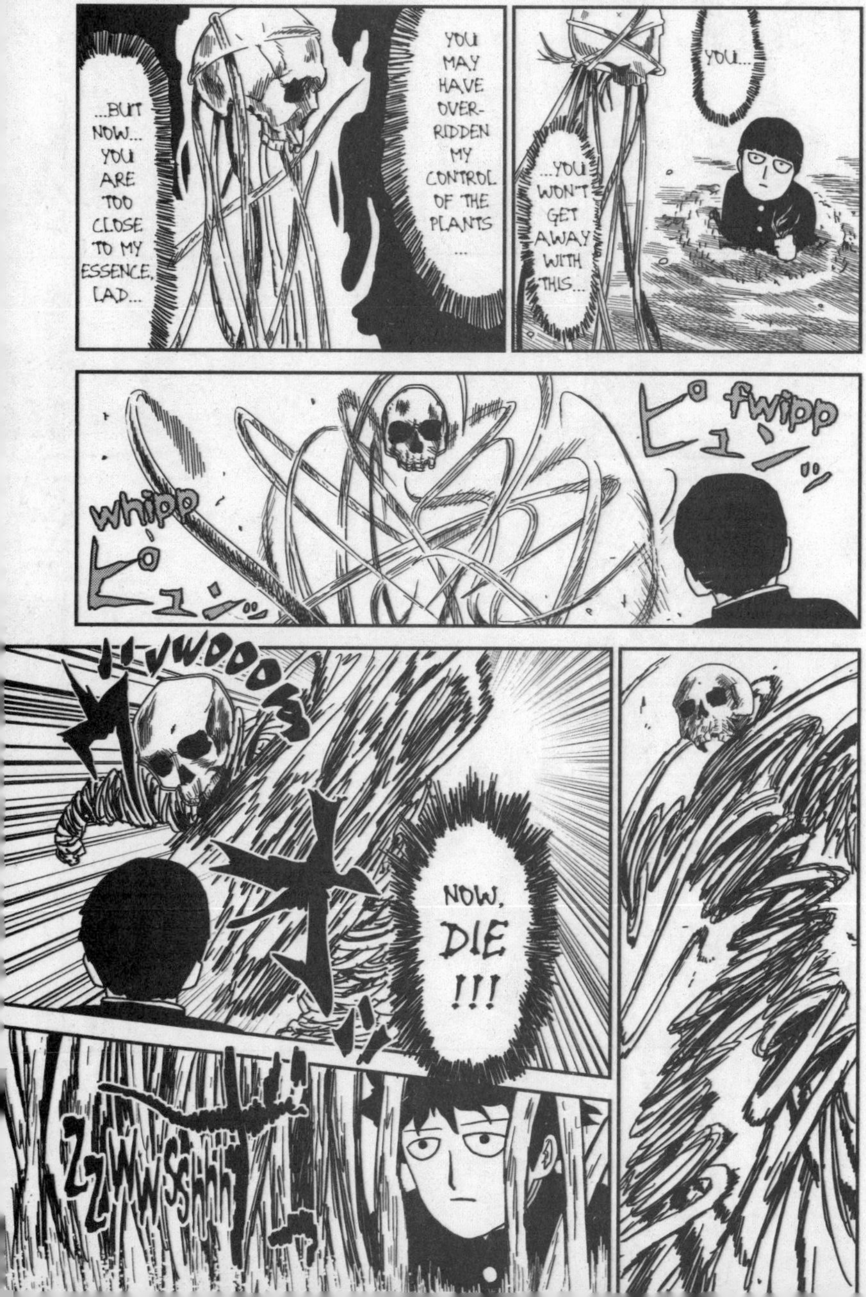
YOU...
...YOU WON'T GET AWAY WITH THIS...
YOU MAY HAVE OVER-RIDDEN MY CONTROL OF THE PLANTS...
...BUT NOW... YOU ARE TOO CLOSE TO MY ESSENCE, LAD...
fwipp
whipp
VWOOOS
NOW, DIE!!!
ZZWWSHHH

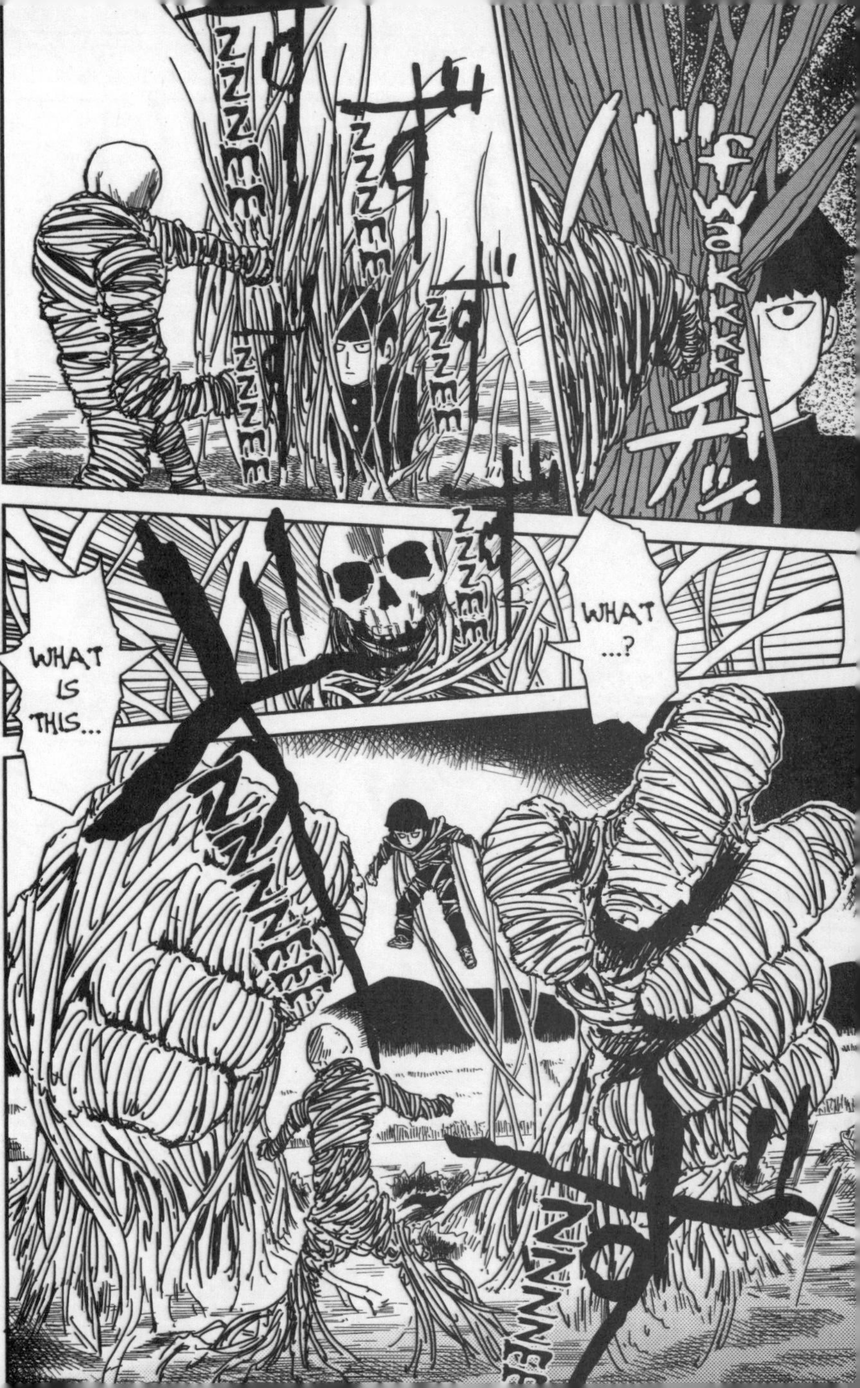
fwakkkk
ZZZmm
ZZZmm
ZZZmm
ZZZmm
ZZZmm
WHAT ...?
WHAT IS THIS...
NNNNEEE
NNNNEEE

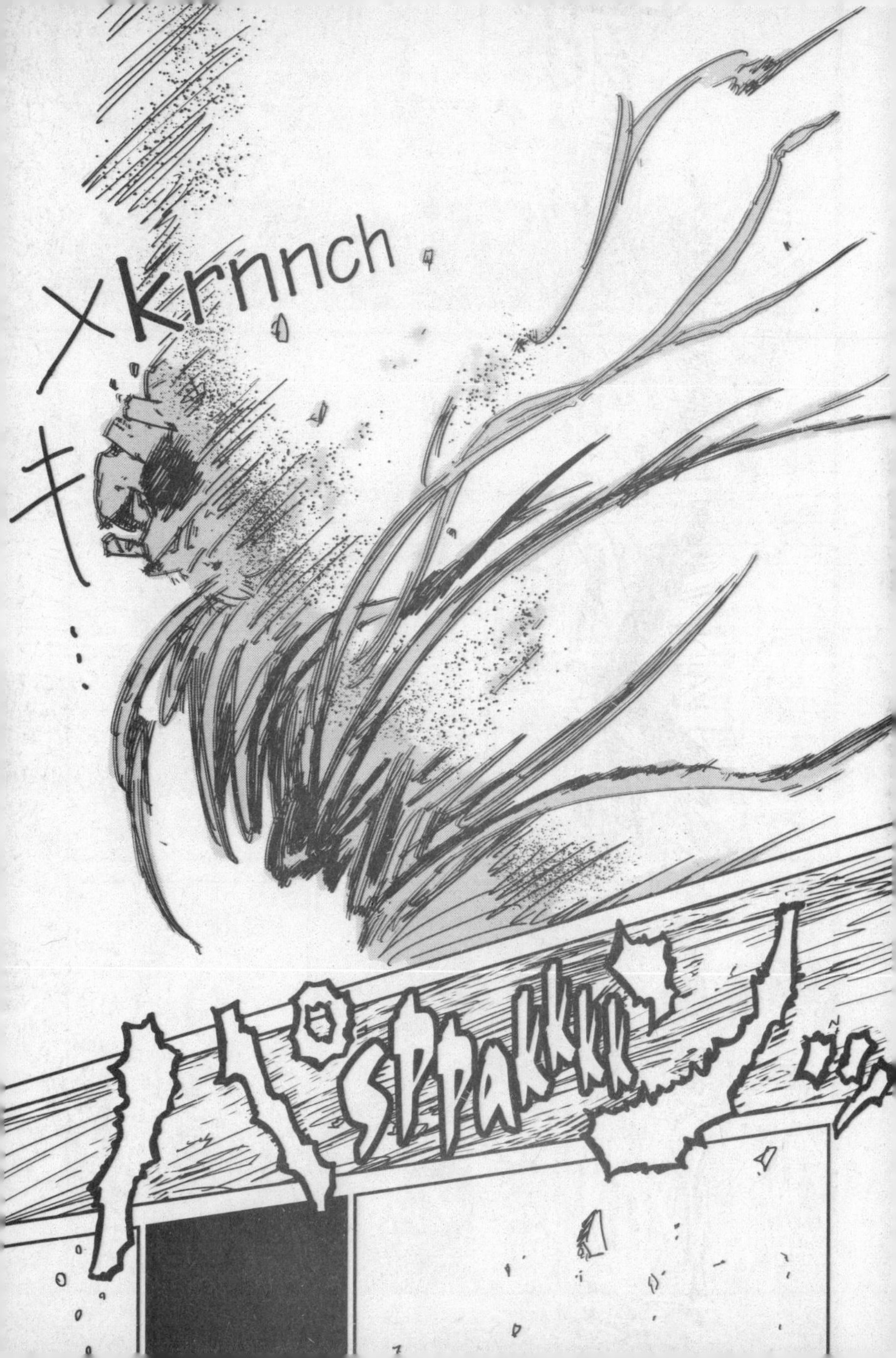
Krnnch
SPPAKKKK

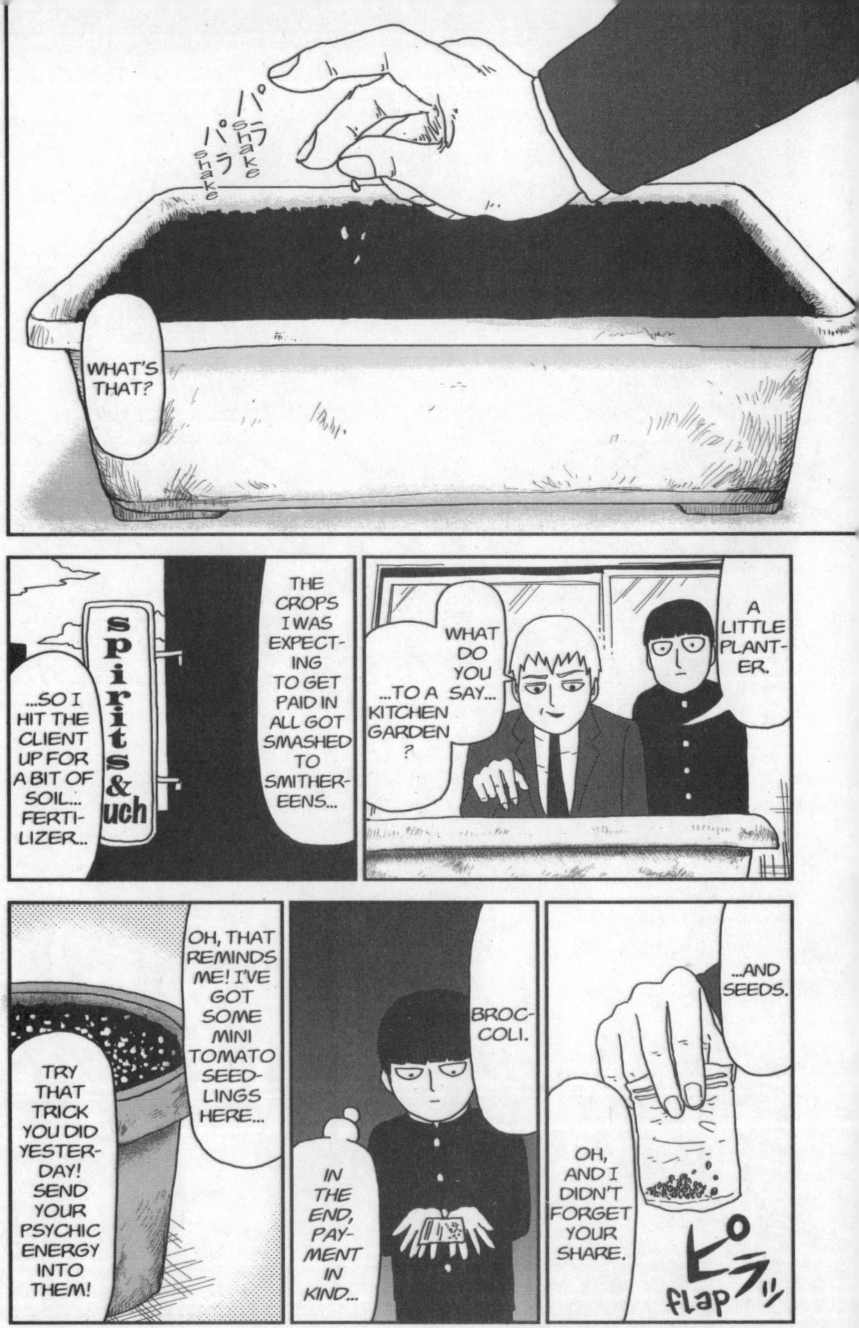
パラ shake
パラ shake
WHAT'S THAT?
A LITTLE PLANTER.
WHAT DO YOU SAY... ...TO A KITCHEN GARDEN?
THE CROPS I WAS EXPECTING TO GET PAID IN ALL GOT SMASHED TO SMITHEREENS...
...SO I HIT THE CLIENT UP FOR A BIT OF SOIL... FERTILIZER...
spirits &
uch
...AND SEEDS.
OH, AND I DIDN'T FORGET YOUR SHARE.
ピラッ flap
BROCCOLI.
IN THE END, PAYMENT IN KIND...
OH, THAT REMINDS ME! I'VE GOT SOME MINI TOMATO SEEDLINGS HERE...
TRY THAT TRICK YOU DID YESTERDAY! SEND YOUR PSYCHIC ENERGY INTO THEM!

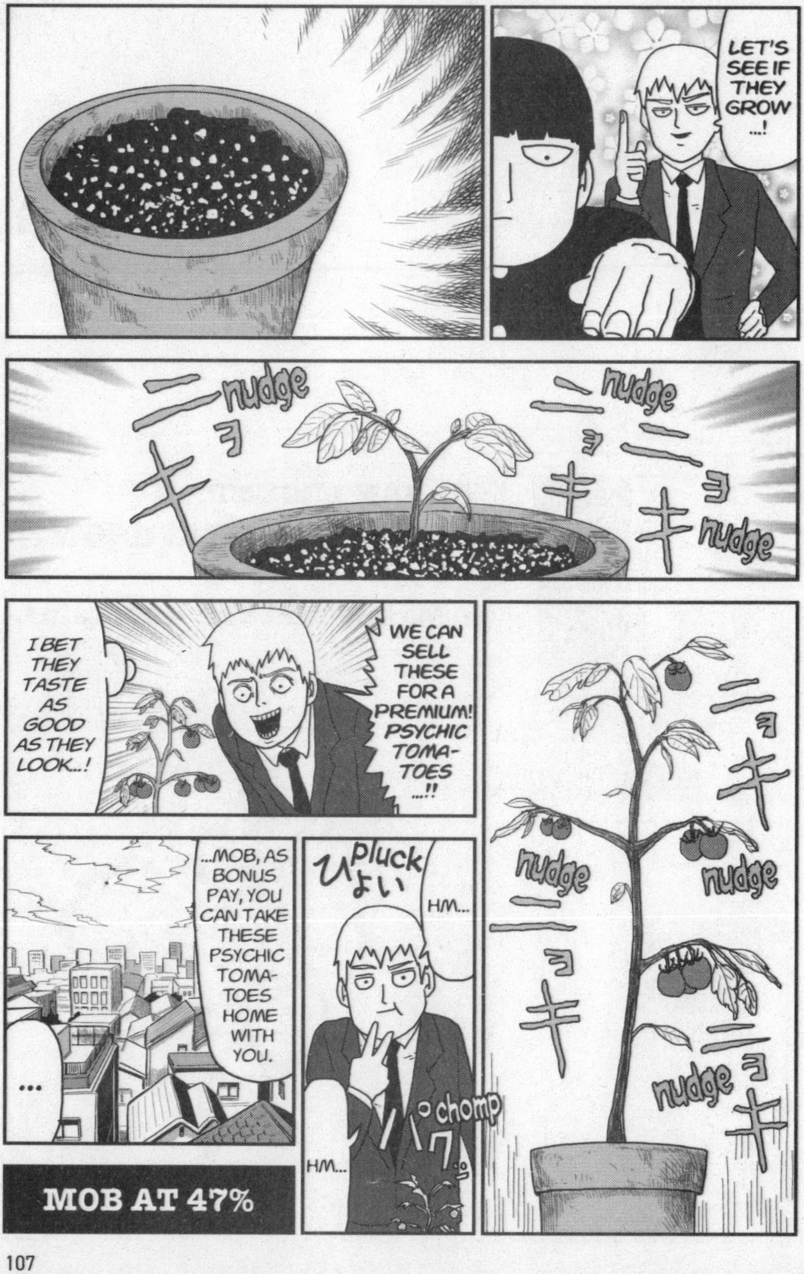
LET'S SEE IF THEY GROW ...!
ニョキ nudge
ニョキ nudge
ニョキ nudge
ニョキ
nudge
nudge
ニョキ
nudge ニョキ
WE CAN SELL THESE FOR A PREMIUM! PSYCHIC TOMATOES ...!!
I BET THEY TASTE AS GOOD AS THEY LOOK...!
ひょい pluck
HM...
ハグッ chomp
HM...
...MOB, AS BONUS PAY, YOU CAN TAKE THESE PSYCHIC TOMATOES HOME WITH YOU.
...
MOB AT 47%

URBAN LEGEND:
THE SPRINTING CRONE
- Fast.
- Mainly takes on mountains.

CHAPTER 58: MOUNTING DANGERS

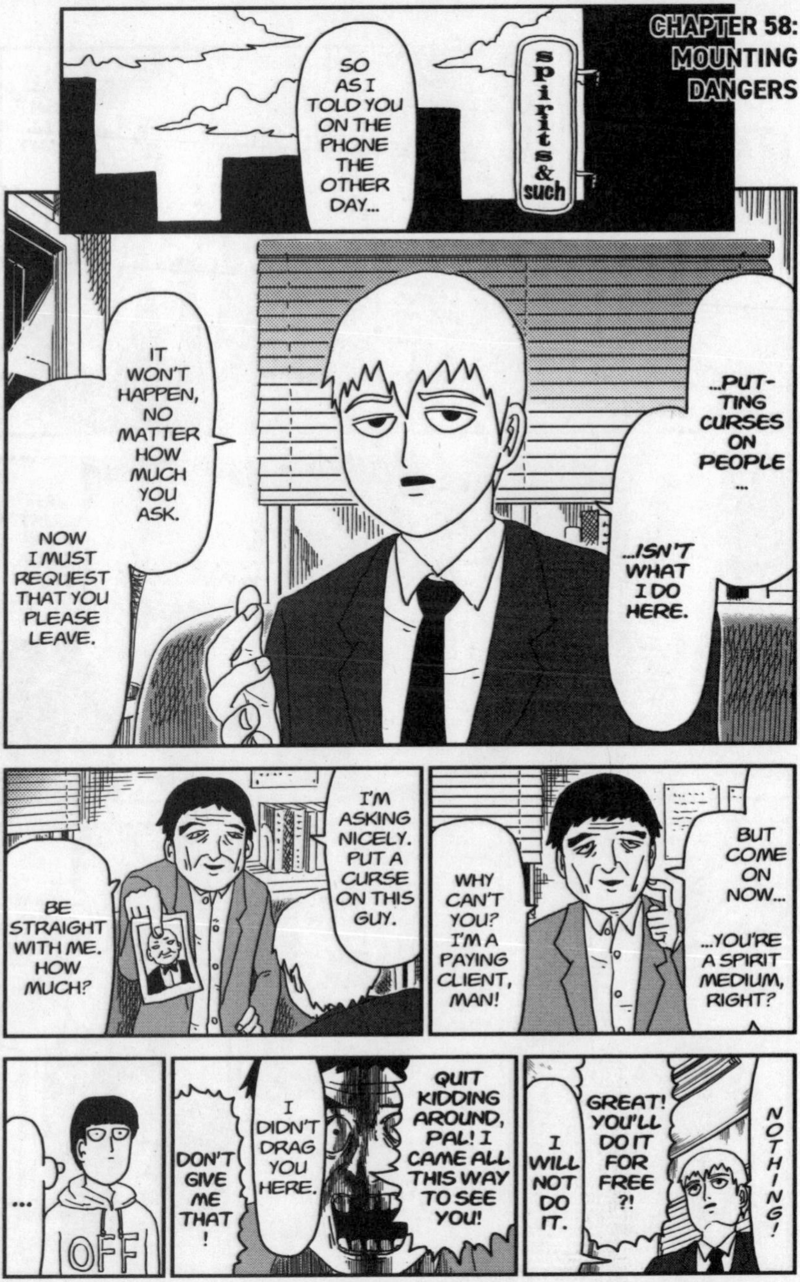
spirits & such
SO AS I TOLD YOU ON THE PHONE THE OTHER DAY...
...PUTTING CURSES ON PEOPLE...
...ISN'T WHAT I DO HERE.
IT WON'T HAPPEN, NO MATTER HOW MUCH YOU ASK.
NOW I MUST REQUEST THAT YOU PLEASE LEAVE.
BUT COME ON NOW...
...YOU'RE A SPIRIT MEDIUM, RIGHT?
WHY CAN'T YOU? I'M A PAYING CLIENT, MAN!
I'M ASKING NICELY. PUT A CURSE ON THIS GUY.
BE STRAIGHT WITH ME. HOW MUCH?
NOTHING!
GREAT! YOU'LL DO IT FOR FREE?!
I WILL NOT DO IT.
QUIT KIDDING AROUND, PAL! I CAME ALL THIS WAY TO SEE YOU!
I DIDN'T DRAG YOU HERE.
DON'T GIVE ME THAT!
...
OFF

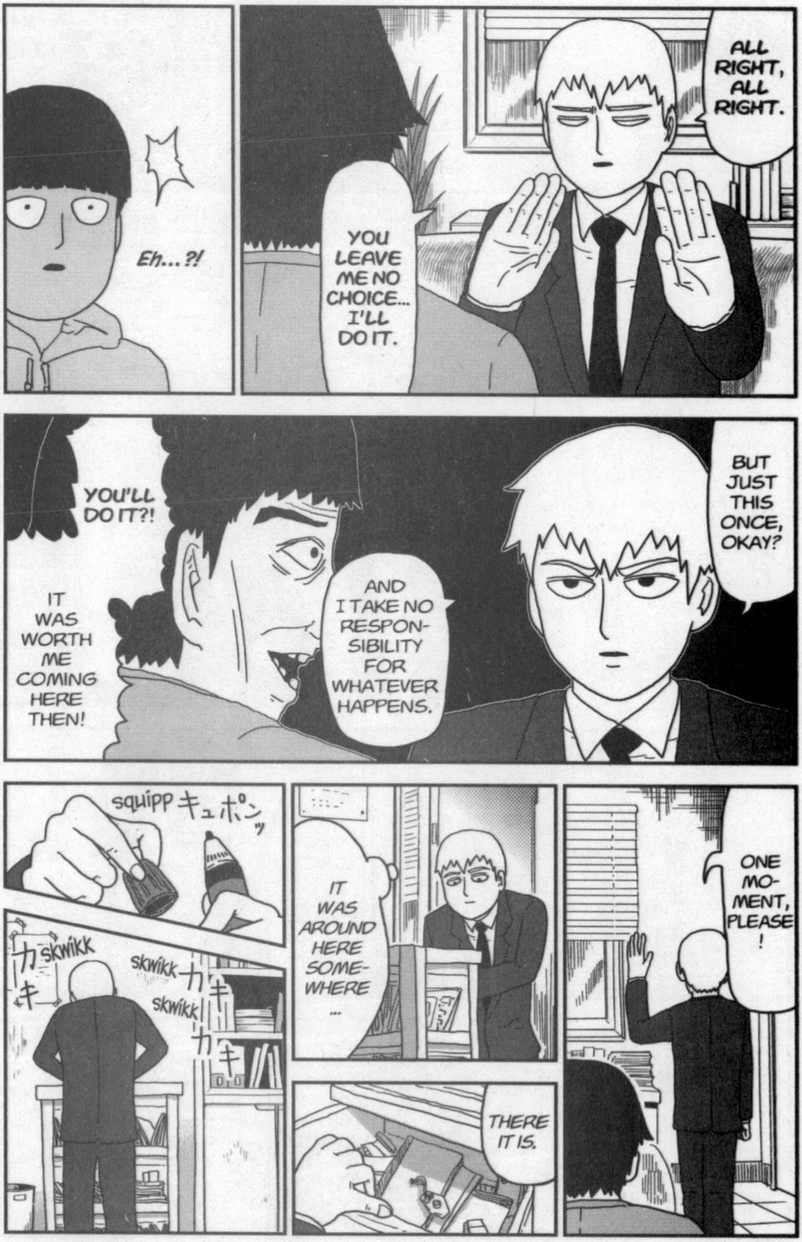
ALL RIGHT, ALL RIGHT.
YOU LEAVE ME NO CHOICE... I'LL DO IT.
Eh...?!
BUT JUST THIS ONCE, OKAY?
AND I TAKE NO RESPON-SIBILITY FOR WHATEVER HAPPENS.
YOU'LL DO IT?!
IT WAS WORTH ME COMING HERE THEN!
ONE MO-MENT, PLEASE!
IT WAS AROUND HERE SOME-WHERE...
THERE IT IS.
squipp キュポンッ
skwikk カキ
skwikk カキ
skwikk カキ

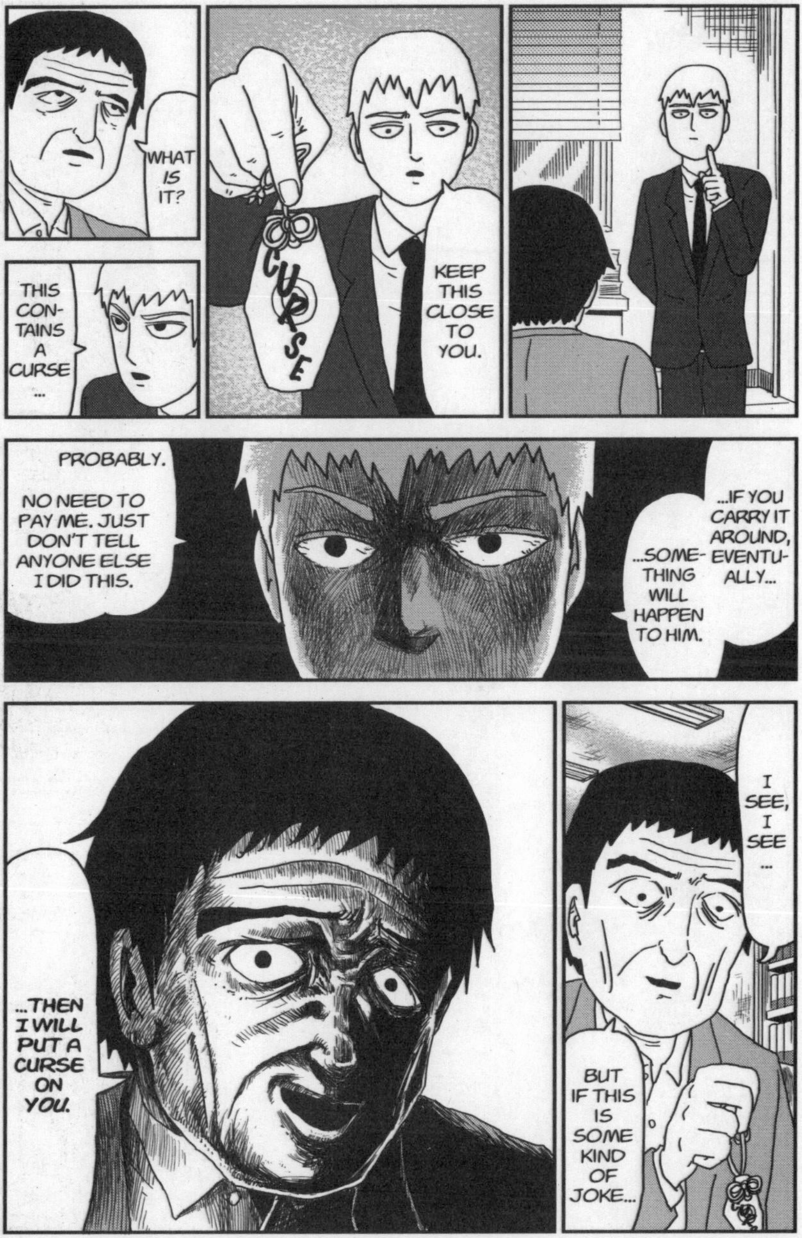
KEEP THIS CLOSE TO YOU.
CURSE
WHAT IS IT?
THIS CONTAINS A CURSE ...
...IF YOU CARRY IT AROUND, EVENTUALLY...
...SOMETHING WILL HAPPEN TO HIM.
PROBABLY.
NO NEED TO PAY ME. JUST DON'T TELL ANYONE ELSE I DID THIS.
I SEE, I SEE ...
BUT IF THIS IS SOME KIND OF JOKE...
...THEN I WILL PUT A CURSE ON *YOU*.

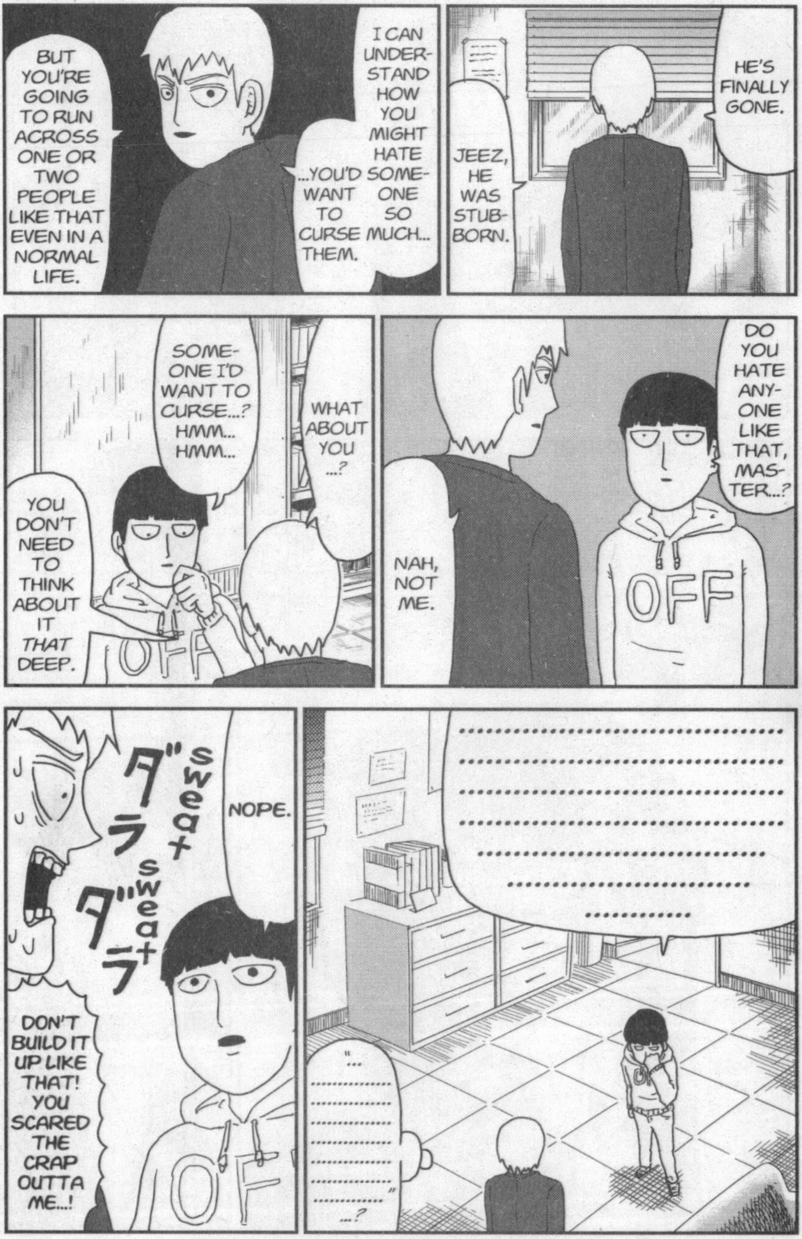
HE'S FINALLY GONE.
JEEZ, HE WAS STUBBORN.
I CAN UNDERSTAND HOW YOU MIGHT HATE SOMEONE SO MUCH...
...YOU'D WANT TO CURSE THEM.
BUT YOU'RE GOING TO RUN ACROSS ONE OR TWO PEOPLE LIKE THAT EVEN IN A NORMAL LIFE.
DO YOU HATE ANYONE LIKE THAT, MASTER...?
NAH, NOT ME.
WHAT ABOUT YOU ...?
SOMEONE I'D WANT TO CURSE...? HMM... HMM...
YOU DON'T NEED TO THINK ABOUT IT *THAT* DEEP.
....
".." ...?
NOPE.
ダラ sweat
ダラ sweat
DON'T BUILD IT UP LIKE THAT! YOU SCARED THE CRAP OUTTA ME...!

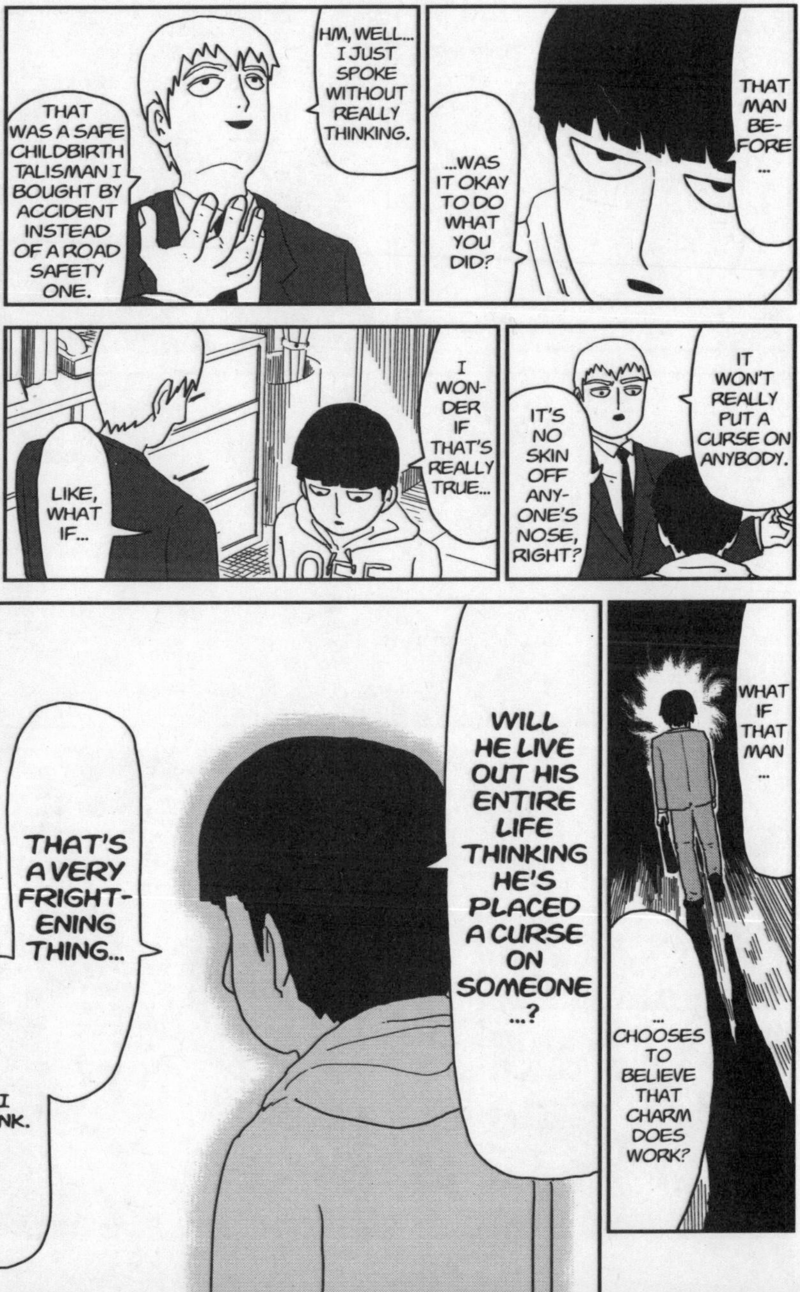
THAT MAN BEFORE...
...WAS IT OKAY TO DO WHAT YOU DID?
HM, WELL... I JUST SPOKE WITHOUT REALLY THINKING.
THAT WAS A SAFE CHILDBIRTH TALISMAN I BOUGHT BY ACCIDENT INSTEAD OF A ROAD SAFETY ONE.
IT WON'T REALLY PUT A CURSE ON ANYBODY.
IT'S NO SKIN OFF ANYONE'S NOSE, RIGHT?
I WONDER IF THAT'S REALLY TRUE...
LIKE, WHAT IF...
WHAT IF THAT MAN...
...CHOOSES TO BELIEVE THAT CHARM DOES WORK?
WILL HE LIVE OUT HIS ENTIRE LIFE THINKING HE'S PLACED A CURSE ON SOMEONE...?
THAT'S A VERY FRIGHTENING THING...
...I THINK.

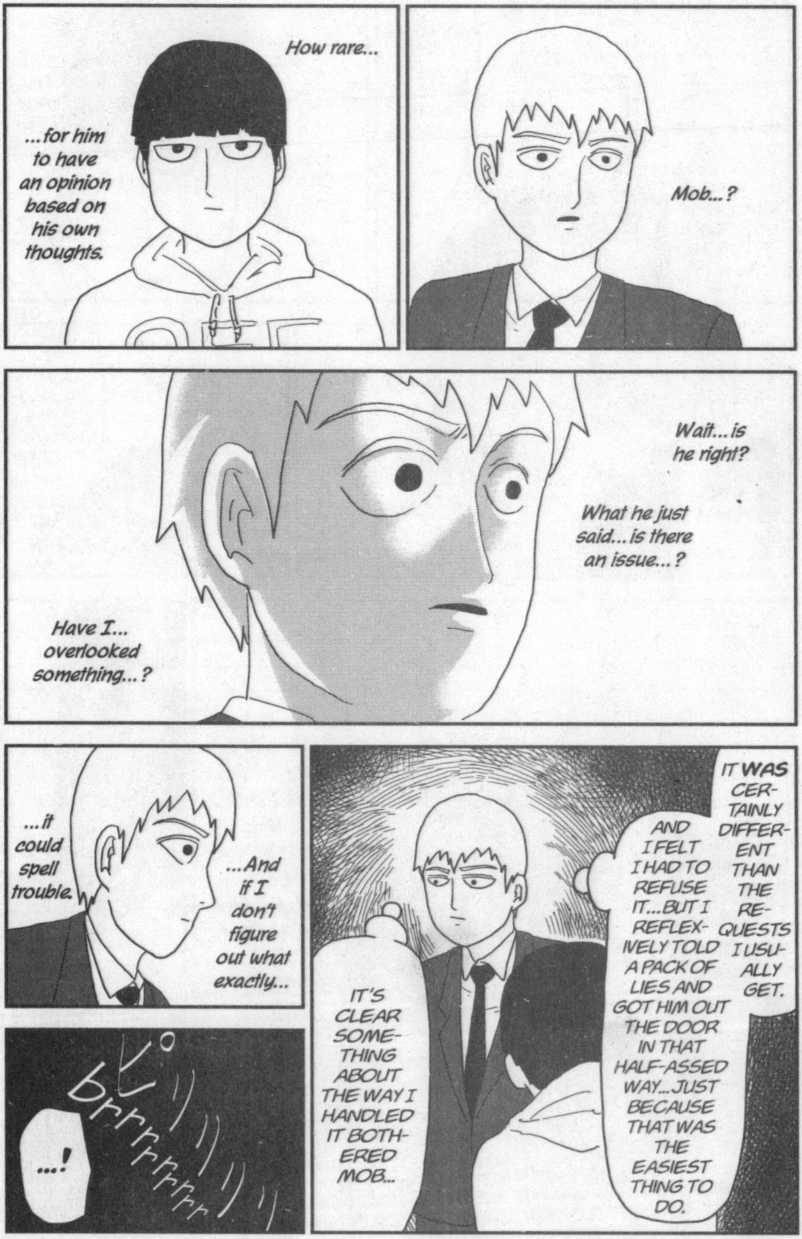
How rare...
...for him to have an opinion based on his own thoughts.
Mob...?
Wait... is he right?
What he just said... is there an issue...?
Have I... overlooked something...?
...And if I don't figure out what exactly...
...it could spell trouble.
IT'S CLEAR SOMETHING ABOUT THE WAY I HANDLED IT BOTHERED MOB...
IT WAS CERTAINLY DIFFERENT THAN THE REQUESTS I USUALLY GET.
AND I FELT I HAD TO REFUSE IT...BUT I REFLEXIVELY TOLD A PACK OF LIES AND GOT HIM OUT THE DOOR IN THAT HALF-ASSED WAY...JUST BECAUSE THAT WAS THE EASIEST THING TO DO.
brrrrrrrr
...!

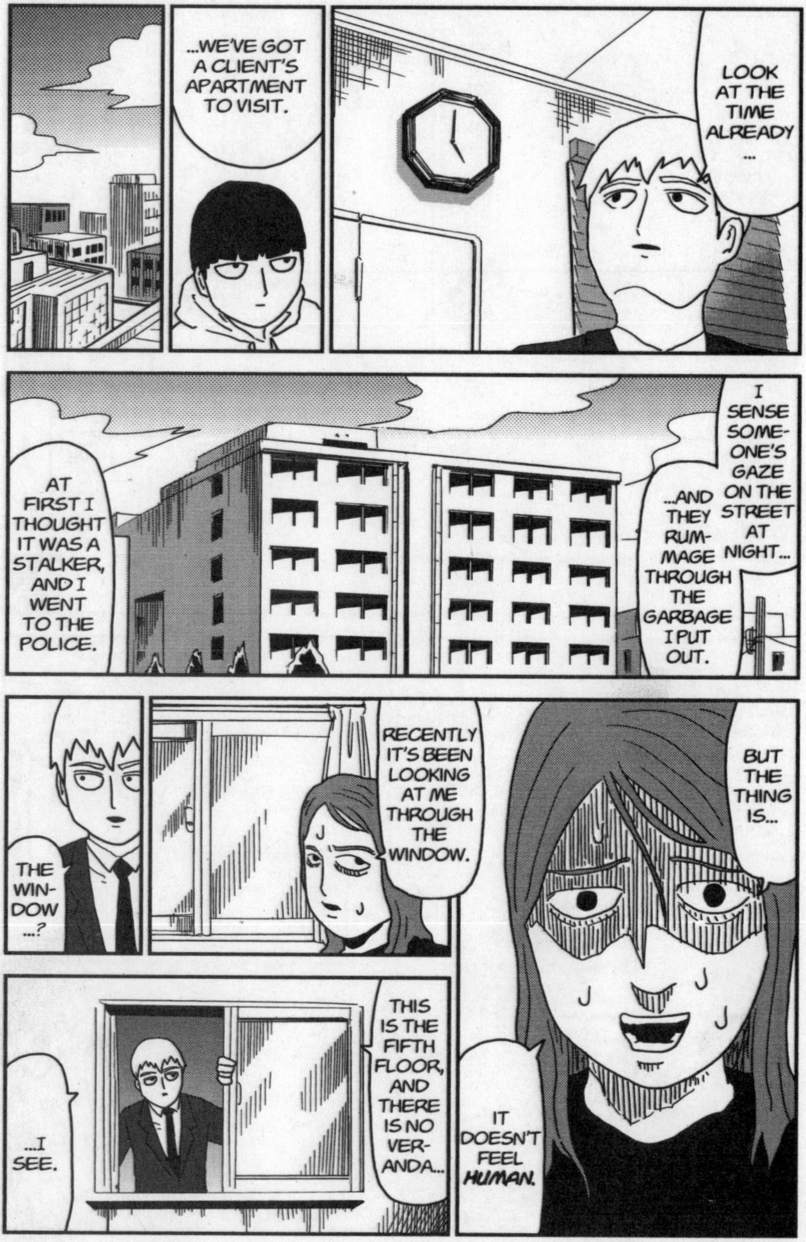
LOOK AT THE TIME ALREADY ...
...WE'VE GOT A CLIENT'S APARTMENT TO VISIT.
I SENSE SOME-ONE'S GAZE ON THE STREET AT NIGHT...
...AND THEY RUM-MAGE THROUGH THE GARBAGE I PUT OUT.
AT FIRST I THOUGHT IT WAS A STALKER, AND I WENT TO THE POLICE.
RECENTLY IT'S BEEN LOOKING AT ME THROUGH THE WINDOW.
THE WIN-DOW ...?
BUT THE THING IS...
THIS IS THE FIFTH FLOOR, AND THERE IS NO VER-ANDA...
...I SEE.
IT DOESN'T FEEL *HUMAN.*

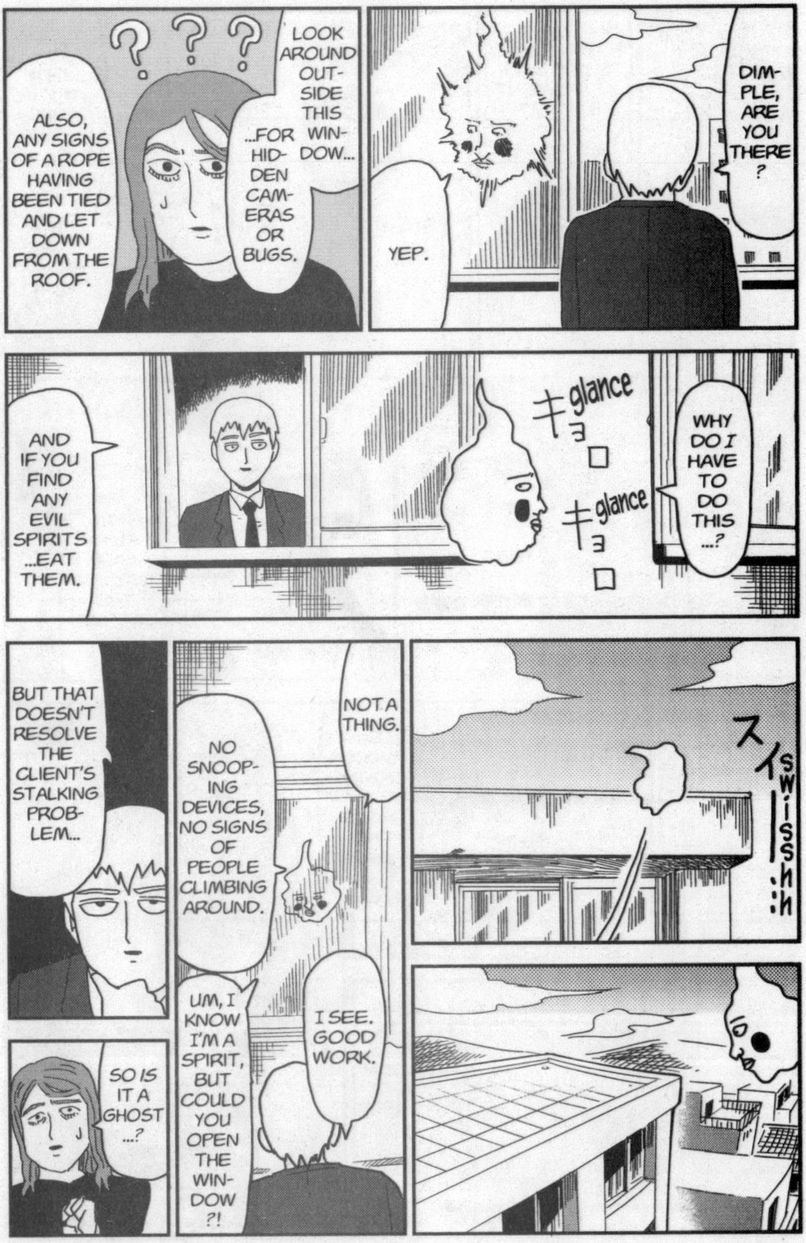
DIMPLE, ARE YOU THERE?
YEP.
LOOK AROUND OUTSIDE THIS WINDOW...
...FOR HIDDEN CAMERAS OR BUGS.
ALSO, ANY SIGNS OF A ROPE HAVING BEEN TIED AND LET DOWN FROM THE ROOF.
WHY DO I HAVE TO DO THIS...?
キョロ glance
キョロ glance
AND IF YOU FIND ANY EVIL SPIRITS ...EAT THEM.
スイ SWISSHH...
NOT A THING.
NO SNOOPING DEVICES, NO SIGNS OF PEOPLE CLIMBING AROUND.
I SEE. GOOD WORK.
UM, I KNOW I'M A SPIRIT, BUT COULD YOU OPEN THE WINDOW?!
BUT THAT DOESN'T RESOLVE THE CLIENT'S STALKING PROBLEM...
SO IS IT A GHOST...?

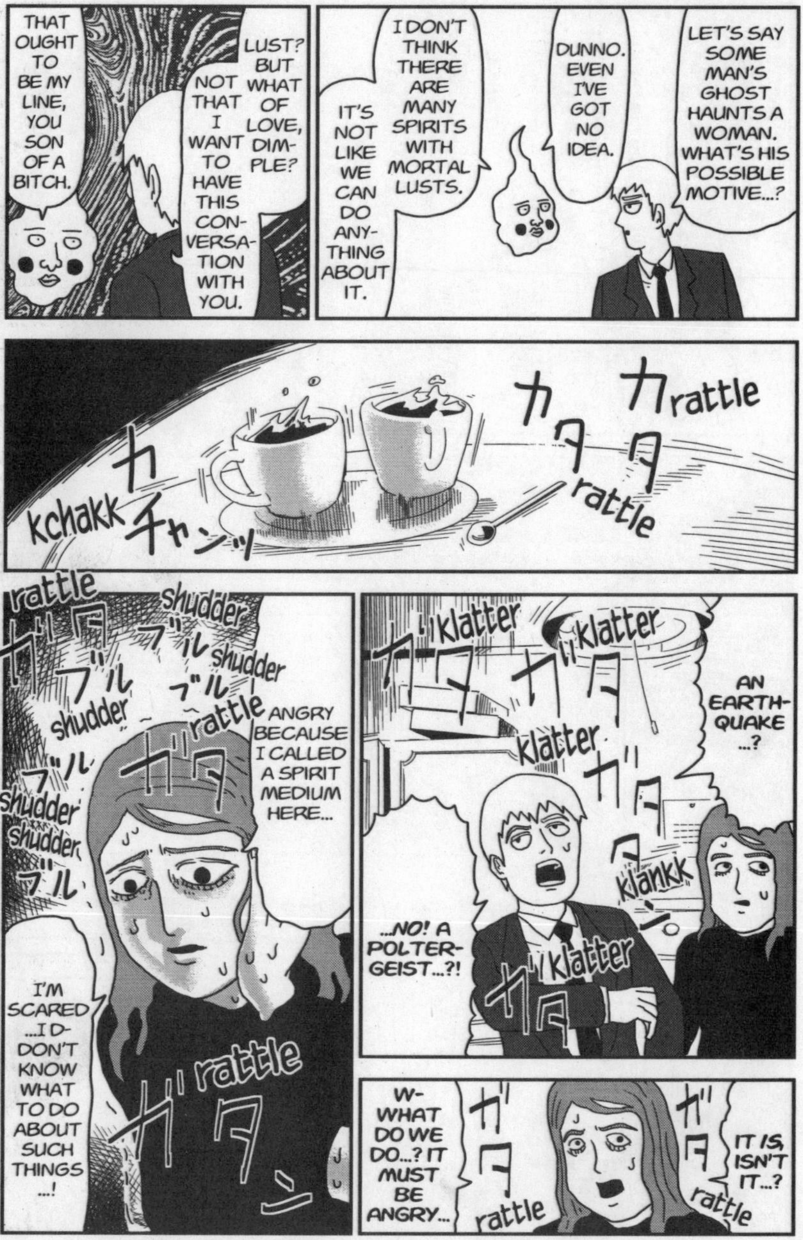
LET'S SAY SOME MAN'S GHOST HAUNTS A WOMAN. WHAT'S HIS POSSIBLE MOTIVE...?
DUNNO. EVEN I'VE GOT NO IDEA.
I DON'T THINK THERE ARE MANY SPIRITS WITH MORTAL LUSTS.
IT'S NOT LIKE WE CAN DO ANY-THING ABOUT IT.
LUST? BUT WHAT OF LOVE, DIM-PLE?
NOT THAT I WANT TO HAVE THIS CON-VERSA-TION WITH YOU.
THAT OUGHT TO BE MY LINE, YOU SON OF A BITCH.
カタ rattle
カタ rattle
カチャンッ kchakk
カタ klatter
カタ klatter
AN EARTH-QUAKE ...?
ガタ klatter
klankk
...NO! A POLTER-GEIST...?!
ガタ klatter
ガタ rattle
ブル shudder
ブル shudder
ブル shudder
ガタ rattle
ブル shudder
shudder
ブル
ANGRY BECAUSE I CALLED A SPIRIT MEDIUM HERE...
I'M SCARED ...I D-DON'T KNOW WHAT TO DO ABOUT SUCH THINGS ...!
ガタン rattle
IT IS, ISN'T IT...?
ガタ rattle
W-WHAT DO WE DO...? IT MUST BE ANGRY...
ガタ rattle

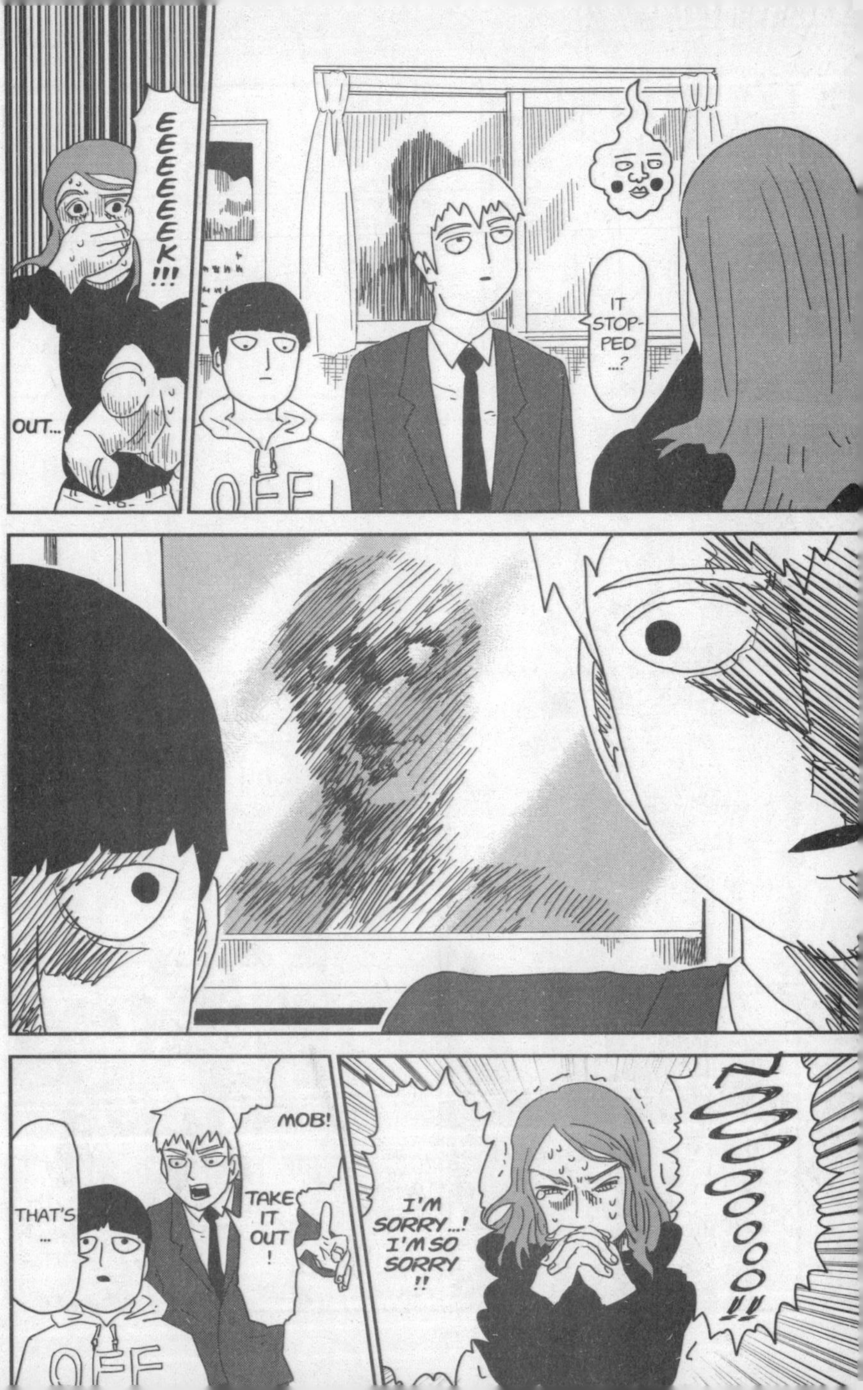
IT STOPPED...?
EEEEEEEK!!!
OUT...
NOOOOOOOOO!!!
I'M SORRY...! I'M SO SORRY!!
MOB!
TAKE IT OUT!
THAT'S...

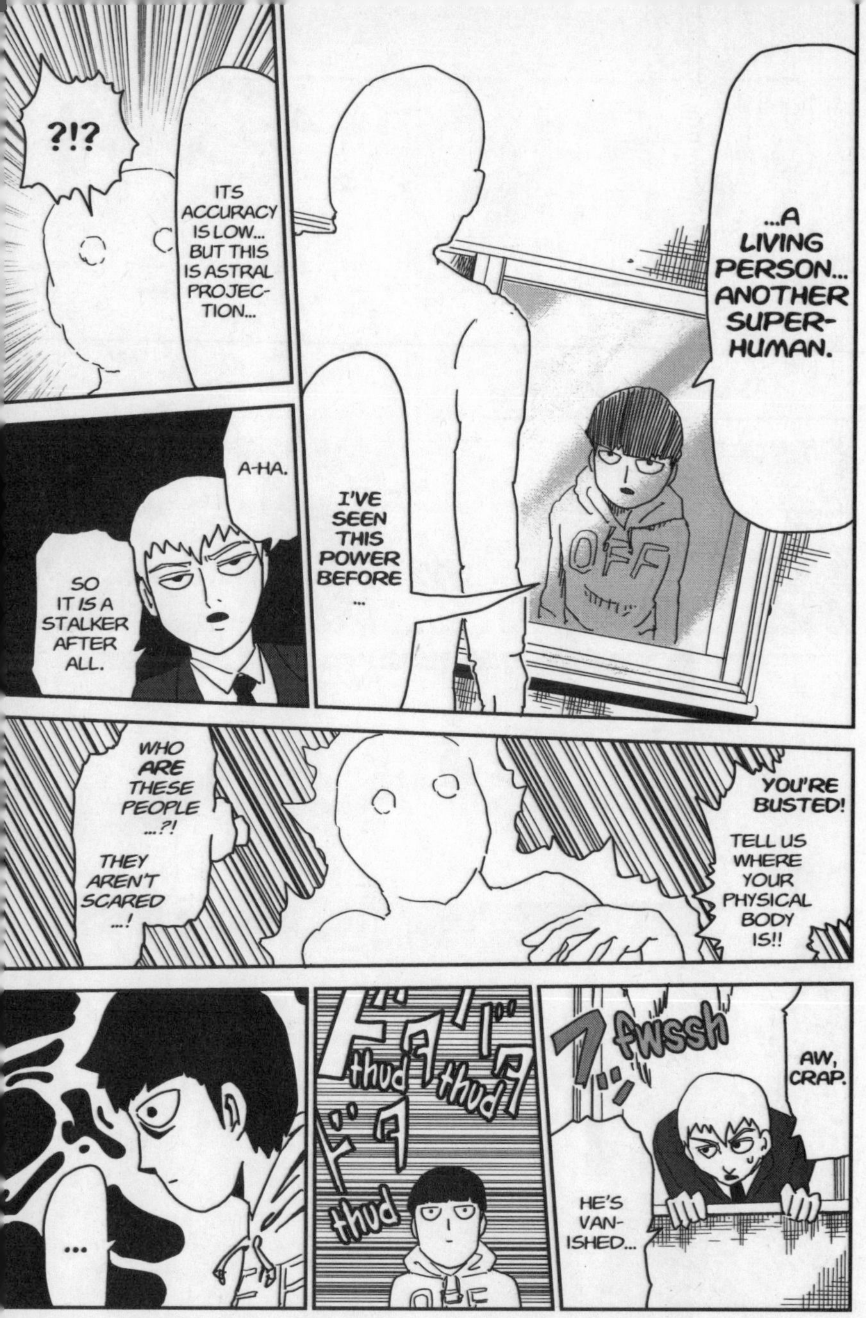
...A LIVING PERSON... ANOTHER SUPER-HUMAN.
I'VE SEEN THIS POWER BEFORE ...
?!?
ITS ACCURACY IS LOW... BUT THIS IS ASTRAL PROJEC-TION...
A-HA.
SO IT IS A STALKER AFTER ALL.
YOU'RE BUSTED!
TELL US WHERE YOUR PHYSICAL BODY IS!!
WHO ARE THESE PEOPLE ...?!
THEY AREN'T SCARED ...!
fwssh
AW, CRAP.
HE'S VAN-ISHED...
thud thud
thud
...

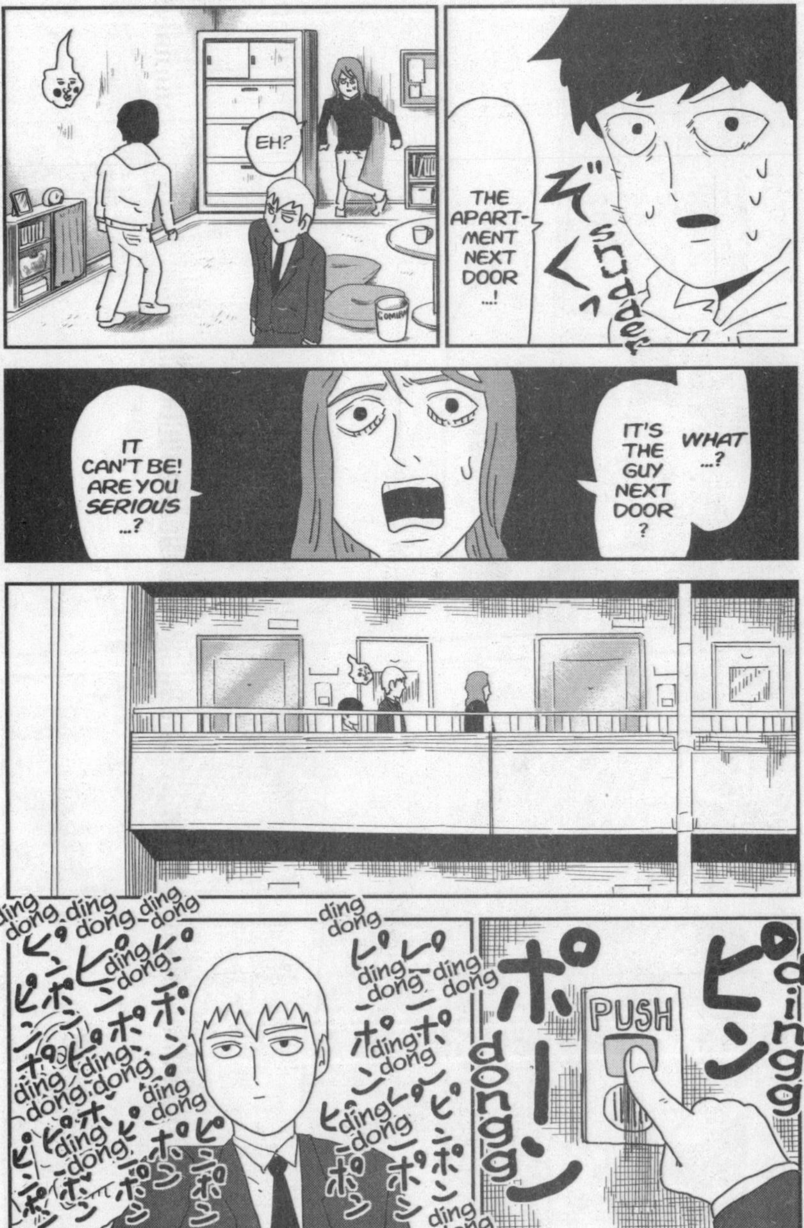
THE APARTMENT- MENT NEXT DOOR ...!
ぞくっ
shudder
EH?
WHAT ...?
IT'S THE GUY NEXT DOOR ?
IT CAN'T BE! ARE YOU SERIOUS ...?
ピンポーン
dingg dongg
PUSH
ding dong
ピンポン
ding dong
ピンポン
ding dong
ピンポン
ding dong
ピンポン
ding dong
ding dong
ding dong
ding dong
ding dong
ding dong
ding dong
ding dong

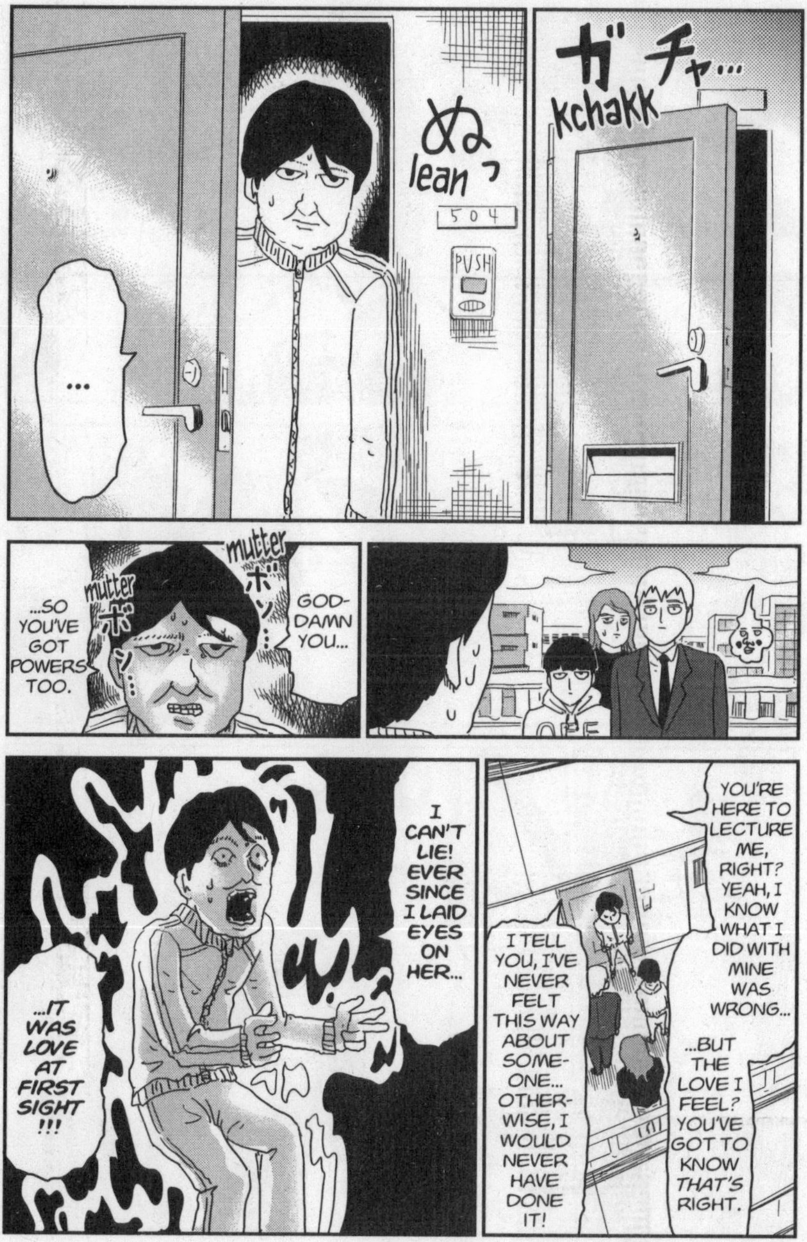
ガチャ…
kchakk
ぬっ
lean
504
PUSH
…
mutter
ボソッ
GOD-DAMN YOU...
mutter
ボソ…
...SO YOU'VE GOT POWERS TOO.
YOU'RE HERE TO LECTURE ME, RIGHT? YEAH, I KNOW WHAT I DID WITH MINE WAS WRONG...
...BUT THE LOVE I FEEL? YOU'VE GOT TO KNOW *THAT'S* RIGHT.
I TELL YOU, I'VE NEVER FELT THIS WAY ABOUT SOME-ONE... OTHER-WISE, I WOULD NEVER HAVE DONE IT!
I CAN'T LIE! EVER SINCE I LAID EYES ON HER...
...IT WAS LOVE AT FIRST SIGHT!!!

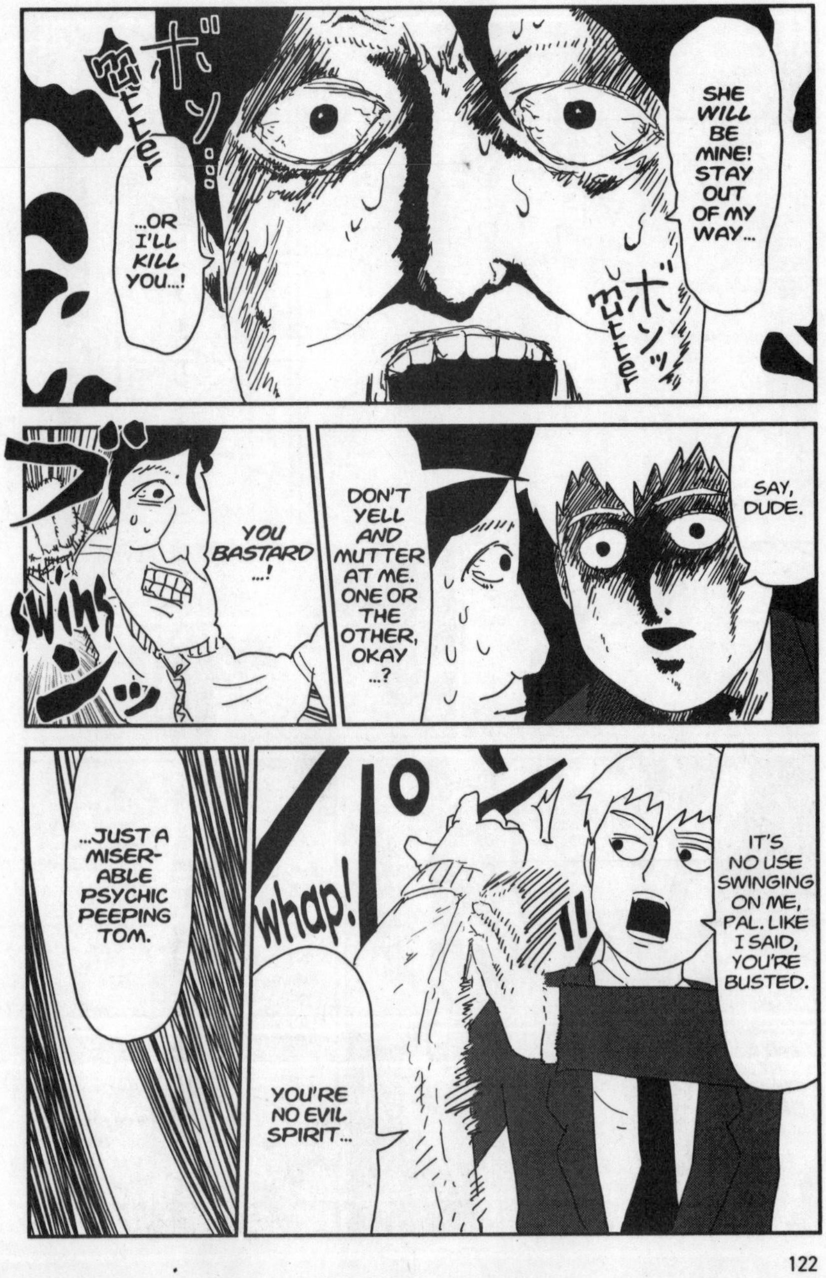
SHE WILL BE MINE! STAY OUT OF MY WAY...
ボソッ
mutter
ボソ...
mutter
...OR I'LL KILL YOU...!
SAY, DUDE.
DON'T YELL AND MUTTER AT ME. ONE OR THE OTHER, OKAY...?
YOU BASTARD...!
swing
IT'S NO USE SWINGING ON ME, PAL. LIKE I SAID, YOU'RE BUSTED.
whap!
YOU'RE NO EVIL SPIRIT...
...JUST A MISER-ABLE PSYCHIC PEEPING TOM.

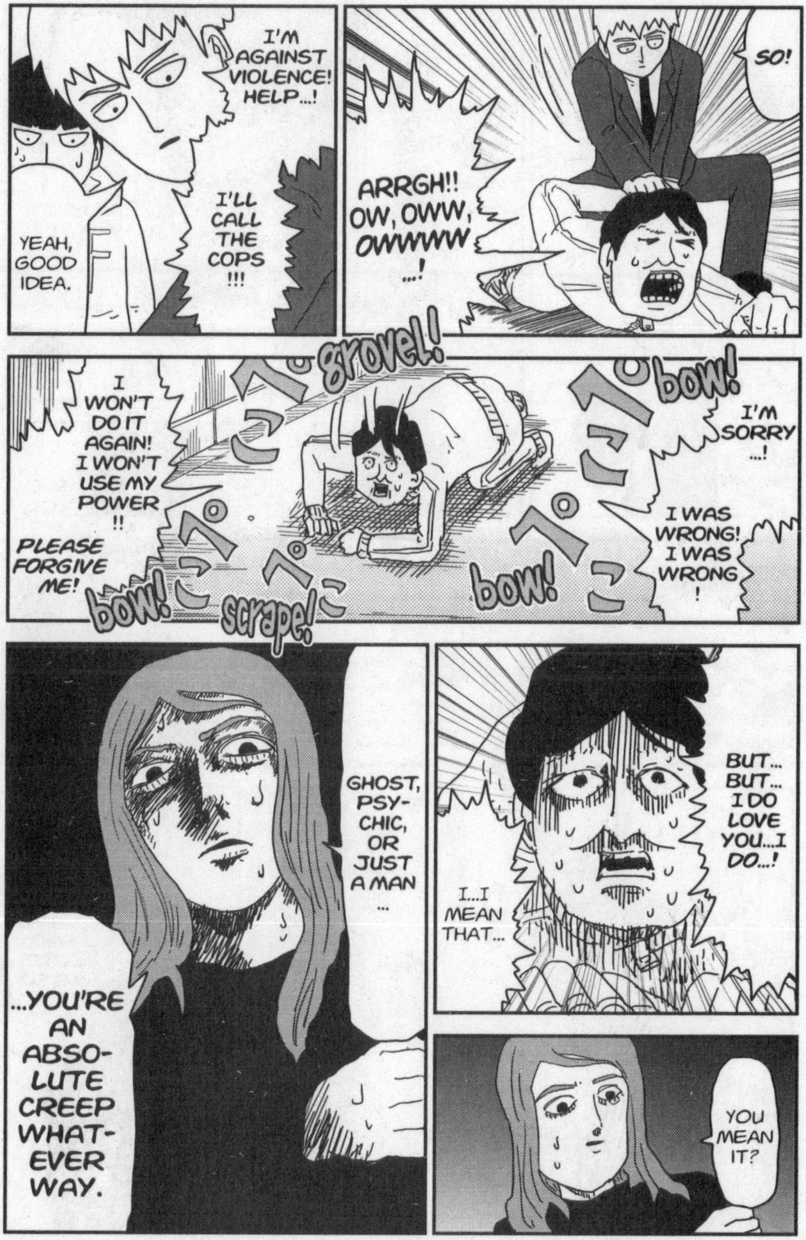
SO!
ARRGH!! OW, OWW, OWWWW ...!
I'M AGAINST VIOLENCE! HELP...!
I'LL CALL THE COPS !!!
YEAH, GOOD IDEA.
bow!
I'M SORRY ...!
I WAS WRONG! I WAS WRONG !
bow!
grovel!
I WON'T DO IT AGAIN! I WON'T USE MY POWER !!
PLEASE FORGIVE ME!
scrape!
bow!
BUT... BUT... I DO LOVE YOU...I DO...!
I...I MEAN THAT...
YOU MEAN IT?
GHOST, PSY-CHIC, OR JUST A MAN ...
...YOU'RE AN ABSO-LUTE CREEP WHAT-EVER WAY.

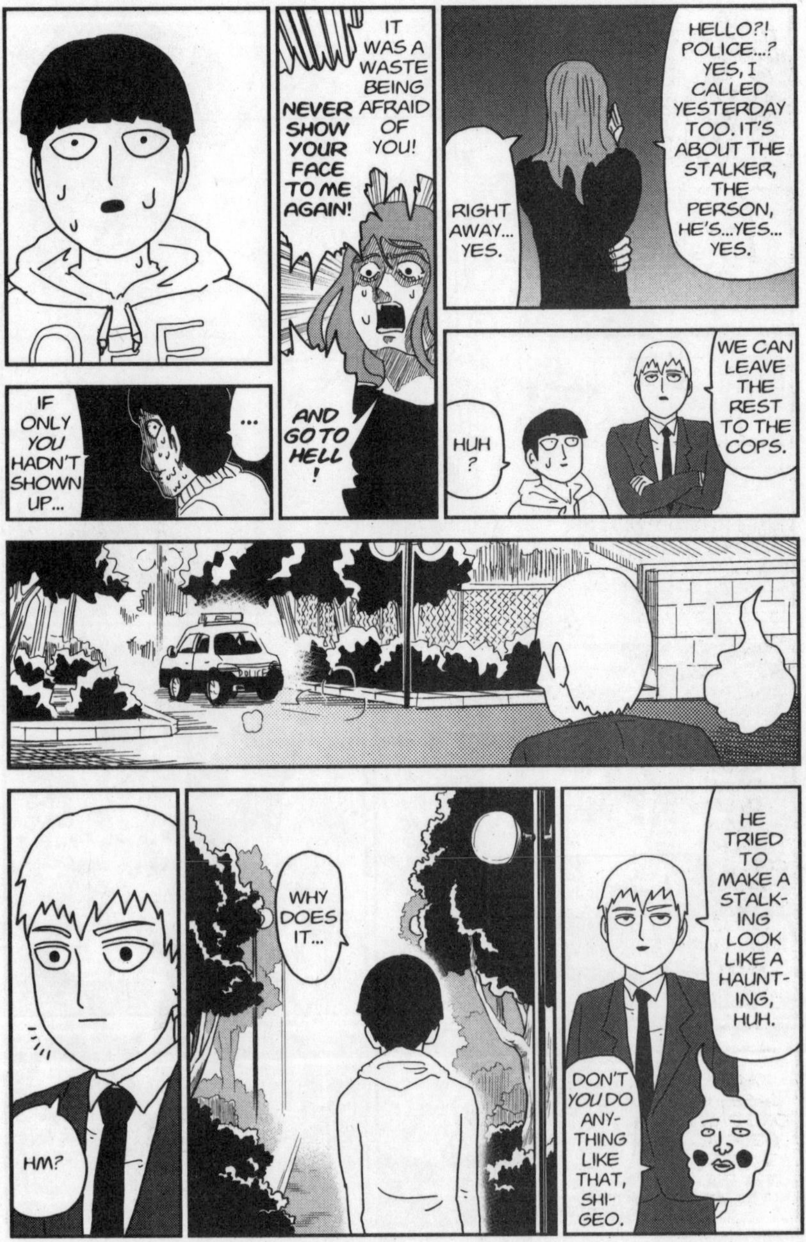
HELLO?! POLICE...? YES, I CALLED YESTERDAY TOO. IT'S ABOUT THE STALKER, THE PERSON, HE'S...YES... YES.
RIGHT AWAY... YES.
WE CAN LEAVE THE REST TO THE COPS.
HUH?
IT WAS A WASTE BEING AFRAID OF YOU!
NEVER SHOW YOUR FACE TO ME AGAIN!
AND GO TO HELL!
...
IF ONLY *YOU* HADN'T SHOWN UP...
HE TRIED TO MAKE A STALKING LOOK LIKE A HAUNTING, HUH.
DON'T *YOU* DO ANYTHING LIKE THAT, SHIGEO.
WHY DOES IT...
HM?

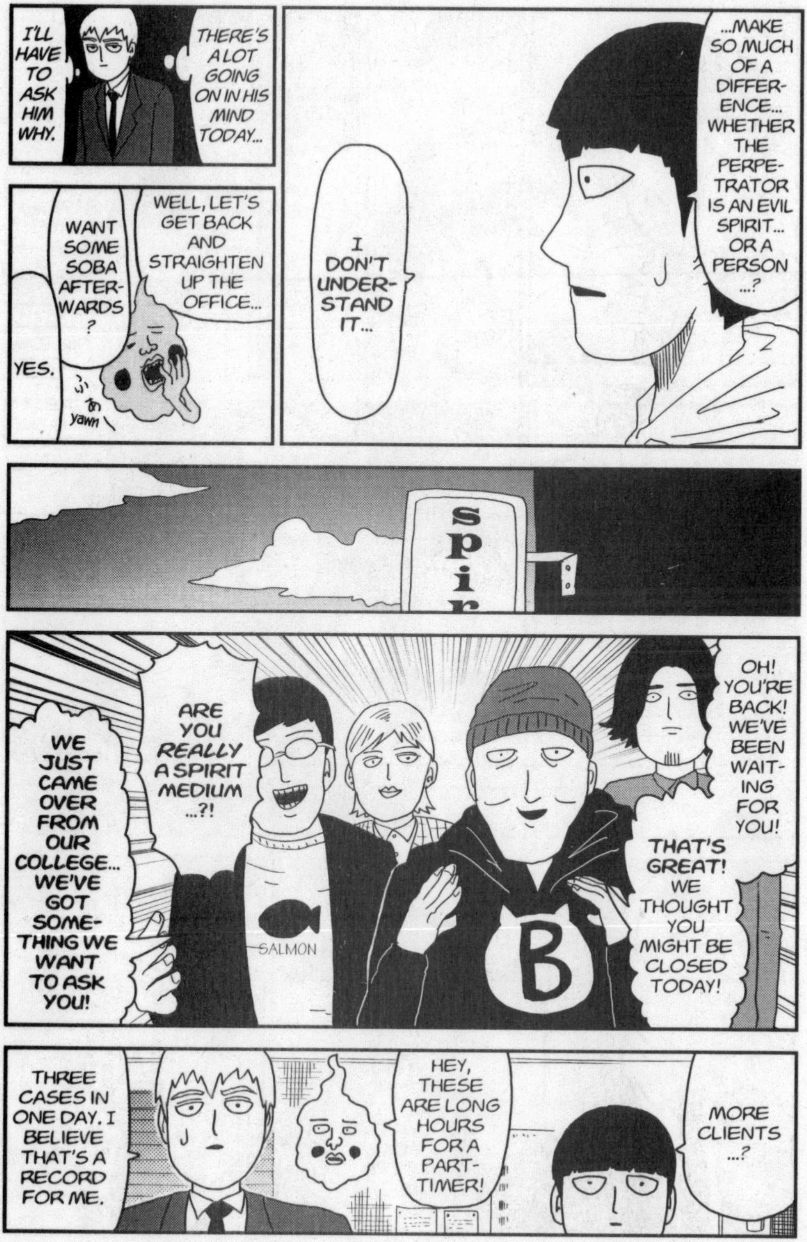
...MAKE SO MUCH OF A DIFFERENCE... WHETHER THE PERPETRATOR IS AN EVIL SPIRIT... OR A PERSON ...?
I DON'T UNDERSTAND IT...
THERE'S A LOT GOING ON IN HIS MIND TODAY...
I'LL HAVE TO ASK HIM WHY.
WELL, LET'S GET BACK AND STRAIGHTEN UP THE OFFICE...
WANT SOME SOBA AFTERWARDS?
YES.
ふあ
yawn
spir
OH! YOU'RE BACK! WE'VE BEEN WAITING FOR YOU!
THAT'S GREAT! WE THOUGHT YOU MIGHT BE CLOSED TODAY!
ARE YOU REALLY A SPIRIT MEDIUM ...?!
WE JUST CAME OVER FROM OUR COLLEGE... WE'VE GOT SOMETHING WE WANT TO ASK YOU!
SALMON
B
MORE CLIENTS ...?
HEY, THESE ARE LONG HOURS FOR A PART-TIMER!
THREE CASES IN ONE DAY. I BELIEVE THAT'S A RECORD FOR ME.

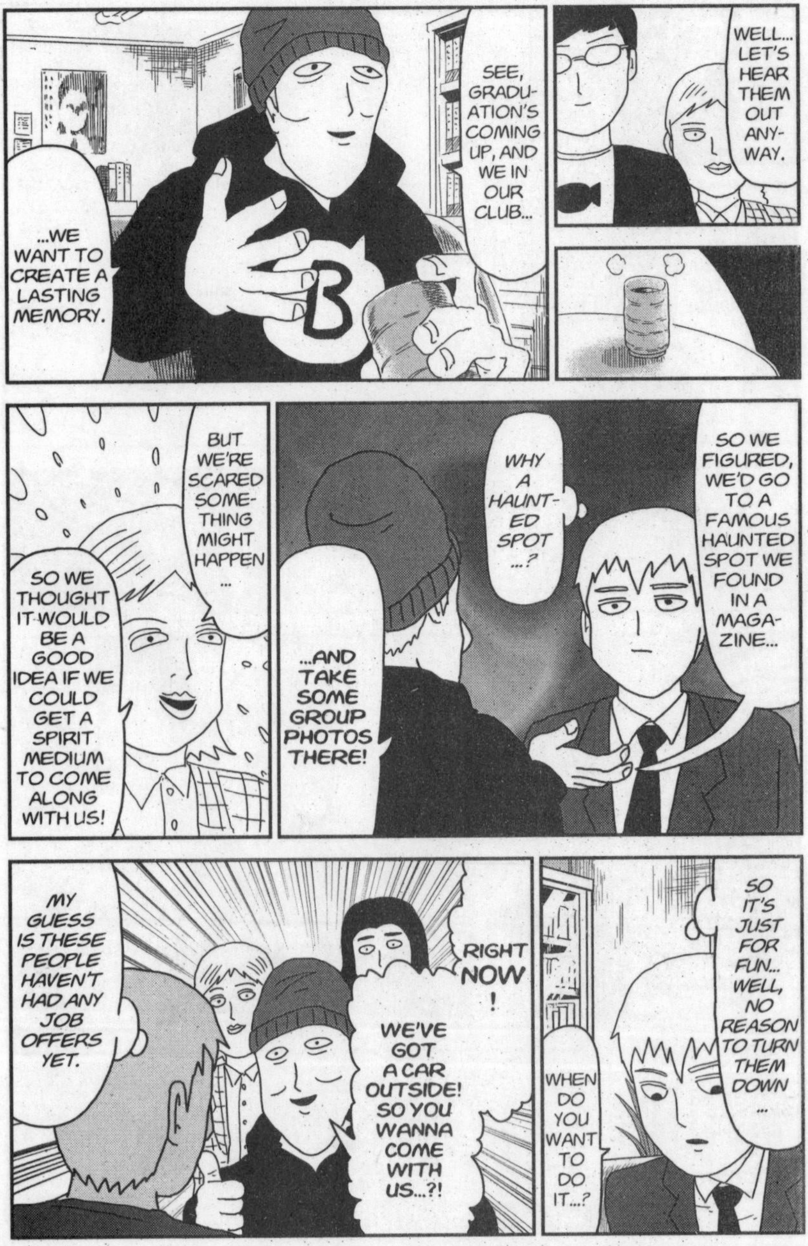
WELL... LET'S HEAR THEM OUT ANYWAY.
SEE, GRADUATION'S COMING UP, AND WE IN OUR CLUB...
...WE WANT TO CREATE A LASTING MEMORY.
SO WE FIGURED, WE'D GO TO A FAMOUS HAUNTED SPOT WE FOUND IN A MAGAZINE...
WHY A HAUNTED SPOT ...?
...AND TAKE SOME GROUP PHOTOS THERE!
BUT WE'RE SCARED SOMETHING MIGHT HAPPEN ...
SO WE THOUGHT IT WOULD BE A GOOD IDEA IF WE COULD GET A SPIRIT MEDIUM TO COME ALONG WITH US!
SO IT'S JUST FOR FUN... WELL, NO REASON TO TURN THEM DOWN ...
WHEN DO YOU WANT TO DO IT...?
RIGHT NOW!
WE'VE GOT A CAR OUTSIDE! SO YOU WANNA COME WITH US...?!
MY GUESS IS THESE PEOPLE HAVEN'T HAD ANY JOB OFFERS YET.

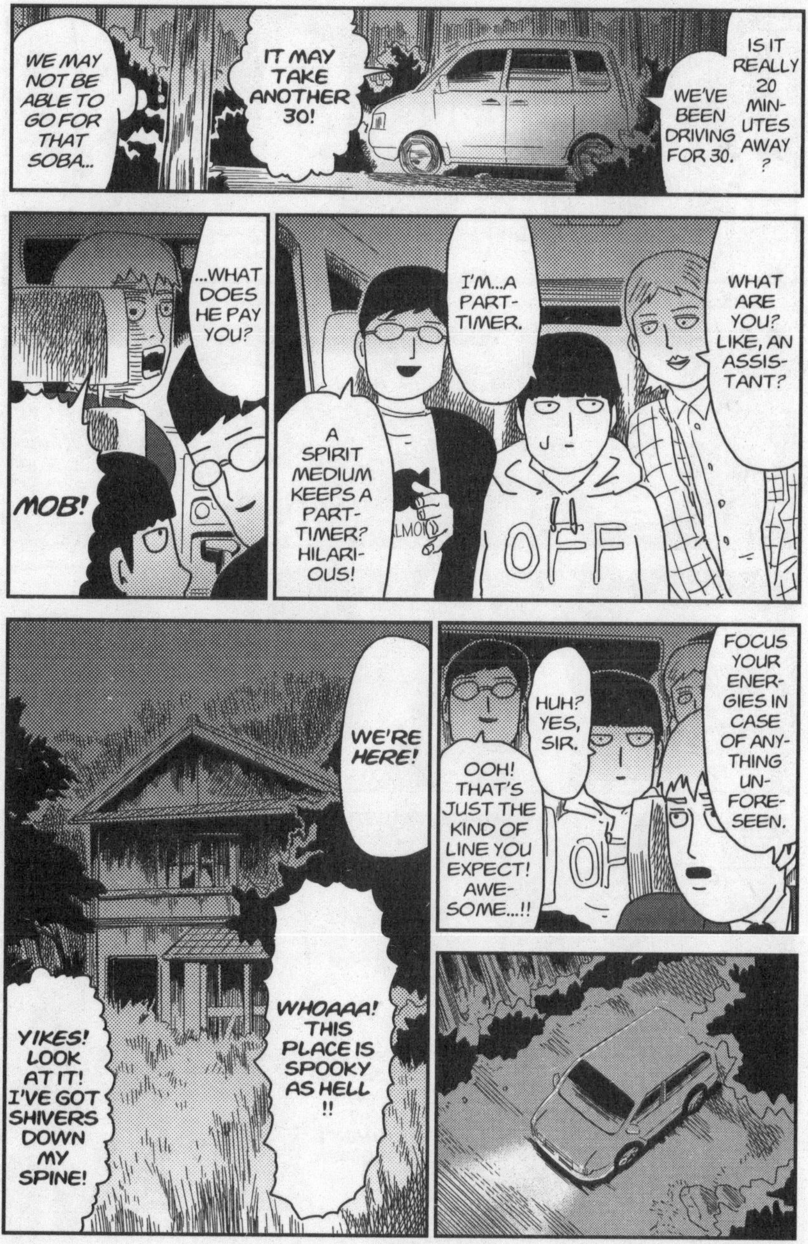
IS IT REALLY 20 MINUTES AWAY?
WE'VE BEEN DRIVING FOR 30.
IT MAY TAKE ANOTHER 30!
WE MAY NOT BE ABLE TO GO FOR THAT SOBA...
WHAT ARE YOU? LIKE, AN ASSISTANT?
I'M...A PART-TIMER.
A SPIRIT MEDIUM KEEPS A PART-TIMER? HILARIOUS!
...WHAT DOES HE PAY YOU?
MOB!
FOCUS YOUR ENERGIES IN CASE OF ANYTHING UNFORESEEN.
HUH? YES, SIR.
OOH! THAT'S JUST THE KIND OF LINE YOU EXPECT! AWESOME...!!
WE'RE HERE!
WHOAAA! THIS PLACE IS SPOOKY AS HELL!!
YIKES! LOOK AT IT! I'VE GOT SHIVERS DOWN MY SPINE!

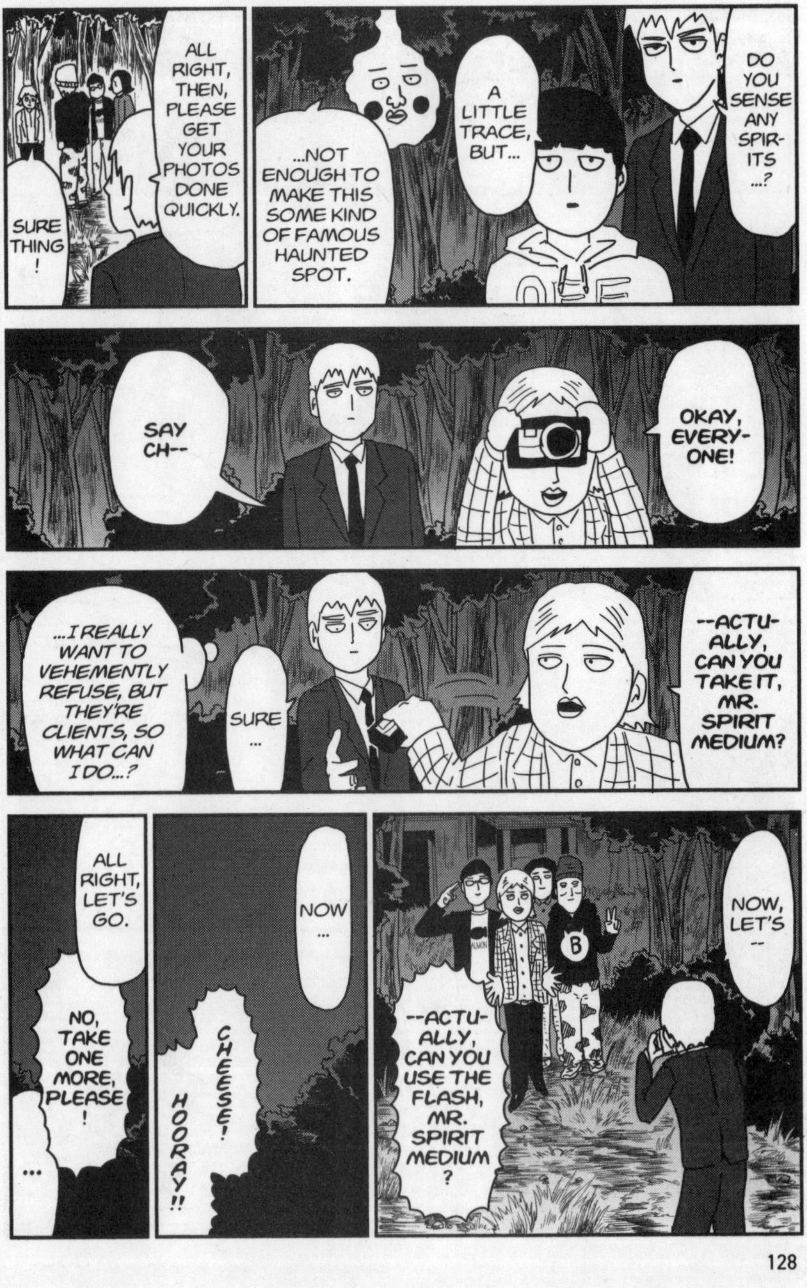
DO YOU SENSE ANY SPIRITS ...?
A LITTLE TRACE, BUT...
...NOT ENOUGH TO MAKE THIS SOME KIND OF FAMOUS HAUNTED SPOT.
ALL RIGHT, THEN, PLEASE GET YOUR PHOTOS DONE QUICKLY.
SURE THING!
OKAY, EVERYONE!
SAY CH--
--ACTUALLY, CAN YOU TAKE IT, MR. SPIRIT MEDIUM?
SURE...
...I REALLY WANT TO VEHEMENTLY REFUSE, BUT THEY'RE CLIENTS, SO WHAT CAN I DO...?
NOW, LET'S--
--ACTUALLY, CAN YOU USE THE FLASH, MR. SPIRIT MEDIUM?
NOW...
CHEESE!
HOORAY!!
ALL RIGHT, LET'S GO.
NO, TAKE ONE MORE, PLEASE!
...

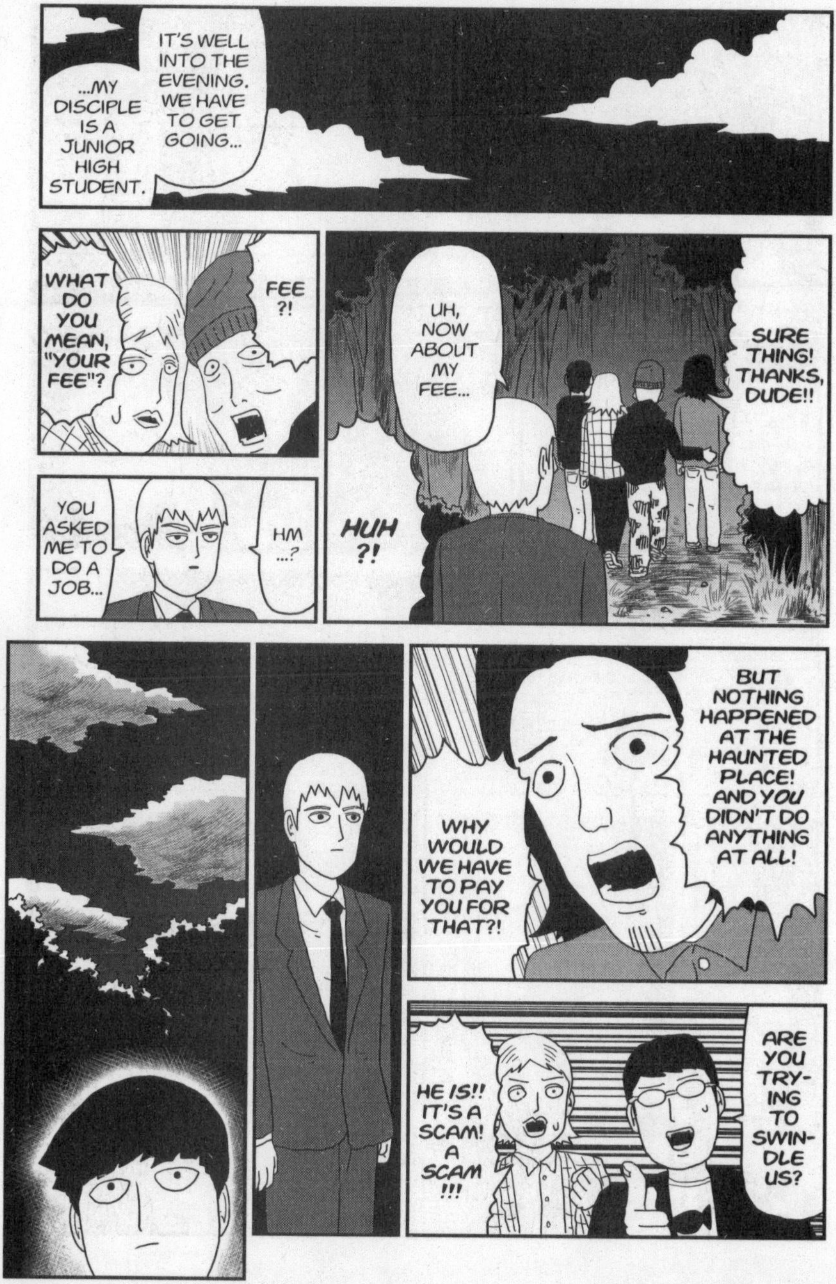

IT'S WELL INTO THE EVENING. WE HAVE TO GET GOING...
...MY DISCIPLE IS A JUNIOR HIGH STUDENT.
SURE THING! THANKS, DUDE!!
UH, NOW ABOUT MY FEE...
HUH ?!
FEE ?!
WHAT DO YOU MEAN, "YOUR FEE"?
HM ...?
YOU ASKED ME TO DO A JOB...
BUT NOTHING HAPPENED AT THE HAUNTED PLACE! AND *YOU* DIDN'T DO ANYTHING AT ALL!
WHY WOULD WE HAVE TO PAY YOU FOR THAT?!
ARE YOU TRY-ING TO SWIN-DLE US?
HE *IS*!! IT'S A SCAM! A SCAM!!!

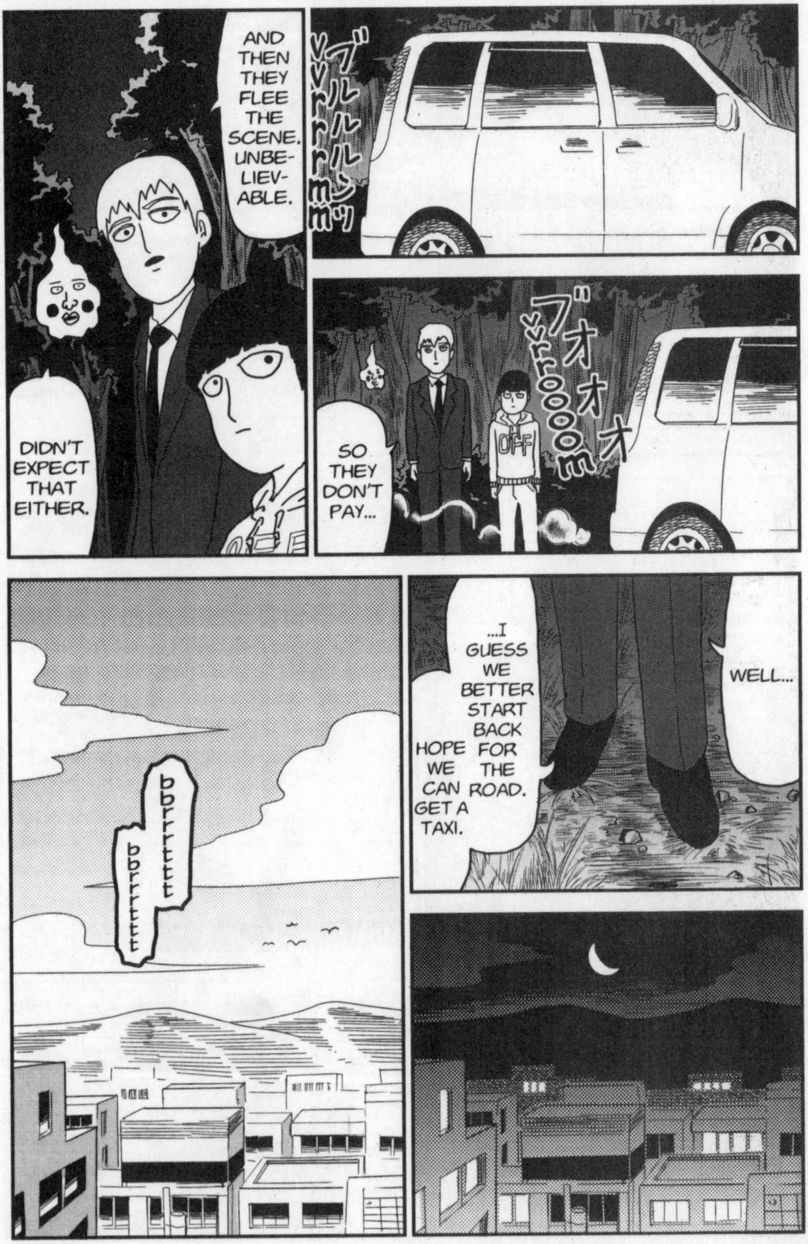
ブルルルンッ
vvrrrmm
ブオオオ
vvroooom
SO THEY DON'T PAY...
AND THEN THEY FLEE THE SCENE. UNBELIEVABLE.
DIDN'T EXPECT THAT EITHER.
WELL...
...I GUESS WE BETTER START BACK FOR THE ROAD.
HOPE WE CAN GET A TAXI.
bbrrrttt
bbrrrttt

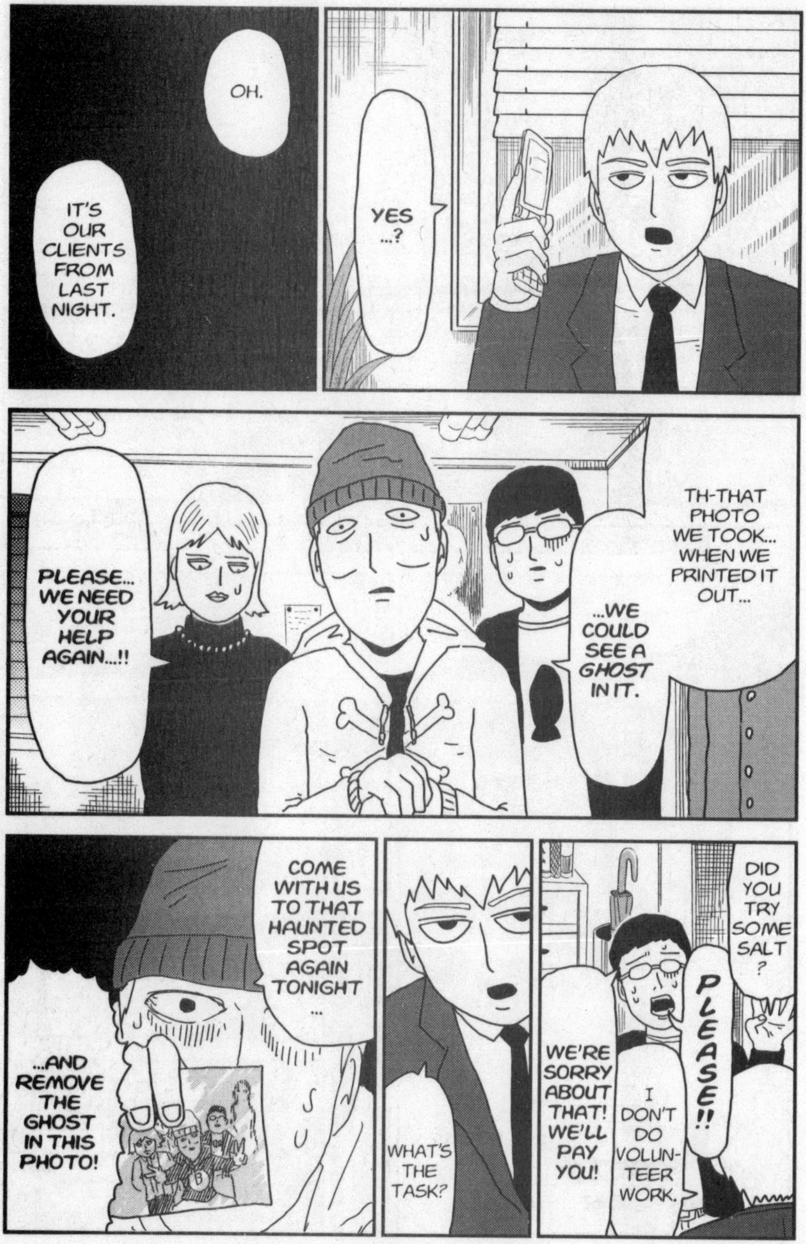
YES ...?
OH.
IT'S OUR CLIENTS FROM LAST NIGHT.
TH-THAT PHOTO WE TOOK... WHEN WE PRINTED IT OUT...
...WE COULD SEE A GHOST IN IT.
PLEASE... WE NEED YOUR HELP AGAIN...!!
DID YOU TRY SOME SALT?
PLEASE!!
I DON'T DO VOLUNTEER WORK.
WE'RE SORRY ABOUT THAT! WE'LL PAY YOU!
WHAT'S THE TASK?
COME WITH US TO THAT HAUNTED SPOT AGAIN TONIGHT...
...AND REMOVE THE GHOST IN THIS PHOTO!

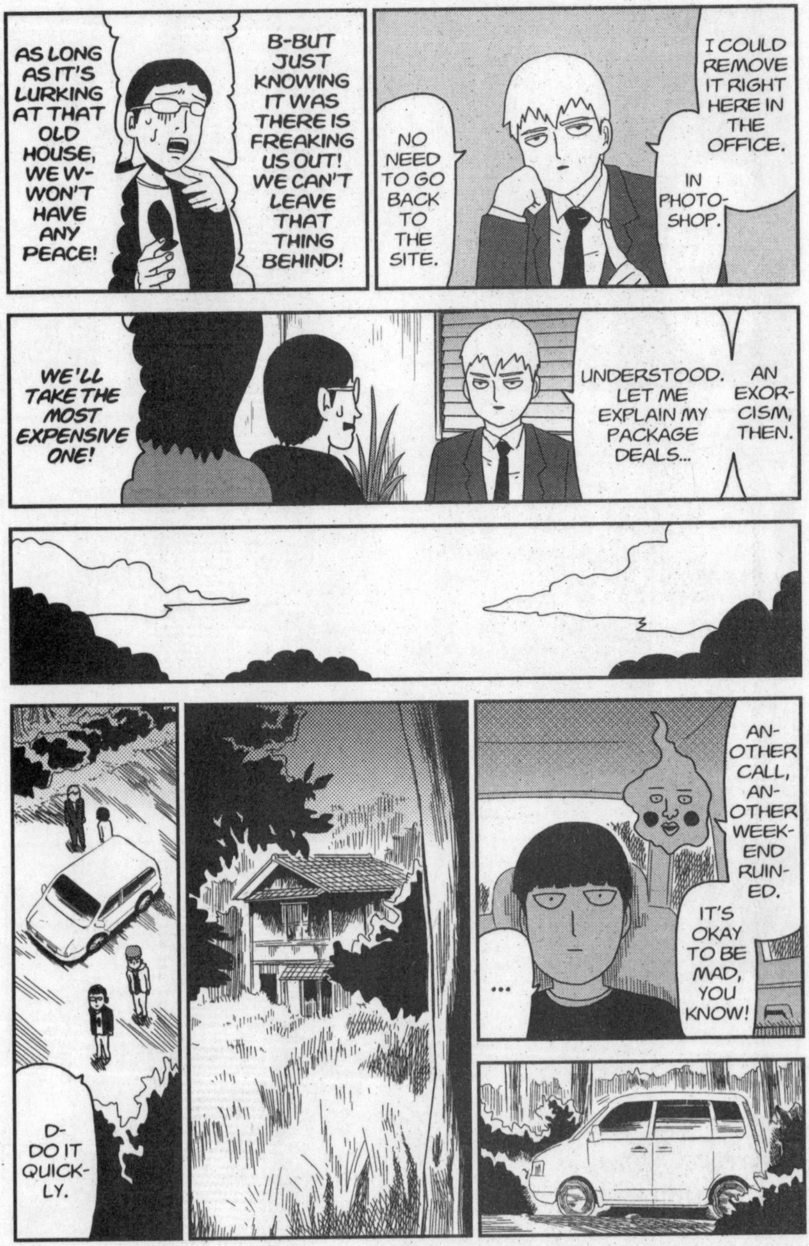
I COULD REMOVE IT RIGHT HERE IN THE OFFICE.
IN PHOTO-SHOP.
NO NEED TO GO BACK TO THE SITE.
B-BUT JUST KNOWING IT WAS THERE IS FREAKING US OUT! WE CAN'T LEAVE THAT THING BEHIND!
AS LONG AS IT'S LURKING AT THAT OLD HOUSE, WE W-WON'T HAVE ANY PEACE!
AN EXORCISM, THEN.
UNDERSTOOD. LET ME EXPLAIN MY PACKAGE DEALS...
WE'LL TAKE THE MOST EXPENSIVE ONE!
AN-OTHER CALL, AN-OTHER WEEK-END RUIN-ED.
IT'S OKAY TO BE MAD, YOU KNOW!
...
D-DO IT QUICK-LY.

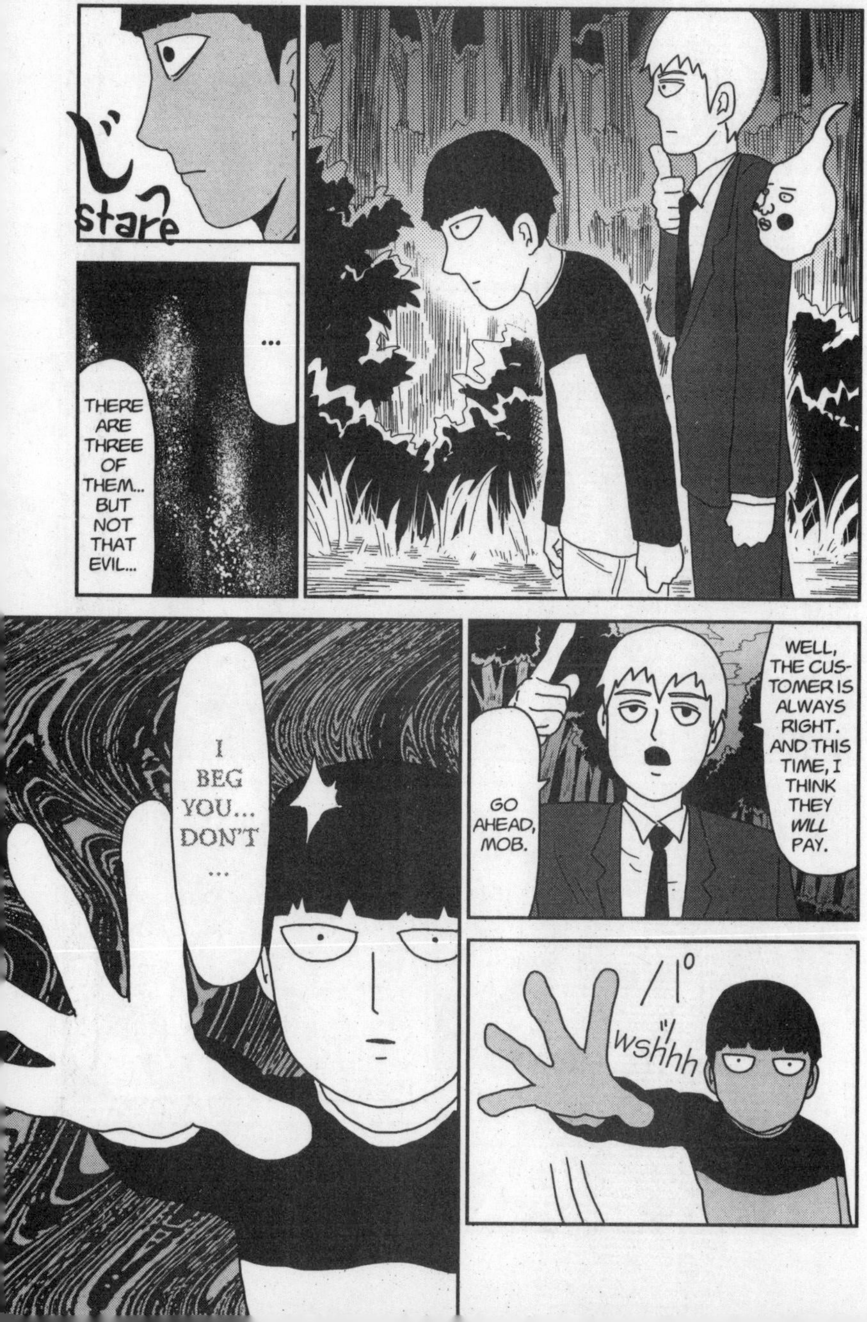
stare
...
THERE ARE THREE OF THEM... BUT NOT THAT EVIL...
WELL, THE CUSTOMER IS ALWAYS RIGHT. AND THIS TIME, I THINK THEY *WILL* PAY.
GO AHEAD, MOB.
wshhh
I BEG YOU... DON'T ...

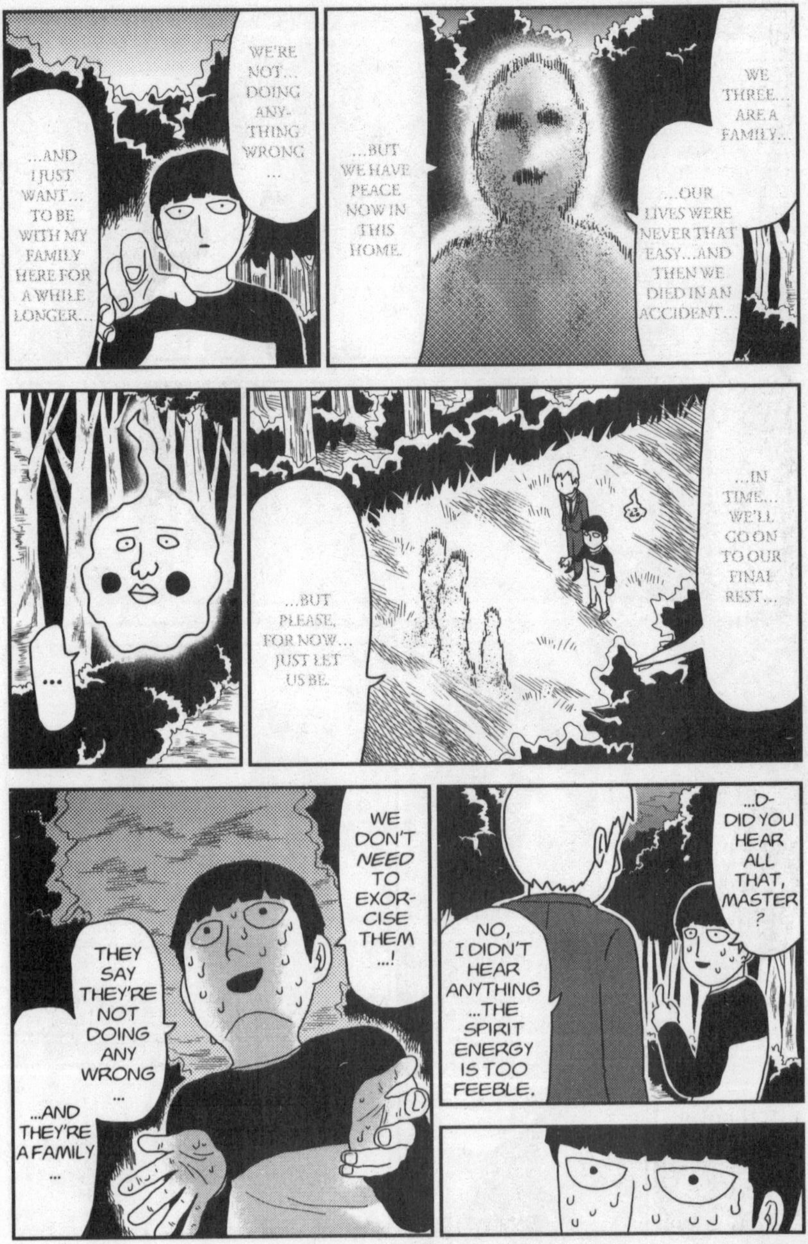

WE THREE... ARE A FAMILY...
...OUR LIVES WERE NEVER THAT EASY...AND THEN WE DIED IN AN ACCIDENT...
...BUT WE HAVE PEACE NOW IN THIS HOME.
WE'RE NOT... DOING ANY-THING WRONG ...
...AND I JUST WANT... TO BE WITH MY FAMILY HERE FOR A WHILE LONGER...
...IN TIME... WE'LL GO ON TO OUR FINAL REST...
...BUT PLEASE, FOR NOW... JUST LET US BE.
...
...D-DID YOU HEAR ALL THAT, MASTER ?
NO, I DIDN'T HEAR ANYTHING ...THE SPIRIT ENERGY IS TOO FEEBLE.
WE DON'T NEED TO EXOR-CISE THEM ...!
THEY SAY THEY'RE NOT DOING ANY WRONG ...
...AND THEY'RE A FAMILY ...

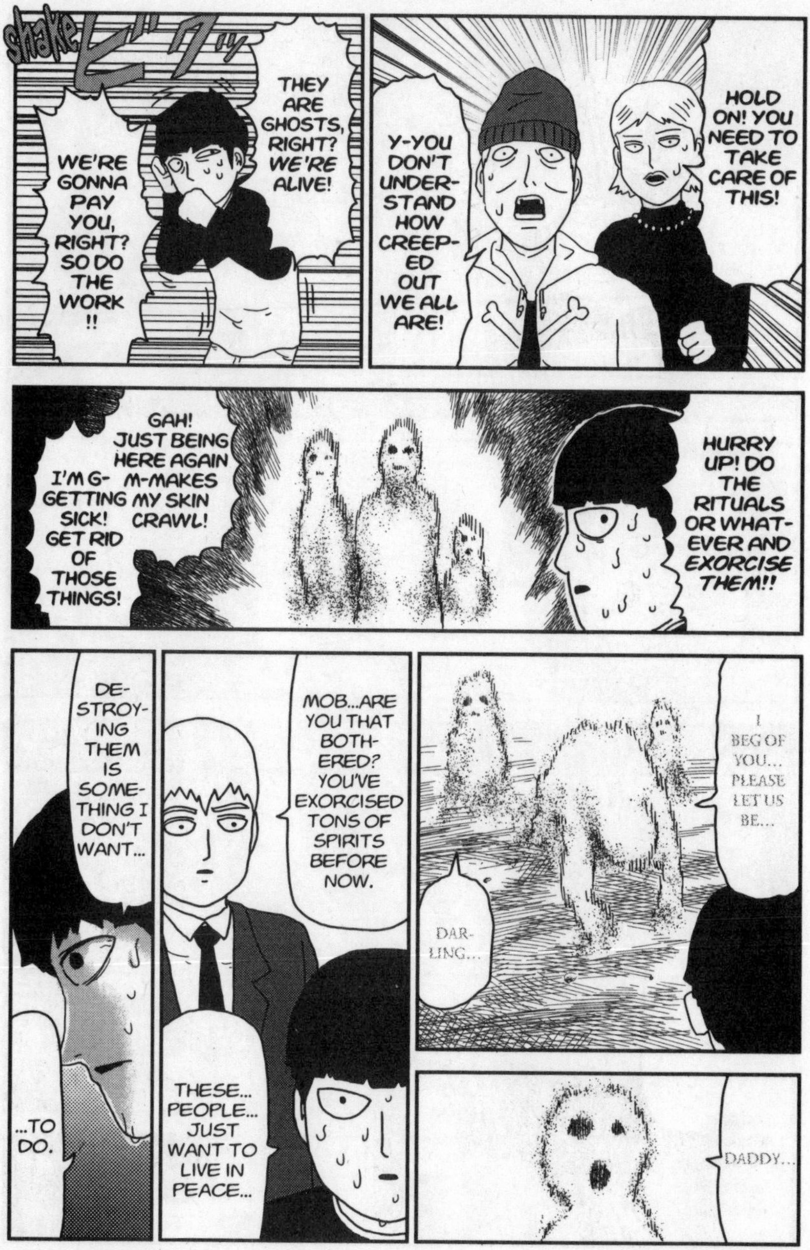
HOLD ON! YOU NEED TO TAKE CARE OF THIS!
Y-YOU DON'T UNDER-STAND HOW CREEP-ED OUT WE ALL ARE!
shake
THEY ARE GHOSTS, RIGHT? WE'RE ALIVE!
WE'RE GONNA PAY YOU, RIGHT? SO DO THE WORK!!
HURRY UP! DO THE RITUALS OR WHAT-EVER AND EXORCISE THEM!!
GAH! JUST BEING HERE AGAIN M-MAKES MY SKIN CRAWL!
I'M G-GETTING SICK! GET RID OF THOSE THINGS!
I BEG OF YOU... PLEASE LET US BE...
DAR-LING...
DADDY...
MOB...ARE YOU THAT BOTH-ERED? YOU'VE EXORCISED TONS OF SPIRITS BEFORE NOW.
THESE... PEOPLE... JUST WANT TO LIVE IN PEACE...
DE-STROY-ING THEM IS SOME-THING I DON'T WANT...
...TO DO.

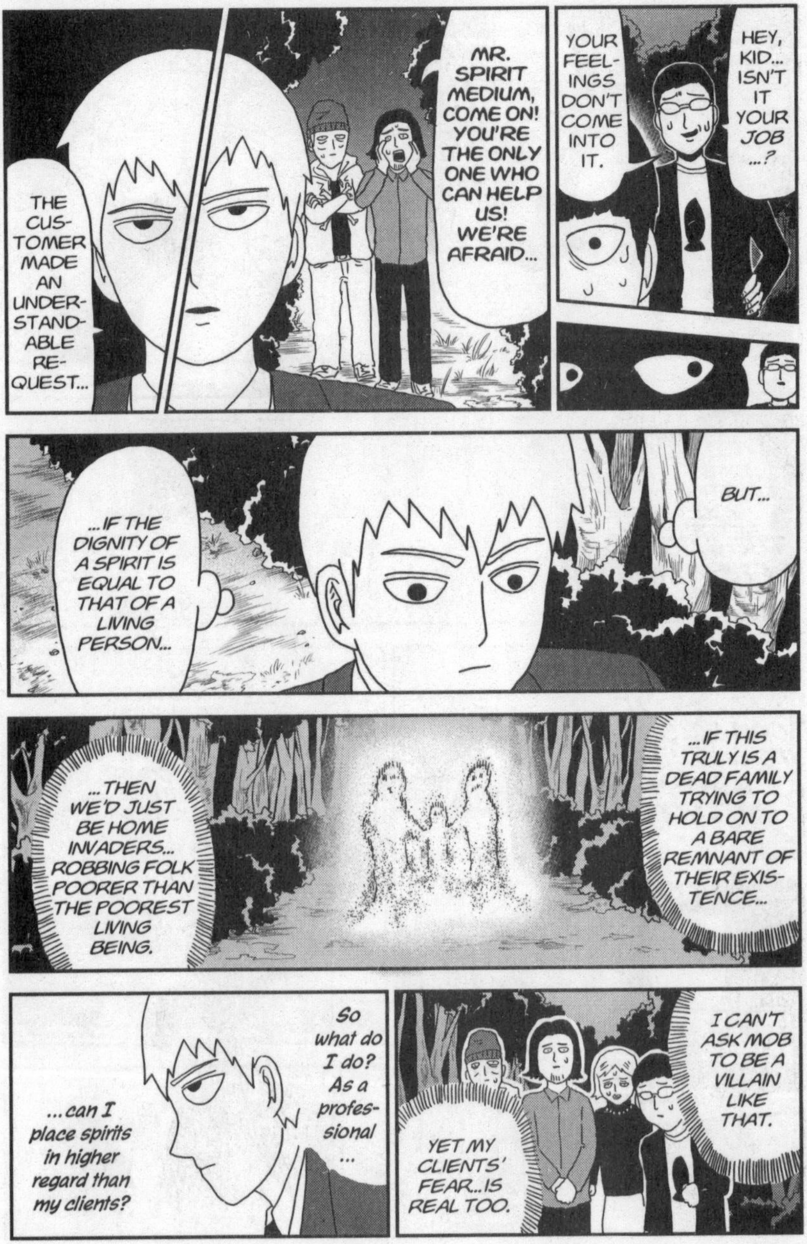
HEY, KID... ISN'T IT YOUR JOB ...?
YOUR FEELINGS DON'T COME INTO IT.
MR. SPIRIT MEDIUM, COME ON! YOU'RE THE ONLY ONE WHO CAN HELP US! WE'RE AFRAID...
THE CUSTOMER MADE AN UNDERSTANDABLE REQUEST...
BUT...
...IF THE DIGNITY OF A SPIRIT IS EQUAL TO THAT OF A LIVING PERSON...
...IF THIS TRULY IS A DEAD FAMILY TRYING TO HOLD ON TO A BARE REMNANT OF THEIR EXISTENCE...
...THEN WE'D JUST BE HOME INVADERS... ROBBING FOLK POORER THAN THE POOREST LIVING BEING.
I CAN'T ASK MOB TO BE A VILLAIN LIKE THAT.
YET MY CLIENTS' FEAR...IS REAL TOO.
So what do I do? As a professional ...
...can I place spirits in higher regard than my clients?

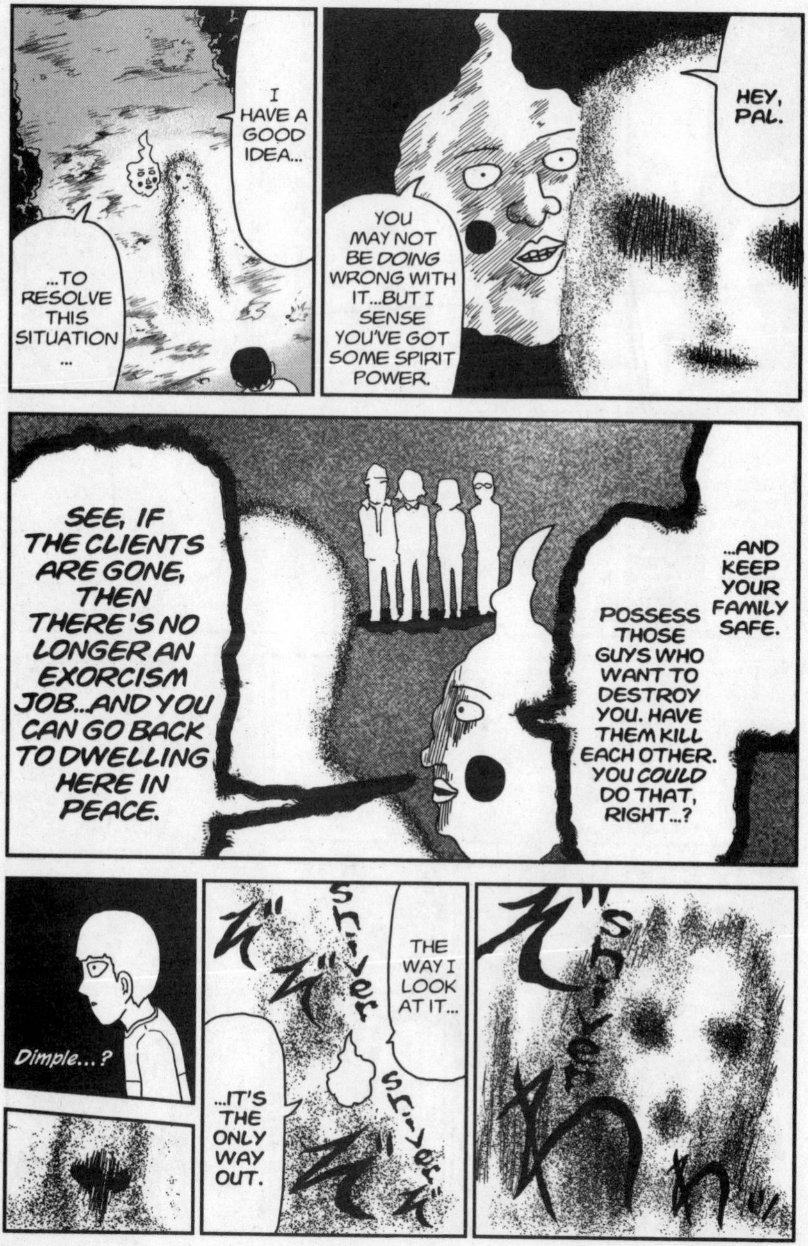
HEY, PAL.
YOU MAY NOT BE DOING WRONG WITH IT...BUT I SENSE YOU'VE GOT SOME SPIRIT POWER.
I HAVE A GOOD IDEA...
...TO RESOLVE THIS SITUATION ...
POSSESS THOSE GUYS WHO WANT TO DESTROY YOU. HAVE THEM KILL EACH OTHER. YOU COULD DO THAT, RIGHT...?
...AND KEEP YOUR FAMILY SAFE.
SEE, IF THE CLIENTS ARE GONE, THEN THERE'S NO LONGER AN EXORCISM JOB...AND YOU CAN GO BACK TO DWELLING HERE IN PEACE.
shiver
THE WAY I LOOK AT IT...
shiver
shiver
...IT'S THE ONLY WAY OUT.
Dimple...?

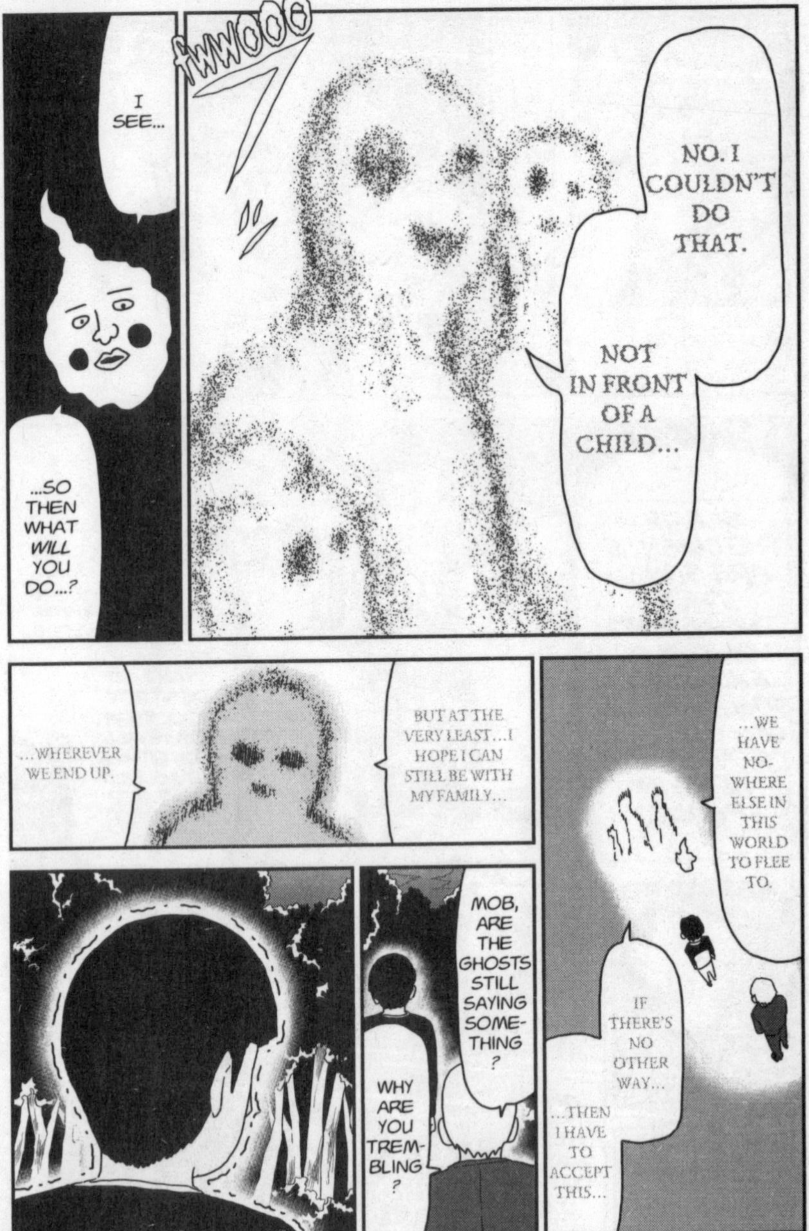
fWWOOO
NO. I COULDN'T DO THAT.
NOT IN FRONT OF A CHILD...
I SEE...
...SO THEN WHAT WILL YOU DO...?
...WE HAVE NO-WHERE ELSE IN THIS WORLD TO FLEE TO.
IF THERE'S NO OTHER WAY...
...THEN I HAVE TO ACCEPT THIS...
BUT AT THE VERY LEAST...I HOPE I CAN STILL BE WITH MY FAMILY...
...WHEREVER WE END UP.
MOB, ARE THE GHOSTS STILL SAYING SOME-THING?
WHY ARE YOU TREM-BLING?

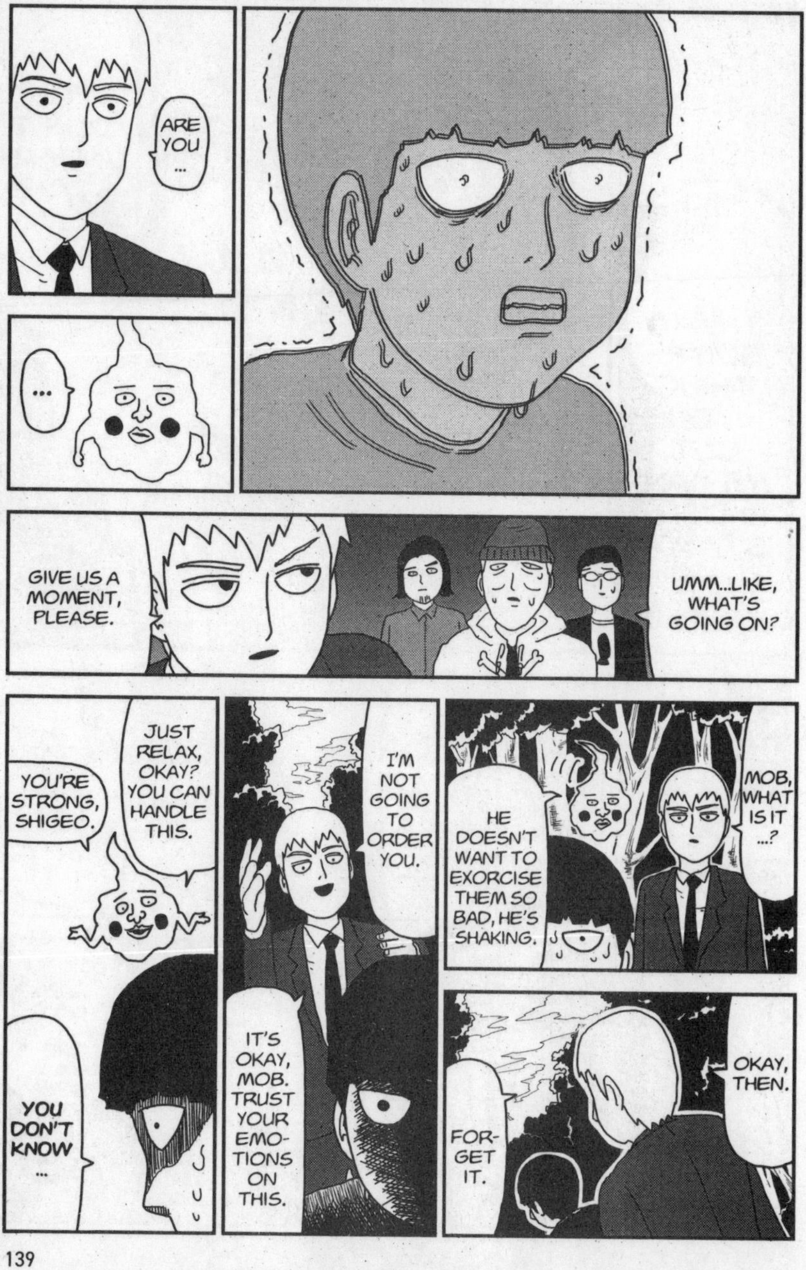
ARE YOU ...
...
UMM...LIKE, WHAT'S GOING ON?
GIVE US A MOMENT, PLEASE.
MOB, WHAT IS IT ...?
HE DOESN'T WANT TO EXORCISE THEM SO BAD, HE'S SHAKING.
OKAY, THEN.
FOR-GET IT.
I'M NOT GOING TO ORDER YOU.
IT'S OKAY, MOB. TRUST YOUR EMO-TIONS ON THIS.
JUST RELAX, OKAY? YOU CAN HANDLE THIS.
YOU'RE STRONG, SHIGEO.
YOU DON'T KNOW ...

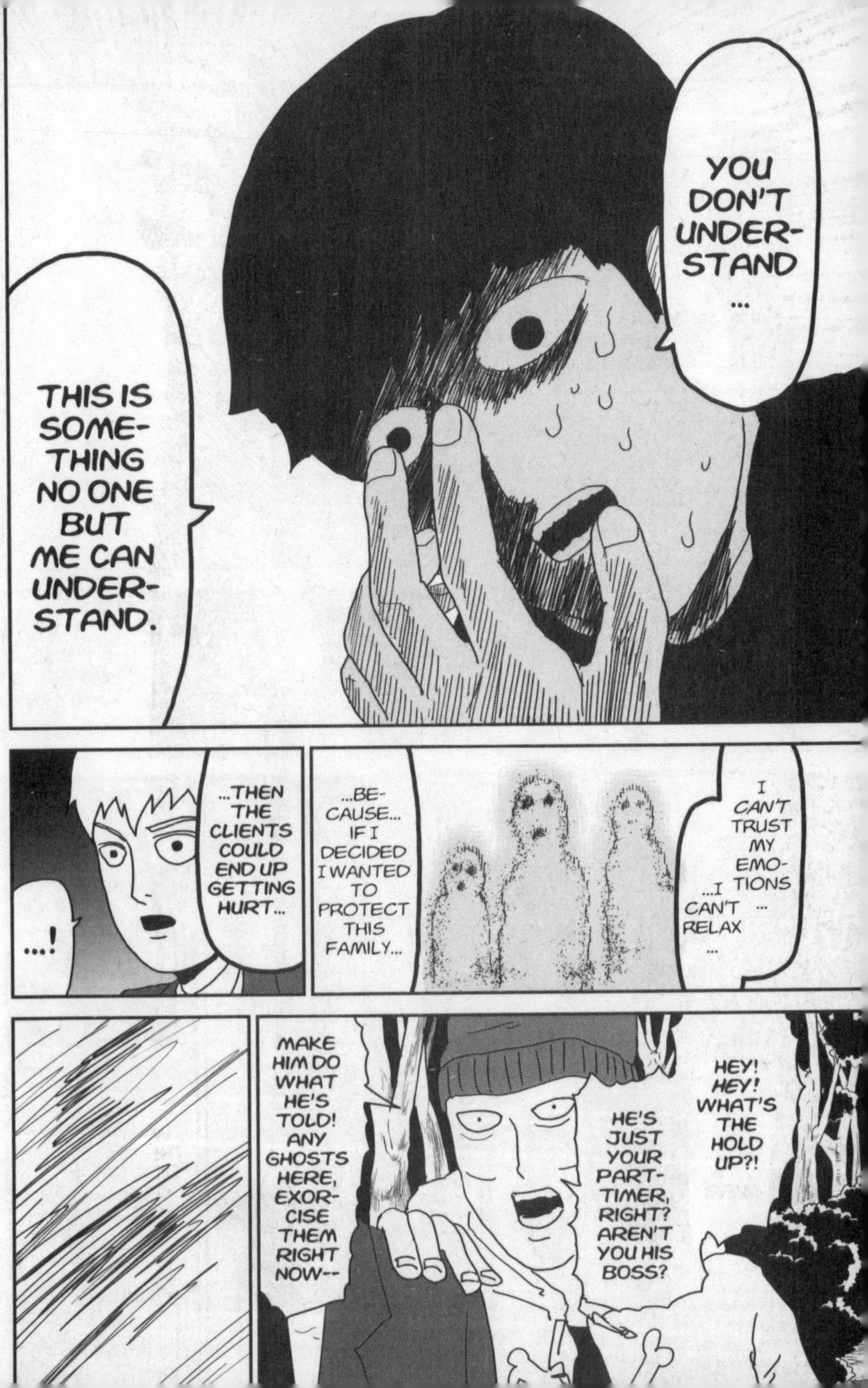
YOU DON'T UNDER-STAND ...
THIS IS SOME-THING NO ONE BUT ME CAN UNDER-STAND.
I CAN'T TRUST MY EMO-TIONS ... ...I CAN'T RELAX ...
...BE-CAUSE... IF I DECIDED I WANTED TO PROTECT THIS FAMILY...
...THEN THE CLIENTS COULD END UP GETTING HURT...
...!
HEY! HEY! WHAT'S THE HOLD UP?!
HE'S JUST YOUR PART-TIMER, RIGHT? AREN'T YOU HIS BOSS?
MAKE HIM DO WHAT HE'S TOLD! ANY GHOSTS HERE, EXOR-CISE THEM RIGHT NOW--

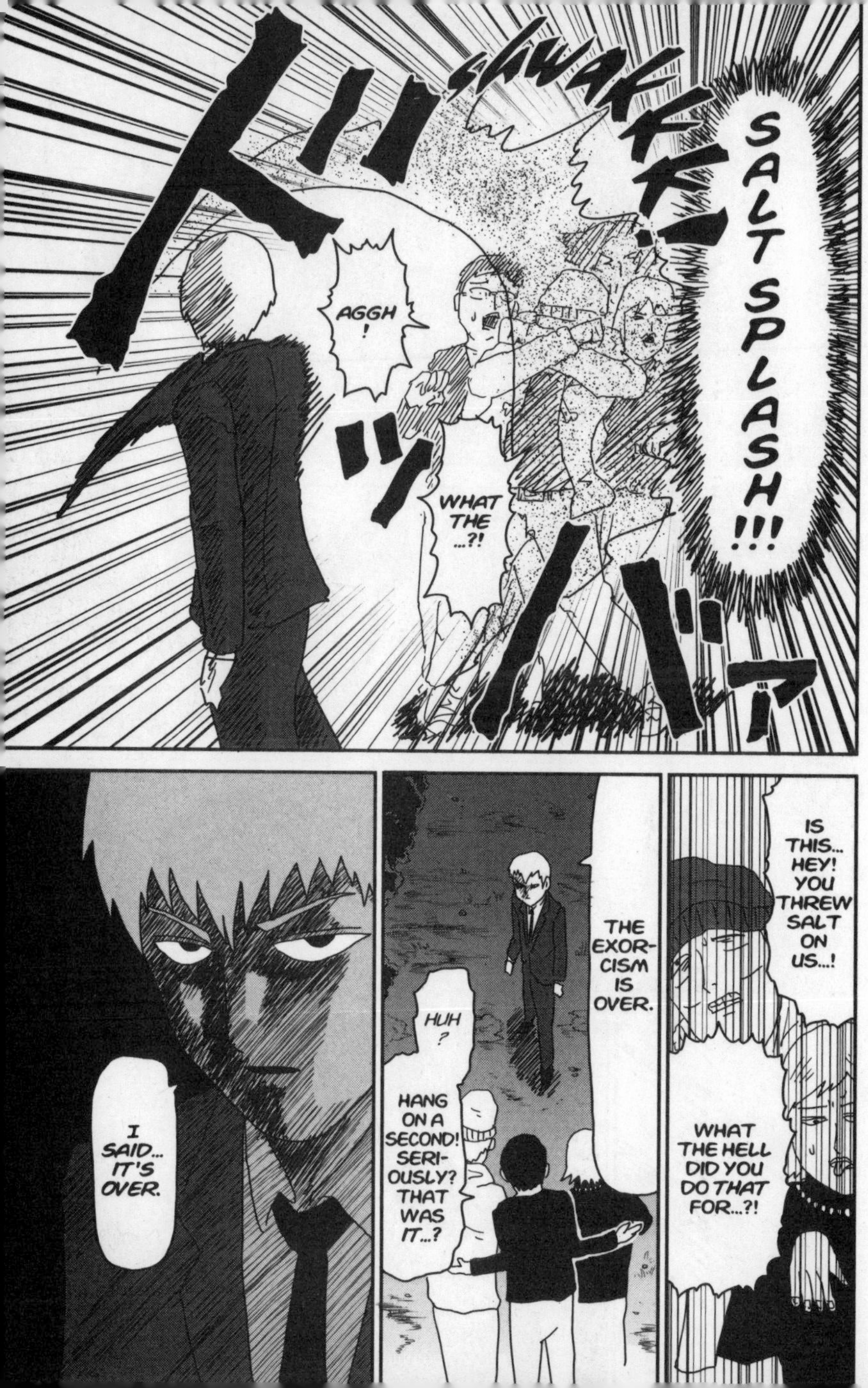
SALT SPLASH!!!
SHWAKK
AGGH!
WHAT THE ...?!
IS THIS... HEY! YOU THREW SALT ON US...!
WHAT THE HELL DID YOU DO THAT FOR...?!
THE EXOR-CISM IS OVER.
HUH?
HANG ON A SECOND! SERI-OUSLY? THAT WAS IT...?
I SAID... IT'S OVER.

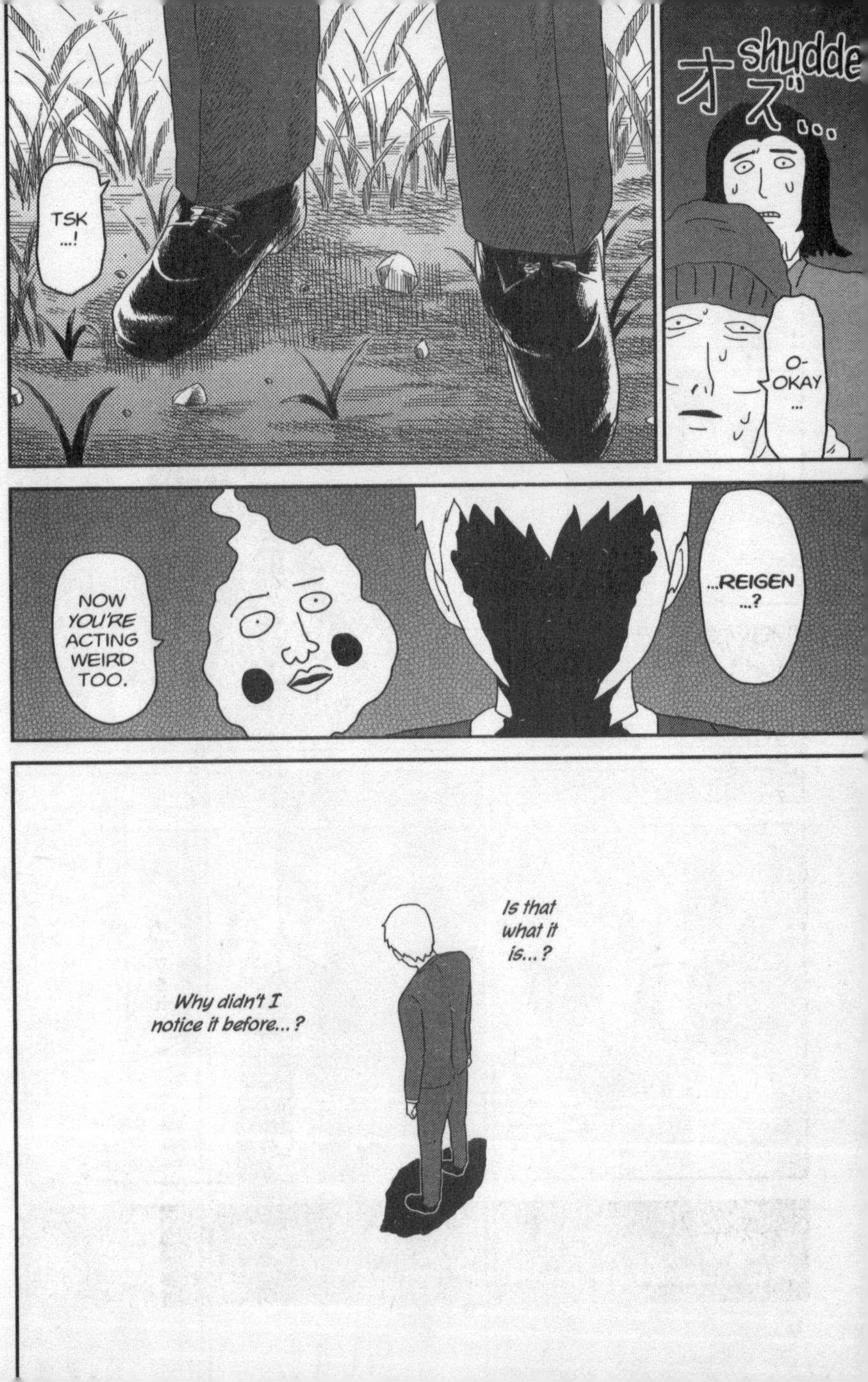
オズ...
shudde
O-OKAY...
TSK...!
...REIGEN...?
NOW YOU'RE ACTING WEIRD TOO.
Is that what it is...?
Why didn't I notice it before...?

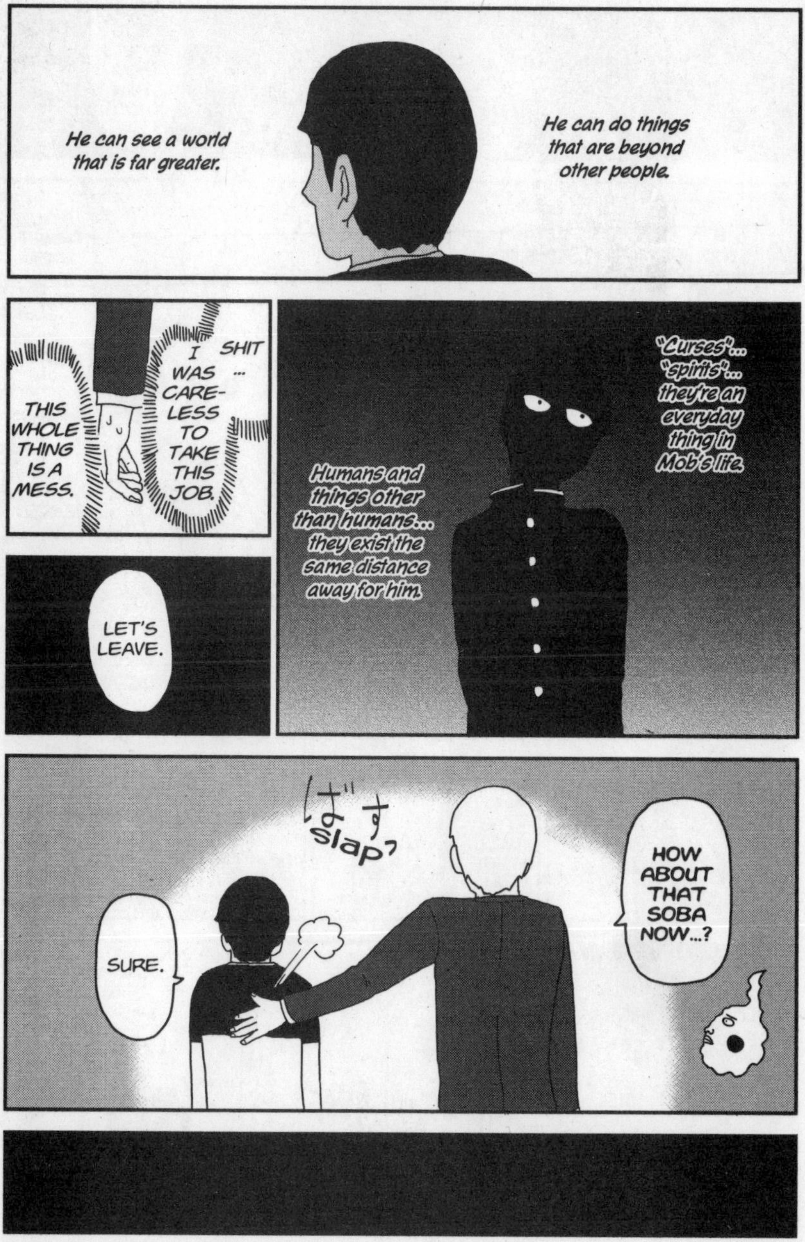

He can do things that are beyond other people.
He can see a world that is far greater.
"Curses"... "spirits"... they're an everyday thing in Mob's life.
Humans and things other than humans... they exist the same distance away for him.
SHIT...
I WAS CARELESS TO TAKE THIS JOB.
THIS WHOLE THING IS A MESS.
LET'S LEAVE.
ばす
slap
HOW ABOUT THAT SOBA NOW...?
SURE.

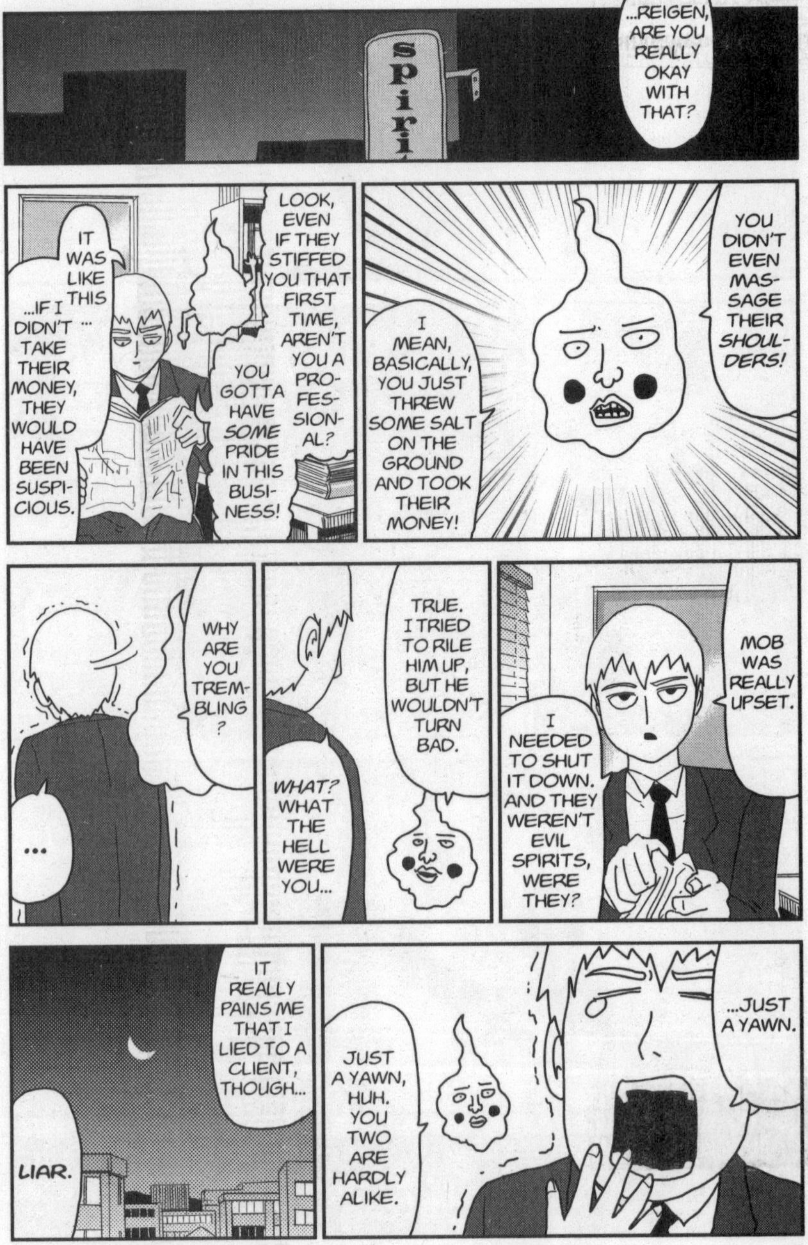
...REIGEN, ARE YOU REALLY OKAY WITH THAT?
YOU DIDN'T EVEN MASSAGE THEIR *SHOULDERS!*
I MEAN, BASICALLY, YOU JUST THREW SOME SALT ON THE GROUND AND TOOK THEIR MONEY!
LOOK, EVEN IF THEY STIFFED YOU THAT FIRST TIME, AREN'T YOU A PROFESSIONAL?
YOU GOTTA HAVE *SOME* PRIDE IN THIS BUSINESS!
IT WAS LIKE THIS ...
...IF I DIDN'T TAKE THEIR MONEY, THEY WOULD HAVE BEEN SUSPICIOUS.
MOB WAS REALLY UPSET.
I NEEDED TO SHUT IT DOWN. AND THEY WEREN'T EVIL SPIRITS, WERE THEY?
TRUE. I TRIED TO RILE HIM UP, BUT HE WOULDN'T TURN BAD.
WHAT? WHAT THE HELL WERE YOU...
WHY ARE YOU TREMBLING?
...
...JUST A YAWN.
JUST A YAWN, HUH. YOU TWO ARE HARDLY ALIKE.
IT REALLY PAINS ME THAT I LIED TO A CLIENT, THOUGH...
LIAR.

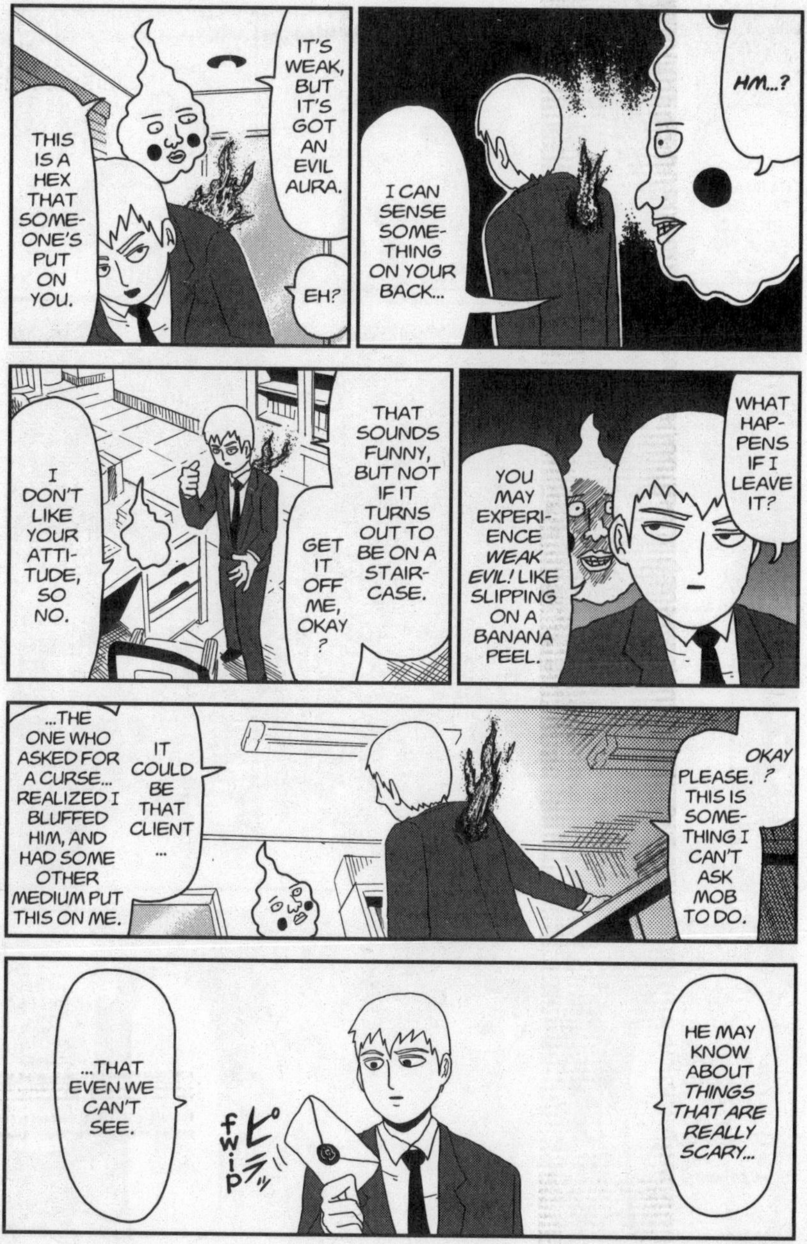
HM...?
I CAN SENSE SOMETHING ON YOUR BACK...
IT'S WEAK, BUT IT'S GOT AN EVIL AURA.
EH?
THIS IS A HEX THAT SOMEONE'S PUT ON YOU.
WHAT HAPPENS IF I LEAVE IT?
YOU MAY EXPERIENCE *WEAK EVIL!* LIKE SLIPPING ON A BANANA PEEL.
THAT SOUNDS FUNNY, BUT NOT IF IT TURNS OUT TO BE ON A STAIRCASE.
GET IT OFF ME, OKAY?
I DON'T LIKE YOUR ATTITUDE, SO NO.
OKAY?
PLEASE. THIS IS SOMETHING I CAN'T ASK MOB TO DO.
IT COULD BE THAT CLIENT...
...THE ONE WHO ASKED FOR A CURSE... REALIZED I BLUFFED HIM, AND HAD SOME OTHER MEDIUM PUT THIS ON ME.
HE MAY KNOW ABOUT *THINGS THAT ARE REALLY SCARY...*
fwip
...THAT EVEN WE CAN'T SEE.

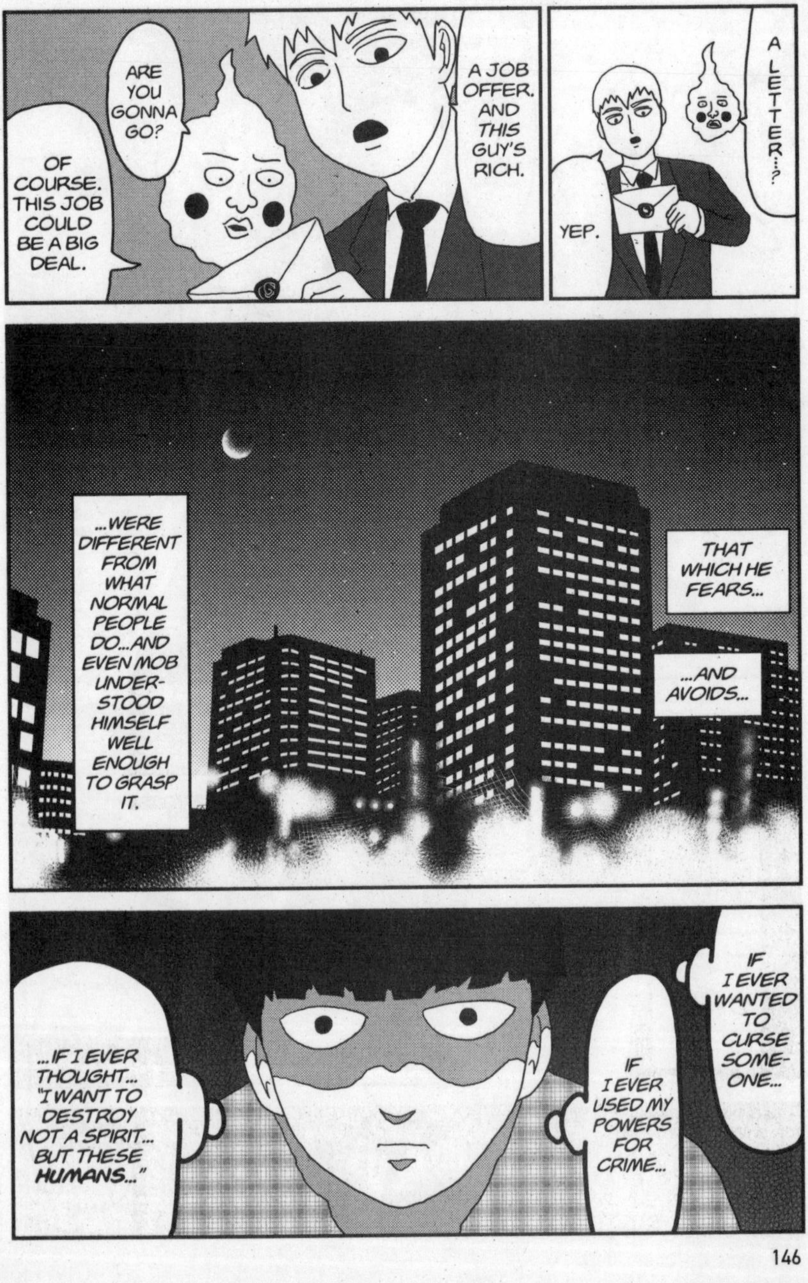
A LETTER...?
YEP.
A JOB OFFER. AND THIS GUY'S RICH.
ARE YOU GONNA GO?
OF COURSE. THIS JOB COULD BE A BIG DEAL.
THAT WHICH HE FEARS...
...AND AVOIDS...
...WERE DIFFERENT FROM WHAT NORMAL PEOPLE DO...AND EVEN MOB UNDER-STOOD HIMSELF WELL ENOUGH TO GRASP IT.
IF I EVER WANTED TO CURSE SOME-ONE...
IF I EVER USED MY POWERS FOR CRIME...
...IF I EVER THOUGHT... "I WANT TO DESTROY NOT A SPIRIT... BUT THESE **HUMANS**..."

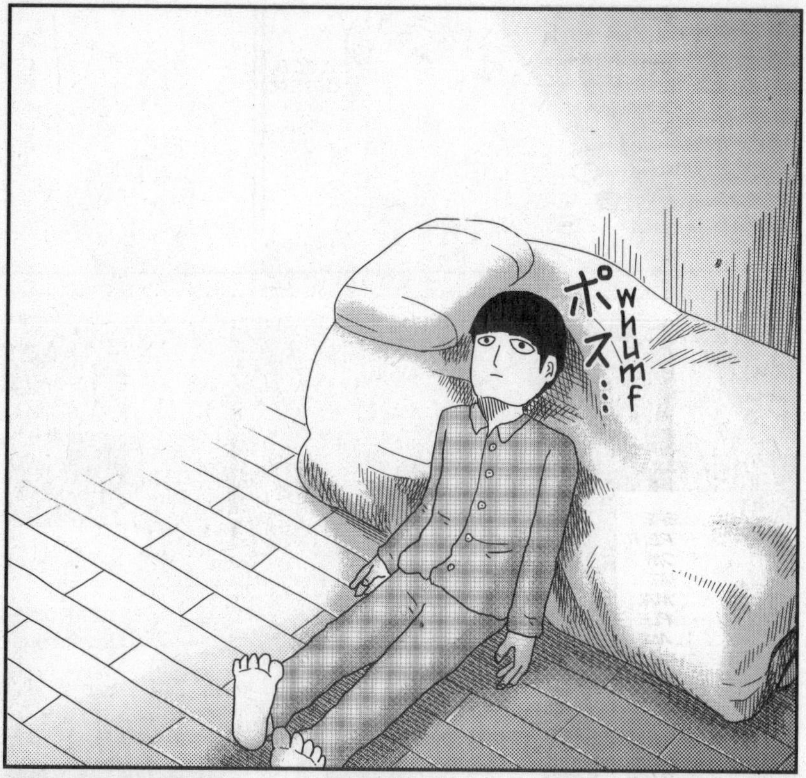
ポス…
whumf

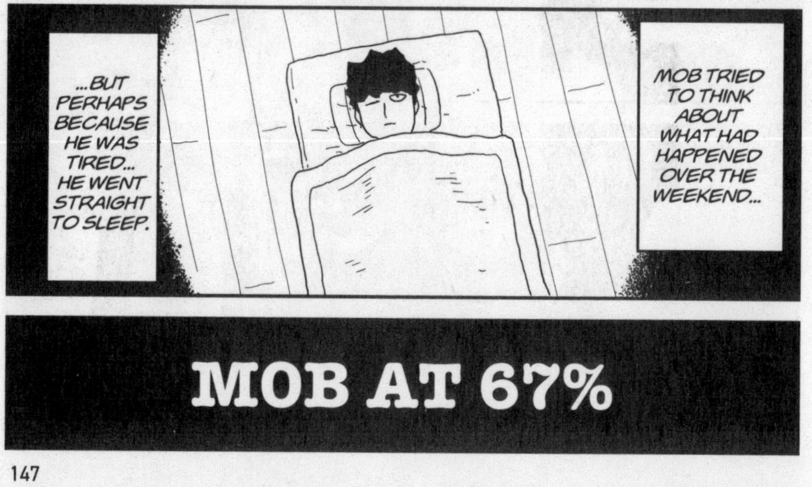
MOB TRIED TO THINK ABOUT WHAT HAD HAPPENED OVER THE WEEKEND...
...BUT PERHAPS BECAUSE HE WAS TIRED... HE WENT STRAIGHT TO SLEEP.

MOB AT 67%

CHAPTER 59: A BIG DEAL

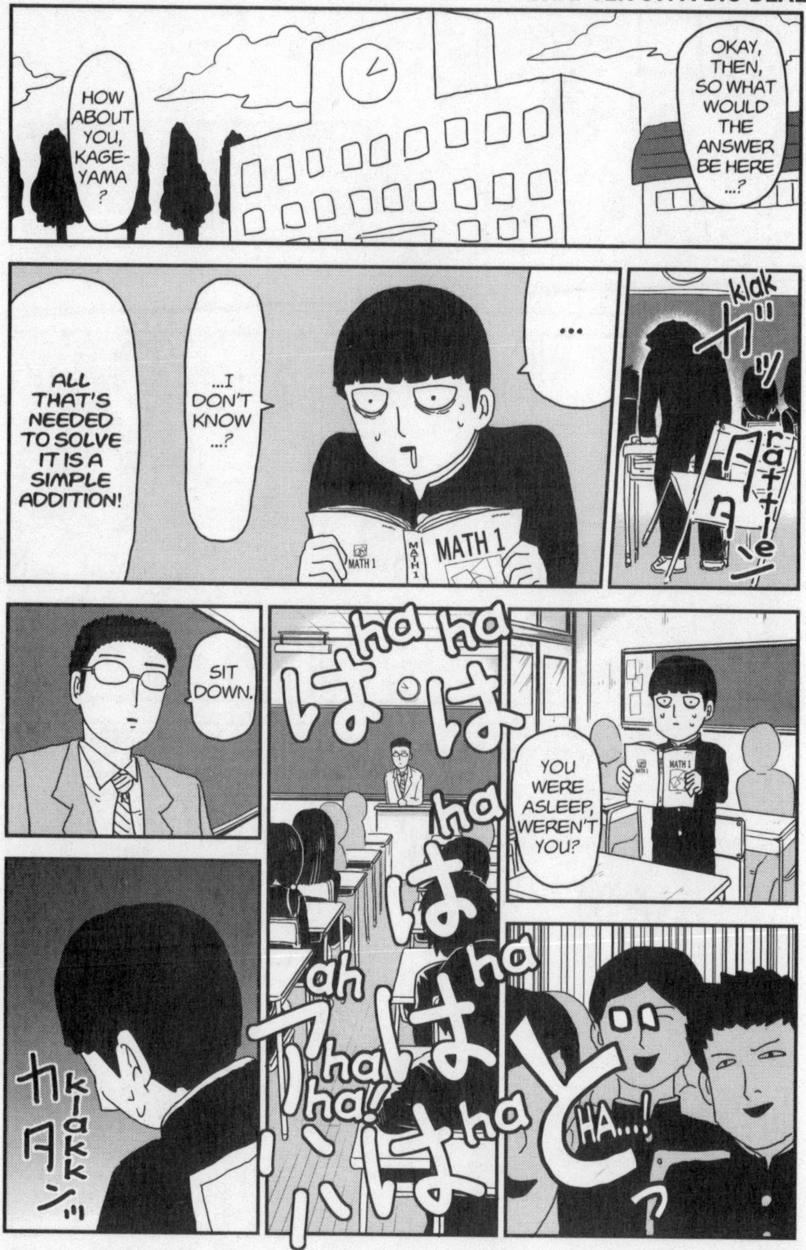
OKAY, THEN, SO WHAT WOULD THE ANSWER BE HERE ...?
HOW ABOUT YOU, KAGE-YAMA?
klak
rattle
...
...I DON'T KNOW ...?
ALL THAT'S NEEDED TO SOLVE IT IS A SIMPLE ADDITION!
YOU WERE ASLEEP, WEREN'T YOU?
ha ha
ha
ha
ah
ha!
ha
ha
SIT DOWN.
HA...!
klakk

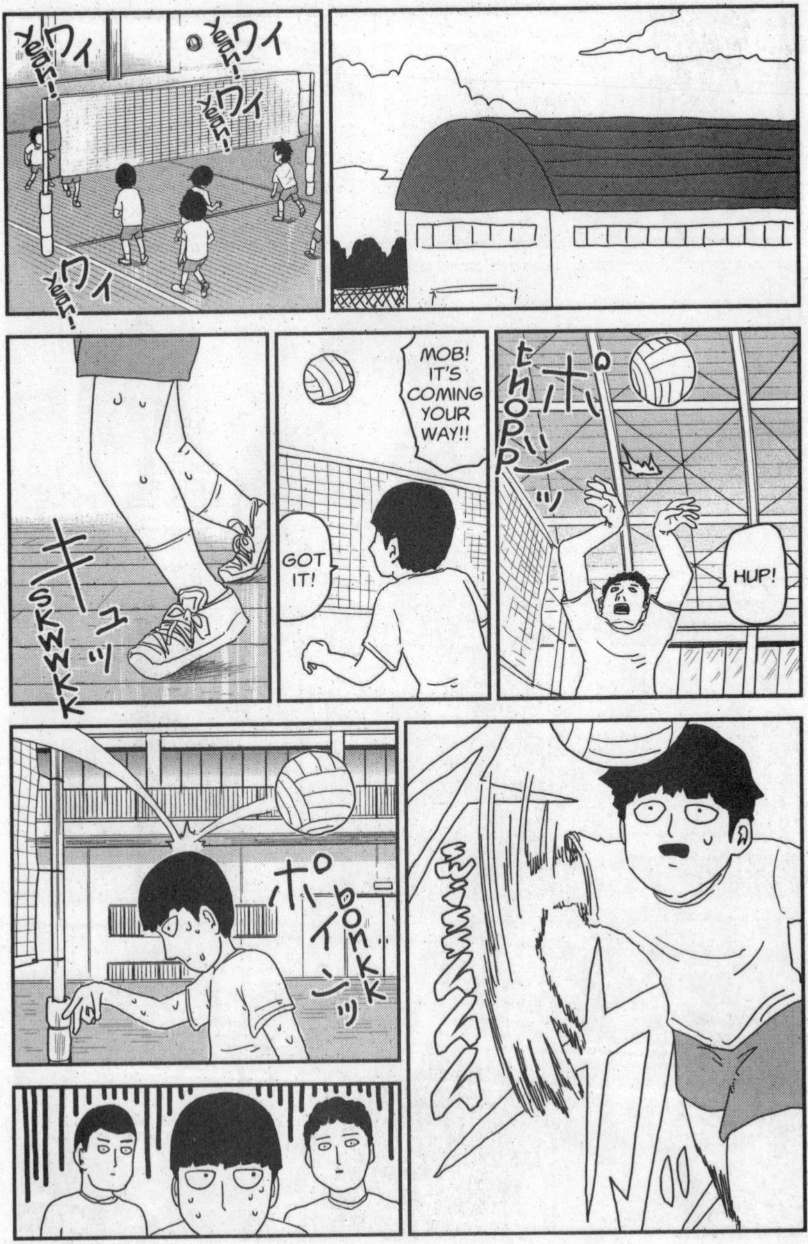
ワイ Yeah!
ワイ Yeah!
ワイ Yeah!
ワイ Yeah!
THOP
HUP!
MOB! IT'S COMING YOUR WAY!!
GOT IT!
キュッ SKWWKK
BONKK

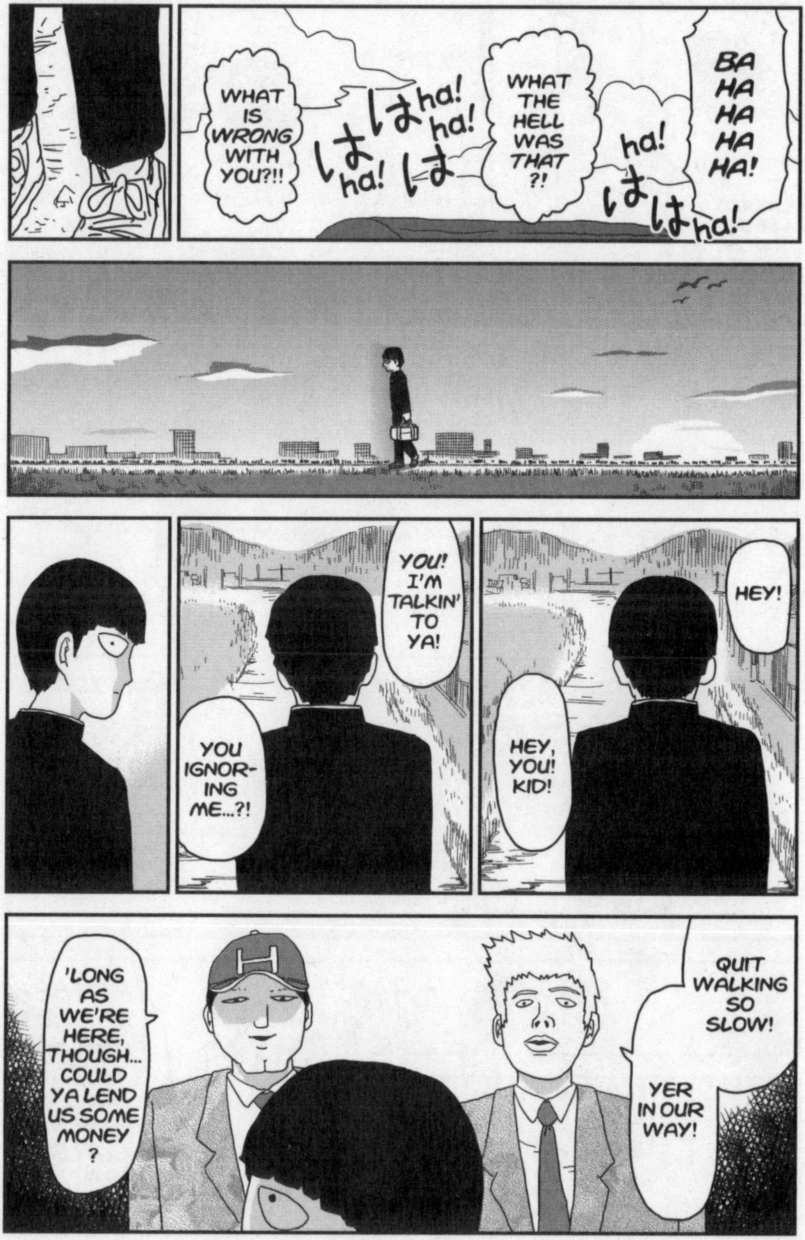
BA HA HA HA HA!
ha! はは ha!
WHAT THE HELL WAS THAT?!
はは ha! ha! ha!
WHAT IS WRONG WITH YOU?!!
HEY!
HEY, YOU! KID!
YOU! I'M TALKIN' TO YA!
YOU IGNORING ME...?!
QUIT WALKING SO SLOW!
YER IN OUR WAY!
'LONG AS WE'RE HERE, THOUGH... COULD YA LEND US SOME MONEY?

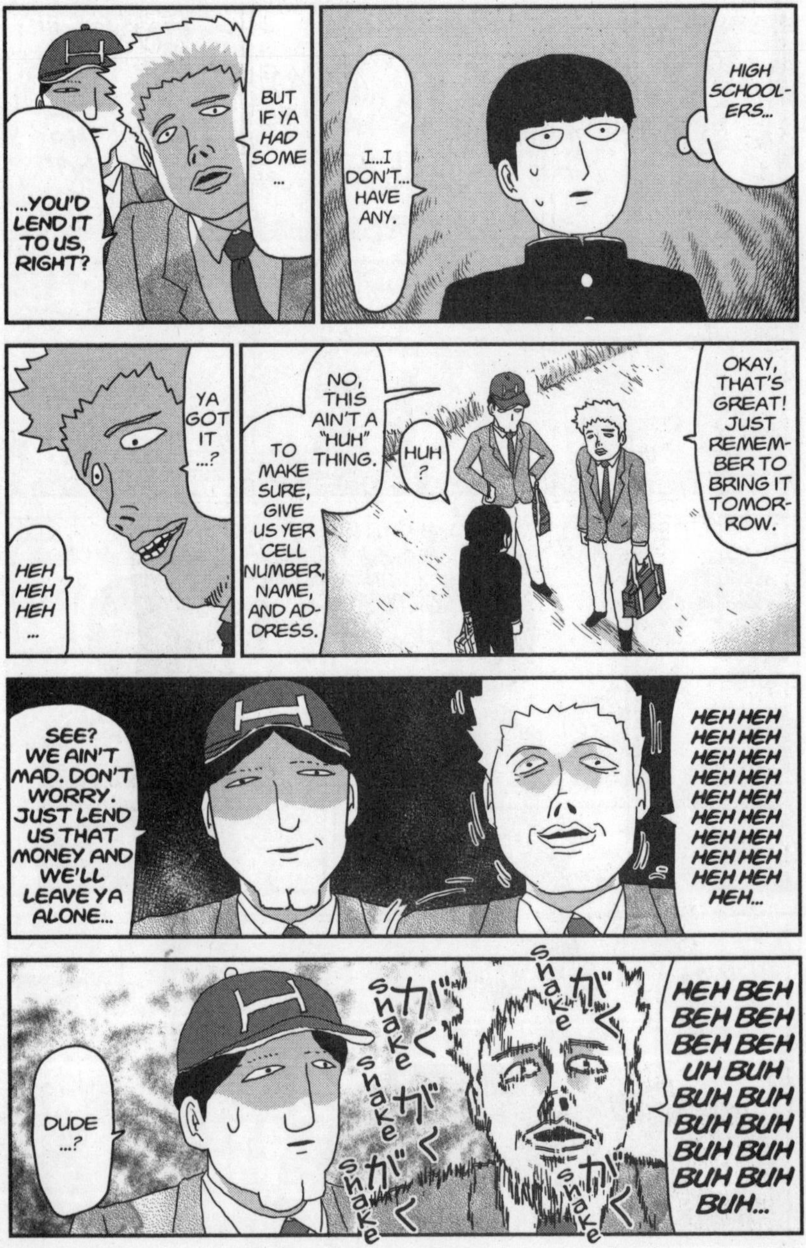
HIGH SCHOOLERS...
I...I DON'T... HAVE ANY.
BUT IF YA HAD SOME ...
...YOU'D LEND IT TO US, RIGHT?
OKAY, THAT'S GREAT! JUST REMEMBER TO BRING IT TOMORROW.
HUH?
NO, THIS AIN'T A "HUH" THING.
TO MAKE SURE, GIVE US YER CELL NUMBER, NAME, AND ADDRESS.
YA GOT IT ...?
HEH HEH HEH ...
HEH HEH HEH HEH HEH HEH HEH HEH HEH HEH HEH HEH HEH HEH HEH HEH HEH HEH HEH...
SEE? WE AIN'T MAD. DON'T WORRY. JUST LEND US THAT MONEY AND WE'LL LEAVE YA ALONE...
HEH BEH BEH BEH BEH BEH UH BUH BUH BUH BUH BUH BUH BUH BUH BUH BUH...
がく shake
がく shake
がく shake
がく shake
がく shake
DUDE ...?

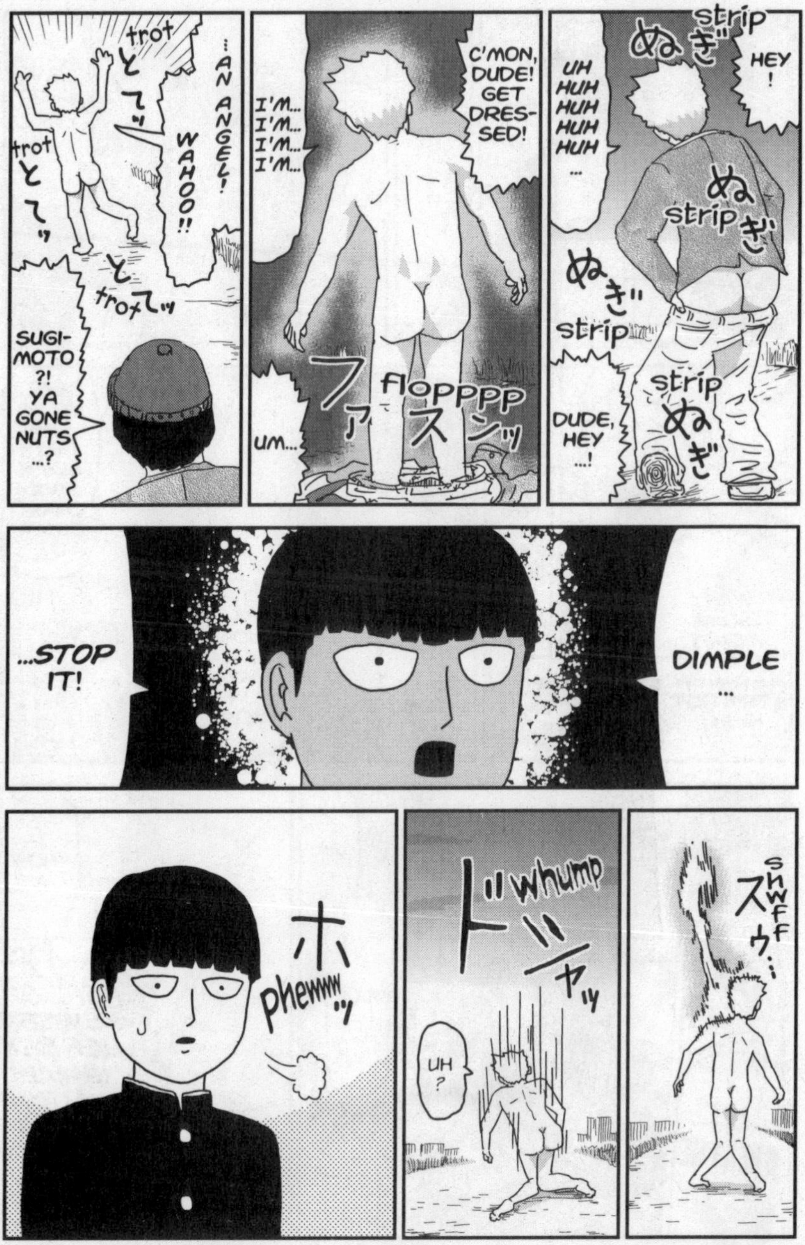
strip ぬぎ
HEY!
UH HUH HUH HUH HUH ...
ぬぎ strip
ぬぎ strip
strip ぬぎ
DUDE, HEY ...!
C'MON, DUDE! GET DRES-SED!
I'M... I'M... I'M... I'M...
floppppp ファスンッ
UM...
trot とてッ
...AN ANGEL!
WAHOO!!
trot とてッ
trot とてッ
SUGI-MOTO?! YA GONE NUTS ...?
DIMPLE ...
...STOP IT!
shwff スウ…
whump ドシャッ
UH?
phewww ホッ

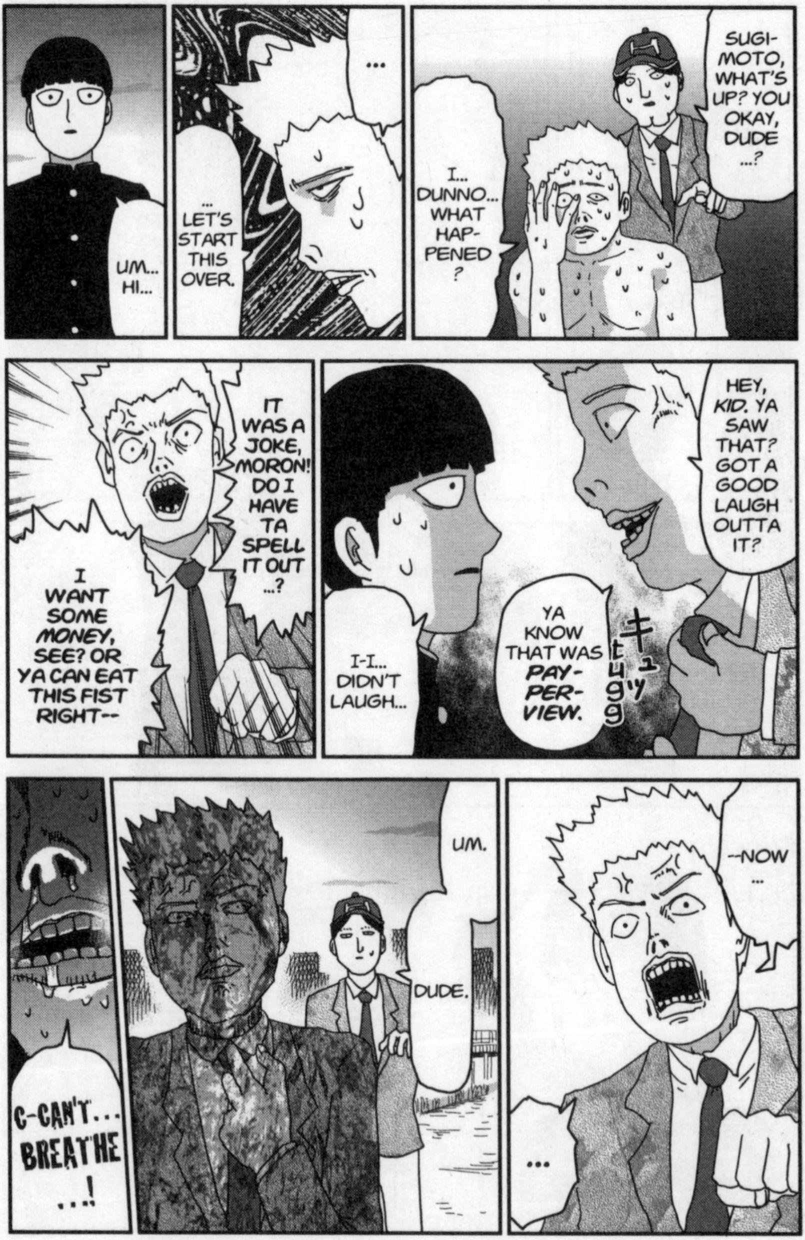
SUGI-MOTO, WHAT'S UP? YOU OKAY, DUDE ...?
I... DUNNO... WHAT HAP-PENED?
...
... LET'S START THIS OVER.
UM... HI...
HEY, KID. YA SAW THAT? GOT A GOOD LAUGH OUTTA IT?
キュ
tugg
YA KNOW THAT WAS PAY-PER-VIEW.
I-I... DIDN'T LAUGH...
IT WAS A JOKE, MORON! DO I HAVE TA SPELL IT OUT ...?
I WANT SOME MONEY, SEE? OR YA CAN EAT THIS FIST RIGHT--
--NOW ...
...
UM.
DUDE.
C-CAN'T... BREATHE ...!

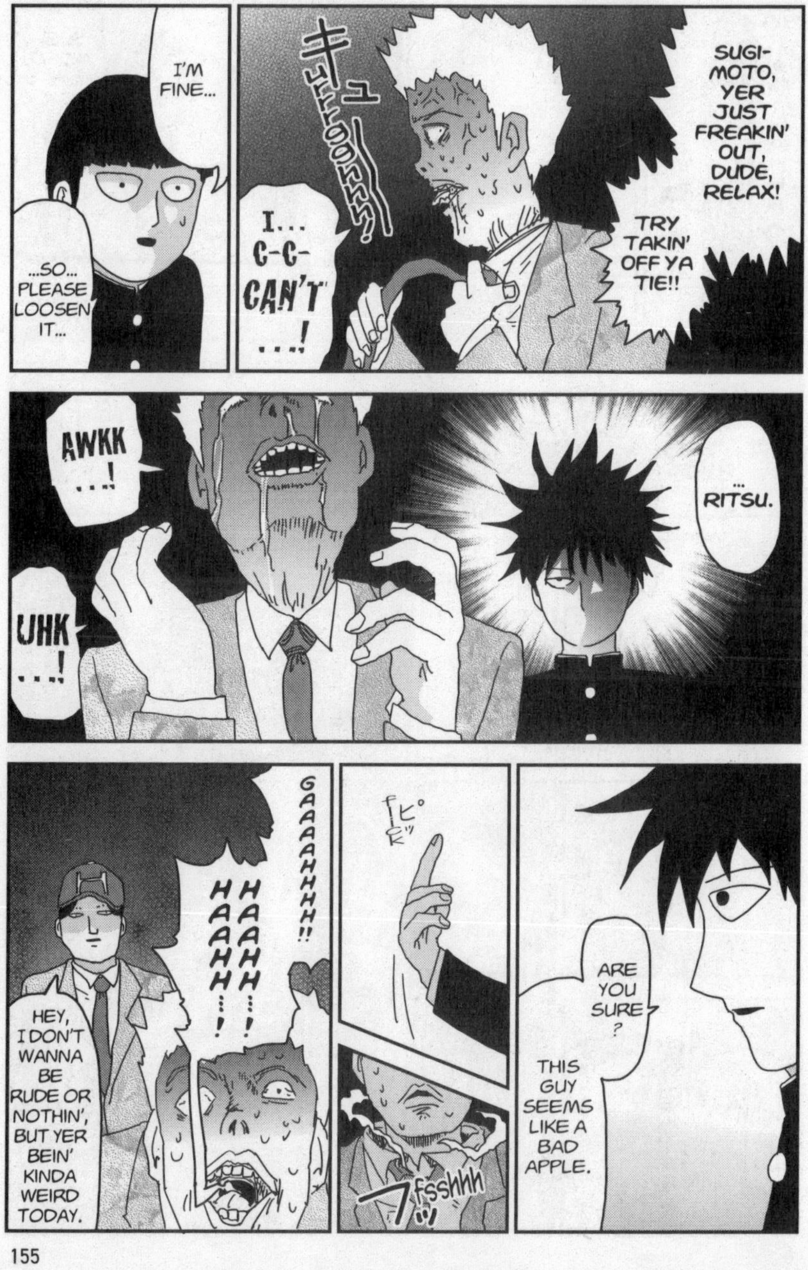
SUGI-MOTO, YER JUST FREAKIN' OUT, DUDE, RELAX!
TRY TAKIN' OFF YA TIE!!
キュ Urrggnnh!
I... C-C-CAN'T ...!
I'M FINE...
...SO... PLEASE LOOSEN IT...
... RITSU.
AWKK ...!
UHK ...!
ARE YOU SURE?
THIS GUY SEEMS LIKE A BAD APPLE.
ピッ flick
フッ fsshhh
GAAAAHHHH!!
HAAAHH...!
HAAAHH...!
HEY, I DON'T WANNA BE RUDE OR NOTHIN', BUT YER BEIN' KINDA WEIRD TODAY.

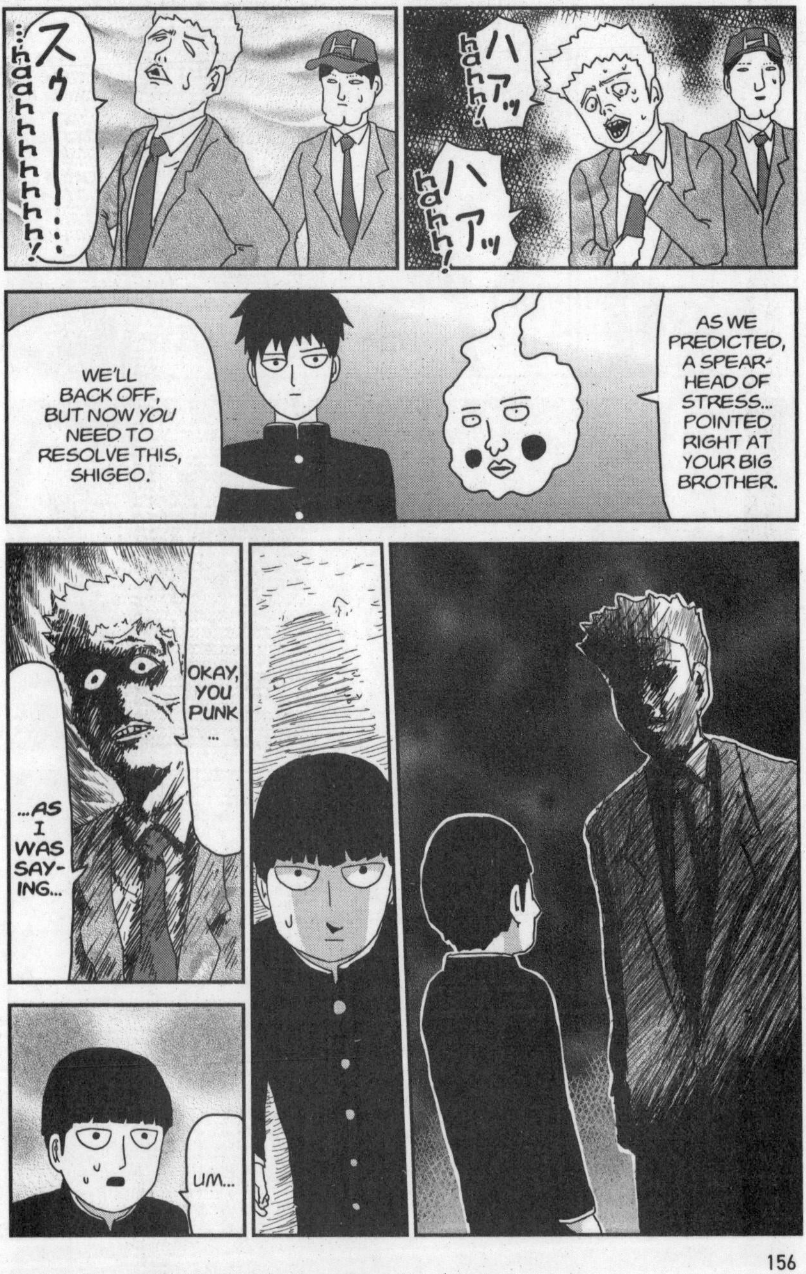
ハアッ
hahh!
ハアッ
hahh!
スゥー……
...haaahhhhhhhh!
AS WE PREDICTED, A SPEAR-HEAD OF STRESS... POINTED RIGHT AT YOUR BIG BROTHER.
WE'LL BACK OFF, BUT NOW *YOU* NEED TO RESOLVE THIS, SHIGEO.
OKAY, YOU PUNK ...
...AS I WAS SAY-ING...
UM...

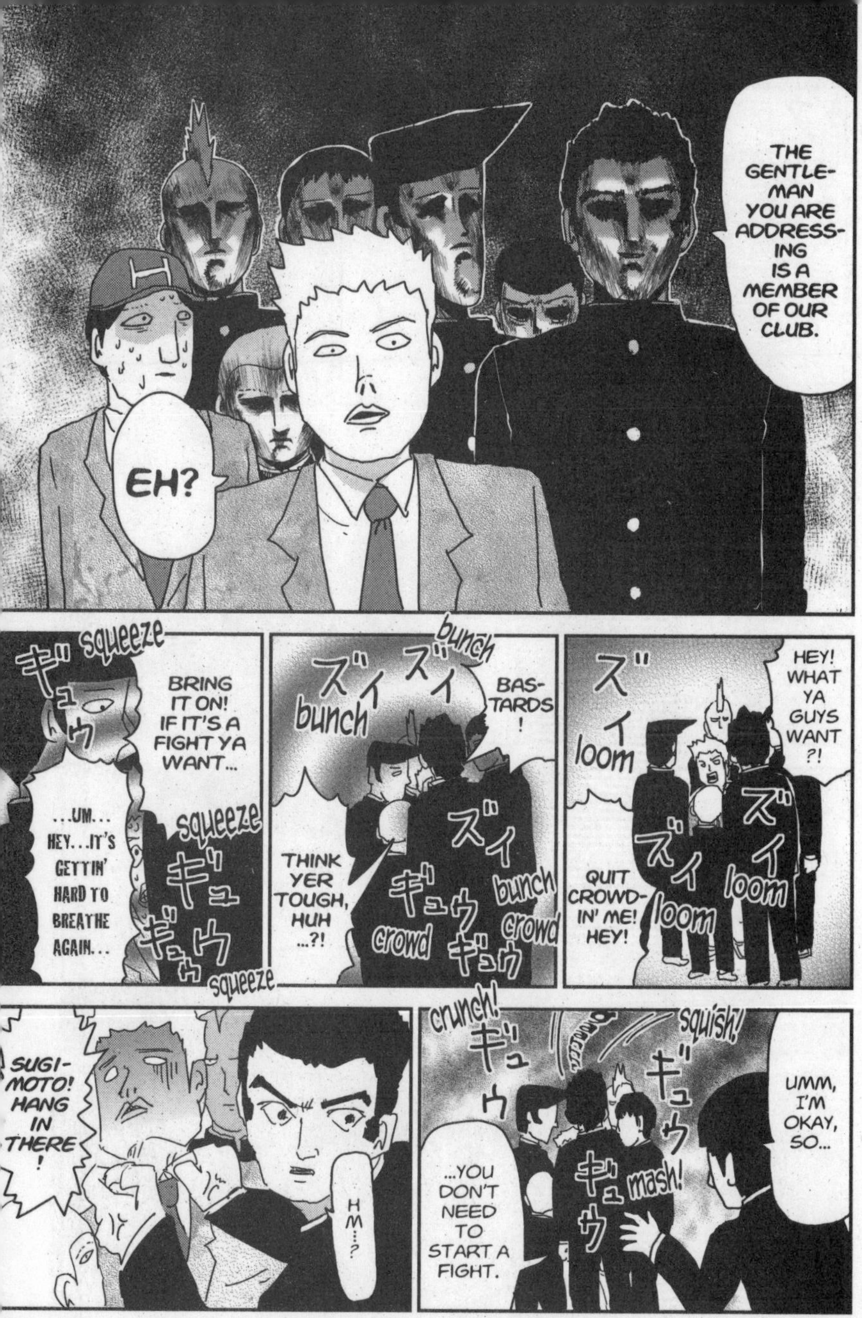
THE GENTLE-MAN YOU ARE ADDRESS-ING IS A MEMBER OF OUR CLUB.
EH?
HEY! WHAT YA GUYS WANT?!
ズイ loom
ズイ loom
ズイ loom
QUIT CROWD-IN' ME! HEY!
ズイ bunch
ズイ bunch
BAS-TARDS!
ズイ bunch
ギュウ crowd
ギュウ crowd
THINK YER TOUGH, HUH ...?!
ギュウ squeeze
BRING IT ON! IF IT'S A FIGHT YA WANT...
ギュ squeeze
ギュウ squeeze
...UM... HEY...IT'S GETTIN' HARD TO BREATHE AGAIN...
UMM, I'M OKAY, SO...
ギュウ squish!
ギュウ crunch!
ギュウ mash!
...YOU DON'T NEED TO START A FIGHT.
HM...?
SUGI-MOTO! HANG IN THERE!

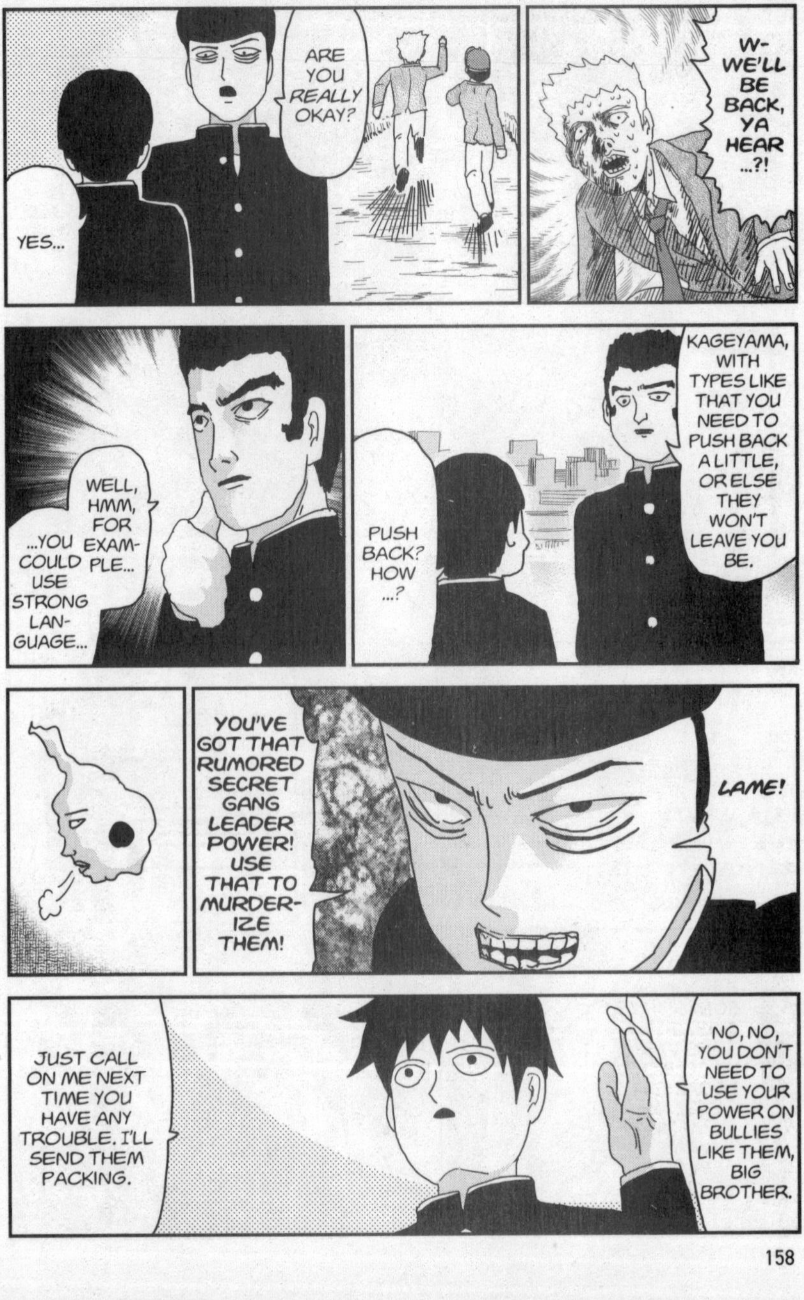
W-WE'LL BE BACK, YA HEAR ...?!
ARE YOU REALLY OKAY?
YES...
KAGEYAMA, WITH TYPES LIKE THAT YOU NEED TO PUSH BACK A LITTLE, OR ELSE THEY WON'T LEAVE YOU BE.
PUSH BACK? HOW ...?
WELL, HMM, FOR EXAMPLE...
...YOU COULD USE STRONG LANGUAGE...
YOU'VE GOT THAT RUMORED SECRET GANG LEADER POWER! USE THAT TO MURDERIZE THEM!
LAME!
JUST CALL ON ME NEXT TIME YOU HAVE ANY TROUBLE. I'LL SEND THEM PACKING.
NO, NO, YOU DON'T NEED TO USE YOUR POWER ON BULLIES LIKE THEM, BIG BROTHER.

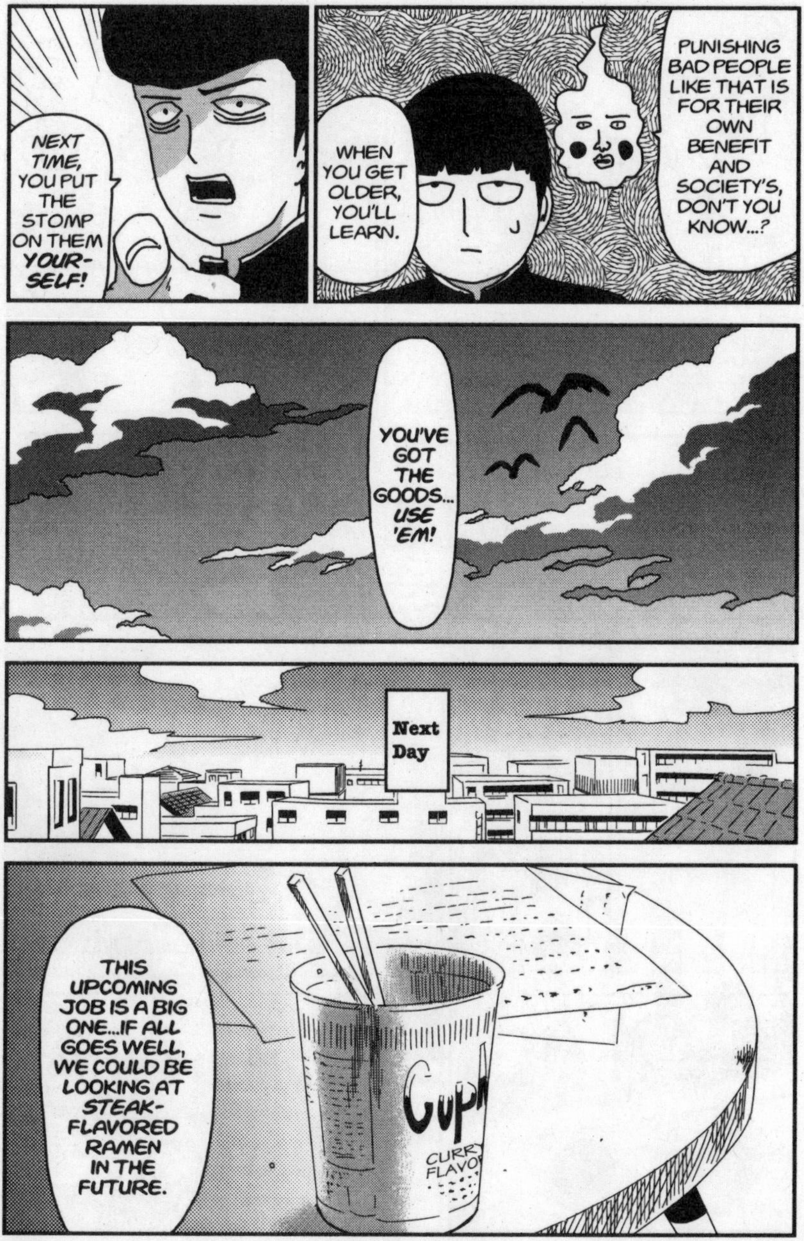
PUNISHING BAD PEOPLE LIKE THAT IS FOR THEIR OWN BENEFIT AND SOCIETY'S, DON'T YOU KNOW...?
WHEN YOU GET OLDER, YOU'LL LEARN.
NEXT TIME, YOU PUT THE STOMP ON THEM *YOURSELF!*
YOU'VE GOT THE GOODS... *USE 'EM!*
Next Day
THIS UPCOMING JOB IS A BIG ONE...IF ALL GOES WELL, WE COULD BE LOOKING AT *STEAK-FLAVORED* RAMEN IN THE FUTURE.

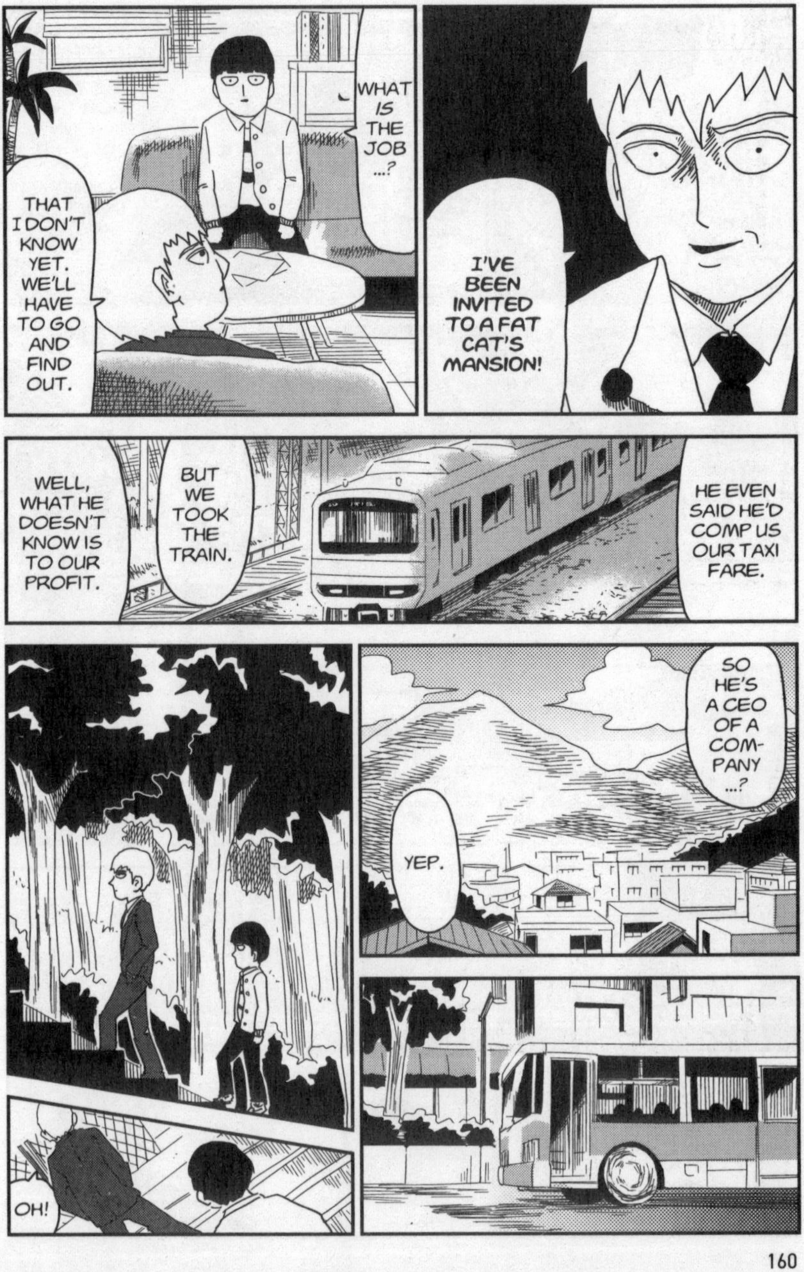
I'VE BEEN INVITED TO A FAT CAT'S MANSION!
WHAT IS THE JOB ...?
THAT I DON'T KNOW YET. WE'LL HAVE TO GO AND FIND OUT.
HE EVEN SAID HE'D COMP US OUR TAXI FARE.
BUT WE TOOK THE TRAIN.
WELL, WHAT HE DOESN'T KNOW IS TO OUR PROFIT.
SO HE'S A CEO OF A COMPANY ...?
YEP.
OH!

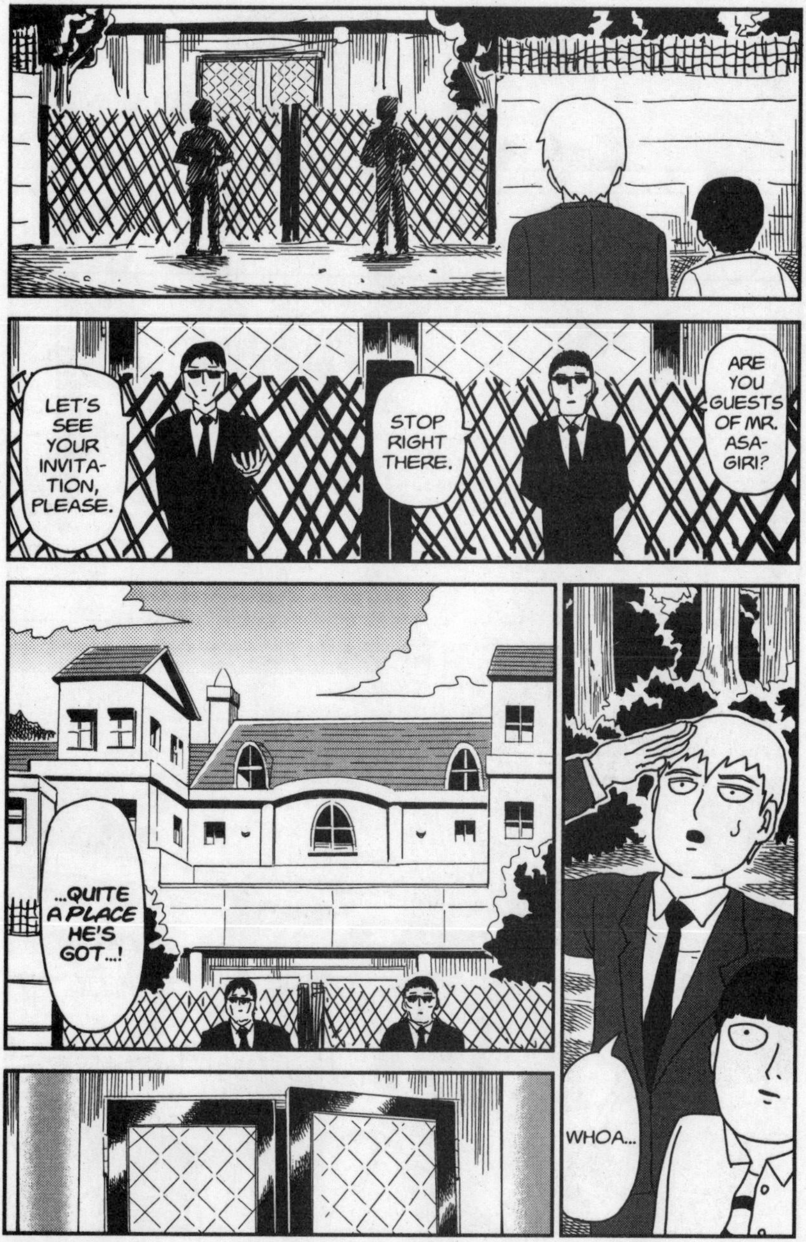
ARE YOU GUESTS OF MR. ASA-GIRI?
STOP RIGHT THERE.
LET'S SEE YOUR INVITA-TION, PLEASE.
WHOA...
...QUITE A PLACE HE'S GOT...!

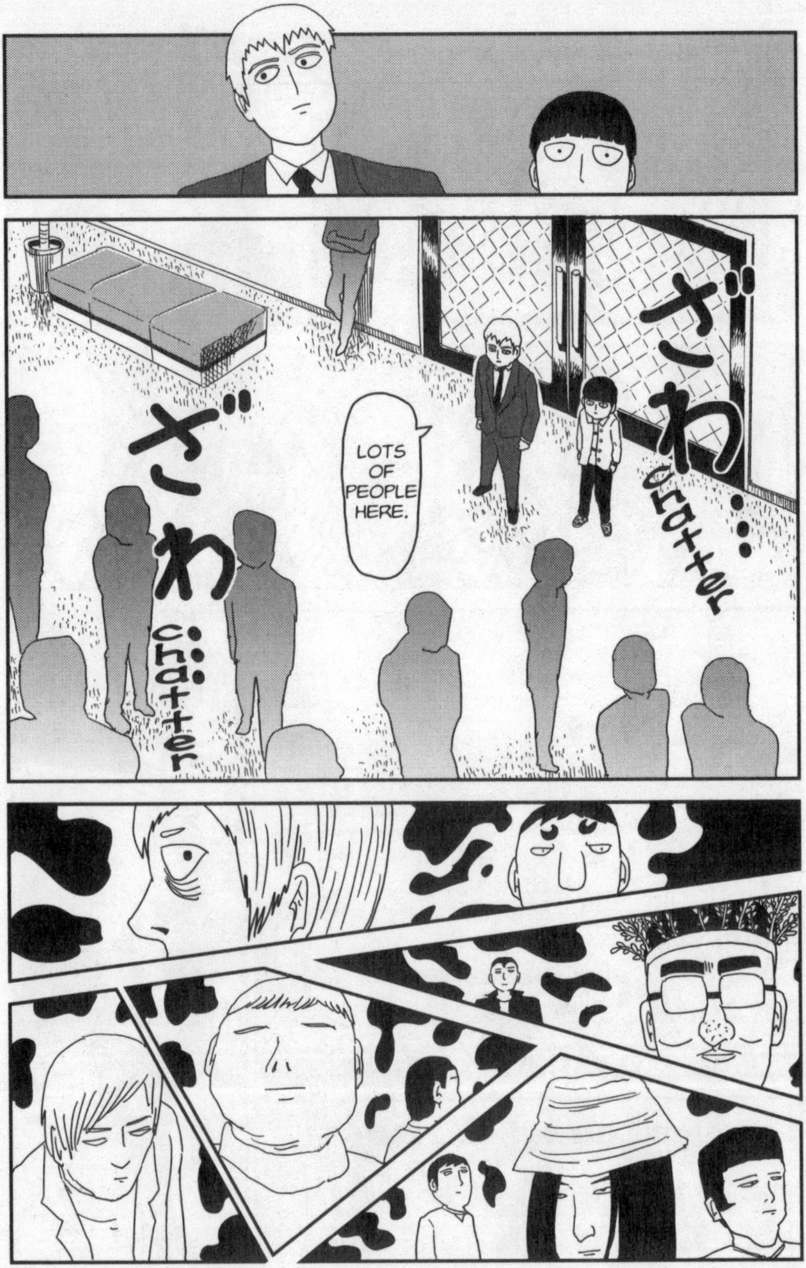
ざわ…
chatter
LOTS OF PEOPLE HERE.
ざわ
chatter

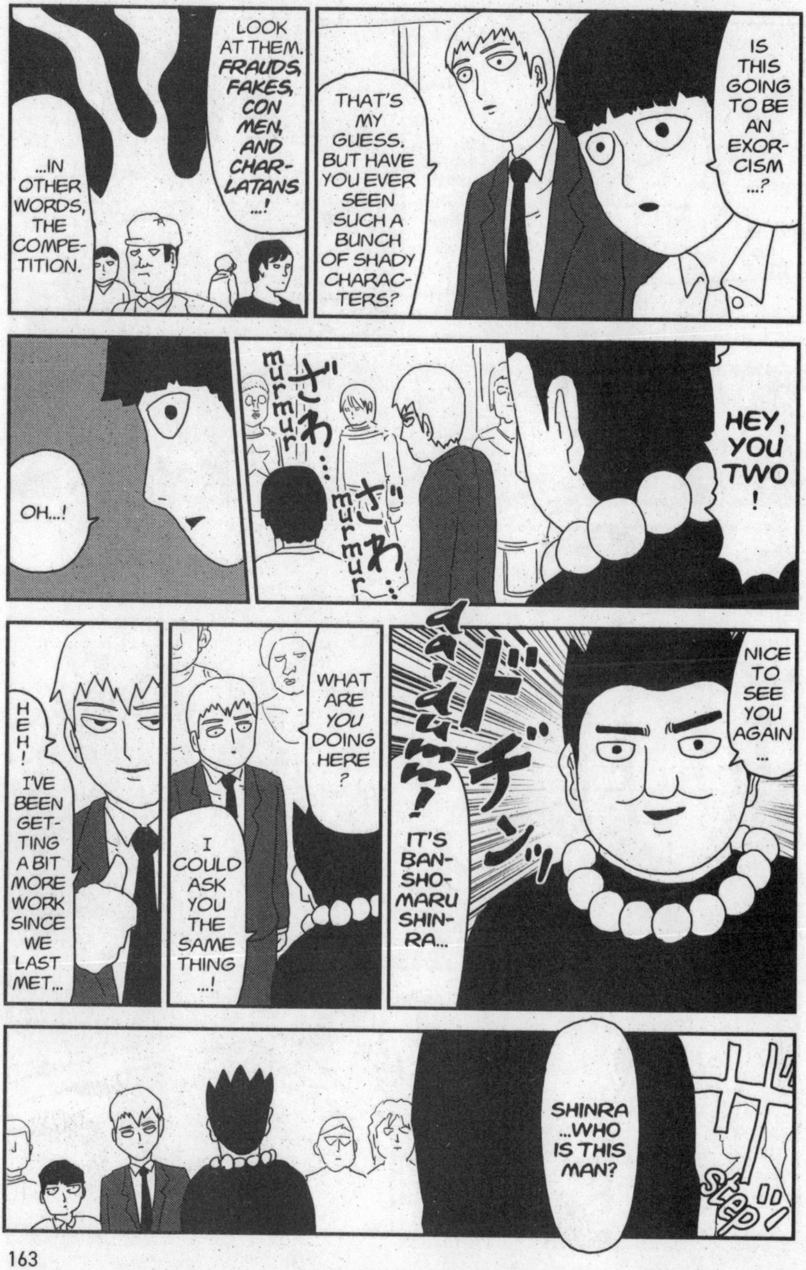

IS THIS GOING TO BE AN EXORCISM ...?
THAT'S MY GUESS. BUT HAVE YOU EVER SEEN SUCH A BUNCH OF SHADY CHARACTERS?
LOOK AT THEM. FRAUDS, FAKES, CON MEN, AND CHARLATANS ...!
...IN OTHER WORDS, THE COMPETITION.
HEY, YOU TWO!
ざわ murmur
ざわ murmur
OH...!
NICE TO SEE YOU AGAIN ...
ドチン
ズイムッ!
IT'S BANSHOMARU SHINRA...
WHAT ARE YOU DOING HERE?
I COULD ASK YOU THE SAME THING ...!
HEH! I'VE BEEN GETTING A BIT MORE WORK SINCE WE LAST MET...
ザッ step!
SHINRA ...WHO IS THIS MAN?

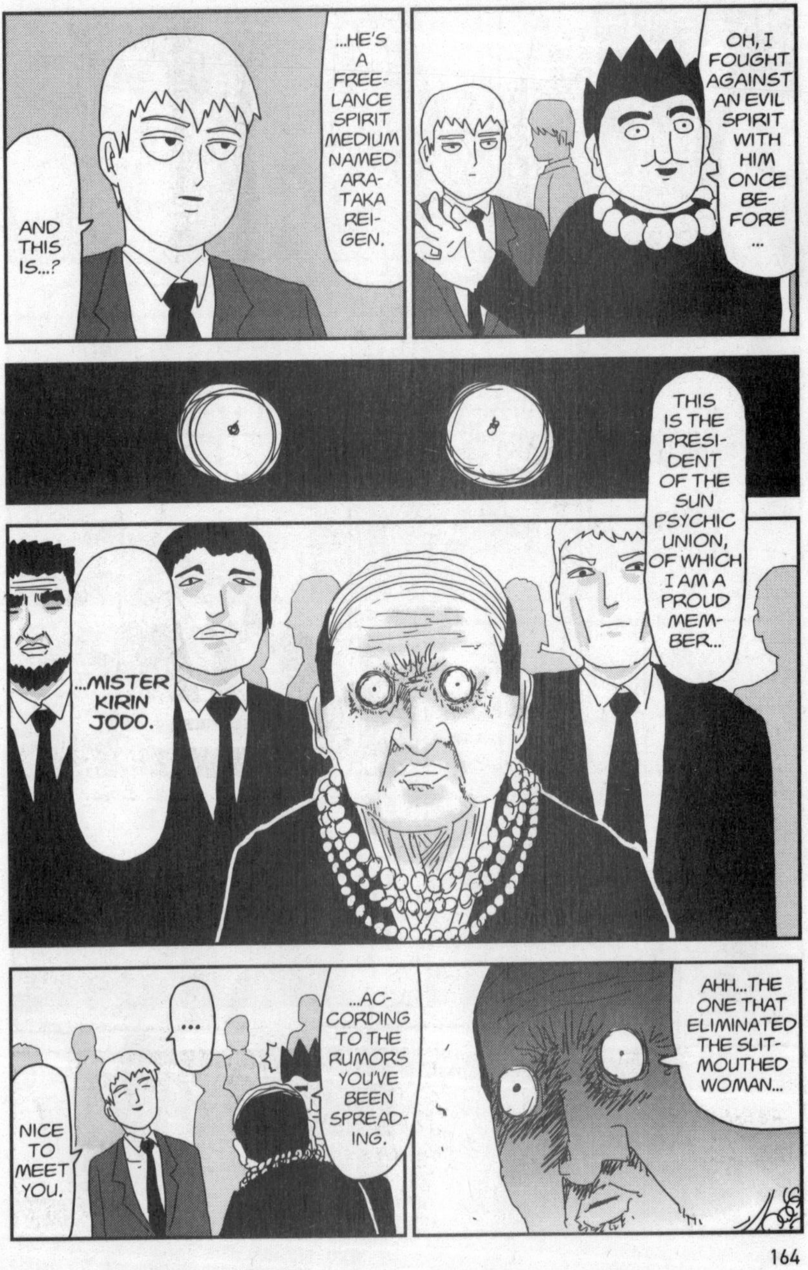
OH, I FOUGHT AGAINST AN EVIL SPIRIT WITH HIM ONCE BEFORE...
AND THIS IS...?
...HE'S A FREE-LANCE SPIRIT MEDIUM NAMED ARA-TAKA REI-GEN.
THIS IS THE PRESI-DENT OF THE SUN PSYCHIC UNION, OF WHICH I AM A PROUD MEM-BER...
...MISTER KIRIN JODO.
AHH...THE ONE THAT ELIMINATED THE SLIT-MOUTHED WOMAN...
...AC-CORDING TO THE RUMORS YOU'VE BEEN SPREAD-ING.
...
NICE TO MEET YOU.

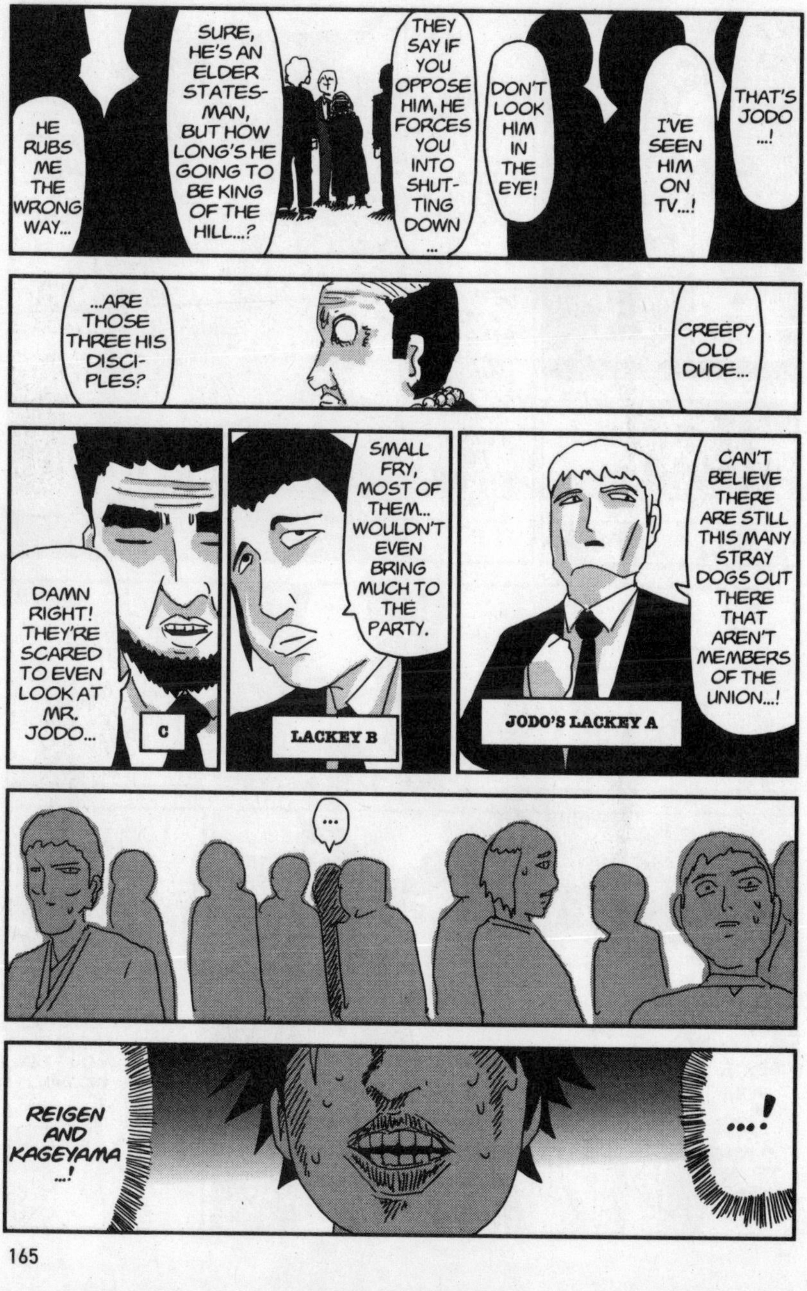
THAT'S JODO ...!
I'VE SEEN HIM ON TV...!
DON'T LOOK HIM IN THE EYE!
THEY SAY IF YOU OPPOSE HIM, HE FORCES YOU INTO SHUTTING DOWN ...
SURE, HE'S AN ELDER STATESMAN, BUT HOW LONG'S HE GOING TO BE KING OF THE HILL...?
HE RUBS ME THE WRONG WAY...
CREEPY OLD DUDE...
...ARE THOSE THREE HIS DISCIPLES?
CAN'T BELIEVE THERE ARE STILL THIS MANY STRAY DOGS OUT THERE THAT AREN'T MEMBERS OF THE UNION...!
JODO'S LACKEY A
SMALL FRY, MOST OF THEM... WOULDN'T EVEN BRING MUCH TO THE PARTY.
LACKEY B
DAMN RIGHT! THEY'RE SCARED TO EVEN LOOK AT MR. JODO...
C
...
...!
REIGEN AND KAGEYAMA ...!

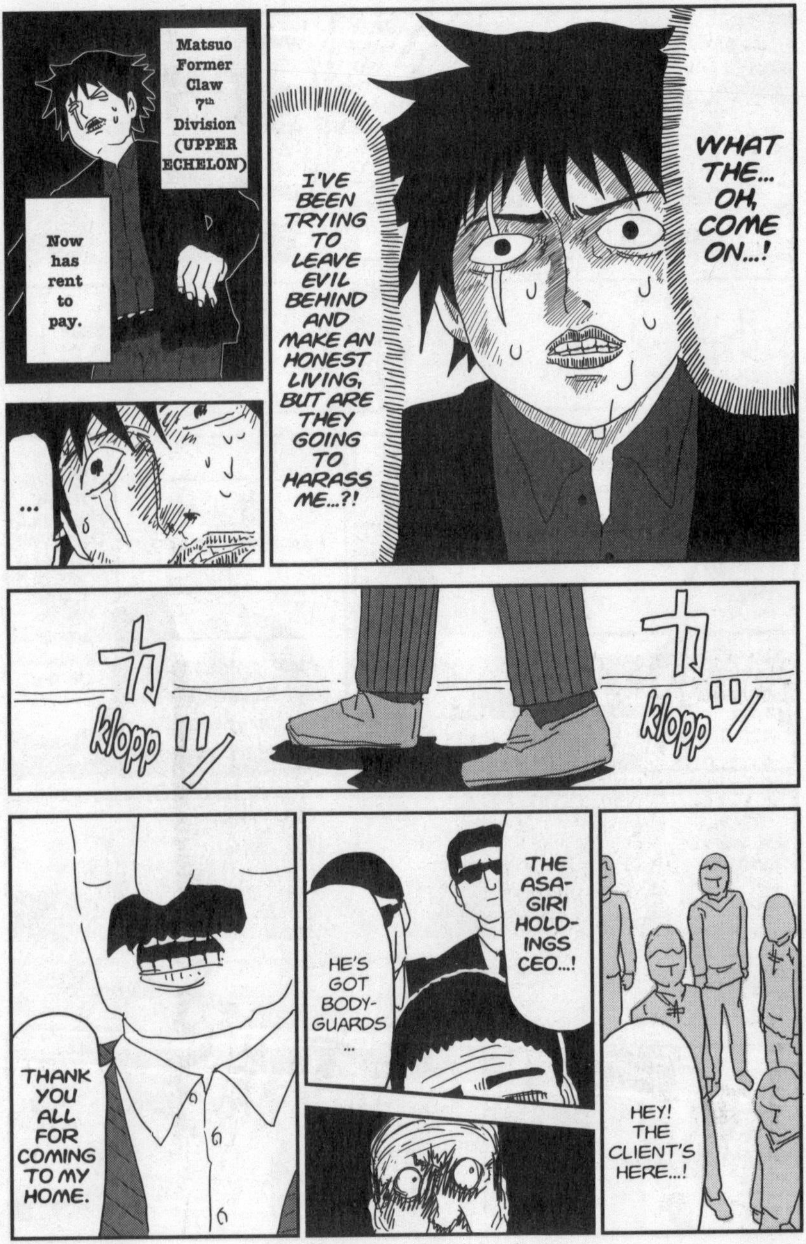
WHAT THE... OH, COME ON...!
I'VE BEEN TRYING TO LEAVE EVIL BEHIND AND MAKE AN HONEST LIVING, BUT ARE THEY GOING TO HARASS ME...?!
Matsuo Former Claw 7th Division (UPPER ECHELON)
Now has rent to pay.
...
カッ
klopp
カッ
klopp
HEY! THE CLIENT'S HERE...!
THE ASAGIRI HOLDINGS CEO...!
HE'S GOT BODYGUARDS...
THANK YOU ALL FOR COMING TO MY HOME.

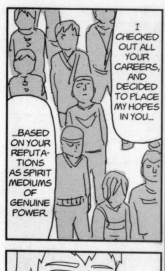

I AM THE ONE...
...WHO ASKED YOU HERE TODAY.
CLIENT MASASHI ASAGIRI
I CHECKED OUT ALL YOUR CAREERS, AND DECIDED TO PLACE MY HOPES IN YOU...
...BASED ON YOUR REPUTATIONS AS SPIRIT MEDIUMS OF GENUINE POWER.
YET EVEN HAVING SAID THAT...
I STILL DO NOT KNOW IF THERE IS ONE AMONG YOU WHO CAN SAVE MY DAUGHTER.
I APPEAL TO YOUR HONOR...
ざわ
murmur
ざわ
murmur
...THAT WHAT I SHOW YOU NOW REMAINS IN CONFIDENCE.
ウィーン...
VWeeeeeeeen

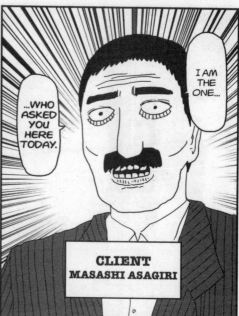

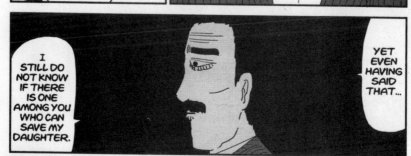

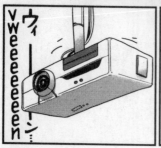

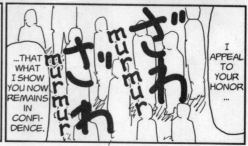

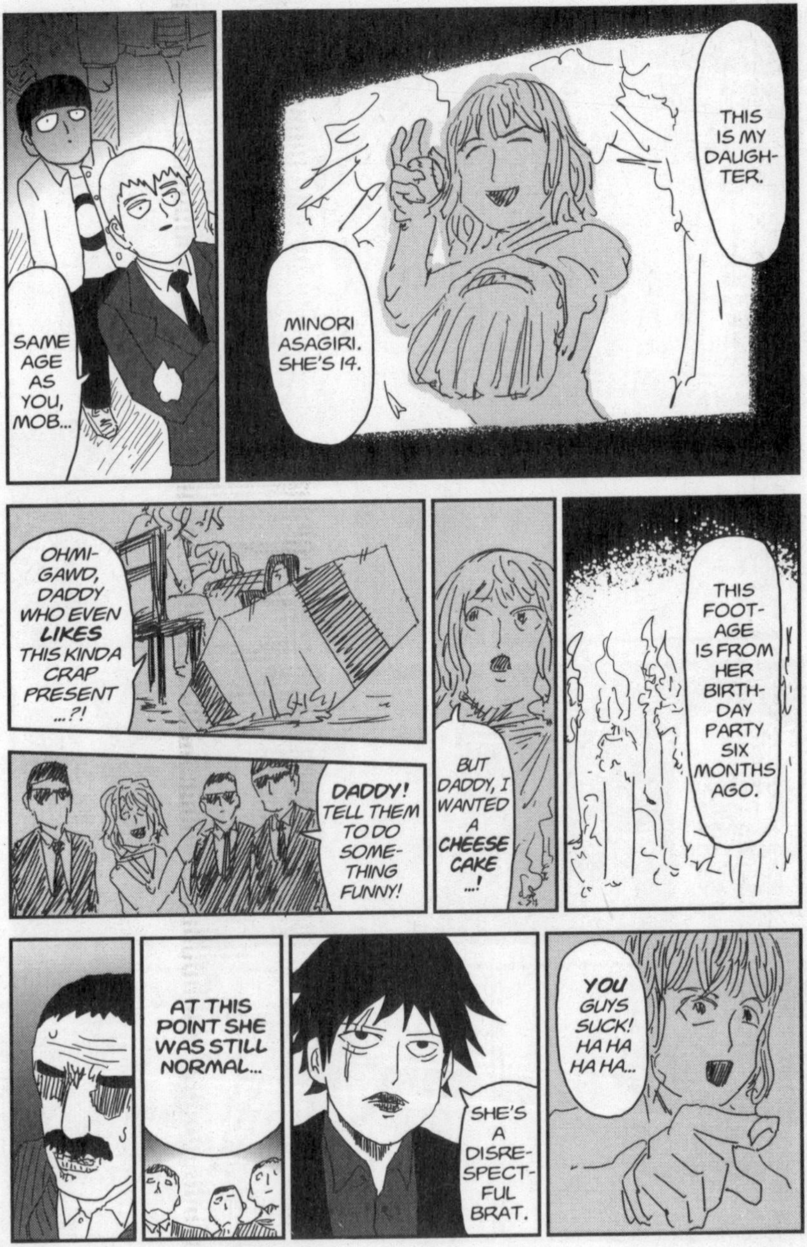
THIS IS MY DAUGHTER.
MINORI ASAGIRI. SHE'S 14.
SAME AGE AS YOU, MOB...
THIS FOOTAGE IS FROM HER BIRTHDAY PARTY SIX MONTHS AGO.
BUT DADDY, I WANTED A CHEESE CAKE ...!
OHMIGAWD, DADDY WHO EVEN LIKES THIS KINDA CRAP PRESENT ...?!
DADDY! TELL THEM TO DO SOMETHING FUNNY!
YOU GUYS SUCK! HA HA HA HA...
SHE'S A DISRESPECTFUL BRAT.
AT THIS POINT SHE WAS STILL NORMAL...

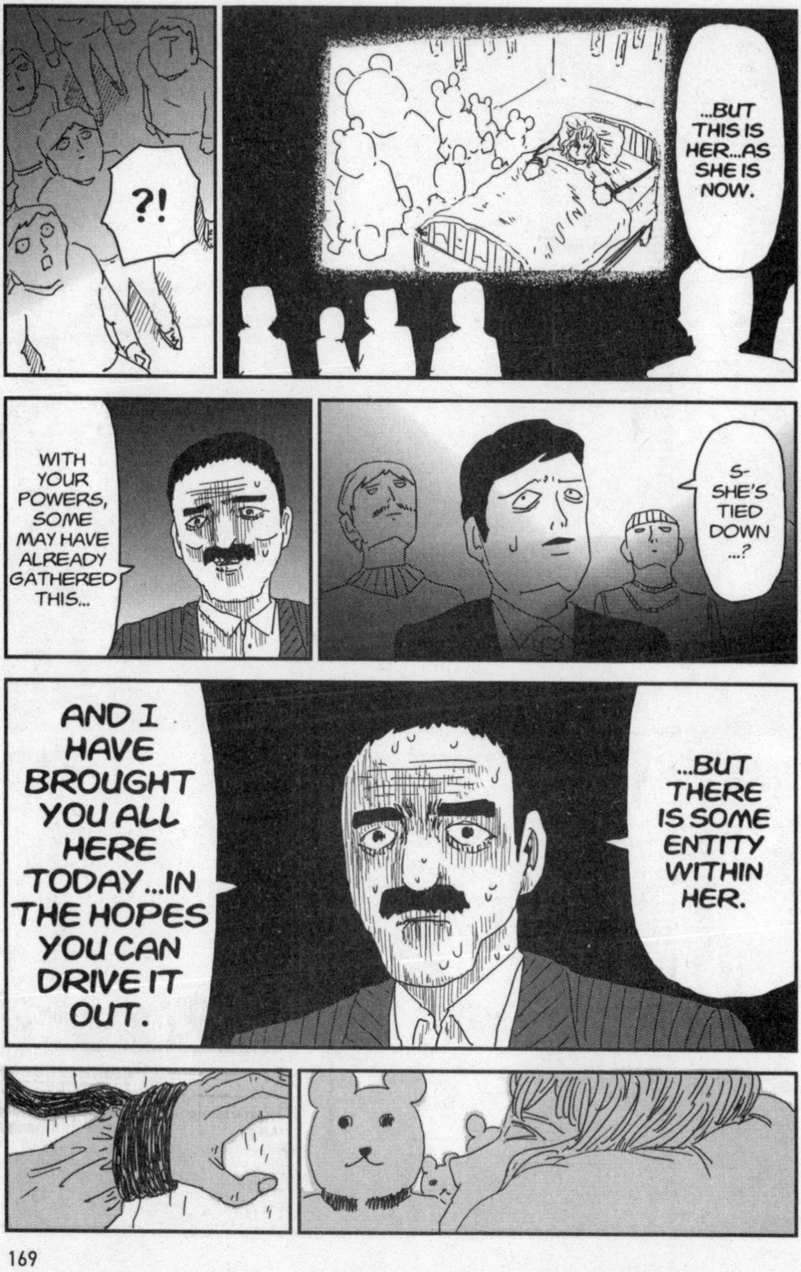
...BUT THIS IS HER...AS SHE IS NOW.
?!
S-SHE'S TIED DOWN ...?
WITH YOUR POWERS, SOME MAY HAVE ALREADY GATHERED THIS...
...BUT THERE IS SOME ENTITY WITHIN HER.
AND I HAVE BROUGHT YOU ALL HERE TODAY...IN THE HOPES YOU CAN DRIVE IT OUT.

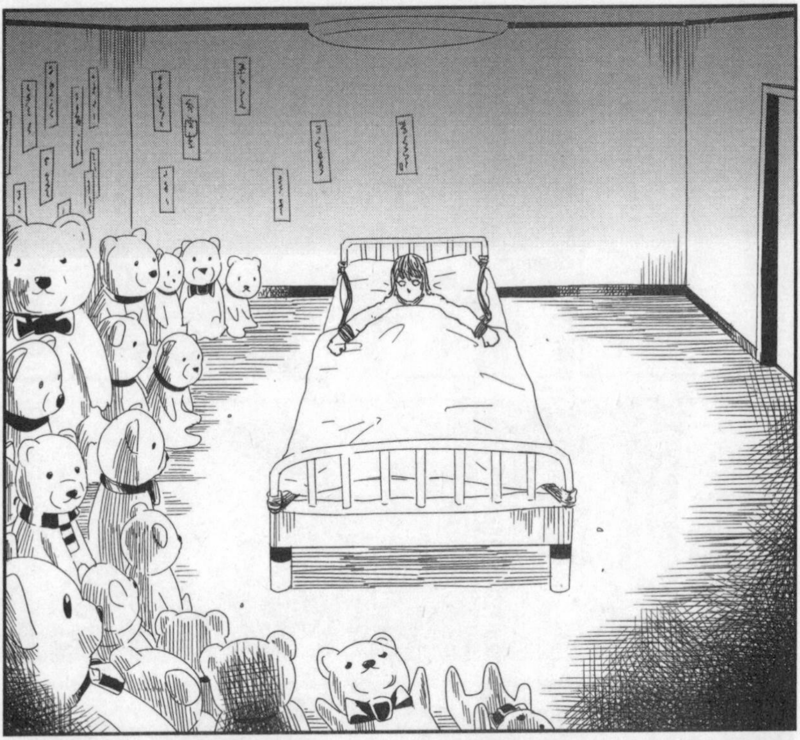

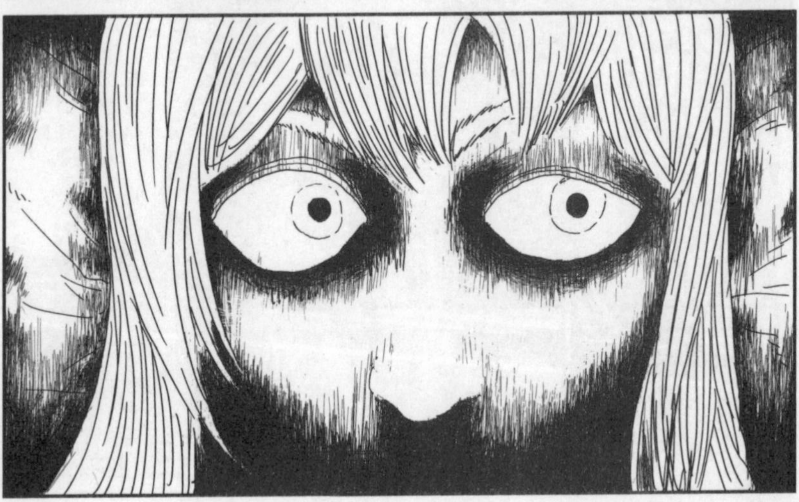

CHAPTER 60: WITHIN

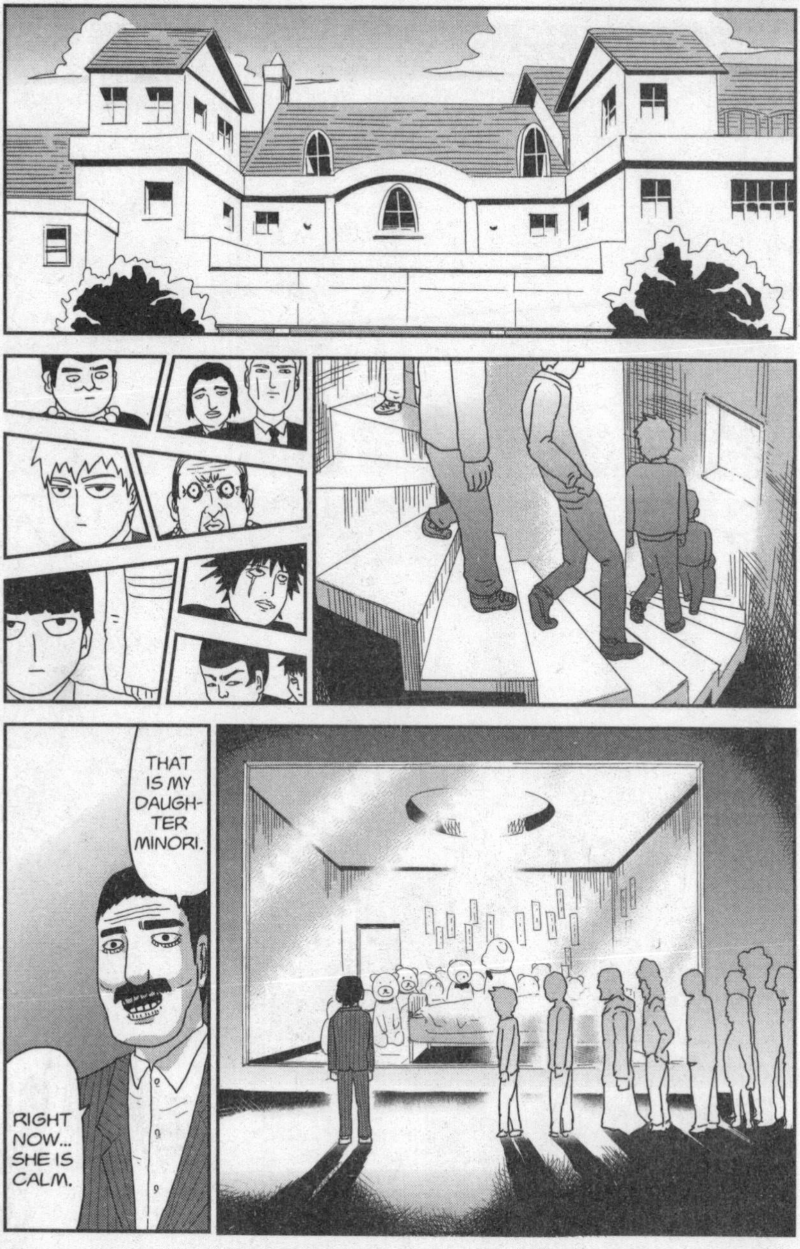
THAT IS MY DAUGHTER MINORI.
RIGHT NOW... SHE IS CALM.

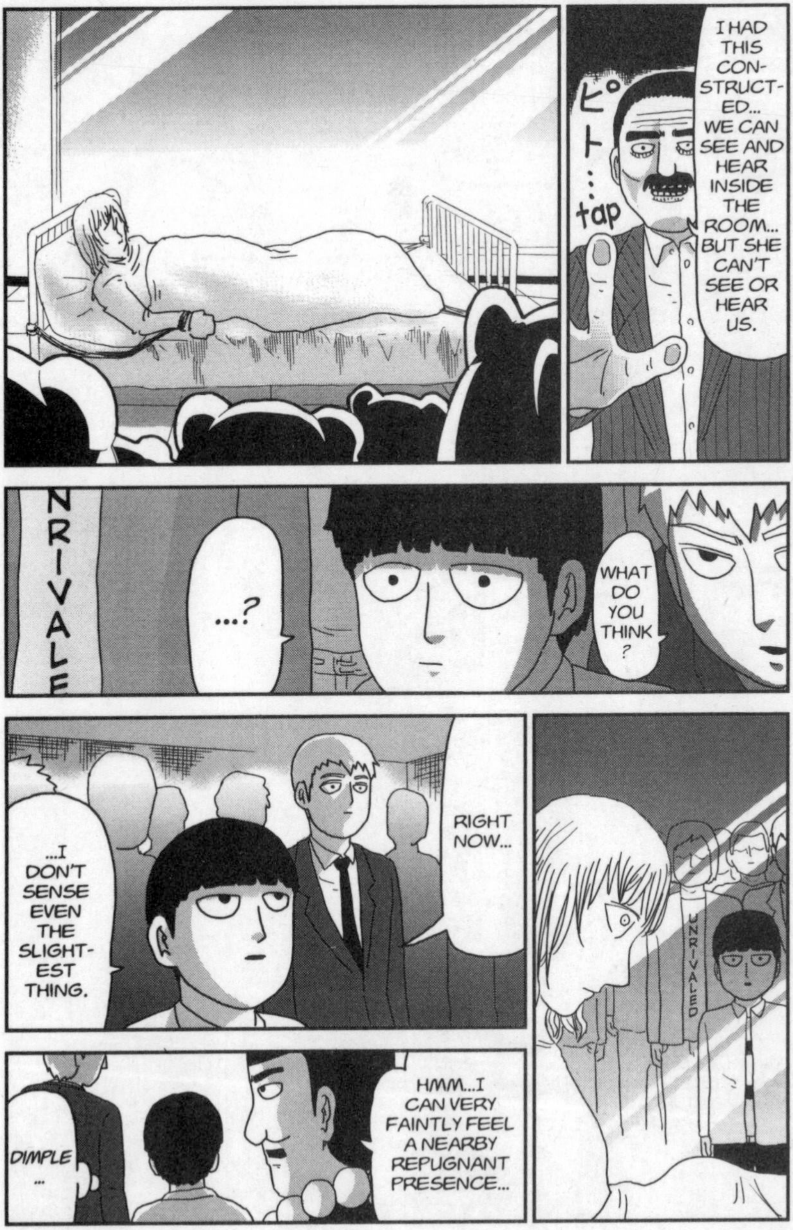
ピ
ト…
tap
I HAD THIS CONSTRUCTED... WE CAN SEE AND HEAR INSIDE THE ROOM... BUT SHE CAN'T SEE OR HEAR US.
WHAT DO YOU THINK?
...?
NRIVALE
UNRIVALED
RIGHT NOW...
...I DON'T SENSE EVEN THE SLIGHTEST THING.
HMM...I CAN VERY FAINTLY FEEL A NEARBY REPUGNANT PRESENCE...
DIMPLE ...

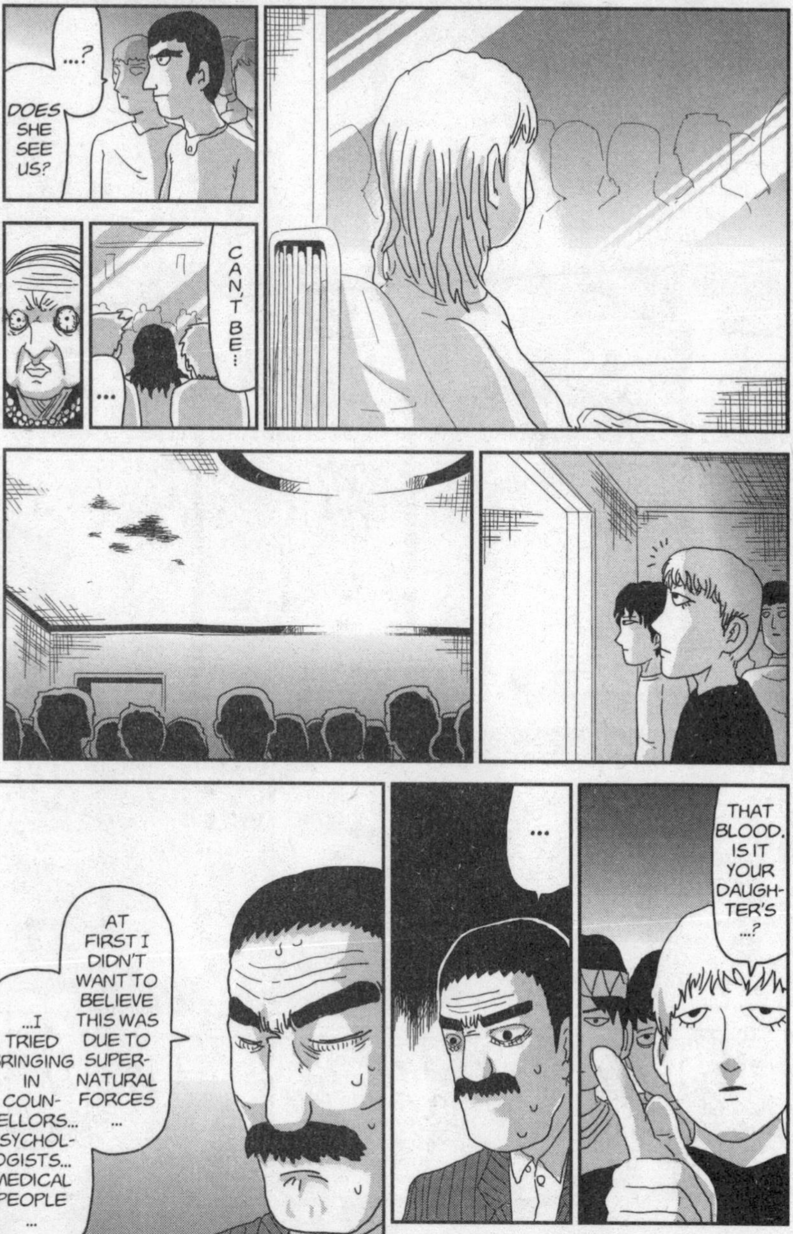
...?
DOES SHE SEE US?
CAN'T BE...
...
THAT BLOOD. IS IT YOUR DAUGHTER'S ...?
...
AT FIRST I DIDN'T WANT TO BELIEVE THIS WAS DUE TO SUPER-NATURAL FORCES ...
...I TRIED BRINGING IN COUN-SELLORS... PSYCHOL-OGISTS... MEDICAL PEOPLE ...

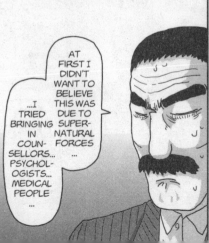

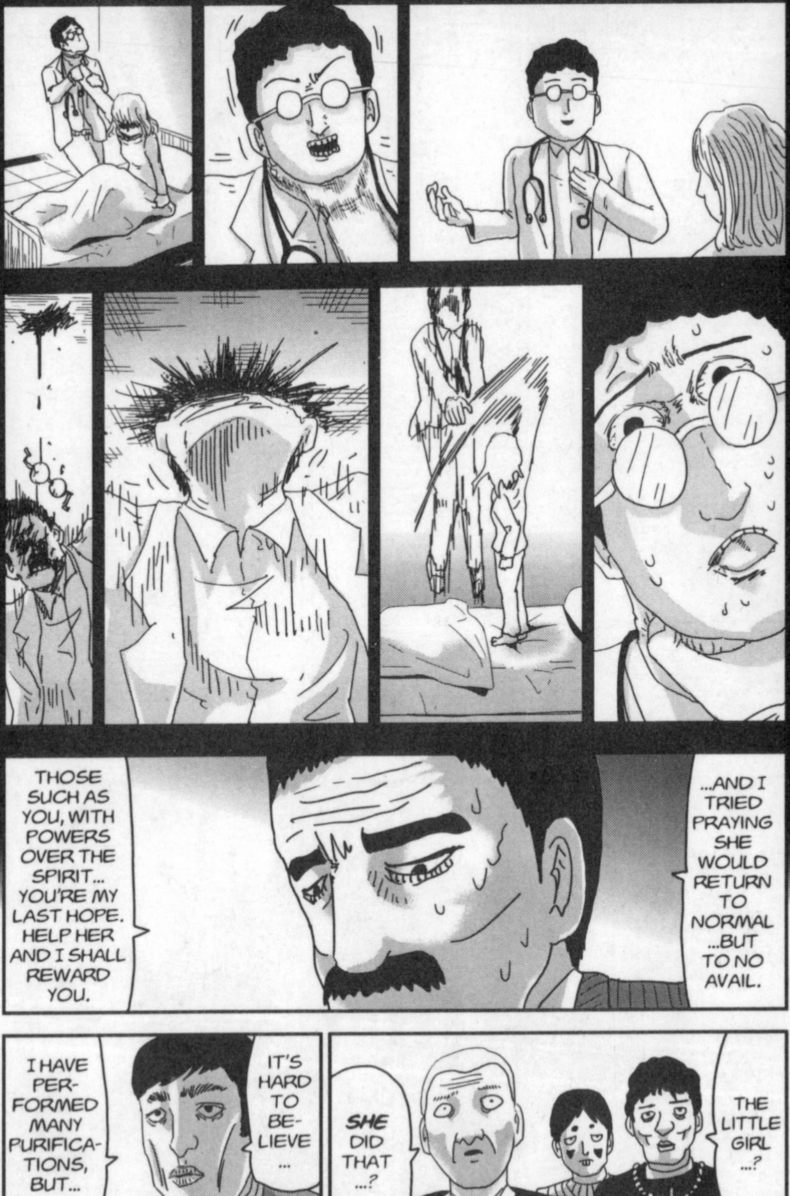
...AND I TRIED PRAYING SHE WOULD RETURN TO NORMAL ...BUT TO NO AVAIL.
THOSE SUCH AS YOU, WITH POWERS OVER THE SPIRIT... YOU'RE MY LAST HOPE. HELP HER AND I SHALL REWARD YOU.
THE LITTLE GIRL ...?
SHE DID THAT ...?
IT'S HARD TO BE-LIEVE ...
I HAVE PER-FORMED MANY PURIFICA-TIONS, BUT...

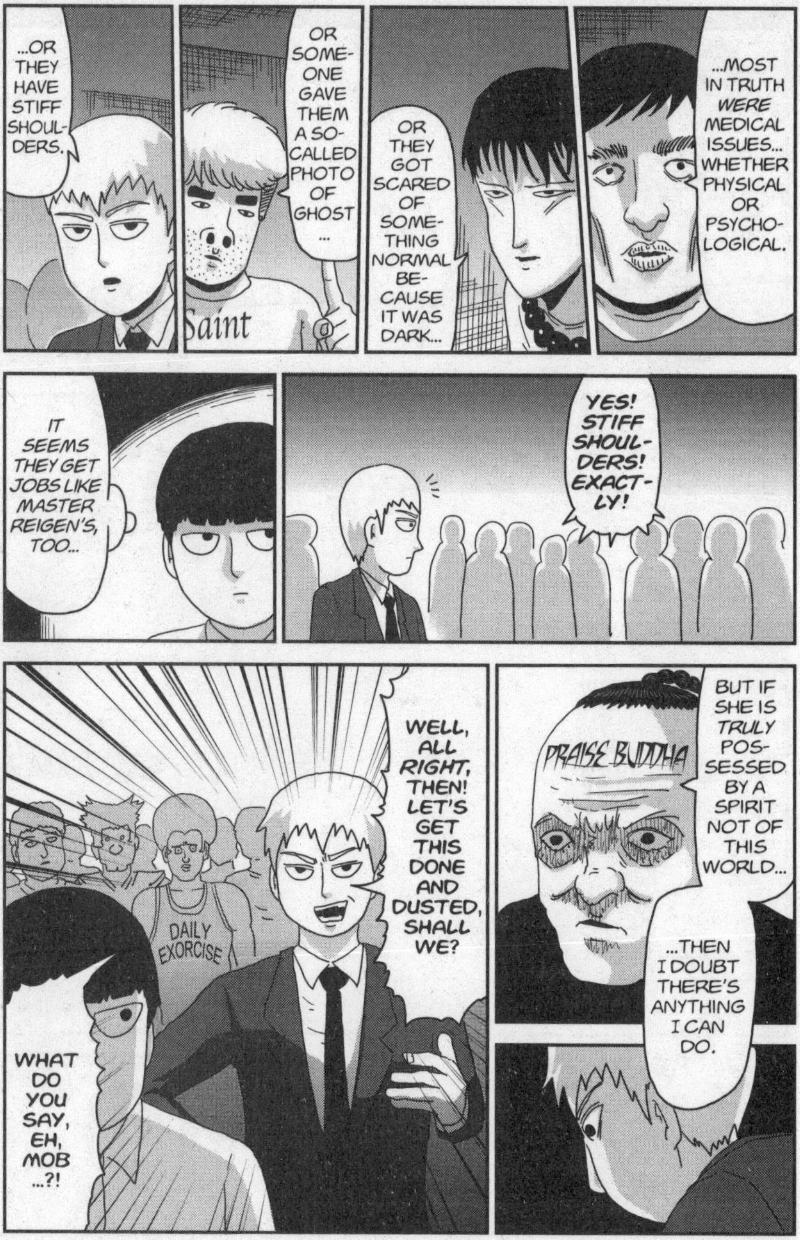
...MOST IN TRUTH WERE MEDICAL ISSUES... WHETHER PHYSICAL OR PSYCHOLOGICAL.
OR THEY GOT SCARED OF SOMETHING NORMAL BECAUSE IT WAS DARK...
OR SOMEONE GAVE THEM A SO-CALLED PHOTO OF GHOST ...
Saint
...OR THEY HAVE STIFF SHOULDERS.
YES! STIFF SHOULDERS! EXACTLY!
IT SEEMS THEY GET JOBS LIKE MASTER REIGEN'S, TOO...
PRAISE BUDDHA
BUT IF SHE IS TRULY POSSESSED BY A SPIRIT NOT OF THIS WORLD...
...THEN I DOUBT THERE'S ANYTHING I CAN DO.
WELL, ALL RIGHT, THEN! LET'S GET THIS DONE AND DUSTED, SHALL WE?
DAILY EXORCISE
WHAT DO YOU SAY, EH, MOB ...?!

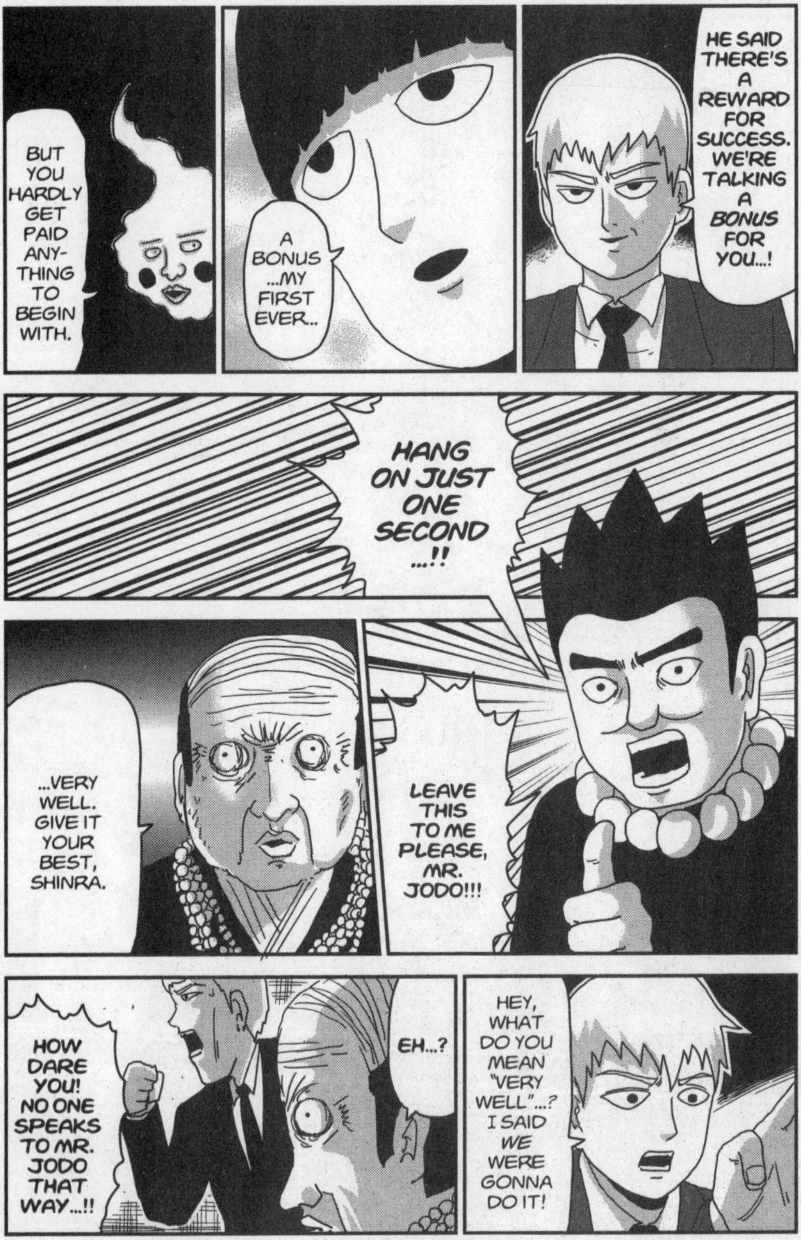
HE SAID THERE'S A REWARD FOR SUCCESS. WE'RE TALKING A *BONUS* FOR YOU...!
A BONUS ...MY FIRST EVER...
BUT YOU HARDLY GET PAID ANYTHING TO BEGIN WITH.
HANG ON JUST ONE SECOND ...!!
LEAVE THIS TO ME PLEASE, MR. JODO!!!
...VERY WELL. GIVE IT YOUR BEST, SHINRA.
HEY, WHAT DO YOU MEAN "VERY WELL"...? I SAID *WE* WERE GONNA DO IT!
EH...?
HOW DARE YOU! NO ONE SPEAKS TO MR. JODO THAT WAY...!!

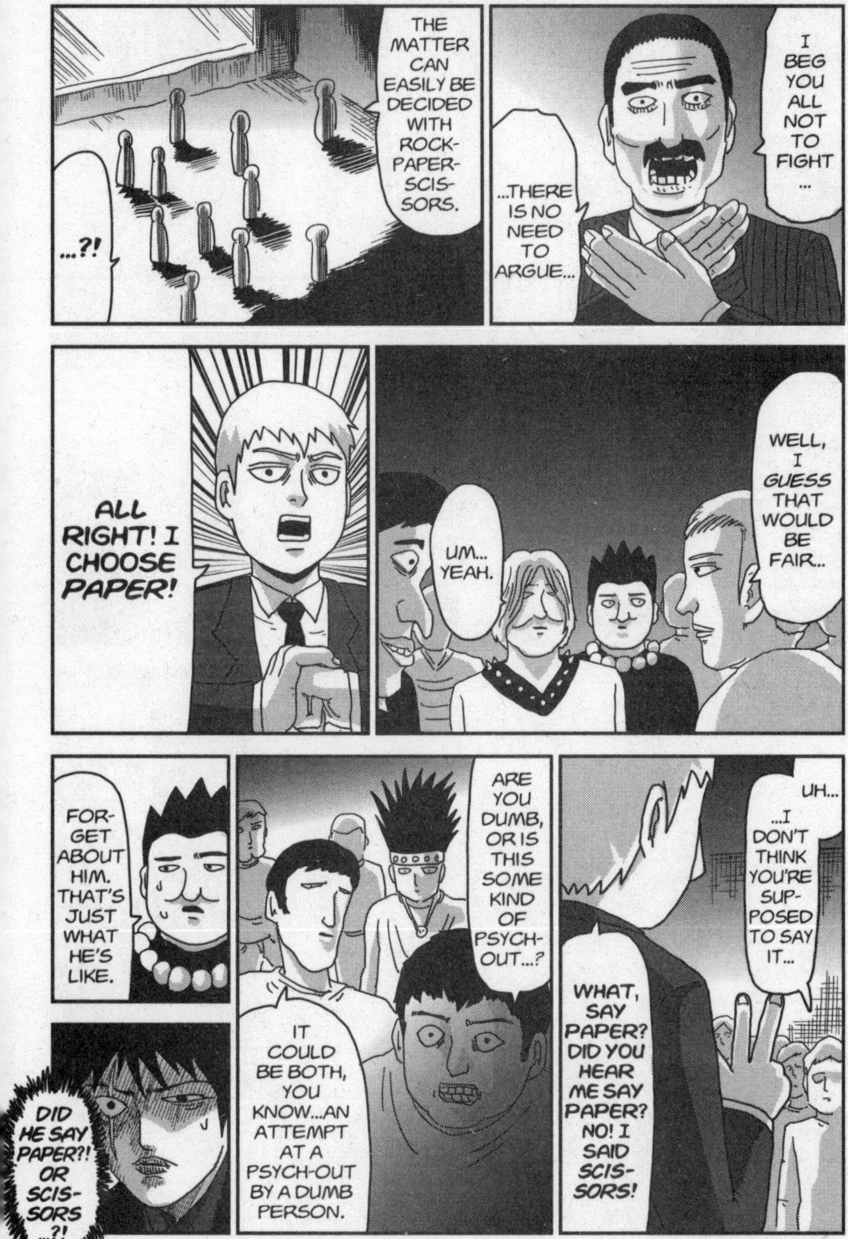
I BEG YOU ALL NOT TO FIGHT ...
...THERE IS NO NEED TO ARGUE...
THE MATTER CAN EASILY BE DECIDED WITH ROCK-PAPER-SCISSORS.
...?!
WELL, I GUESS THAT WOULD BE FAIR...
UM... YEAH.
ALL RIGHT! I CHOOSE PAPER!
UH... ...I DON'T THINK YOU'RE SUPPOSED TO SAY IT...
WHAT, SAY PAPER? DID YOU HEAR ME SAY PAPER? NO! I SAID SCISSORS!
ARE YOU DUMB, OR IS THIS SOME KIND OF PSYCH-OUT...?
IT COULD BE BOTH, YOU KNOW...AN ATTEMPT AT A PSYCH-OUT BY A DUMB PERSON.
FORGET ABOUT HIM. THAT'S JUST WHAT HE'S LIKE.
DID HE SAY PAPER?! OR SCISSORS...?!

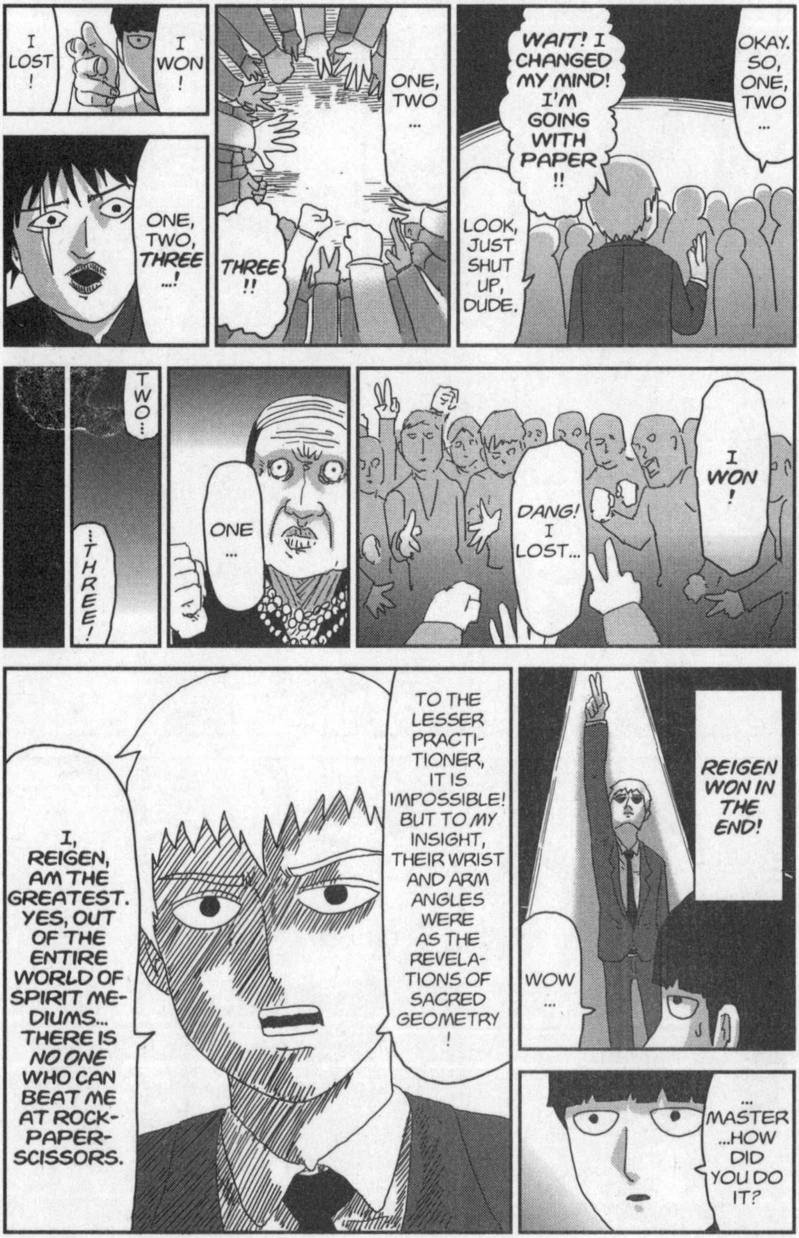
OKAY. SO, ONE, TWO ...
WAIT! I CHANGED MY MIND! I'M GOING WITH PAPER !!
LOOK, JUST SHUT UP, DUDE.
ONE, TWO ...
THREE !!
I WON !
I LOST !
ONE, TWO, THREE ...!
I WON !
DANG! I LOST...
ONE ...
TWO...
...THREE!
REIGEN WON IN THE END!
WOW ...
... MASTER ...HOW DID YOU DO IT?
TO THE LESSER PRACTI-TIONER, IT IS IMPOSSIBLE! BUT TO MY INSIGHT, THEIR WRIST AND ARM ANGLES WERE AS THE REVELA-TIONS OF SACRED GEOMETRY !
I, REIGEN, AM THE GREATEST. YES, OUT OF THE ENTIRE WORLD OF SPIRIT ME-DIUMS... THERE IS NO ONE WHO CAN BEAT ME AT ROCK-PAPER-SCISSORS.

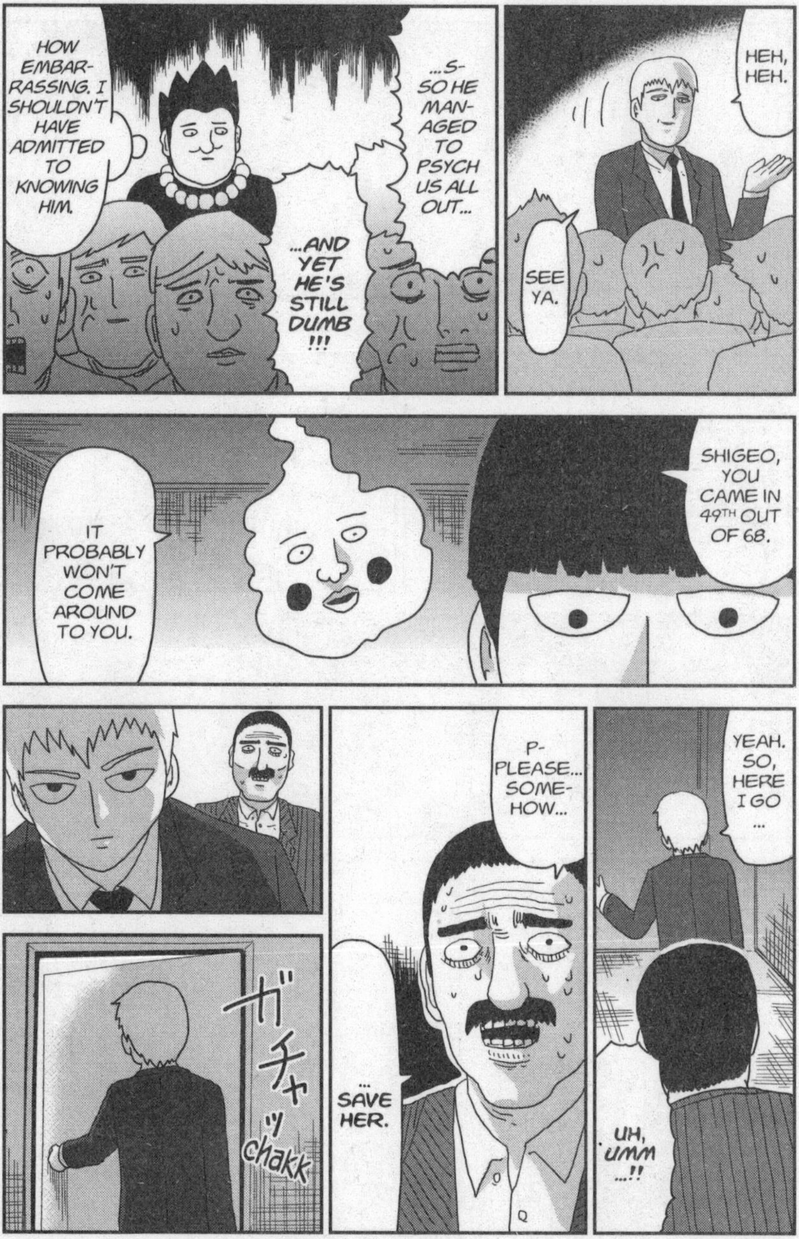
HEH, HEH.
SEE YA.
...S- SO HE MAN- AGED TO PSYCH US ALL OUT...
...AND YET HE'S STILL DUMB!!!
HOW EMBAR- RASSING. I SHOULDN'T HAVE ADMITTED TO KNOWING HIM.
SHIGEO, YOU CAME IN 49TH OUT OF 68.
IT PROBABLY WON'T COME AROUND TO YOU.
YEAH. SO, HERE I GO ...
UH, UMM ...!!
P- PLEASE... SOME- HOW...
... SAVE HER.
ガチャッ
chakk

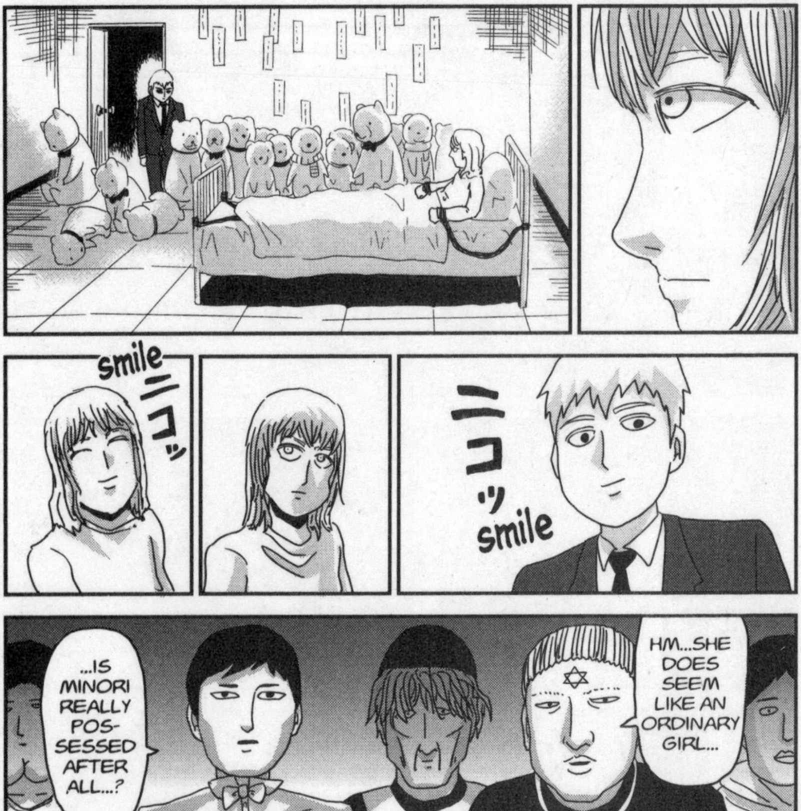
ニコッ
smile
smile
ニコッ
HM...SHE DOES SEEM LIKE AN ORDINARY GIRL...
...IS MINORI REALLY POSSESSED AFTER ALL...?
THIS IS CLEARLY SERIOUS... AND IF IT **DOES** TURN OUT TO BE A MENTAL HEALTH ISSUE, I'M NO EXPERT.
AND I CAN'T TELL HER I'M A SPIRIT MEDIUM... BECAUSE IF IT TRULY **IS** POSSESSION, I CAN'T HELP HER EITHER...!
HI!
...LET'S JUST SEE HOW IT GOES.

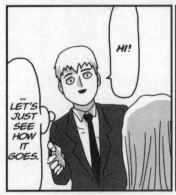

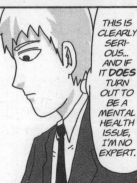

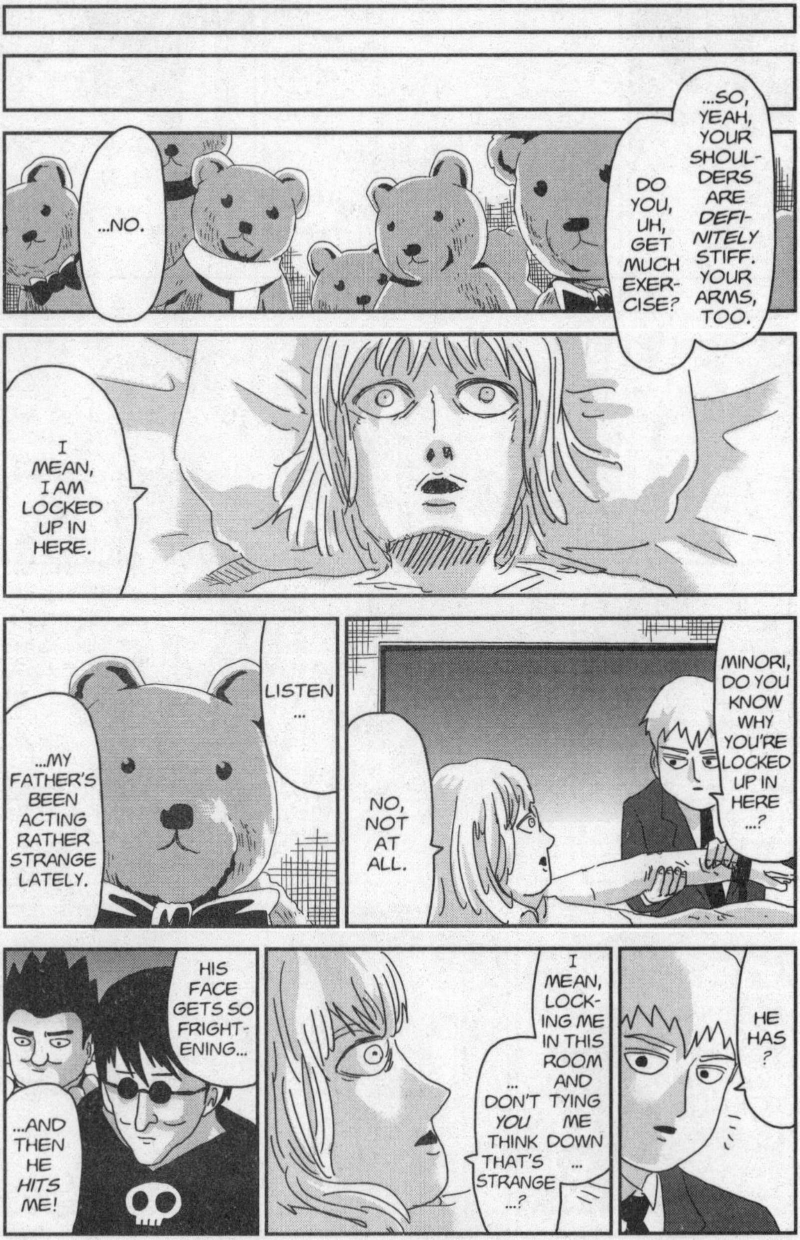
...SO, YEAH, YOUR SHOULDERS ARE *DEFINITELY* STIFF. YOUR ARMS, TOO.
DO YOU, UH, GET MUCH EXERCISE?
...NO.
I MEAN, I AM LOCKED UP IN HERE.
MINORI, DO YOU KNOW WHY YOU'RE LOCKED UP IN HERE ...?
NO, NOT AT ALL.
LISTEN ...
...MY FATHER'S BEEN ACTING RATHER STRANGE LATELY.
HE HAS?
I MEAN, LOCKING ME IN THIS ROOM AND TYING ME DOWN ...
... DON'T *YOU* THINK THAT'S STRANGE ...?
HIS FACE GETS SO FRIGHTENING...
...AND THEN HE *HITS* ME!

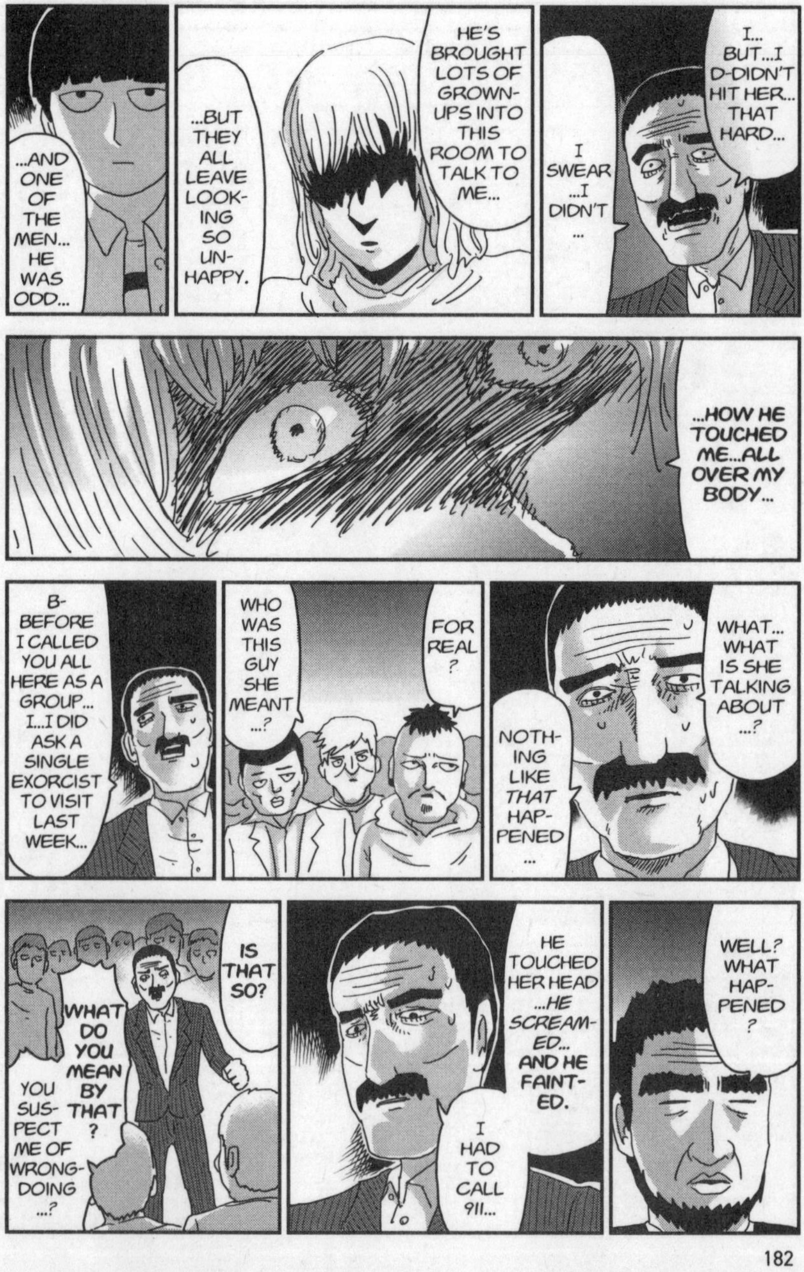
I... BUT...I D-DIDN'T HIT HER... THAT HARD...
I SWEAR ...I DIDN'T ...
HE'S BROUGHT LOTS OF GROWN-UPS INTO THIS ROOM TO TALK TO ME...
...BUT THEY ALL LEAVE LOOKING SO UNHAPPY.
...AND ONE OF THE MEN... HE WAS ODD...
...HOW HE TOUCHED ME...ALL OVER MY BODY...
WHAT... WHAT IS SHE TALKING ABOUT ...?
NOTHING LIKE THAT HAPPENED ...
FOR REAL ?
WHO WAS THIS GUY SHE MEANT ...?
B-BEFORE I CALLED YOU ALL HERE AS A GROUP... I...I DID ASK A SINGLE EXORCIST TO VISIT LAST WEEK...
WELL? WHAT HAPPENED ?
HE TOUCHED HER HEAD ...HE SCREAMED... AND HE FAINTED.
I HAD TO CALL 911...
IS THAT SO?
WHAT DO YOU MEAN BY THAT ?
YOU SUSPECT ME OF WRONGDOING ...?

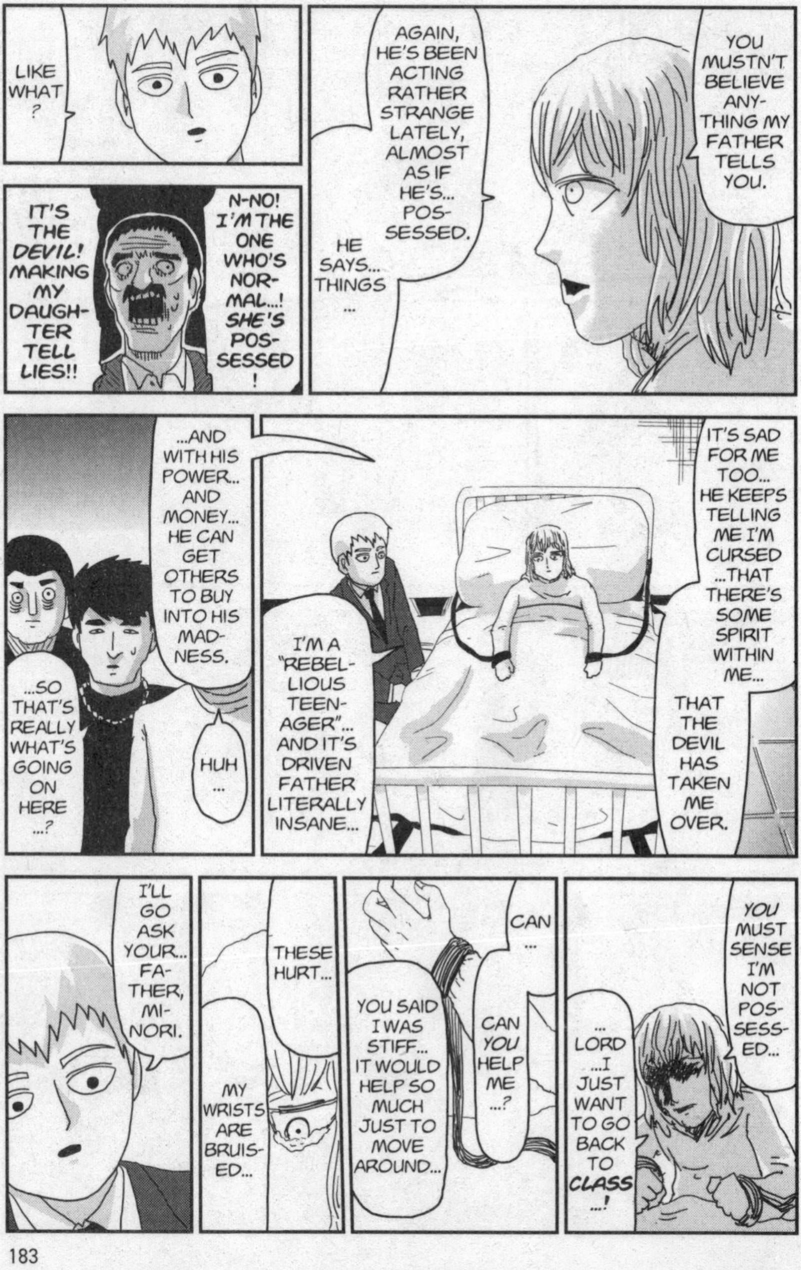
YOU MUSTN'T BELIEVE ANYTHING MY FATHER TELLS YOU.
AGAIN, HE'S BEEN ACTING RATHER STRANGE LATELY, ALMOST AS IF HE'S... POSSESSED.
HE SAYS... THINGS ...
LIKE WHAT ?
N-NO! I'M THE ONE WHO'S NORMAL...! SHE'S POSSESSED !
IT'S THE DEVIL! MAKING MY DAUGHTER TELL LIES!!
IT'S SAD FOR ME TOO... HE KEEPS TELLING ME I'M CURSED ...THAT THERE'S SOME SPIRIT WITHIN ME...
THAT THE DEVIL HAS TAKEN ME OVER.
I'M A "REBELLIOUS TEENAGER"... AND IT'S DRIVEN FATHER LITERALLY INSANE...
...AND WITH HIS POWER... AND MONEY... HE CAN GET OTHERS TO BUY INTO HIS MADNESS.
HUH ...
...SO THAT'S REALLY WHAT'S GOING ON HERE ...?
YOU MUST SENSE I'M NOT POSSESSED...
... LORD ...I JUST WANT TO GO BACK TO CLASS ...!
CAN ...
CAN YOU HELP ME ...?
YOU SAID I WAS STIFF... IT WOULD HELP SO MUCH JUST TO MOVE AROUND...
THESE HURT...
MY WRISTS ARE BRUISED...
I'LL GO ASK YOUR... FATHER, MINORI.

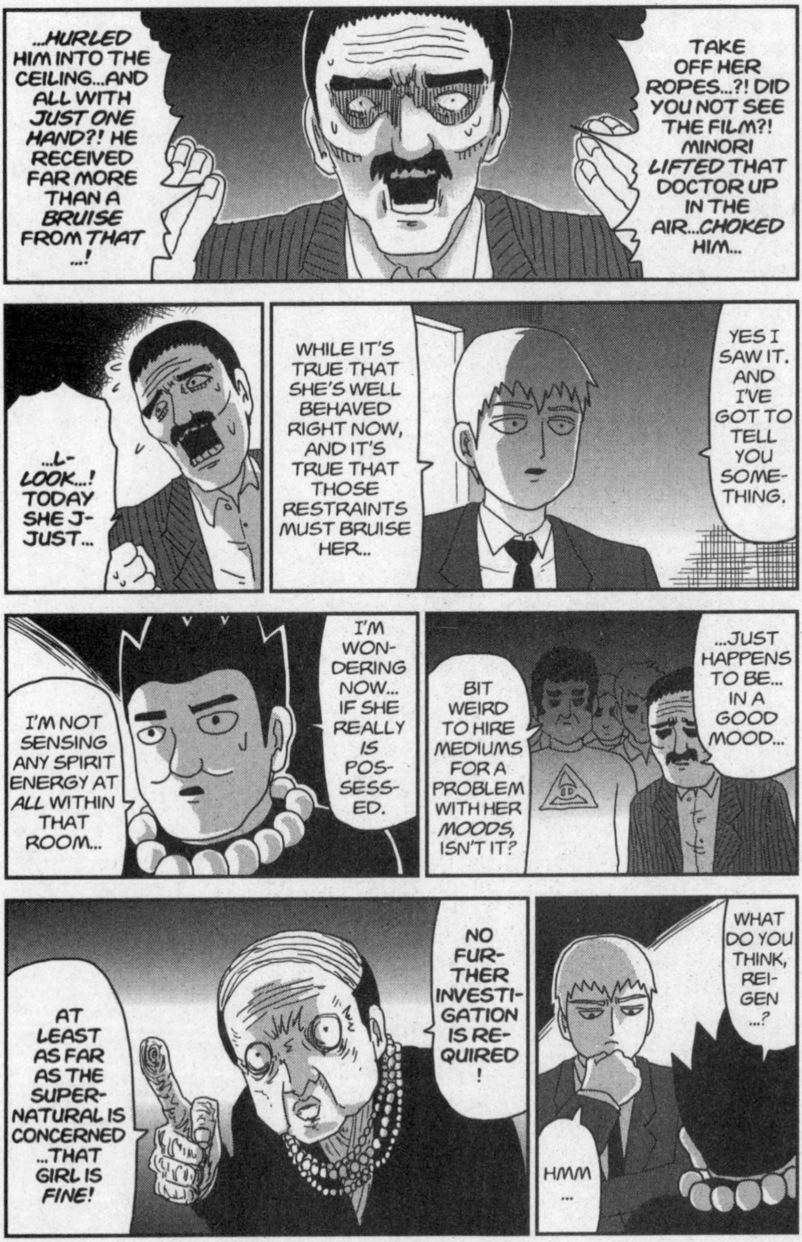
TAKE OFF HER ROPES...?! DID YOU NOT SEE THE FILM?! MINORI *LIFTED* THAT DOCTOR UP IN THE AIR...*CHOKED* HIM...
...*HURLED* HIM INTO THE CEILING...AND ALL WITH *JUST ONE HAND?!* HE RECEIVED FAR MORE THAN A *BRUISE* FROM *THAT* ...!
YES I SAW IT. AND I'VE GOT TO TELL YOU SOME-THING.
WHILE IT'S TRUE THAT SHE'S WELL BEHAVED RIGHT NOW, AND IT'S TRUE THAT THOSE RESTRAINTS MUST BRUISE HER...
...L-*LOOK*...! TODAY SHE J-JUST...
...JUST HAPPENS TO BE... IN A GOOD MOOD...
BIT WEIRD TO HIRE MEDIUMS FOR A PROBLEM WITH HER *MOODS,* ISN'T IT?
I'M WONDERING NOW... IF SHE REALLY *IS* POSSESSED.
I'M NOT SENSING ANY SPIRIT ENERGY AT *ALL* WITHIN THAT ROOM...
WHAT DO YOU THINK, REIGEN ...?
HMM ...
NO FURTHER INVESTIGATION IS REQUIRED !
AT LEAST AS FAR AS THE SUPERNATURAL IS CONCERNED ...THAT GIRL IS *FINE!*

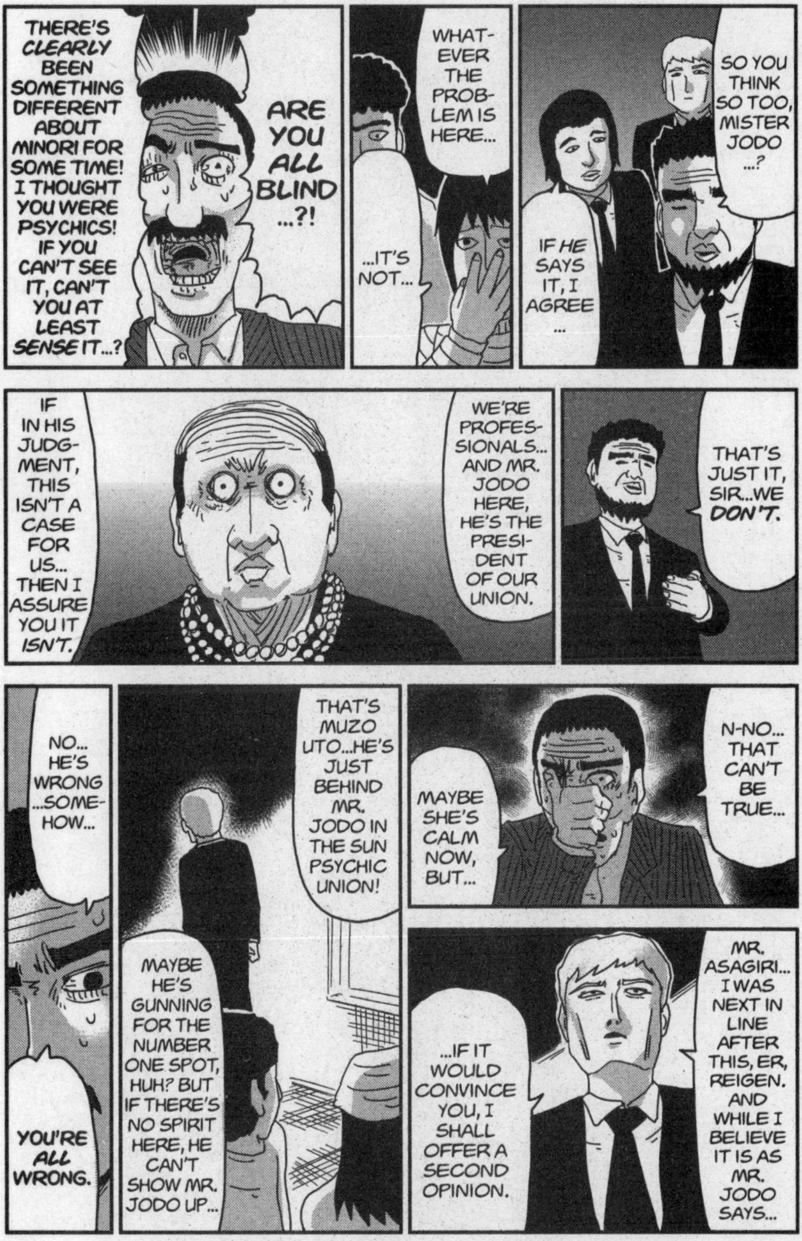
SO YOU THINK SO TOO, MISTER JODO ...?
IF HE SAYS IT, I AGREE ...
WHATEVER THE PROBLEM IS HERE...
...IT'S NOT...
ARE YOU ALL BLIND ...?!
THERE'S CLEARLY BEEN SOMETHING DIFFERENT ABOUT MINORI FOR SOME TIME! I THOUGHT YOU WERE PSYCHICS! IF YOU CAN'T SEE IT, CAN'T YOU AT LEAST SENSE IT...?
THAT'S JUST IT, SIR...WE DON'T.
WE'RE PROFESSIONALS... AND MR. JODO HERE, HE'S THE PRESIDENT OF OUR UNION.
IF IN HIS JUDGMENT, THIS ISN'T A CASE FOR US... THEN I ASSURE YOU IT ISN'T.
N-NO... THAT CAN'T BE TRUE...
MAYBE SHE'S CALM NOW, BUT...
MR. ASAGIRI... I WAS NEXT IN LINE AFTER THIS, ER, REIGEN. AND WHILE I BELIEVE IT IS AS MR. JODO SAYS...
...IF IT WOULD CONVINCE YOU, I SHALL OFFER A SECOND OPINION.
THAT'S MUZO UTO...HE'S JUST BEHIND MR. JODO IN THE SUN PSYCHIC UNION!
MAYBE HE'S GUNNING FOR THE NUMBER ONE SPOT, HUH? BUT IF THERE'S NO SPIRIT HERE, HE CAN'T SHOW MR. JODO UP...
NO... HE'S WRONG ...SOMEHOW...
YOU'RE ALL WRONG.

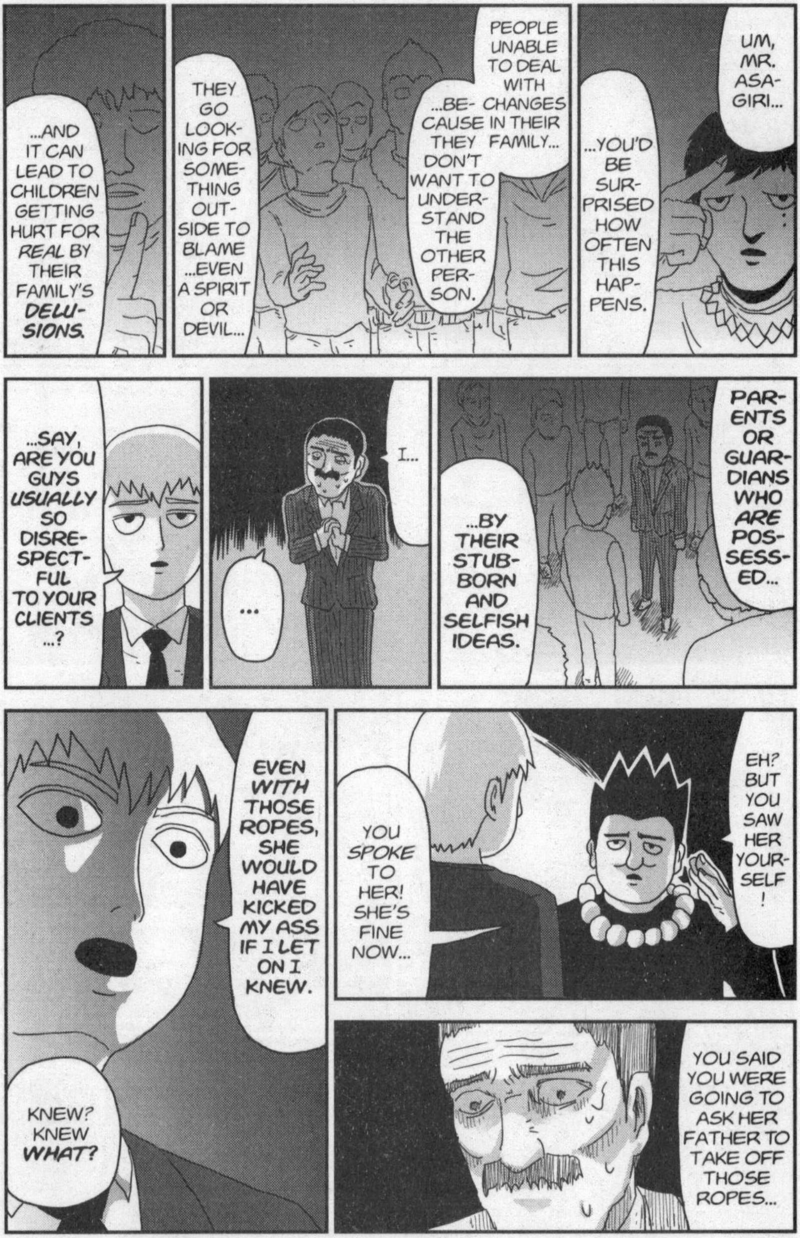

UM, MR. ASAGIRI...
...YOU'D BE SURPRISED HOW OFTEN THIS HAPPENS.
PEOPLE UNABLE TO DEAL WITH CHANGES IN THEIR FAMILY...
...BECAUSE THEY DON'T WANT TO UNDERSTAND THE OTHER PERSON.
THEY GO LOOKING FOR SOMETHING OUTSIDE TO BLAME ...EVEN A SPIRIT OR DEVIL...
...AND IT CAN LEAD TO CHILDREN GETTING HURT FOR *REAL* BY THEIR FAMILY'S **DELUSIONS.**
PARENTS OR GUARDIANS WHO *ARE* POSSESSED...
...BY THEIR STUBBORN AND SELFISH IDEAS.
I...
...
...SAY, ARE YOU GUYS *USUALLY* SO DISRESPECTFUL TO YOUR CLIENTS ...?
EH? BUT YOU SAW HER YOURSELF!
YOU *SPOKE* TO HER! SHE'S FINE NOW...
YOU SAID YOU WERE GOING TO ASK HER FATHER TO TAKE OFF THOSE ROPES...
EVEN *WITH* THOSE ROPES, SHE WOULD HAVE KICKED MY ASS IF I LET ON I KNEW.
KNEW? KNEW ***WHAT?***

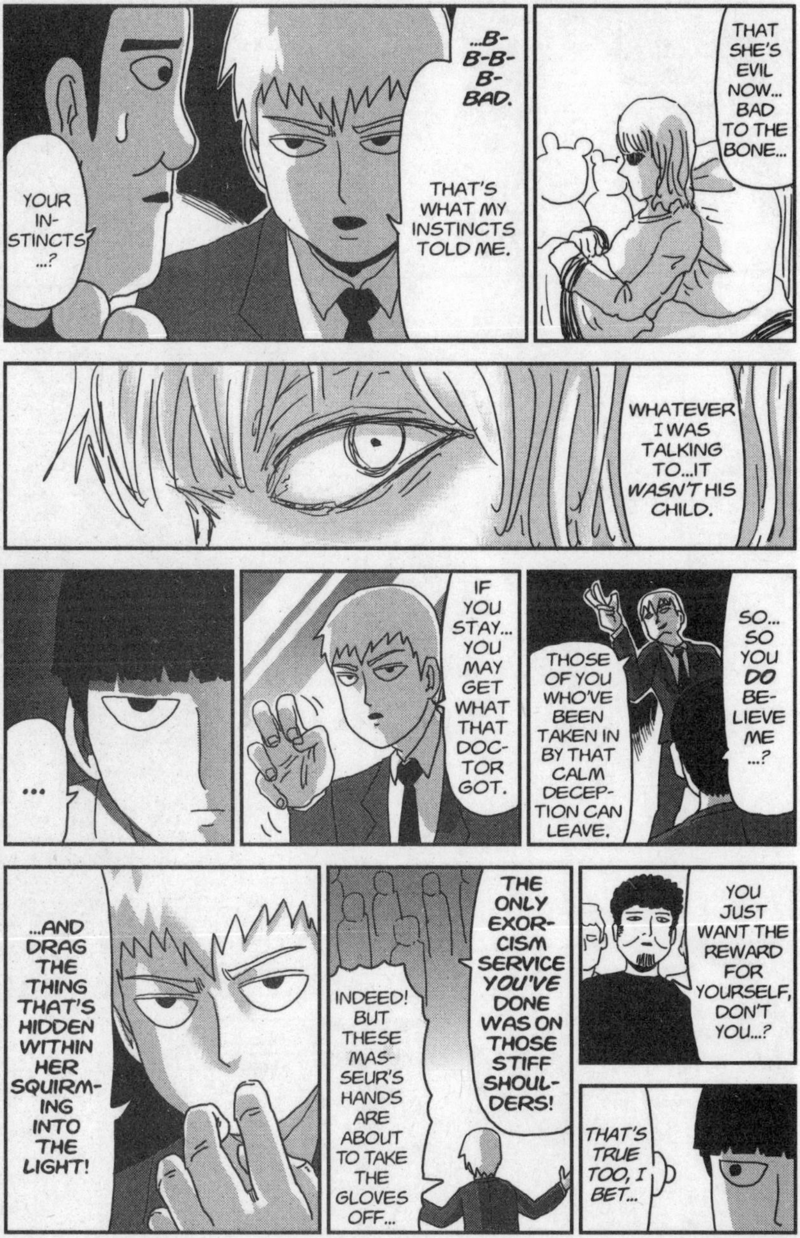
THAT SHE'S EVIL NOW... BAD TO THE BONE...
...B-B-B-B-BAD.
THAT'S WHAT MY INSTINCTS TOLD ME.
YOUR INSTINCTS ...?
WHATEVER I WAS TALKING TO...IT *WASN'T* HIS CHILD.
SO... SO YOU **DO** BELIEVE ME ...?
THOSE OF YOU WHO'VE BEEN TAKEN IN BY THAT CALM DECEPTION CAN LEAVE.
IF YOU STAY... YOU MAY GET WHAT THAT DOCTOR GOT.
...
YOU JUST WANT THE REWARD FOR YOURSELF, DON'T YOU...?
THAT'S TRUE TOO, I BET...
THE ONLY EXORCISM SERVICE *YOU'VE* DONE WAS ON THOSE STIFF SHOULDERS!
INDEED! BUT THESE MASSEUR'S HANDS ARE ABOUT TO TAKE THE GLOVES OFF...
...AND DRAG THE THING THAT'S HIDDEN WITHIN HER SQUIRMING INTO THE LIGHT!

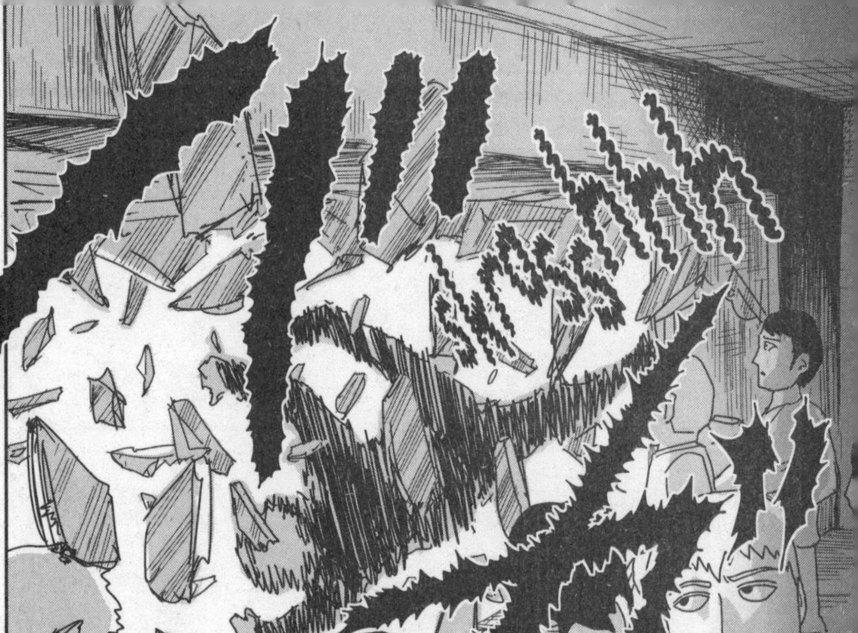

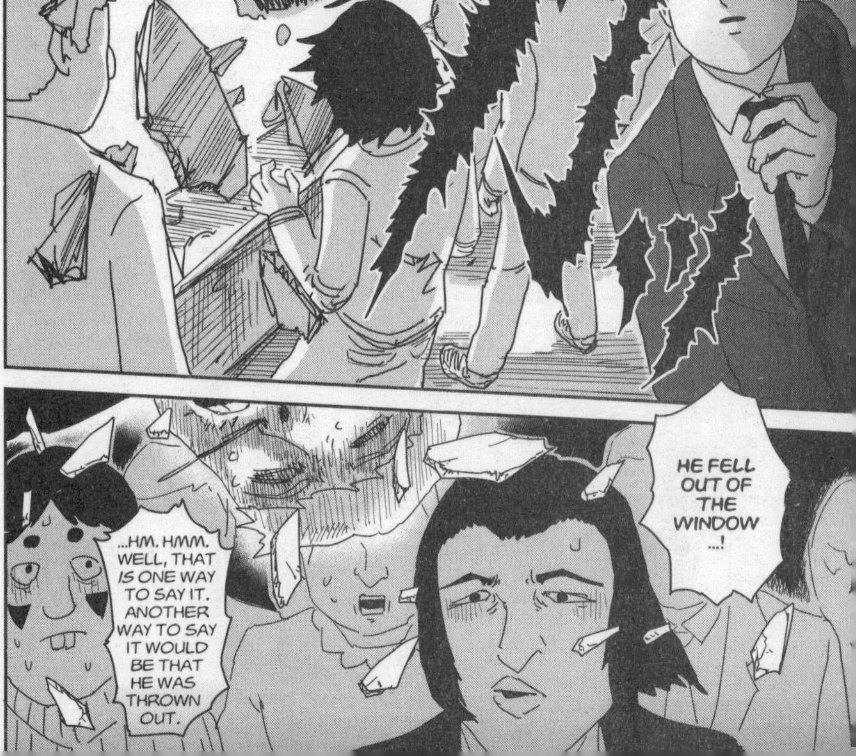
HE FELL OUT OF THE WINDOW ...!
...HM. HMM. WELL, THAT *IS* ONE WAY TO SAY IT. ANOTHER WAY TO SAY IT WOULD BE THAT HE WAS THROWN OUT.

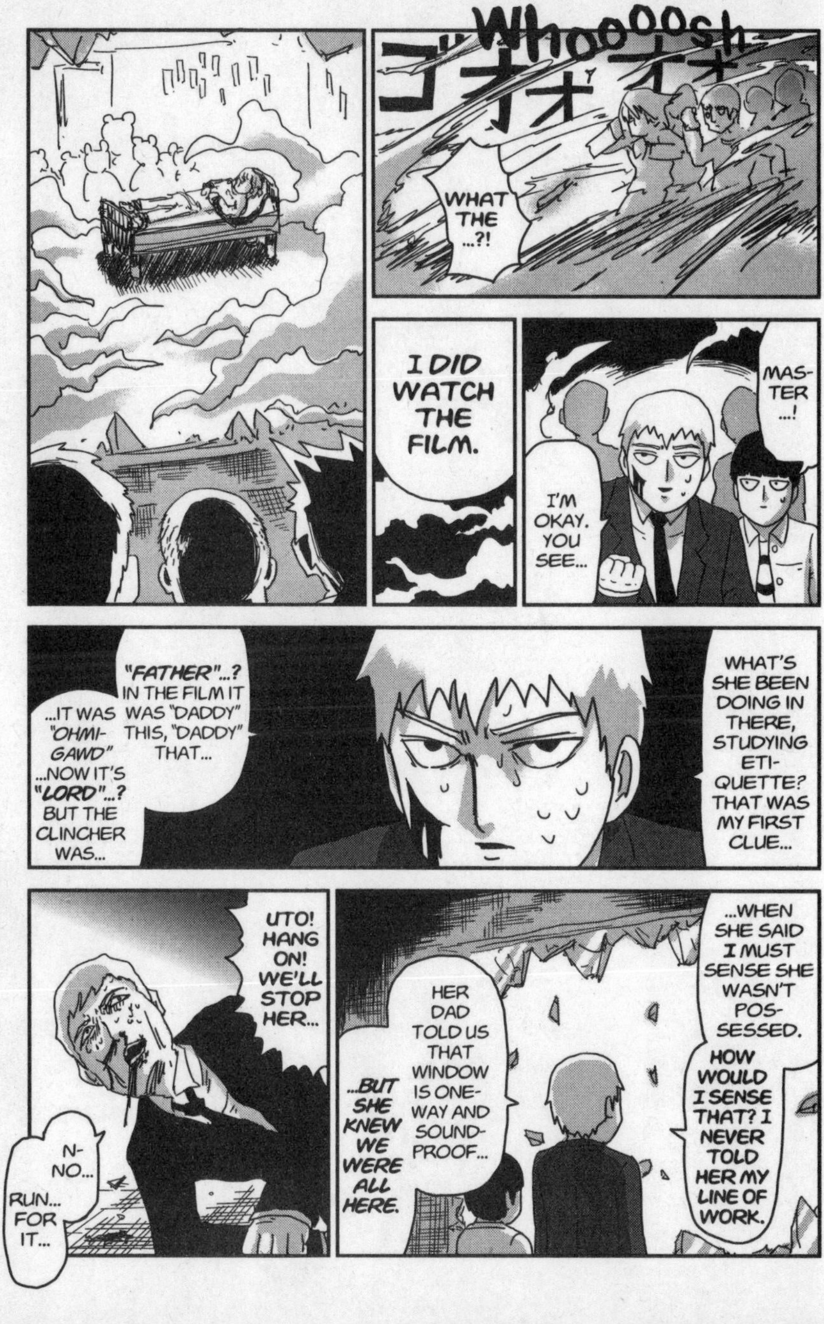
Whoooosh
WHAT THE ...?!
MAS-TER ...!
I'M OKAY. YOU SEE...
I DID WATCH THE FILM.
WHAT'S SHE BEEN DOING IN THERE, STUDYING ETI-QUETTE? THAT WAS MY FIRST CLUE...
"FATHER"...? IN THE FILM IT WAS "DADDY" THIS, "DADDY" THAT...
...IT WAS "OHMI-GAWD" ...NOW IT'S "LORD"...? BUT THE CLINCHER WAS...
...WHEN SHE SAID I MUST SENSE SHE WASN'T POS-SESSED.
HOW WOULD I SENSE THAT? I NEVER TOLD HER MY LINE OF WORK.
HER DAD TOLD US THAT WINDOW IS ONE-WAY AND SOUND-PROOF...
...BUT SHE KNEW WE WERE ALL HERE.
UTO! HANG ON! WE'LL STOP HER...
N-NO... RUN... FOR IT...

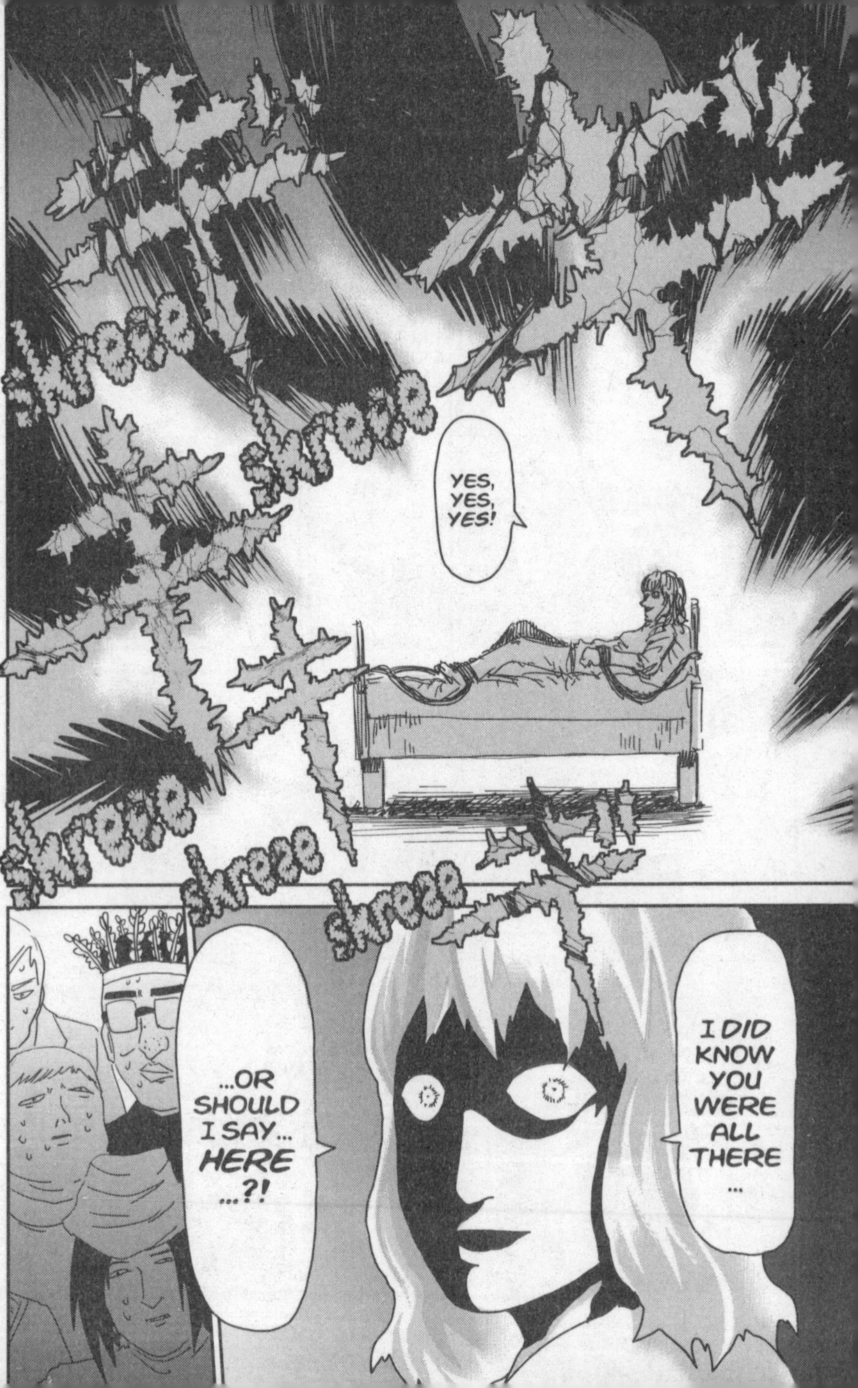
YES, YES, YES!
skreee
skreee
skreee
skreee
skreee
I DID KNOW YOU WERE ALL THERE ...
...OR SHOULD I SAY... HERE ...?!

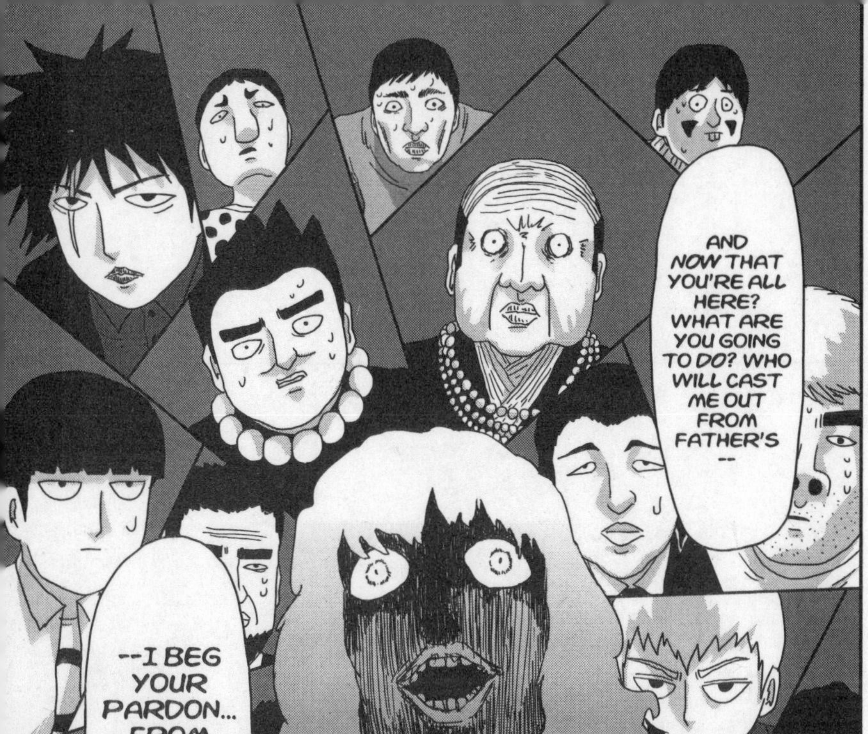
AND NOW THAT YOU'RE ALL HERE? WHAT ARE YOU GOING TO DO? WHO WILL CAST ME OUT FROM FATHER'S --
--I BEG YOUR PARDON... FROM DADDY'S LITTLE GIRL...?!

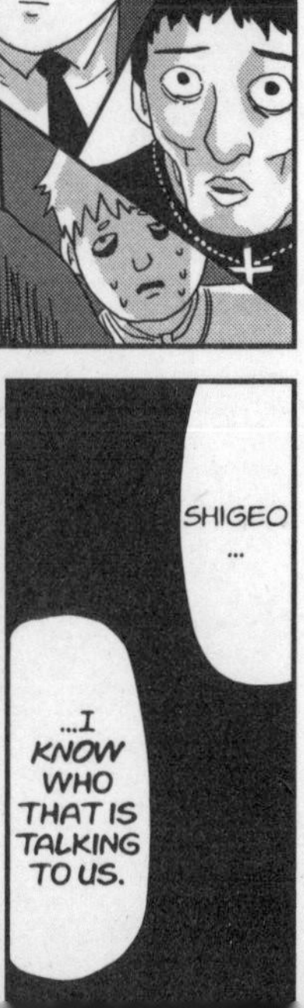
SHIGEO ...
...I KNOW WHO THAT IS TALKING TO US.

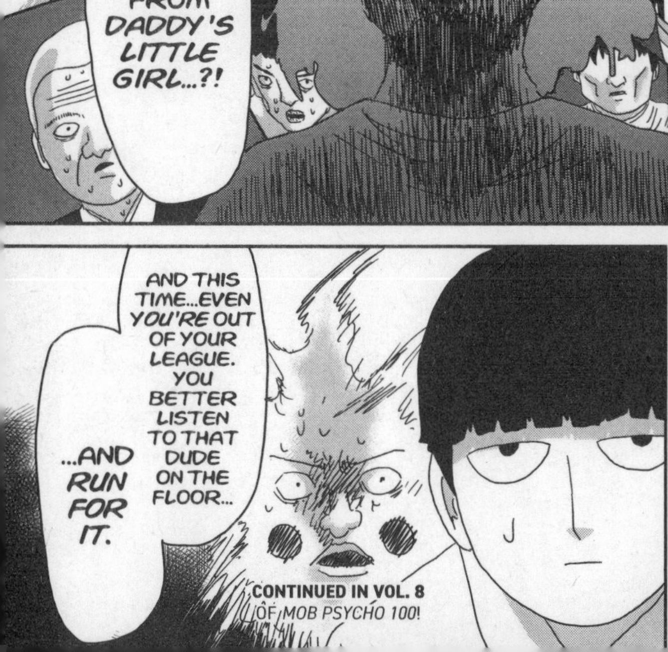
AND THIS TIME...EVEN YOU'RE OUT OF YOUR LEAGUE. YOU BETTER LISTEN TO THAT DUDE ON THE FLOOR...
...AND RUN FOR IT.

CONTINUED IN VOL. 8 OF MOB PSYCHO 100!

ONE

I'd like to go to the beach.
Or even the mountains.
Or even a rice paddy.

president and publisher
MIKE RICHARDSON

editor
CARL GUSTAV HORN

designer
BRENNAN THOME

digital art technician
CHRIS HORN

English-language version produced by Dark Horse Comics

MOB PSYCHO 100

Published by Dark Horse Manga
A division of Dark Horse Comics LLC
10956 SE Main Street, Milwaukie, OR 97222

DarkHorse.com

To find a comics shop in your area, visit comicshoplocator.com.

First edition: September 2021 | ISBN 978-1-50672-759-2 | eBook ISBN 978-1-50672-777-6

3 5 7 9 10 8 6 4 2

Printed in the United States of America

KEEP YOUR HANDS OFF EIZOUKEN!

By Sumito Oowara

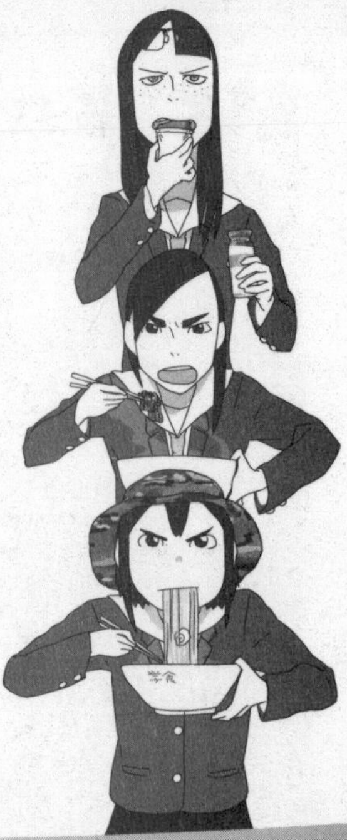

Asakusa loves to design worlds. Mizusaki loves to animate. Kanamori loves to make money! And at Shibahama High, they're known as Eizouken—a club determined to produce their own science fiction anime! But with no budget and a leaky warehouse for a studio, Eizouken is going to have to work hard—together!—and use their imaginations if they want to create their vision of the ultimate world.

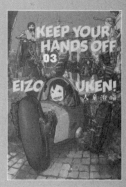

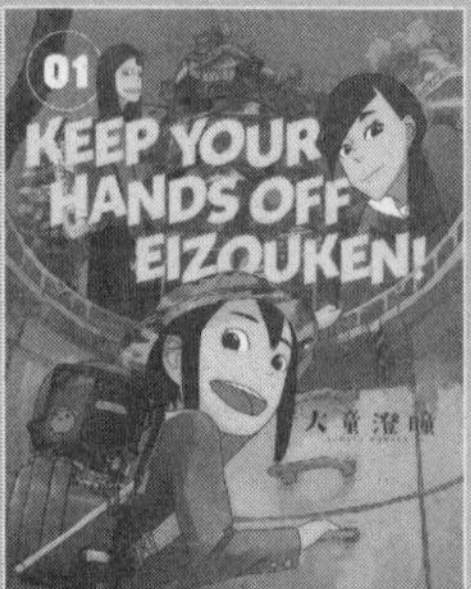
01
KEEP YOUR HANDS OFF EIZOUKEN!

VOLUME 1
ISBN 978-1-50671-897-2
$12.99

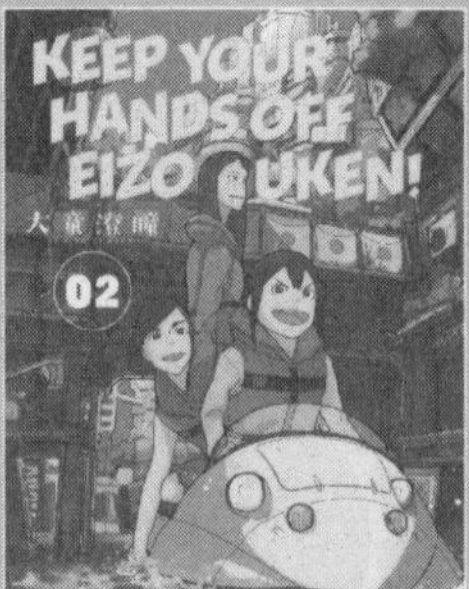
KEEP YOUR HANDS OFF EIZOUKEN!
02

VOLUME 2
ISBN 978-1-50671-898-9
$12.99

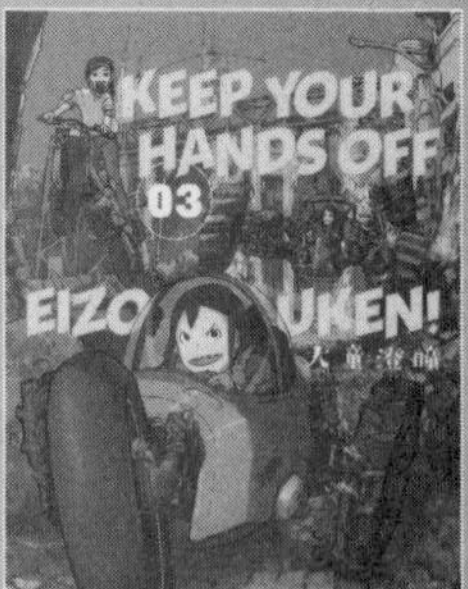
KEEP YOUR HANDS OFF
03
EIZOUKEN!

VOLUME 3
ISBN 978-1-50671-899-6
$12.99

AVAILABLE AT YOUR LOCAL COMICS SHOP OR BOOKSTORE

To find a comics shop near you, visit comicshoplocator.com. For more information or to order direct, visit darkhorse.com. *Prices and availability subject to change without notice.

Ms. Koizumi loves ramen noodles.

The original manga that inspired the anime series from Crunchyroll!

$10.99 EACH!

Ms. Koizumi loves ramen noodles . . . and Yu likes Ms. Koizumi! But she soon discovers that the only way to get closer to this cool, mysterious transfer student is to become her pupil on the path of ramen!

Translated by Japanese chef Ayumi Kato Blystone, *Ms. Koizumi Loves Ramen Noodles* is a fun food manga that shows you all around the authentic ramen culture of everyday Japan, from crazy home-cooked versions to famous restaurants reached by bullet train! Do you know about sauce vs. broth? How to pair sushi with ramen? Or even sweet ramen dishes like chocolate, pineapple, and ice cream? You soon will—and with bonus notes on real ramen shops to visit, this manga will leave you hungry for more!

VOL. 1 | ISBN 978-1-50671-327-4 | 136 pages ▼ **VOL. 2** | ISBN 978-1-50671-328-1 | 136 pages
VOL. 3 | ISBN 978-1-50671-329-8 | 136 pages

EMANON

FROM KENJI TSURUTA, THE ARTIST OF THE EISNER-NOMINATED *WANDERING ISLAND*, **AND THE AWARD-WINNING JAPANESE SCIENCE FICTION AUTHOR SHINJI KAJIO!**

Emanon is the eternal stranger who belongs here more than any of us— a woman possessing a mind that evolved over the entire history of life on earth, and who carries within her over three billion years of memories. Set in 1960s and 70s Japan, *Emanon* tells of her encounters with the lives of people who can no more forget her, than she can forget any person. Drawn in both Tsuruta's elegant black-and-white linework and his signature painted color, *Emanon* is a literary SF manga at the intersection of life, memory, family, and existence.

VOL. 1: MEMORIES OF EMANON
ISBN 978-1-50670-981-9 - 192 pages

VOL. 2: EMANON WANDERER PART ONE
ISBN 978-1-50670-982-6 - 216 pages

VOL. 3: EMANON WANDERER PART TWO
ISBN 978-1-50670-983-3 - 240 pages

$14.99 EACH!

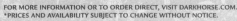

the KUROSAGI corpse delivery service
黒鷺死体宅配便

OMNIBUS EDITIONS

Five young students at a Buddhist university find there's little call for their job skills in today's Tokyo. . . among the living, that is! But their studies give them a direct line to the dead—the dead who are still trapped in their corpses, and can't move on to the next incarnation! Whether death resulted from suicide, murder, sickness, or madness, the Kurosagi Corpse Delivery Service will carry the body anywhere it needs to go to free its soul!

"Nobody does horror-comedy comics better than Otsuka and Yamazaki"
—Booklist

Each 600+ page omnibus book collects three complete volumes of the series!

Vol. 1:
Contains vols. 1–3, originally published separately.
ISBN 978-1-61655-754-6 $19.99

Vol. 2:
Contains vols. 4–6, originally published separately.
ISBN 978-1-61655-783-6 $19.99

Vol. 3:
Contains vols. 7–9, originally published separately.
ISBN 978-1-61655-887-1 $19.99

Vol. 4:
Contains vols. 10–12, originally published separately.
ISBN 978-1-50670-055-7 $19.99

GOU TANABE

These moody and evocative manga volumes strike directly at the dark heart of the Cthulhu mythos, with all the fear and wonder for which they have become famous! These graphic adaptations of some of H.P. Lovecraft's most infamous stories of cosmic horror (and the intrepid adventurers who just can't leave well enough alone) will unsettle and delight in equal measure!

H.P. LOVECRAFT'S AT THE MOUNTAINS OF MADNESS
VOLUME 1 | ISBN 978-1-50671-022-8 | $19.99
VOLUME 2 | ISBN 978-1-50671-023-5 | $19.99

H.P. LOVECRAFT'S THE HOUND AND OTHER STORIES
ISBN 978-1-50670-312-1 | $12.99